Bahadur

Also by ***Kalpish Ratna***

Fiction

- Synapse
- The Quarantine Papers
- The Nalanda Chronicles

Non-fiction

- Gastronama—*The Indian Guide To Eating Right*
- A Crown of Thorns—*The Coronavirus & Us*
- Fat—*The Body, Food & Obesity*
- The Secret Life of Zika Virus
- Room 000
- Once Upon A Hill
- Uncertain Life & Sure Death—*Medicine & Mahamaari in Maritime Mumbai*
- A Compendium of Family Health

For Children

- A Pandemonium in Pakshila
- Nyagrodha—*The Ficus Chronicles*
- Doctor Wrasse of Crystal Rock

Bahadur

Shah of Gujarat

Kalpish Ratna

London · New York · Sydney · Toronto · New Delhi

First published in India by Simon & Schuster India, 2023

1 3 5 7 9 10 8 6 4 2

Simon & Schuster India
818, Indraprakash Building, 21, Barakhamba Road,
New Delhi 110001.

Simon & Schuster: Celebrating 100 years of Publishing in 2024

www.simonandschuster.co.in

Hardback ISBN: 978-93-92099-94-6
Ebook ISBN: 978-93-92099-95-3

Typeset in India by Chandrakant Neman, Mumbai
Printed and bound in India by Replika Press Pvt. Ltd.

Simon & Schuster India is committed to sourcing paper that is made from wood grown in sustainable forests and support the Forest Stewardship Council, the leading international forest certification organisation. Our books displaying the FSC logo are printed on FSC certified paper.

In memoriam

Savithri Swaminathan

29 August 1930 — 23 February 2014

Bahadur

Contents

ابتداء

Why would anybody want to read about Bahadur Shah of Gujarat? Few have even heard of him. At first mention he is invariably confused with a far more sympathetic figure.[1]

Every schoolchild knows Bahadur Shah Zafar was the last of the Mughals. Very few know that the Mughal dynasty had its beginning in a whim of Bahadur Shah of Gujarat.

How could a rebellious teenager from far off Gujarat be a deciding factor in the change of power at Dilli?

The year is 1526. Bahadur, 19, is a prince in exile from the richest kingdom on the subcontinent. Bitter, heartbroken, he is unconscious that others see him as a king in search of a kingdom.

Dilli is up for auction, and the bidding factions are seasoned warriors all: Lodi, Mughal, Rajput. Why would they clamour to sign up a hot-headed teenager? And why would the rebel Lodis offer him the throne?

Unbelievable, right?

It was to me too, when I came across the story. It was my second reason for pursuing Bahadur, but I mention it first, as it is of universal interest.

My first reason was deeply personal.

I live on Shashti Island, which today is western suburban Mumbai. The documented history of this island goes back to the 10th century. In the 15th century, it was part of the territory of the Gujarat Sultâns. It had a syncretic culture: Saivite, Buddhist, Jain and Muslim shrines flourished. It was on the trade route from the Dakshin to the port, and caravans passed through its bazaars. It was renowned for its mangoes and rice. The silk looms of Thana supplied the world.

This was Shashti as the Portuguese found it in 1500, when they began their raids on the western coastline. In his famous *Lusiad,* Luís de Camões described Shashti as the Isle of Love, and transformed a real event of plunder, rape and rapine into a lyrical idyll that would be read as allegory. Within twenty years Shashti was reduced to a wasteland, the people terrorized, the women raped, the men enslaved. But it wasn't yet occupied by the Portuguese, not until twenty years after Alfonso de Albuquerque's massacre of Goa in 1510.

---

1 Urdu … ابتداء [*ibteda*]; the beginning.

On 23 December 1534, a Gujarat Sultân signed away the seven islands of Bombay to the Portuguese, inaugurating centuries of religious persecution, enslavement and dispossession. That Sultân was Bahadur Shah.

Why did he do that?

Portuguese historians had a ready answer: Bahadur was a dissolute drunkard, incapable of governing, insatiably greedy, and of course—like the rest of the pagans—thoroughly treacherous. He sold his people to get Portuguese help against the Mughal. Their stories about the events that led to Bahadur's death were simply ridiculous.

By now I was used to the general acceptance of the Portuguese point of view. 19th and early 20th century British historians had uncritically bought into it. So had the tertiary sources—standard historical narratives of our own time. When Bahadur was noticed at all, it was with a sneer.

Almost immediately, stories opened kaleidoscopically.

These were Indian historians talking about what had happened to their own people—perhaps removed in time by a century or so, but always able to connect with a verifiable anecdote.

As pieces of the jigsaw came together, Bahadur emerged as an intriguing young man. He could have been the quintessential hero. The valour of Arjun, the stamina of Bheema, the boyishness of Nakul and Sahadev—all these he had, but in lacking utterly the judgment of Yudhishtra, history damned him. And then, there was the terrible crime of *jauhar* laid at his door twice over. Was there truth in that accusation?

The only advocate I found for Bahadur was the sane voice of the Portuguese savant Garcia da Orta. Garcia's boon companion Martim Affonso Sousa had a personality very like Bahadur's, and not surprisingly, the two men became friends.[2] Garcia was already a person of interest to me—I had, in the past few years, tracked him back to his birthplace in Portugal, and was presently engaged in unravelling his mysterious book *Colóquios dos Simples e Drogas da India*[3] and his many references to Bahadur only served to deepen its mystery.

I couldn't let it pass, so I went to Diu where Bahadur was murdered on 14 February 1537.

I stood at the scene of crime, and followed the dead man on his last days through landmarks that had stayed the hand of time.

And there I saw the hokka, the tree that fringed every crevice of the island.

It was the hokka that explained Bahadur to me. The son of a Rajput princess and a Muslim Sultân, he was the land itself, balanced between two languages, two cultures, two beliefs. He transcended all these categories by asserting his own identity: in his military prowess and in his ability to inspire loyalty and courage, he was unique. The dichotomy was forced on him, but in Bahadur the two strands wound naturally as the helix of his DNA.

---

2 'This [Sultân Bahadur] is naturally a conqueror, and of great heart, and the most indefatigable man that I've ever seen, and an extraordinarily great lord, save now that Fortune goes against him [...]'
—Martim Affonso de Sousa to Dom João III (1535)

3 *Colloquies on the Simples & Drugs of India*, published in Goa in 1563, is a book of botany and pharmacognosy.

Nobody understood this better than the peasants of Gujarat. When he lost the throne to Humayun, the peasants funded a new army for the king they believed in. The more I thought about Bahadur, the more he seemed like a teenager in this polarized land of ours today—robbed of opportunity, tutored in hate and prejudice, and yet asserting his natural sense of justice. Dispossessed, yet unwilling to be bribed out of his right to belong. Unlettered, yet daring to pit not just his army but his wits against the scholar Humayun, his alter ego, his nemesis.

I saw also in Bahadur the story of a man unjustly accused and forced to bear the guilt of heinous crimes he did not commit.

The histories from which I sourced Bahadur's story were not direct narratives. They were circular, oblique, telescopic, allusive. Puranic might be the best word to describe them. They were adventurous, prophetic, exaggerated and frankly fantastical.

Western historians were dismissive about them. They could be endured as fables or travellers' tales, but not as histories. I didn't think so. These histories shaped the imagination and explained how memory is retained. Modern histories are just as questionable—school textbooks are busy preparing new narratives of a freedom struggle just 70 years old. What cannot be reimagined across a span of five centuries?

I decided to tell Bahadur's story using the footnotes, fables and anecdotes contained in these histories as embellishments to the main narrative strand. For these, I chose different styles to retain the antic caper as well as the hushed wonder in these histories. You will find here the story of the marvelous kamarband which gave Sulaiman the Magnificent his cognomen, the tale of those famous fried carrots that poisoned the Padshah, the song that called a stop to Humayun's *qatl-e-aam,* and the Revolt of the Pen Pushers that nearly cost Humayun his new kingdom. And weaving in and out of these silken stories runs the homespun thread of Bahadur's tormented life.

Kalpish Ratna
[*Kalpana Swaminathan & Ishrat Syed*]

Part One

Kalpish Ratna

1

Damu

Mulgaon, Shashti Pranth, North Kokan, 1536

Light before daybreak, a yellow flicker on the edge of dreams, a roar in the doorway, ash, tears, screams. On land, a cindered village. From the retreating boat far out at sea, an island fringed with fire. When the smoke clears on the island, every man is a slave.

An hour before dawn Damu contemplates his place in this universe. Standing twenty feet above ground, balancing the fulcrum of the water pump, he treads its wide wooden arms. He watches the iron pitcher sink and rise out of a well as black as the night sky, and as invulnerable. It taps a secret artery of water deep beneath the rock. This inexhaustible pulse is now the village's only certainty.

Mulgaon is patrolled by men with guns. The *azaan*[4] has fallen silent. Temple bells are muffled, lest they offend. Women keep within doors. The Khan bleeds to death in a gutter, his sons are hanged.

In nearby Kondiviti, the market flourishes. Merchants speak in hushed tones of new taxes, new routes, more money. In Thana, silk looms clatter again.

Damu treads the fulcrum, worrying why.

His eyes chart the dark as if they can see beyond the fields, past the smoke of the coastline, far out to sea. His father says, 'We are slaves so that there may be no more burnings, so that the looms may work again, so that the merchants may make more money, so that our land is saved. This is the price we pay.'

'Who decided that?' Damu asks the Maulvi.

The Maulvi has been in hiding for a week from the men with guns.

Damu's family has sheltered him. If he is discovered, the Firangi[5] will torch their hut.

The Maulvi says their fates have been altered by the drunken stroke of a pen.

What does he mean by that?

---

4 Urdu … اذان … the call to prayer.

5 The Urdu word فرنگی [*Firangi*] is borrowed from the Arabic فرنج [*firanj*] meaning the French or Franks. It emerged during medieval interactions between the Arabs and the European Crusaders, who were almost all from France or the Frankish Kingdom. The word later came to mean *foreigner*, as all Europeans were in the Muslim world.

'The Maulvi is a fool,' his father says. 'Listen to the caravans, they bring all the good stories.'

Where do the caravans come from? Where do they go?

Lands are named by stuff the caravans bring, dream stuff, stuff for Rajas and Khans, too precious to be unpacked on the road, but wending its way somehow to the Shaniwar Bazaar. Here, rejects unacceptable at the depot because of their very pettiness, the smallness of their grandeur, are dusted off like a crush of mica. Silks fragmented as rainbows, ribbons and brocade sold as piece-goods, lusted after by women who never wear them but hoard them as dreams, and gift them as dower. Fistfuls of gemstones, cracked, tainted, clouded, but spitting fire just the same, or sulking with concealed colour, morose till the light provokes a gleam of purple, rose, green or gold. These are avidly bought by the poor as amulets for their children. Rich folk who can afford the Vasai jewellers disdain these treasures, but Damu still wears a small garnet strung around his waist.

If you don't want the flash and flicker of jewels, you still go to the bazaar, just for the smell of it. You can fill your lungs with the scent of a Raja's kitchen—pepper, cinnamon, nutmeg, mace, cloves, cardamom, star anise—fragments and twigs that smell of heaven. You never exhale those smells, they keep looping through your brain, singing in your blood when you chew at your bhakri-chutney.

And the horses!

Cavalcades that get the villagers lining the roads swooning in wonder.

Black, silver, brown, no matter what their colour, the horses' coats are like silk. They step like dancers, straining and rebelling at the strange air, wild with relief at pacing solid ground again after the terror days at sea.

Children run after them for gifts of coins or candy, for the riders are always generous.

The horses are for royalty, this Raja or that Sultân. They come from beyond the sea, from Makkah and the countries of sand, from Zanj, from places that have no name. They go to all the Sultâns and Rajas, but mainly to Mulgaon's own Sultân in Gujarat who has the pick of the finest since the white men came.

Before that, the Raja of Vijayanagar had the best horses, and his men led them with such sweet music that the whole village, not just the children, ran after the cavalcade.

Their masters may be at war, but the horse merchants are a noisy, back-slapping, friendly crew, always ready with a laugh. Rough fellows, but they warm Damu's heart. They have stories too, but the best stories come at night when the bazaar has folded up, and the horses led away to the stables. Then the villagers bring out their welcome, food and fruit and sweetmeats, baskets of mango, sacks of rice. And the sweetest toddy in the world. These are gifts, thanksgiving, for the privilege of living on the caravan route.

And such a short route it is too!

It can be walked in a day, from the Ulhas to Mahim, from Vasai to Bandra.

The merchants come from the mainland across the creek from Thana and Turbhe, or over the ghats from the Dakshin. From the Mahim river they sail to the harbour at Mumbai where the bigger boats lie moored. From there they sail to Chaul, or where they will! Some say beyond Zanj, south around the land, past the ocean demons into a bigger ocean so cold, so vast and so peaceful that the crew pass on into eternal sleep.

What good is a story without demons and magic? Like the Vasai Rakshasi,[6] like Devis all around the island, like Mumba Rakshas[7] who disappointingly turned out to be only Mubarak Khan.

Stories judge the truth, not the other way around.

The village gathers for the stories on the large maidan cleared of bales and carts for the occasion. When everybody has eaten, and the musicians have tired the listeners out, stories begin around the fire.

Nobody knew when a story ended or a new one began, they fit one within another, as all good stories should.

Sometimes, when he was a boy, Damu would fall asleep and wake to find a sky full of wheeling stars and the storyteller's voice seemed to stream down from their immeasurable distance.

The stories come in many tongues, but the village has an interpreter who takes up when the visitor stops for breath—and lets fly a tale so florid that Damu doubts if it is the same as the visitor's. It must be, for the village knows the interpreter well enough by light of day. He is a Brahman so stupid he couldn't be trusted with the scriptures, and so was left to learn the many languages of trade, and learn them well he did. Perhaps he wasn't so stupid after all. But he certainly is a dull fellow, and invention is beyond him.

Damu believes the stories. Treading the pump leaves his mind free to think about them. He wonders if the Maulvi knows that story, the last one he heard before he became a slave, and the Maulvi a fugitive. It is a story about slaves and fugitives and it is called ...

6 Sanskrit ... राक्षसी ... female demon.

7 Sanskrit ... राक्षस ... male demon.

2

The Shining Sword of Samarqand

The wheel of Time turns, friends, follow its tread we must! Old books, old stories have vanished with other yugas! Kali is upon us, and who will rescue us from its demons, bhoot, rakshas, djinn, afreet, unless we hear their stories? Blessed be the good merchant Ghazanfar who brings us this tale! Blessed be our noble Sultân whose road brings the merchant to us! Blessed be his father, and his forefathers, may Allah give him increase!

This story, my friends, is from the mountains, the great Himalaya, of which the tallest as we all know, is Kailasa. Our friend here has not seen Kailasa. He brings his story from another mountain. There are hundreds of mountains, thousands of mountains, lakhs of them in the Himalaya. You and I would be lost, brothers, if we ventured there to test his tale!

Mountain slopes are thick with tigers, triple-headed beasts whose fangs drip venom that will freeze a man's heart to stone. Serpents thicker than palm trunks, quicker than lightning in their strike, they glide about with jewels so bright on their flat heads, no lamps are lit by night! The rocks are steep and sharp and kill with coldness even before they pierce your feet! No! It is no place for us Shashtikars!

Leave it to the demons, say I!

Leave them their land, but listen to their story!

In Dilli—Ah! Allah! Who does not know Dilli?

Dilli, city of shaitans, where rakshas after rakshas has built palace and tower and masjid and wall so strong they're mistaken for mountains.

Now Dilli had a Sultân,[8] a sad and timid man who trembled when the wind blew, and shuddered when he heard the drumbeats of war.

One day, his wazir told him there was a tumult in the mountains, beyond the land of fruit and roses, behind the rocky peaks where the wind blew on thousands of miles of empty land.

'Are there no people in this land?' the Sultân asked.

'No,' said the wazir, 'emptiness is the nature of this land.'

---

8 *Sultân* [Arabic … سلطان] derives from the Semitic root *salaṭa* [سلاطا] which means 'to be strong, resolute.' As a noun *sultân* initially designated moral authority and spiritual power (not political power) and is used in this sense in the Qur'an.
At the end of the 10th century, *sultân* began to be employed to describe individual rulers with sovereign authority and the territories and state ruled by such a sultân became his *sultanate* [سلطنت].

'Then be silent for it does not interest me,' thundered the Sultân.

So the wazir was silent, but saddling his horse, he rode out north to listen.

And where did he go?

Why, he went to a bazaar, to the very bazaar our good merchant Ghazanfar comes from. Ghazanfar rubbed shoulders with the wazir as they listened to the wind whisper:

How many heads did he bring home today?
Yesterday?
And how many more tomorrow, pray?
How many heads did he bring home today?

'Who is this *he*?' the wazir asked.

And the bazaar answered, 'The Shining Sword of Samarqand!'

The Shining Sword of Samarqand leaps from his sheath when you shed a tear, you should know that, Shashtikars, maybe he'll come to wipe ours!

Ghazanfar here says it is an old story.

And I ask: How old?

Do stories age, wrinkle, and creak at the joints, like you?

No?

Then tell it as it is happening, unroll it like one of the carpets you carry, throw at our feet flowers, fruits, birds, the very scents of Paradise.

Listen, then, to the tale of the Shining Sword of Samarqand!

When he was twelve, in the Holy Month, his blessed father, the King, climbed up the ramparts and stretching his arms heavenward, he prayed. The pigeons from the dovecote rose in a milk-white cloud as he called out his son's name, and such was the magic of that name, the King was transformed into a falcon. His wings were striped with gold and scarlet, his beak shone like steel, his talons mighty like Jatayu's,[9] he rose in an arc over the setting sun, then down he swooped over the fortress, seeking out his son. With his retinue of pigeons the Falcon King circled the courtyard where the boy was practicing his archery. Birds ringed the courtyard with shifting shadows. The boy's aim never wavered. Every arrow pierced the weaving shadows and found its mark.

Is this really my son, wondered the Falcon, Or is it Arjun,[10] returned?

And up he rose for his karma was complete, and breaking past the clouds like Garuda[11] hurrying home to Vaikuntha,[12] became a small black dot against the sinking sun and was seen no more.

[9] Sanskrit … जटायु … In the epic *Ramayana*, Jatayu is a vulture who defies Ravana as he abducts Sita. Rama, distracted with grief at the loss of Sita, meets the wounded Jatayu whose dying narrative leads to Sita's rescue.

[10] Sanskrit … अर्जुन … In the epic *Mahabharat*, Arjun, one of the five Pandava brothers, is an archer nonpareil.

[11] Sanskrit … गरुड … Garuda is a kite, Vishnu's ride and companion.

[12] Sanskrit … वैकुण्ठ … literally, 'without anxiety.' The residence of Vishnu; heaven.

The boy put away his toys and became king.

King, yes, but not king enough for him!

The name of his country was Farghana.

Ghazanfar tells me the pomegranates there are full of Badakhshan rubies, and as for the melons, their flesh is solid honey, four fingers thick. Streams warble like birds as they hurry to join the holy Ganga, birds sing like the flute, and the veena there captures all the melody of nature in its strings.

This Farghana, the country of the Boy King, was fat with grain and fruit and flower, but in the west was—Samarqand!

The boy played the veena and sang with the voice of the koel, but he sang only of Samarqand.

Every night he asked his Grandmother, 'And when shall we take Samarqand?'

'Not yet,' she answered.

From the south and the east and the north enemies thundered in, each with his sword upraised, ready to skin the stripling and seize the throne.

'Welcome!' the boy called out, 'enter as kings and leave as my subjects!'

Two turned back at the boy's words, but the third army charged up the river towards the fort.

At the boy's command the clear water became a swirling morass. The little bridge—swarmed so suddenly with men, horses, camels—splintered and gave way. Horses and men swam helplessly, but with every stroke the water drew them in. Round and round whirled the horses in its churning current, sucked noisily into its muddy funnel, leaving a stink so evil it shrivelled the fruit ripening on trees and cindered the roses to ash.

'Now, shall we take Samarqand?' the boy asked impatiently.

'Not yet,' said the Grandmother.

Samarqand had a new king—Kans![13]

What?

How did Kans turn up there, when Krishna slew him in the *Mahabharat*?

That was in another age. This is Kali, bhau, Kali, everything that happened then will happen again, only much worse.

What did that Kans do? He dashed Devaki's babies down on the rocky floor of her prison and shattered their skulls, once, twice, seven times!

What did this Kans do, this Kans of Samarqand? He didn't touch the babies, he let the babies alone, but I'll tell you what he did. H*e picked the boys*.

That's right, you heard me.

Not a boy was left in Samarqand but had served his time as the King's catamite.

Yatha raja, tatha praja![14]

---

13 Sanskrit ... कंस ... In the Krishna legends, Kans is Krishna's maternal uncle. Fearful of a prophecy that his nephew will usurp the throne, he imprisons his sister Devaki and her husband for years. During this time, Devaki bears seven children. Kans kills each infant at birth. Kans is a byword for insensate cruelty.

14 Sanskrit aphorism which means: *The subjects mirror their ruler.* The English equivalent would be: *Like father, like son.*

Each man in court had his band of boys, blinded, imprisoned, tormented into doing things of which, being a Brahman, I may not speak, although I have heard every detail from Ghazanfar, yes!

[No, you may fall at my feet, but I will not tell you.]

Shut your eyes instead and listen.

Can't you hear the wailing? Can't you hear the piteous cries of those parents?

No?

That is because you're listening to the silence of those boys.

In Farghana, the Boy King heard both.

'Shall we not take Samarqand now?' he demanded angrily.

But the Grandmother answered, 'Not yet.'

This Kans was rewarded, like that Kans, with fear. Death haunted him. His sons died. His wives died. His concubines and catamites died. They all died cursing him. The people cursed him and clamoured for the Boy King.

'The Falcon is not swifter than his son!' they shouted. 'He will be here before you know it!'

At Samarqand, Kans staggered about in terror. Half crazed in panic, he ordered his soldiers to attack the Boy King at the ramparts where the falcon had flown up to Heaven.

And so they marched on Farghana!

Maddened and confused by the drunken orders of the Samarqand Kans, they sent forth a swarm of arrows that turned inwards on the archers themselves.

Perhaps it was the wind, for all the thrice-sixty Maruts[15] that powered the Fathering Falcon's flight returned to protect his son. Perhaps it was the Night, for Chandrika hid herself in terror from the rapist.

Whatever the force that turned the arrows, it sent one straight at the wicked Kans of Samarqand, and impaled him! Transfixed his very shame. The arrow threaded him from orifice to orifice.

'Now shall we take Samarqand?' the Boy King asked wearily, for he was sickened by so much evil.

'Not yet,' said his Grandmother.

Now you may ask, he was a King, wasn't he? Why did he have to listen to his Grandmother? What kind of King does that?

I will answer you.

He was a King, true, but he was also a child of twelve. He was a child, true, but he was a King too, and well read in this and that shastra you and I have not even heard of, not being kings ourselves! Like our own Sultân, the Boy King was a Rajarshi[16] and treated his elders with respect. That is the sign of greatness!

The Boy King didn't question his Grandmother, but his heart ached, and he fell ill.

The illness of kings, my brothers, is quite different from our small complaints.

---

15 Sanskrit … मरुत … The deity of storms.

16 Sanskrit … राजर्षि … A king of great spiritual attainments.

Your son and mine may get fevers, but as for the Boy King, Agni[17] roared like a *havan* inside him.

Vaids and hakims buzzed around like flies, but not a bead of sweat could they wring out of his hot shiny skin.

His lips grew slack, his limbs motionless. Only his restless eyes roved west, always west, towards Samarqand.

A wick of cotton soaked in milk was dripped on his tongue, but swallow he could not.

Shadows gathered around him. Yamraj[18] beckoned from the south. Samarqand beckoned from the west. Enemies from the north and east.

And at that moment, the Grandmother said, 'Tomorrow we set out for Samarqand!'

Dashing the milky cotton from his lips, up he sprang, and called for his horse Tipchak [which was Vayudev[19] himself, disguised] and away he galloped, towards the west.

And what of Yamraj, do you ask?

There's the wonder of it all!

Yamraj trundled after him on his buffalo. Quite out of breath, he pursued the Boy King till they came to a great maidan. There, as the Boy King rested on the soft grass, Yamraj twitched his noose.

'Not so soon,' implored the Boy King. 'It is but an hour's ride to Samarqand. Come with me, and once I have Samarqand, I will go with you.'

Now we know that Yamraj was no longer bhola after Savithri[20] tricked him, but the Boy King's courage pleased him, so he said, very kindly, 'Alright, get some rest. When you're feeling stronger, let's go to Samarqand, get you crowned, and after that—'

'After that, I'm yours,' the Boy King said, and shutting his eyes against the soft sunshine, he fell into a deep sleep.

Flowers covered him with fragrant petals, butterflies opened and shut their silky fans, birds stopped singing lest he wake and flocked all around him. Yamraj too found a convenient tree, and in its shade, fell fast asleep.

While they slept the maidan was filling up slowly with tired people who had walked all the way from Samarqand to welcome the Boy King. So desperate were they in their misery, that when they heard the news the Boy King was on his way, they dropped everything and took to the road to meet him half way.

And now they were all here, camped on the road to the maidan, waiting for him to wake, chattering and gossiping, buying and selling, eating, arguing, quarrelling, no different from us Shastikars at Shaniwar Bazaar.

Indeed, the entire place had been converted into a large bazaar.

---

17 Sanskrit ... अग्नि ... The God of Fire. In Ayurveda, the word is also used for metabolism.

18 Sanskrit ... यमराज ... The God of Death and Justice.

19 Sanskrit ... वायुदेव ... The God of Wind.

20 Sanskrit ... सावित्री ... Mythic heroine, regarded as the ideal woman. She beguiled Yamraj with a wily logic that won him over and he restored her dead husband Satyavan to life.

The cacophony woke up Yamraj who, in turn, prodded his quarry awake. 'I don't have much time, so get going Rajkumar,' he urged.

But the Boy King laughed and huddled deeper in his cloak. 'What's the hurry?'

'Aren't you in a hurry to get to Samarqand?'

'No longer! The Samarqandis have come here, haven't they? I'm not going to Samarqand for a few years, but do wait here if you want to, we'll try to make you comfortable.'

For the second time in his long career, Yamraj had been outwitted.

He is the Lord of Justice, isn't he, and he begins by judging himself. And here he was defeated by a child! He laughed and blessed the Boy King with the largest kingdom in the world—and vanished.

The Boy King did go to Samarqand, but he was never easy about it, he never stayed long. He blamed it on enemies, but that wasn't true. He didn't trust Yamraj to keep his word, and to remind himself, he named that maidan Yam, and to this day that's the name it goes by.

Finally, after five long years, he decided to trust Yamraj after all and unsheathed his shining sword and went on to conquer the greatest kingdom in the world.

That's the story the wazir carried back to the timid Dilli Sultân, and that's the story Ghazanfar has brought to us! It is an old story, but for us, it is new! Our own Sultân has heard it many times, when he sits like you and me beneath the stars, tasting not our toddy, but two-headed toddy, from the two-headed *tād* of the Sultâns.

What, do you think the toddy has gone to my head that I should speak of a two-headed *tād*?

No, it is true!

The Sultân's *tād* is a two-headed tree, and when its nectar drips on the tongue, it makes a man two-headed, which is what a Sultân needs to be. He has to think for himself, true, but he must think for us too.

And where is this two-headed *tād*?

Ghazanfar has seen it on an island.

What island?

An island is an island.

And what is the tree called, this two-headed *tād*?

'Hokka?' Right. 'Hokka!'

Say it after me. Hokka. Yes, that's what it is.

Hokka.

3

Hokka

Hokka.

That's me.

That's my name in my time.

My ancestors had different names, because they came from a different country, from across the ocean.

I am the ocean's omphalos.

To my west, Africa.

To my south, a frozen land, unnamed.

Approaching me, a sail.

Everything passes through me. That's my heritage.

You might object to that and point out I'm just a tree. A freakish palm tree.

True.

A freak anywhere except on this island, and in my ancestral place of which I have no more than the memory passed on by seeds, and from what I know, that's a very long memory.

We trees are older than men, yet our memory has a human scale.

Is that not strange?

Perhaps that's because you, a human, are listening to me, a tree, and our common ground for understanding must be Time, the universal matrix.

Trees see further than men can, and a tree on an island can see beyond the sea. Ships drift in and out, battles are fought, men die.

All this we observe without any real sense of time.

The pulse of the seasons measures us.The rhythms of the ocean, the crumble of rock into anchoring soil, these are our determinants.

On the human scale, you and I have known each other for at least 5,000 years, from the time of the Pharoahs who were the Sultâns and

Padshahs[21] of the land of my ancestors, which you insist on calling Misr, Egypt, forgetting that land is really its water.
The pulse of the land, like that of your body, is the rushing tide of its conduits.
The artery of Misr is Iteru, Hpi, Nahal, Al-Neel, Al-Azraq, the Nile.
My ancestors thought of their land not as Egypt but as the Nile. And I, nourished by the ocean's tang, I too was once, they tell me, a creature of the Nile.
Who cares?
Not I!
So many men of Africa have walked past me without a look. Surely, they should know me. Their children suck my nectar, it is sweeter than their mothers' milk. My leaves shelter them. My wood is the spine of their civilization. The hard ivory of my kernel gave them joy—as toys, as jewels.
I healed their sick.
I made floating bridges for their kings to walk across rivers.
I was mother, father, doctor, jeweller, turner, architect—for a hokka can be hired to do the impossible.
That's what we do. It is the diktat of the seed.
When defeat is inevitable, a hokka always wins. Men have known that for millennia.
When it gets rough, they look to a hokka to provide. In the desert, moisture. In famine, fruit. For the hearth, fuel. For the wanderer, a roof. For the unfordable river, a bridge. For the man who pisses blood from the parasite that bites the bladder, ease. For the man whose brain threatens to explode, the calming ebb of blood tides. For rash, sore, itch, pustule, abscess, imposthume, balm. For apathy, coldness and impotence, heat.
All these things we provide.
The hokka is the one tree left standing after a forest fire.
All this the men of Africa know. But—do they know me?
A hokka has two heads, for my trunk bifurcates and then divides again, and yet again.
I have eight fans of two heads each, and I've just turned thirty.
Two streams of thought, one being.
A hokka must use both to survive. Cut off one, the other dies.

I'm not interested in heritage, see?
There's plenty in the here and now to occupy me.
I own this island now.
The people eat my fruit, burn my wood, weave my leaves.

---

21 *Padshah* [Farsi … پادشاه] … protecting lord, supreme.

Children play with the nuts once they've sucked my fruit dry.
They don't make toddy from my fruit, because I've made my peace with the tād[22], the coconut, the supari. I allow them here, but in small doses.
And I don't take away their importance.
The wine is theirs, but the island belongs to me.

People. People and their comings and goings make up Time, as I told you earlier.
On this island, nobody notices a hokka, but I suppose we'd be prized elsewhere.
I'm prized here by only one man.
I've known him for years, and not a year goes by without his coming to see me.
Like me, he's two-headed.
I'm the only two-headed palm in this part of the world, and he's the only two-headed man I know. Like a hokka, he's hired for impossibilities.
A two-headed man is a curiosity in the country of the two-headed tree. When I first saw him, I recognized him, as he recognized me.
We were of the same age. We became friends.
Trees are invisible to humans except in their moments of leisure, or perhaps when, thrilled by a stray current of curiosity, they pause in question.
It is very rarely that a human looks at us as he would at another human face. The two-headed man did that the day we met, and I knew straight away that he was one of us. He had sought me out. It was only logical that a two-headed man should need a two-headed tree.
He travelled here, looking for me.
It was the Firangi year 1524. For him: 930 Hijri and 81, Vikram Samvat.
Then, he knew nothing at all about this place, this island.
Listen to the air if you want to know about the island, I told him. Hang about the wharf. Everything vibrates, like aftershocks from an earthquake concealed in the ocean, in ever-widening circles of story.
Listen—

22 The Asian Palmyra palm, *Borassus flabellifer*, பனைமரம் in Tamil, ताड़ [*tād*] in Hindi.

4

Diu

Diu!

Infinitesimal, ink dot overlooked, comedo on Gujarat's jowly gape—from whose point of view?

Dweep. Divya. Dwip. Dev-Diu. Dio. Diu. Div.

Call it what you want. Acknowledge that it is bigger than the mainland. It conjures up ships from nothingness. Piercing the invisible walls of the ocean they ride in from nowhere west and somewhere south, floating libraries encyclopaedic with life. And Diu, besotted bibliophile, jingles its coins. Its pockets go deep, deeper than memory, which on Diu is a much abbreviated article, no older than a century, ignoring the clock set 178,000 years ago for the patient accretion of generations of sea creatures, the laminate perforate miliolite and acidulated karst that make the bones of the island. Ignoring also the equally patient accretion of human thought, like the thinkers, soon lost in the wind. Memory is selective on Diu as it is everywhere. It begins with Shahzada Jalal Khan, afterwards Sultân Qutubuddin, remembered on the mainland for Kankaria Lake with its floating Nagina, but overlooked for his valour in driving away the Chinese fishing boats that sailed up from Cochin, right to Gujarat's chin. Nothing tells us why he was on this island of pirates, what pickings he had come to glean, but Jalal Khan swooped down on the Chinese boats, and in sending them spinning into splinters, he fortuitously noticed the location of this most insignificant of his possessions, and set about making a city of it in the usual way, by building a wall around it and taxing the people. But after he became Sultân, his wars and skirmishes, his wild amours, his brilliant gardens, his quarrels with the Sufi Sheikh who sheltered his hated half-brother and married his bed-tricked bride, all these, we are told with malicious relish, murdered him in his twenty-eighth year. And having begun the city, he left Diu to its own devices, which were not lacking, for rumour flies faster than the Sultân's word, and when ships on the Makkah route put in for water, they found a growing body of merchants, middlemen, money-changers, interpreters and slave dealers swarming the quay, confident their wares would reach Hormuz and Aden, from there to find the vast bazaars of white men, or else to go further west from Socotra and trawl the African markets with musical names, Malindi, Mogadishu, Mozambique, or east to Malacca, to China and who knows where. They mobbed the wharf for quicksilver chance, nibbles, dribbles, leavings, scraps, until everything changed because of a bird. A common crow that did the uncommon thing by a cloacal squirt of pungent lime-green slime on the upraised brow of the Sultân as he scanned the heavens on the eve of war. No ordinary Sultân he, but Two Forts Mahmud, prodigious of appetite, canny of judgement, Sultân Mahmud Begada, a man who ate one *maund* of rice a day and breakfasted on a cup of honey, a cup of butter, and one hundred and fifty golden bananas. This man who was formerly the hated half-brother of Diu's founder, and now the man with the largest Kingdom in history, this man, enraged, bawled angrily that he would reward the man who would shoot that upstart bird. No sooner said than an arrow pinioned the crow to a tree, and the archer, Ayaaz, till then slave in a merchant's retinue, was gifted freedom and the Sultân's ear, which he used most ably to direct campaigns with his military skill and got Mahmud Begada his second *gadh*, Pavagadh of Champaner. Subsequently the story changed; the common crow was transformed into a hawk to give status to its royal salute and Ayaaz the slave became Malik Ayaaz. And as reward, the Sultân offered him the wilderness of Diu, the most paltry jagir in the kingdom, not guessing that Ayaaz, [now Gujarati but formerly Russian, by way of Istanbul and Basra; now Mussalman, but formerly Christian; now a soldier, but he had served with merchants] would see on the crowded wharf at Diu no rabble of hopefuls but merchants, bankers, capitalists, as worthy as any in the counting-houses of Hormuz and Aden and Bharuch, lacking but the respectability of a mercantile city to back the port. So Ayaaz secured the port, gathered an army and built a fortress on a rock in the harbour and fashioned chains to limit entry. This fort, the Sangal Kotha, was but his first step to secure the island. Walls went up like thoughts at every creek, and within these he partitioned the city into streets for different trades, and let it be known that all trades were welcome and men and their families would be housed and fed until trade picked up. As he made no difference of tongue or colour or religion, the streets were soon full of people whose many languages made pleasant music, whose many colours spoke of many nations, whose diverse faiths continued diverse, but whose loyalties were all one with his own, prosperity. And how they prospered! Malik Ayaaz the most of all. Diu was noticed by ships from Hormuz and Aden. The Makkah trade was now shipped by the one thousand importers and exporters who had their offices around the Sangal Kotha, By the end of the first year, one hundred ships on the Red Sea route had called at Diu, and Malik Ayaaz bought their merchandize by paying them in gold, no barter, and then he traded with the importers and exporters, sending and receiving, dealing with honesty and expecting the same in return. Yet he kept his army close, so no man dared chicanery of any kind on the island. But mind you, this was half a century ago, and at Diu they did not yet know what the next two years would bring: the Portuguese whose hearts were all for the ocean, and for nothing else; whose greed was a bottomless abyss that Malik Ayaaz would foolishly attempt to appease. The news came soon enough from Cochin when the pepper failed to arrive. The ship *Miri* full of Hajjis was burnt, the Firangi da Gama stood by unperturbed as children wailed for mercy, the Brahman envoy was sent back to the Samudri with his legs and arms cut off and a sack full of ears and noses and genitals harvested from the Nairs sent out with him. These stories came to Diu. And Malik Ayaaz, resolving there was much to do, began by publishing his luxuries so that Firangi heard of the table he kept every day with the richest dishes from all known cuisines so that stranger or friend, all may eat: Brahman, Jain, Mussalman, Rumi, Siddi, Chinese, Firangi, for there were at that time in Diu, very many Firangi about. Stories travelled of the gardens he had laid with fountains and rare flowers, of the roses he cultivated for *itr*[23] so intense that it could be smelt far out at sea, of the monopoly he held on silks and ivory, on gemstones from Khambat, from Vijayanagar, from the Tamil country, from Lanka, and by the land route from Badakhshan and beyond. And then there were textiles, Gujarat's prized prints and richly embroidered weaves no Raja or Sultân could reign without. Spices from Malacca he held in his palm for the Arab traders dealt with him alone. And horses, horses by the thousand, for every kingdom in Hindustan. But Ayaaz now considered what had been recently achieved: a larger entrepôt that could bypass the Red Sea, go south of Mozambique, round the Horn of Africa, grab the *volta do mar* and waft directly to Europe, and considering the Firangi friends worth having, he sent word inviting them to sell copper at Diu. In answer came alarm from Hormuz, port taken, city plundered, people massacred, ships burnt, including one of his own. The name was a new one, Alfonso d'Albuquerque, but the pattern was familiar to this former slave who knew this Albuquerque would not stop at Hormuz; and firangi ships loaded with canon, patrolled the coast from Cochin, firing at Anjediva, at Bhatkal, at Goa, some said as far north as Vasai, frightening away the Aden ships, none of which dared venture after Hormuz was taken. From that moment on, Malik Ayaaz was a pauper despite his income of 1 lakh 60,000 cruzados a year and the fortunes of Diu began to vacillate between prosperity and war. With Venice, Cairo and Istanbul joining the Samudri in defying the firangi, Malik Ayaaz won one war against the firangi and lost another in the time of the next Sultân whom he served with the kind of intelligence and loyalty that is always suspect, and becoming a target of malice and envy, he died dishonoured far away from his beloved island. But our Sultân, the Sultân of these times, finding the injustice intolerable, kept on the son of Ayaaz, Malik Toghan, as the ears and eyes of Diu. Taking counsel from another tycoon, Khwaja Zafar; once Albanian, now Gujarati, and always a merchant; the young Sultân first quarreled and then pacified and bartered with the Firangi.

So now Diu has been stood on its head, for in the time of Malik Ayaaz no firangi ship dared enter the harbour without his permit, and now in the time of Sultân Bahadur, no ship at all may enter the harbour without a permit from the firangi. And who can say what all this will lead to, especially now as Ramzan begins, and men grow quarrelsome rather than peaceful, and the air is thick with whispers for Diu is a place of pluralities and from a man's skin or faith it is impossible to judge his loyalties. Lights burn like warnings on the massive fort the Firangi have built as if the land belongs to them. When the Sultân ordered a wall to be built to protect the town from the firangi and compelled them to pay permits to enter, there was much bad blood, and the Sultân had the wall dismantled. And so they have continued uneasy even though the Sultân has embraced their Captain of the Sea and called him friend, their eyes continue wary,

23 Urdu ... عطر ... perfume, essence; *itr* has entered English as the mondegreen 'attar.'

and they say the Captain of the Fort awaits the firangi governor, Nuno da Cunha,[24] by all accounts an evil man, more Pirate than Governor, having burnt Surat and Rander and Gogha and Vasai, and has set greedy eyes, some say, on the Sultânate itself. These may be rumours, yet daylight will bring truth, for the wharf has been busy all night, and the bridge of Malik Ayaaz that leads to the town of Goghla on the mainland is being patrolled by the firangi although they have no right to police the island, it being under the rule of Sultân Bahadur, with Malik Toghan as Governor. Rumour even says the Sultân himself is Malik Toghan's guest at Una this week, but nobody can predict the Sultân who is like a vein of quicksilver, so swift is he and so many times has he been shattered and joined whole again. Only daylight can tell if a firangi ship treads water, and what manner of men have disembarked, so I'll go to the wharf, and stealing a line from a play not yet written, cry out, 'You are welcome, Sir, to Diu. Goats and monkeys!'[25]

24 Nuno da Cunha, the Portuguese admiral who was the governor of Portuguese possessions in India from 1529 to 1538.

25 William Shakespeare was born twenty-seven years after Bahadur's murder. He wrote *The Tragedy of Othello, the Moor of Venice* in 1603. The play is set during the Ottoman-Venetian War of 1571-73 for the control of the island of Cyprus.

5

14 February 1537 [Part i]

On the third day of Ramadan, an hour before dawn, a rider thundered down the Una road towards the sea. He sat light in the saddle, leaning forward to urge his steed.

Night wrapped everything. Even the sea was out of sight.

The man relaxed, gentling the horse's neck with his fingertips. This was how he liked it. Just the three of them: him, the horse and the road, and the world could go hang.

This was how he liked it, and usually, it was enough to restore him. Usually, the blood tides beating in his skull retreated, leaving his thoughts clear and shining. In a little while, he would have a plan, and by the time they stopped, the joy of it would break out in a laugh. Anything was possible!

Not today.

His eyes strained for starlight. He stopped the horse, scanned the heavens. Not a scintilla showed. Like the darkness, the silence was absolute.

He felt the horse's skin change. It no longer fell soft and pliant, a satin paniculus with the secret intelligence of muscle. It had become mail, tensile as silk, tough as steel.

That pleased him. The beast had sensed his discomfort, and responded with alertness as Barq would have.

Barq.

An icy fist punched his chest at the name. Memory was a bitch. It brought up Barq's soft neigh, his warm smell. He waited for the pain to pass. That was a trick he had learnt recently. All pain passes, eventually. One simply has to wait.

He would name this young one for his father. Barq.

'Barq,' he whispered the name against the silvery mane. The horse smelt sweet and milky, like a child. His hand hovered, then drew back. It would not do to fondle the beast. A slight pressure from his thighs served to soothe the horse's nervousness.

The horse was easily disciplined.

Not so the melancholy growing in him.

He eased the horse to a canter.

Night still wrapped everything, shut out the world, kept them safe. But it was no longer enough: him, the horse and the road.

The road always found him. No matter how rough, or how featureless the terrain, the road always revealed itself. His blood thrilled to that moment when the impassable yielded passage, closed off all the rest, drew him deeper down a road of his own making. Even in the Rann where the air crackled with salt and hooves ground down bone dust, the road awaited him.

For solitude he often set out at nightfall, having sent the rest a few stages ahead. He had heard it whispered that he had the eyes of a cat. Make that a cheetah, he amended grimly, then stopped himself. He was jealous of the animal. He had yet to find a horse as fast as a cheetah.

Last week, he had refused Malik Toghan's cheetah for the hunt. It was a magnificent beast, nearly six feet long. It advanced at an amble, slow and languorous, each step invoking a ripple in the velvet haunch. The carnelian eyes, lined with collyrium, were hard and calculating. Toghan had dressed it like a courtesan. The black satin cape on its shoulders was embroidered with gems, the solemn wink of garnet and emerald relieved here and there by an iridescent flash of diamond. Its feral reek had been sweetened with rose water. It was muzzled with an iron mask, but its chains were of gold. It stood staring contemptuously, ears pinned back against its flat skull.

Upon Toghan's urging, he was forced to say he had yet never needed a cheetah to land his prey.

Such statements, Haridas had warned him, would be recorded as boastful and vain. And he had never heeded Haridas.

But that was long ago.

Where was Haridas now when he needed caution?

He had thrown away caution as he had thrown away Haridas, a fistful of ash on the desert wind.

Boastful or not, he had done without the cheetah. He patted the horse in approval. Nanu, now Nanu Barq, had done well. His arrow had missed the neck and wounded the nilgai on the shoulder, but Nanu had caught up with the fleeing beast and his dagger had done the rest. He had the carcass dressed and sent to the Firangi. Toghan had muttered about that too. The venison should have been cooked, he said, he had the finest cooks in Hindustan, the Firangi were barbarians, their dinners were inedible. Then let them eat like barbarians, he had retorted. Malik Toghan was easily offended, so it would be best to invite them to a feast. That put the smile back on Toghan's face. A simple fellow at heart, but Toghan did like ostentation. Right now, he needed the man. Malik Toghan's word was law in Diu, even his royal guest must abide by it.

'Nanu Barq,' he whispered. The horse twitched an ear in response. Barq's firstborn too hadn't been named for him, but once the young stallion measured up to his father's speed, he was called Kuchak Barq, Little Barq. Kuchak, like Barq, had died honourably, in battle.

Nanu was still untried. Barq's blood was sound, but the dam could not be trusted.

Nanu had speed, but it was stamina that counted in horses, as in men.

This was a short ride, five kos,[26] half an hour. Besides, the horse knew the road. They had made this trip last evening at *maghrib*. He should be quicker.

The rider cupped the horse's right ear, gently. It had been his usual signal to Barq—would his grandson read it as easily?

---

[26] A measure of distance, one *kos* is about 3000 meters or 1.8 miles.

Nanu was still skittish and headstrong as his Arab dam. Like himself, this horse was a doum.[27]

Doum.

The first time he had heard that term, it was meant as insult.

The word had been unfamiliar. The speaker was a man of Misr, his speech slurry with *afim*[28] and wine. Later, when he understood the insult mocked his heritage, he got level with the man with a boy's cruelty, vengeful, wanton, ferocious. Now he wished the deed undone. In that man's land doum was the name of a tree, a twinned tree, two disparate trees growing out of a common trunk. When he discovered the tree for himself, the word ceased to be an insult.

The tree grew on this island, the place was thick with it. He had never seen it any other place, desert, coast, hill or plain. But it grew here, as if it owned rights to every inch of the island. It had ambushed him on his first visit. When was that? Nine—no, ten years ago. The tree had two divergent heads, two fans of palm. It branched beyond into two more and so on until its canopy was a cluster of tassels, all of them twinned.

It was a tree, but it was himself he saw.

Everything that made him was twinned.

Hindavi-Rumi. Hindu-Mussalman. Farsi-Gujarati.

These streams ran parallel, immiscible, making up one identity that could unravel at a thought.

What then?

They swung free, these threads, each one a loyalty for hire.

The tree was stronger. It could not be unravelled. Its twin heads depended on their shared origin. The doum was above price, and so, had inherited the land. It had assumed the identity of the land. No longer doum, it was *hokka.*

A tree could do it. A horse could do it. What stopped a man?

Nothing would stop him. He would not be unravelled for hire. He would stay rooted like the hokka. He would stay Bahadur, Shah of Gujarat.

The ocean was audible now.

Suddenly, the sound was everywhere. It had swallowed the dark.

Bahadur felt its suction, compelling him deeper into its vortex. He had a moment of terror, felt it gather him in, enfold and squeeze him in a tightening torque down its muscled gullet. He shook away the thought.

For the millionth time he told himself that fear was the price of neglect.

He had neglected the ocean.

He had ridden through every inch of land he ruled, but he had never yet ventured far out to sea. Brief sailing expeditions out of Gogha in the company of mariners was the most he had done. Eighty-seven ports. *Eighty-seven*! All bringing in wealth and fortune, and he had neglected them all by trusting them to men who knew the business of commerce. None of them knew the business of war at sea.

27 Urdu … دوم … twinned.

28 Urdu … افیم … Opium; laudanum.

He had been a long time conceding that. Finally, he sent for help. He didn't like the Rumi, but there, now, the deed was done. Asaf had left two days ago. His precious cargo was enough to turn the head of an emperor. Humayun would have sold his children to possess one hundredth of it. But Asaf Khan could be trusted. Not one ashrafi would be missing when the tally was made in Istanbul.

Greed. He had his share of it, if not for gold, for the luxuries it bought: not just libraries, musicians, horses, dogs, but loyalties. Obligations.

This was a land where men still traded on honour.

But the Firangi came from another land. They talked money, and the idiom of honour was unknown in their tongue.

Yesterday, he had visited Pani Kotha[29] with two amirs. There was no doubt the Firangi grew fat on the duty they levied.

As was his custom when away from court, he was dressed like a commoner and had done away with ceremony. Nothing but the polite deference with which he was treated, identified the Sultân.

The amirs who accompanied him were forced to adopt the same ease, but they were seated as persons of quality, on rich cushions on the dais.

Bahadur sat with the port officers, interviewing men from the boats that had made port from Malabar, from Bhatkal, Dabhol, and Chaul. He spoke with the mariners first and gave a careful hearing to their complaints.

All of them complained about the *cartaz*,[30] the pass issued by the Firangi.

Their fathers had sailed these waters for centuries, *they* hadn't seen these white faces before.

'Tell me, huzoor,' a weathered sailor demanded. 'Was there a battle we missed? No? Then what made the Firangi masters of the sea?'

Captain after captain grumbled at the loss. They were not allowed to carry pepper. There was a special cartaz required for other spices. The same was true of small dealers. Nobody had denied them their profits till now, they answered to the market alone. Now it appeared the market was closed to them. It would make better sense to sell directly to the Firangi.

The bigger merchants had a different story—or no story at all. 'If it has to be paid, it will be paid' was the cant.

That meant trouble. It meant they were already making deals with the Firangi.

He meant to get the truth out of Malik Toghan, and wondered if the fat fellow gave the situation much thought.

Toghan had inherited his father's magnificent fortune and seemed bent on squandering every tanga of it.

The Firangi knew their man. As long as they kept him in a flutter of expectation, pandering to his insatiable taste for luxuries, Malik Toghan asked no questions.

---

29 Urdu ... پانی کو تھا ... a bastion and landing stage built by Malik Ayaaz, it acted as a fortification to control traffic into Diu harbour.

30 *Cartaz* ... A permit issued by the Portuguese.

The resentment against the cartaz was the burden of every man's song. The Firangi who sat across the hall could not have been unconscious of the contempt with which the coin was slapped down as each man was issued his scrap of paper.

After hearing the same story repeated by at least a hundred men, Bahadur had lost interest. His eye strayed to the window, and for the next hour he saw nothing beyond the square of ocean it framed. It was a small window, recessed deep in two feet of dense stone, yet the constant motion beyond, now blue, now turquoise, now iridescent, gave the window the shimmer of a Kashmiri sapphire, the wave-forms became facets refracting light. The shifting waterscape mocked the bastion's solidity.

Bahadur was reminded of the quality of rock on this island: fragile phyllodes of stone, glued like a Turkish sweet, not with syrup but the shells of tiny sea-creatures.

What a pretense it was, the land's rootedness!

The ocean was simply biding its time.

He should have noticed that before.

He should have befriended the ocean as the Firangi had. Their ships were at ease in these waters, even miles away from home. He was surprised to learn about the new Firangi routes from the *mallams*[31] in Gogha. Around the horn of Africa? Even the Chinese sailors with their floating castles hadn't dared those waters.

The *pothi*[32] of Gogha mariners did not know these Firangi routes.

Our ships cannot withstand those currents, they told him.

Build better ones, he snapped.

But they knew he wasn't serious.

The Firangi had more than ships and guns and instruments to read the stars. They had a madness he understood all too well. It thundered in his own veins, he knew its smell.

The difference between them was elemental. His madness was land. Theirs, the ocean.

Land had its limits.

The ocean broke all limits and claimed the horizon.

If that made them stronger, he did not resent it.

That was his mistake.

Was it in admiration, or in envy, that he gave his birthright away?

The ocean brought them, and the ocean took them away, their ships moved like pendulums, like the seasons, like heartbeats. They brought in paltry goods, and carried away the lifeblood of his land.

Money. Every port was being bled white.

The Makkah trade was dwindling rapidly. The Venetians, desperate to keep it going, were courting Istanbul.

And now, so was he.

---

31 Urdu … معلّم … though here it means a master sailor, the word *Mallam* is an honorific given to Islamic scholars in Africa. The Arabic … مولانا… *maulãna* … means 'master,' and on the subcontinent it is used as a respectful address for scholars of Islam.

32 Gujarati … પોથી … Traditional naval tables of Gujarati mariners.

These angry men, they had no idea why their fortunes were so bound up with the Firangi. Ten years ago, he would have told them the simple truth: *It was me. I did this to you.*

It was easily said then. Defiance, not confession.

I did this to you also dared *so what are you going to do about it?*

He was too old now for such arrogance.

He left the hall abruptly to a flutter of alarm among the officials.

Boats crowded the jetty, fragile shells of wood with fluttering pennants. On the horizon, galleons trod water awaiting goods from Malabar and the hinterland. Eschewing Makkah they would now make their way around Africa, defy giant waves of the south and cross another ocean to a land whose resplendence he could only imagine. Gold and silver, pearls and ivory, exquisite silks, thousands of tons of pepper—these would make port in some Firangistan. Treasures or trifles? Haridas would have told him the truth.

But Hari was gone.

Hari and Barq, his two eyes, both gone.

What was the use turning over pages of lost time? There was no time to be lost now, not today. As if in assent, the horse neighed softly, voicing its impatience. Bahadur laughed in the dark.

It was long since he had laughed that old laugh. Always, it signaled an end to bewilderment. It would be light very soon, and he meant to be on the beach at dawn.

'Fly, Nanu!'

He didn't have to say the words aloud. At his thought the horse took wing. The air roared as if they were lofted on the very waves that mocked him.

Ghoghla.

The place was named for the shells that washed up on the strand. No pearls here, just pretty shells, though some of them had rainbows trapped in their grey hardness. He found these enchanting, and last year he had his windows paned with them. They let in a soft pearly light that soothed his headaches. Soothed, not stopped. Nothing stopped them.

The Firangi hakim had assured him the headaches would stop if he gave up wine and afim.

The Persian hakim said afim was medicinal in his case, and stopping it would be fatal.

The vaid swore by wine, just a little Firangi wine, enough to raise his spirits, no more.

Idiots, the lot of them.

He had left on an empty stomach, but there was some fruit in the saddlebag, and water. Best breakfast now, while there was time. In the mist the hour might take one by surprise, and it would be *fajr* long before light crept up.

He ate and drank without dismounting. When it was time for namāz he would say whatever came to his lips as he rode. On the horse, he could still be Bahadur. When he dismounted, he was Sultân. Of late, the two strained further and further apart.

He no longer felt subsumed by the ocean. He was still uneasy. He was here this morning to counter that unease. He reminded himself of a drawing Haridas had made after one of their sailing trips. They had circumscribed his kingdom beginning at its southernmost point at the Mahim river, visited the scatter of islands around Mumbai, then north to Vasai, Daman, Navsari, Surat, Bharuch, Khambhat, then west to Lothal, and then south to Ghogha, Delvada, Una. At Diu they sailed around the island, passed northwest to Veraval, Porbandar and on to the western extremity at Bet Dwarka. There, turning into the Gulf of Kutch at Okha, they travelled east to Kandla, then Mandvi, then north to Narayan Sarovar, and finally, past the ancient temple of Koteshwar to the very edge of the Rann.

Haridas had drawn a line connecting the ports and it had made a surprising shape. In Haridas's drawing, Gujarat was a monstrous jaw, opened wide to swallow the ocean.

'A bird might see it like that,' mused Bahadur. 'A bird of prey, a kite or vulture circling very high might mistake Gujarat for a monster and think it competition.'

'It wouldn't be mistaken. Look at it! Gujarat, the world's gular pouch! Swallows everything, digests everything. Desert, ocean, hills, plains. Hindu, Mussalman, Sufi, Jain, and whatever's next on the list.'

'And then, in one grand regurgitation, spits them all far out to sea. Socotra, Africa—'

'Africa is the dam that walls the ocean and limits our mallams.'

'But the Firangi came around it. You think our ships aren't good enough?'

'Ships can be built. That's not our worry. Our worry is this land. Gujarat, Malabar, Tamil, no matter where your sailor comes from, his true north is his home. The magnetic tug of this land is something no man can resist.'

'They have homes too, in Firangistan.'

'Maybe, but their magnet is the ocean.'

Bahadur laughed at that. 'No, my innocent, their magnet is also our land. It was the Chaghtai's[33] magnet, Taimur's before him, and Mahmud of Ghazni's, and who knows how many before that?'

'Why? Is it just our wealth they want?'

'Just? It is all they want. It is all we want, warring and plundering each other.'

'You speak as if it sickens you.'

'It does. And yet I war and plunder. It is never enough.'

'You put wealth to good use. Some of the time.'

'Sometimes, yes,' he agreed with a laugh and they went off to inspect a Kutchi stallion he had heard about.

A skin of grey wrinkled the east into hills, into dark stands of trees. The ocean was still a blank.

Bahadur dismounted. Throwing the reins on the horse's back he schooled it to match his meditative stride. Once the horse learned this, words would no longer be

---

33 The Chaghtai … چغتائی … are descendants of Genghis Khan's second son Chaghtai Khan.

needed. From time to time he put a hand to the withers and wondered if the horse felt the same ease of companionship.

He was easy with horses and dogs.

Never with women.

The thrill of desire never came without dread these days.

Dead women haunted him.

He did his duty by his wives, perfunctorily. They put down his tepidity to wine, to afim, to his headaches, to the burdens of state.

He let them think what they wanted. He did not like them. There would be no more children, and he did not regret that.

Last week, he had appointed his heir publicly. If people wondered why a man of thirty, in vigorous health, should presume he would never have a son, they did not wonder aloud.

Dawn.

I've been watching you all night, said the ocean. *You never guessed, did you?*

'Coward! Come out and fight!'

Perhaps the ocean read him, perhaps he shouted out the words.

The tide hurtled in a rush of light, roaring its battle cry. But it lost heart as it neared, slumped and flattened abjectly in the sand.

It was playing him, like that girl had played him.

Why did he always think of her as 'that girl'?

There had been a dozen others, but he had forgotten their names, their faces. That girl had a name. He did not want to say it. It described her, described the last shocked look he had surprised, and described his shame.

At that moment, he had felt no shame, just fear. Terror of the sort he never felt in battle, for never had a foe terrified him like this. He could not confront his fear. How do you confront the enemy who has infiltrated, occupied, and suborned your will?

He made a truce. Now he lived with the enemy every breathing moment. They had this pact for life. He kept the enemy lulled on opium and wine. He only thought clearly when the enemy slept.

She was asleep now, that enemy, even though he was clearsighted and sober. It was the month. Bahadur recalled Sheikh Jiu's words: *Prayer is the state of being.*

'What does that mean?' Bahadur asked.

'You will learn, with time, if you're lucky.'

'And if I'm not?'

'Then you will die in the ignorance in which you've lived.'

In that case, Bahadur thought, I'm doomed to die in ignorance, damned if I know what those words mean: *Prayer is the state of being.*

Here he was then.

Labbaik!

I have arrived. I am here! Do with me what you will!

But the tide had retreated. *Don't hurry me,* it grumbled, *I'll get you in my own good time.*

With light came colour. Water became a mirror, an optical instrument to examine what he was here to see.

Diu.

Div.

Divya dweep.

Diva Dandi. Lighthouse.

Ghoghla beach was an outstretched finger of the mainland stopping just short of the island.

The creek in between had been bridged fifty years ago by Malik Ayaaz.

The creek contained the Pani Kotha, also built by Malik Ayaaz.

Malik Ayaaz built the harbour and a wall around the island, planned the roads, gardens and palaces. The very air of the island, scented delicately by the roses he cultivated for itr, owed its fragrance to Malik Ayaaz. The bustle of the island, its rainbow population, its music of many tongues, all these were his doing.

Who was this man? wondered Bahadur.

The usual responses did not quite answer the question—he was Russian, captured by the Rumi, enslaved, bought by a merchant who traded with Gujarat. Thus had Malik Ayaaz arrived in his grandfather's court. The rest was legend—he was a brilliant archer, a daring businessman, a lordly host, a generous employer, a canny diplomat.

These too did not answer the question, What had driven Malik Ayaaz to render his vision real? He had found Diu a jungle and he had left it a cosmopolis, the richest port on the coast of Gujarat.

Until the Firangi arrived.

Malik Ayaaz had called the Rumi to rid Diu of the Firangi. Now Bahadur had taken the same step.

Malik Ayaaz had died in disgrace, shunned by Bahadur's father on the advice of his amirs. Few remembered him now, and fewer still remembered his generous hospitality. His son Toghan was living out the pretense of being Malik Ayaaz. Very soon the scales would fall from his eyes, and he would see himself for the hollow man he was. Bahadur was in no hurry to unmask him. Malik Toghan held Diu in his palm, no matter how Khwaja Zafar looked at the matter.

Khwaja Zafar worried Bahadur. He did not doubt the man, but the feeling that he was being manipulated was inescapable. Initially, Khwaja had spoken for the Firangi. He regretted following Khwaja's counsel about Vasai. Then he had done worse with the second treaty. And now the man had reversed his stand.

They were both on the same side now, intent on throwing out the Firangi. He could feel Khwaja's cautious pressure on his neck, not quite the Firangi's foot pressing down squarely on his nape, but discernible still.

Khwaja Zafar had over six million cruzados invested in Diu, twice the annual income the Firangi earned out of their shameful slave trade. Bahadur's chief consolation was Khwaja's wealth. As long as the Firangi threatened those millions, Khwaja could be trusted.

But Khwaja was only a merchant by opportunity.

Weren't they all?

Khwaja Zafar was, first and foremost, a soldier, and he knew more about guns than the perfidious Rumi Khan.

And, he knew Diu.

He knew it as well as Malik Ayaaz had, and in a fashion Malik Toghan never would.

Khwaja Zafar knew the merchants, the ship owners, the many nations that flocked to Diu, but he, Bahadur, knew its people.

He knew, for instance, the figures emerging from the dark shape of the hills of Nandan. He knew them not by name, or face, but from their appointed place in the rhythm of the land.

They were still smudges on the slate grey horizon.

The sea had absorbed all the colours of dawn and dissolved them into a shining spectrum: bronze, gold, saffron, amber.

A Firangi galleon, massive as a house, bobbed like a toy on the horizon.

Grassia, Bhil, Mina. He could not guess who they were, these tribal women advancing from the hills. They must have left their homes in the forest hours ago, walked with the same instinct with which he found his way in the dark. They belonged to this land the way the hills and forests did, their place appointed in a time beyond memory. No war, no passing Raja or Sultân, no Firangi law could uproot them.

There was a name Haridas used for them: *Adivasi.* The first inhabitants.

'In that case, Haridas, they are the true kings of this land,' he had remarked.

Here they came now, nine women, aged between six and sixty. The child was a woman already, swathed in the rags of her elders, balancing carefully a bundle of twigs on her small round head, trying to keep pace with her mother.

The sight smote him in a way he could not explain. Their stride was fierce and free, they were but keeping the rhythm of life, why should the sight wring him so?

These days he was often disturbed by strong emotions inappropriate to the moment. He put it down to afim, as he did with all his ills. He ought to get rid of the habit. Humayun too was a slave to it, like his father before him.

The women passed him.

He ignored them, knowing his presence had stilled their happy chatter.

Sunlight fell on their retreating backs, making goddesses of them, gilding their rags, polishing their gracile limbs into Dakshin statuary.

It was easy to understand why this country had so many gods and goddesses, they grew out of the land. He wondered what gods and goddesses came out of the ocean.

Haridas would have told him. Perhaps, he had. Oh yes, that tale about the ocean of milk. This was an ocean of Firangi wine. The ship on the horizon carried enough in its hold to satisfy the thirst of all his amirs. He would buy up the lot. He grimaced as he realized Khwaja Zafar probably had purchased it already. Zafar would purchase them all: his amirs, his court, by making a magnificent gift of the shipment. It would leave Malik Toghan fuming.

Enough! He would teach Nanu a trick or two about treading water and ride him through the shallows to Diu.

Nanu Barq was unhappy with the decision. He moved not unwillingly, but with a sudden coyness of step, a delicacy of haunch that irritated Bahadur.

Dismounting, he led the horse out into the water, taking no notice of the protesting neigh. He tightened the rein and walked forward.

Did the horse have heart enough to follow, or would he stay rooted mulishly in dread? If he did that, Bahadur was finished with him. He had no patience with cowardice in men or in horses, and yet, he had heard that word murmured yesterday. They were talking about him, of that he had no doubt.

'He ran from the Mughal and now he'll run from the Firangi.'

They were common fellows, men of no account, on their way to the tavern to get drunk. The Firangi had opened six taverns on the island, and it was no secret that their wine was the best in the world. His amirs urged him to shut them down, even as they shared his wine.

Bahadur continued walking. The tide came in, waist high now. The reins were no longer tense. The horse followed him silently although it exhaled the rank odour of fear. Pleased with its nerve, he began to talk encouragingly as he advanced. The shoreline here was predictable. Once the water reached his navel, he would mount and lead the horse further out. If Nanu didn't baulk it would mean he had won the animal's trust.

Nanu did not baulk. He carried Bahadur bravely forward, and trod water with more confidence now.

Bahadur stopped to let the horse get his bearings.

The tide brought in a boat. A small sailboat, a *ghurab*, not one of the locals. It looked as if the fragile craft was out of control. A lone figure was struggling to keep it afloat. It would be a miracle if he got to shore without capsizing.

Bahadur looked back. The bay was empty.

The boat had disappeared too.

Then Bahadur discerned a red dot in the tide. An arm shot up and was lost in the wall of water. If only he wasn't on horseback—

Barely had the thought registered when Nanu startled him by plunging forward, swimming with ease, his head pointed in the direction of the flailing figure. They reached the sailor before he went under and Bahadur pulled him up without effort. He was an elderly man, exhausted almost to last breath, but he would survive.

Elated with his horse, Bahadur busied himself over Nanu Barq. He took off the soaked accoutrements and briskly rubbed him down. He salvaged dates from the saddlebag and the horse took them daintily off his palm. As he rubbed the withers, Nanu nuzzled him affectionately.

Bahadur felt a joy he hadn't experienced since Barq died.

'You have a brave horse.'

Bahadur turned around. The rescued man was sitting up.

He greeted Bahadur with a trembling namaste. 'You saved my life, huzoor. I am your bondsman.'

'His bondsman, not mine,' Bahadur laughed, and patted Nanu.

'Does he have a name? You should name him Bahadur.'

'Why?'

'They say the Sultân has a heart like this one. Acts first, thinks afterwards.'

'Rest yourself, Kaka, you're still shaky. Here—' Bahadur wrung out the damp saddle-cloth and rolled it up like a bolster. 'Ease your head on that, and we can be Sultâns together in the sand.'

The man did not argue. He fell back, content.

Bahadur gave in to his own exhaustion and stretched out on the sand.

It was still cold, still misty, but in half an hour their wet clothes would be steaming on them. He was sliding into a pleasant reverie when the man startled him.

'Have you seen him? They say he's here.'

'Who?' asked Bahadur wearily.

'Why, the Sultân of course.'

'What do you want with him?'

'I've come a long distance to see him. If he isn't here, I'll have to seek him out.'

'What for?'

'I've come to ask him a question.'

Bahadur rose and shook sand off his clothes. 'You would question the Sultân?'

'Why not?'

Bahadur shrugged.

'You think he won't see me? I think he will, unless his guards and amirs obstruct me.'

'Oh?' Bahadur laughed. 'That can be taken care of.'

'You laugh as if you had them all in your hand.'

'One may assume anything!'

'But you know them, right?'

'Some of them, yes.'

'Will you help me get to the Sultân? I have come very far, I may never see my home again, but I must have an answer to my question. It is the purpose of my life. If I can take back his answer to my people I will die content.'

'You have many years left in you, Kaka.'

'You address me as Kaka. You saved my life. My purpose is now your responsibility.'

Bahadur was silent.

'I fear I have offended you, huzoor. I was too familiar.'

'No, it isn't that.' Bahadur sat down heavily next to the man. 'I can't be burdened with your life, Kaka. My own is almost too heavy to bear.'

Why had he said that?

'Heavy? And you so young? Too young to have seen the world.'

Bahadur shook that off with a laugh. 'Never mind me, tell me where you've come from.'

'Mulgaon.'

'Where is that?'

'Shashti Pranth.'

'Is that in the Sultân's kingdom?'

'I have come to remind him that it was.'

'What is your nearest port?'

'Thana, Vasai, Bandra, Mahim, Mumbai.'

'Yes, I recollect—'

'My village is near Bandra.'

'I've been there.'

'You have? When was that? Where did you stay?'

'I simply passed through, sailed from Mahim river.'

'Ah. My village is on that island. That is Shashti Pranth.'

'Your boat is from Mahim?'

'This boat? No. It is from Vesawe. That's north of Mahim. I'm not a fisherman, not a nakhoda. I'm a farmer.'

'You sail well for one who tills the land.'

'We must all learn new ways when old ways are taken from us.'

'Why, who took away your land?'

'The Sultân sold us to the Firangi. He sold the island, the people, the fields, the produce. Sold may be the wrong word. I don't know what he got in return. He gave us away. Nobody knows why. We could have asked our Khan. He was a good man. He would accept nothing without fair payment, not a bag of rice, not a basket of mango. We grow the finest rice. We grow the finest fruit. Now the Firangi has it all.'

'Why is your Khan keeping quiet about this?'

'Oh he is so quiet he will never speak again. They killed him.'

'What?'

'Oh yes, him and many others. My farm is now owned by a Firangi. My sons are his slaves. The fields are still their responsibility. A man with a whip watches them work. Another guards the fields with a gun. Why did the Sultân do this to us? What harm did we cause him? Nobody on our island knows the answer. My son asked a friendly Firangi and his answer was an insult to the Sultân.'

'Why, what did he say?'

'Does it matter? Why repeat slander? We have known nothing but good of the man. I am certain if I ask the Sultân my question, he will answer me. I decided to come in search of him because somebody should find out the truth. I refused a companion because the journey is perilous and its outcome uncertain. What do you think? Will the Sultân see me?'

'Stay here awhile. Within the hour someone will be here to take you to a rest house where you will be fed and clothed. Depend upon my word, I will make certain the Sultân sends for you tomorrow morning.'

'You can do that?' The man stared at Bahadur uncertainly.

'What's your name, Kaka?'

'Krishna. Krishnaji More.'

'Very well, Krishnaji More, I will send for you tomorrow.'

'And you will take me to the Sultân?'

'Yes, you have my word.'

'Huzoor, I can see from your horse that you are a great amir. How should I address you?'

'You have named my horse, that's good enough for now!'

He leapt on Nanu and rode away.

The encounter disturbed him. It had raised the lid on the tumult that churned in him. *What now,* it went. *What now? What now? What now?*

That question must be answered today, it could be put off no longer. He would decide this hour, one way or another.

His reverie brought him to the bridge Malik Ayaaz had built to connect Diu and Ghoghla. This morning, Portuguese guards in their strange pajamas paced at the Diu gate.

Bahadur rode up to the guard house and summoned the Captain..

'What is the Firangi guarding here?'

'I don't know, Huzoor,' he replied, recognizing Bahadur. 'I have asked them, they don't answer. The word is their Governor is come by night.'

'Is he camped at the gate that they must guard him?'

'Huzoor, they are ten men, but they have muskets, and stroll as if they are taking the air.'

'Why have you not driven them away?'

'Khwaja Sahab advised me not to.'

'Very well, bring their captain to me. Send your men to the beach with a stretcher. They will find a tired sailor there. Carry him to the Malik and say I sent him. I will be there tomorrow to see how he's recovering.'

Bahadur could not argue with Khwaja Zafar's decision to refrain from hostilities. But it had encouraged the Firangi bullies.

The Firangi captain, a man of Bahadur's own age, approached with a defiant look.

Bahadur's hard stare shamed him into a salaam.

'Can you find no other place to exercise your men, Captain?' Bahadur enquired pleasantly. 'Surely there is enough space within your fort.'

'I take my orders from the Captain of the Fort.'

'And he, from me. Go tell Emmanuel de Souza that the Sultân of Gujarat wishes his men good health in times of peace, and so returns them to the fort where they may rest and refresh themselves.'

Bahadur turned and rode in the direction of the dargah.

The dargah was beyond the grove. Nanu Barq had been fed and watered, and it would do him good to rest in the shade. He spoke quietly to the horse and tethered him to a large hokka.

Even without the tether the horse and the hokka were one beast. The horse's wild eye had quieted with Bahadur's voice. It was inward now, as self-absorbed as the tree. He could walk away from them confident he would find them unchanged when he returned. Horse and tree were compacted in loyalty. Had they been men they would be compacted in treachery.

He walked through a fallow field waist-high in purple plumes of loosestrife, yellow thistle, and white-pink trumpets of datura. He reached for a spiny fruit. It broke off bleeding sap.

He was wrong about the tree. Treachery could lurk there too, as it did in this bubble of poison.

He held the fruit gingerly, it was replete with barbs. A horse would have kept away from the bush. A man could pick the fruit, guard his fingers from injury, and use it to draw blood elsewhere. Bahadur flung the thornapple away angrily. He tore up a fistful of grass and scrubbed his palms with it. No telling how long the poison lingered. He recalled his mother's admonition. *'Don't go near it!'*

There was a time when she had been crazed with fear that everything they brought to him was poisoned. Every glass, every dish, had to pass her tester before it reached him. He had escaped, of course. He always escaped. It was the only way to live.

The sun was high.

There would be a *surahi*[34] of water waiting for him. The scent of roses welcomed him already, billowing over the cruel smells of crushed grass and mud.

The dargah was deserted.

They had left hastily, noticing his approach.

The place was orderly enough, but he knew that air of sudden abandonment.

He touched the wooden bench in the shade—the seat was warm.

He washed his hands and feet in ritual *wazu*,[35] refreshed by the scent of tulsi that stirred in every splash. He wet his kerchief and buried his face in it.

As he began *salaat*, a heaviness overcame him. The words of the *ayah* buzzed in his brain like doom.

Tired, that's what he was.

He stretched out on the bench and stared at the sky.

Lazy boy, the Pir would have remonstrated, lying flat on your back in the middle of the day?

Nobody dared say that to him now.

The Pir was dead.

Yet it seemed he would never go away.

34 Urdu … صراحی … carafe, pitcher.

35 Urdu … وضو … ablution before prayers.

6

Batoh

1510–1519

The first, and most impressive, thing about the Sheikh was his age. His face was a crumpled page of lines. He walked with difficulty, back bent, joints swollen.

Bahadur looked down on Sheikh Jiu from the imposing elevation of his grandfather's shoulders, and thought him a joke. He was surprised and disappointed when his grandfather made a humble salaam.

'Why are you doing that?' he whispered fiercely into the Sultân's ear. 'You are the king!'

'The child is right. You are the king of the land, I'm just king of the air.'

'True. My feet are in my kingdom, but my head intrudes in yours. It is only polite that it should bow to you.'

Bahadur hastily made his own salaam to the King of Air.

'You, little one, you are a subject of my kingdom too as you ride on your grandfather's shoulders. When I ride on my grandfather's, I shall be a subject of yours.'

This puzzled Bahadur even more.

'Your grandfather must be very very old,' observed Bahadur. 'Are you sure he will be able to carry you on his shoulders?'

'Easily, for he rides on his father's shoulders and he on his father's shoulders, and so on.'

'Who is walking? He must be very strong to carry so many people on his shoulders.'

'Wise child. He is immensely strong, which is why he is called Shafiullah, because Allah chose him for his perfection.'

'My grandfather is stronger than Shafiullah. Aren't you?' Bahadur twirled his grandfather's moustache. He was immensely proud of Sultân Mahmud's moustachios and considered them his particular property. 'Shafiullah did not have my grandfather's moustache.'

'That he did not,' agreed the Sheikh.

'I'm going to grow a moustache right away,' Bahadur assured him. 'It will be the biggest moustache in Gujarat.'

'Inshallah!'

'I'm going to have a horse and an elephant and a sword and a moustache.'

'That's all you need to be king of the land. But you must be king of the sea as well, or the sea will make you his subject.'

'Then I shall have a boat as well!' cried Bahadur, and the Sultân, delighted, tossed him so high he thought he was one with the clouds. He came hurtling down, eyes shut tight, terrified he would hit the ground hard. But he was swept up again till sky and earth lurched through him and he cried, 'Stop! Stop!'

It was Sultân Mahmud who first told Bahadur he must be Sultân.

Even at three, Bahadur knew his grandfather had got the succession wrong, just as he got the simplest sums wrong.

'I was on the battlefield when I should have been at school!' the Sultân often told Bahadur. 'Mind you don't make that mistake. You'll make a bad Sultân if you can't count.'

'You're a good Sultân, and you can't count.'

'I manage because I've got you to count for me.'

That was true.

Still, Bahadur felt constrained to point out that he would never be Sultân because his father wouldn't have the throne.

'Let's see about that,' said Sultân Mahmud.

It didn't take long.

Sultân Mahmud Begada's older sons Ahmad and A'aba both fell out of favour.

Ahmad attempted a coup.

A'aba was a wastrel and a brainless voluptuary. He was caught in bed with the wife of an amir. The irate husband strangled his wife, but there was nothing he could do to her royal lover.

Sultân Mahmud could. He had A'aba Khan hanged.

That brought Bahadur's father, Khalil Khan, to the throne.

In no time at all, the new Sultân was being celebrated as Muzaffar Haleem, the Clement. Bahadur, though, caught the full blast of his father's inclemencies.

'Keep out of your father's way,' his mother Lakham Bai advised.

'Why?'

'I keep out of his way too.'

'Why doesn't he like us?'

'Of course he does.'

But he didn't.

Bahadur could never please him.

Sikandar, Aashiya and Ruqaiyya were his pets. They were all Rani Bibi's children, and like their mother, plump and white.

'He doesn't like you because you look like us,' Haridas informed him.

They were hidden beneath a table in the darbar, watching the Sultân. Bahadur often did that, but he liked it better when he had Hari for company.

'Us?' Bahadur was puzzled. 'Hindu?'

'No. Common folk all look alike, Hindu or Mussalman. All of us are black. Like you.'

'That's rubbish. My father's black too.'

'Yes, but he doesn't want you to be like him. He wants you to be like a Farsi or Qizilbashi[36] or Firangi.'

'How do you know?'

'I just do.'

'Why? Does your father want you to be like a Qizilbashi too?'

'No. He wants me to be like a pandit, going *Om hreem groom swahaa!*'[37]

'I like that. Tell you what, let's exchange.'

'What, fathers?'

'No. You be Qizilbashi, I'll be a pandit.'

'Done!'

It lasted a week. Bahadur went about making loud punditry, and Haridas wore a red cap.

Neither of their fathers noticed.

They were under the table again.

A pair of legs cut off Bahadur's view of his father. A pin in the fleshy bulge of the pajama might be just the way to dislodge the obstruction. The man's words caught his attention.

'The young Prince will show off his archery tomorrow. Will you be there?'

'Yes, or lose my head.'

'He is Arjun reborn, if rumour be true.'

'With the bowstring guided by the Sultân's hand, no doubt.'

'Be kind. He's a little fellow.'

'Not so little. His brother is the better shot. There's an Arjun for you.'

'What? *Bahadur Khan*? He runs about with the ragamuffins of the bazaar.'

The other fellow laughed. 'Maybe,' he said. 'But he's as fine a marksman as I know, to my peril.'

'His name's not on the list of competitors.'

'I noticed.'

'Next year, then.'

'Not if he has the mettle. What's to stop him from storming the ranks?'

'No eight year old has the courage to do that.'

'We'll see.' The legs moved off.

Bahadur ignored Haridas' questioning look.

'Why can't you go, Bahadur?'

'He didn't ask for me.'

'Maybe he doesn't know. You need to show him.'

'They won't let me.'

---

36 *Qizilbash/Qizilbashi* [Farsi … قزلباش] dates to late 15th century Turkey when the head of the Safaviyya Sufi order Shaikh Haydar organized his followers into a militant mercenary group. They wore a distinctive twelve-gored crimson headwear called titled تاج حیدر [*Tāj-e-Ḥaydar*], Haydar's Crown.
Qizilbash literally means 'red head.' The appellation was a pejorative label given to them by their Sunni Ottoman foes, but they adopted it as a provocative mark of pride.

37 This is Hari's saucy take on *Bija-mantra*, the chant of mystic syllables.

'They will, if you change your pajama.'

The whole world was at that pageant. And it was his father, the Sultân, the world had come to see.

Haridas' father had taken his place among the scholars and pandits waiting to honour the Sultân. He had composed an epic about the Sultân's ancestors—in Sanskrit, naturally, explained Haridas, so that he could say whatever he wanted, as long as it sounded learned.

Haridas dragged Bahadur to the archery court, but he shook free and ran away.

Later, Hari spotted him among the contestants—in the line for commoners.

As Hari expected, Bahadur won easily. He would now be pitted against the winner from the sons of nobles.

It was a given that Sikandar would win that, though there were at least six boys who were better shots.

Hari was wrong.

Sikandar did not win, and Bahadur was pitted against a fierce fellow of sixteen, Muqbil, the son of Alp Khan.

Bahadur had not been recognized yet. In his usual crumpled and muddy clothes he wasn't much of a prince.

Muqbil sneered visibly and took his shot at the moving target, and missed twice in six attempts.

Bahadur hit the target all six times.

Hari and his friends went wild. They whistled and tossed their caps in the air. Their cries of '*Shabaash Bahadur!*' were taken up by the onlookers.

Bahadur stepped down, and waited.

It sounded as if the whole world was shouting his name, and the only one who couldn't hear it was his father.

He couldn't remain deaf for long, could he?

No, the master of ceremonies was announcing the scores now, and here it came, *Shahzada Bahadur Khan.*

Bahadur's heart was thumping like a tabla gone wild as he looked up at the dais.

But the Sultân was looking elsewhere. He was in earnest conclave with the master of ceremonies. As that lackey, bowing obsequiously, backed away, the Sultân returned to his abstraction, his lordly gaze fixed in mid-air as if he were holding communion with a djinn of pure and smokeless flame.

Now—what's *this?*—the wretch he had defeated, the butter-fingered squinty Muqbil whose arrows had gone so awry, Muqbil, *Muqbil* was swaggering up the dais.

Bahadur couldn't believe his eyes. He waited for the announcement.

The miserable *qaasid*,[38] the herald, kept on endlessly with his florid praise of the Sultân in a chant that made no sense.

And then suddenly, his words fell in place and Bahadur heard him say, '... in his great and generous mind the spirit of justice rules above all else, and so the Sultân

[38] Urdu ... قاصد ... messenger, envoy, courier, emissary, letter-carrier, herald.

has decreed that Shahzada Bahadur Khan be disqualified from the competition. Since he disrespected the rules and joined the ranks of the commoners instead of the *amir*, he misrepresented himself. In view of his tender years the Sultân mercifully forgives this transgression, but he no longer deserves the prize. The champion is Muqbil, son of Amir Alp Khan.'

Everything stilled.

Bahadur thought he had gone deaf.

The whole world was hushed.

Then, his father's voice rang out. '*Shabaash*, Muqbil Khan!'

The world roared in his ears.

Bahadur ran.

He fought his way out till he was past the throng. Like a squirrel, he ran up the gnarled *bargad*[39] at the edge of the pavilion. Settling in its high fork, he drew his catapult and took aim.

The pebble caught Muqbil in the left eye.

Bahadur watched Haridas leave the crowd and pick his way towards him.

He waited till the tabla inside him had quietened. Then he slid down the tree and joined his friend.

Had it started then?

The roar he had heard that afternoon had got into him somehow. Most of the time it was a low buzz, like that of a weevil trapped in a mango stone. It did not bother him, but he was always aware of it. And, now and then, it broke loose and raced like fire through every inch of him, thundering, screaming, till it seemed to have drawn into itself all the noise in the world. Everything outside would turn silent as long as the roar kept up its fury within him. He tried all sorts of things to make it stop. He ran, but it pursued him. He rode, but it was in the wind that winged his horse. He fought, pummeled and punched anything that came in his way, and that made it retreat a little. He realized that to be free of it he had to be free of the world.

Haridas was speaking. 'They're sending us to school.'

'Who is?'

'Fathers. Yours and mine.'

'That's settled then. I won't go.'

'Like they're asking our permission, ha!'

The Sultân lined up his sons, Sikandar, Bahadur, Latif, Chand, Nasir and Ibrahim. He handed each of them a silk purse.

Sikandar couldn't wait to open it. The Sultân stopped him with a gesture. 'This is a gift. But not for you. This is a gift from you.'

Sikandar was puzzled. 'To whom should I give it?'

'I will tell you when the time comes.'

The Sultân did not encourage conversation, even with his beloved Sikandar.

---

39 Hindi ... बरगद ... Banyan tree [*Ficus bengalensis*].

They had been riding for about an hour when Bahadur spotted a company ahead of them on the road. A silken canopy gleamed. Persons of some eminence, for certain.

Bahadur was absorbed in noticing how thin and weak his father looked after the recent illness. This was his first public appearance in a while.

Haridas said the Sultân's vaid had sought advice from his father on some texts too complicated for his understanding. The pundit advised the vaid not to waste his time on miraculous cures as the Sultân's horoscope destined doom.

'That means your father's going to live for a hundred years,' explained Haridas. 'My father's horoscope readings are always wrong.'

'Doesn't he know that yet?'

'Oh, he does, but he can't help hoping he'll be right the next time. Sometimes he lets me read them.'

'You?'

'Sure. I'm good.'

Bahadur believed him. There was no book Haridas couldn't read. He had done all Bahadur's school work as far as they could remember. What was he going to do if they were sent to different schools?

He shook off that dread as they neared the welcome committee.

A tall darvesh in silken robes awaited them beneath a canopy.

As he stepped forward, the Sultân, much to Bahadur's surprise, dismounted to greet him.

'How is it that you're expecting me?' asked the Sultân.

'He informed me. I was told you would be coming at this hour, and that the ride would have tired you. Rest and refreshment await you, after you have paid your respects.' A certain steely formality set this last phrase apart from the ease of his welcome.

If the Sultân noticed this, he did not react, and asked with great humility to be escorted to the grave of Sheikh Ahmad Qutb-ul-Qutab.

The tall darvesh was the head of the Batoh Bukhariyat Sayyads.

When the *fateha* was recited, the Sheikh escorted them into his *khanquah*[40] where a modest meal was laid out.

Bahadur, finding his staple of rotla and buttermilk, bolted down his food as usual and slipped away.

The khanquah was a big place, and not all its inhabitants had been summoned to the meal. There were scholars hard at reading, ravening in unison, while others sat *qalam*[41] in hand awaiting an inner command to start writing on the blank parchment before them.

Bahadur tiptoed past them all. He seemed to know where to go though he was a stranger here.

---

40 *Khanquah* [Farsi … خانقاه] also known as a *ribāt* [رباط].
A khanquah is a place for spiritual retreat and for congregations of Sufi orders. Khanquahs serve as refuges for *Sāliks* [Sufi travellers], *Murids* [Sufi initiates] and *Tālibs* [Islamic students].
Khanquahs are often found adjoining a *Dargah* [shrine of a Sufi saint], a *masjid* [mosque] or *madarsa* [Islamic school].

41 Arabic … [قلم]… a reed pen.

One courtyard led to another. The floor lit up in pretty patterns where sunlight filtered in through the jaali.

Bahadur ran along the corridor, exulting in a sudden surge of freedom. He hated riding at a solemn trot in cavalcade. Only the thought of being with his father consoled him sometimes on these occasions, and today not at all.

All morning the buzz in his brain had tormented him. Now, magically, it was gone.

It was transformed into a drone outside him, something that belonged among the lush creepers and laughing flowers. A bee, probably.

As he pushed open a door without thought, the drone seized and hurtled him into the room.

The room was empty except for an old man.

The drone came from him.

Although his cap marked him as a Mussalman, his forehead sported a broad stripe of ash like a jogi's.

Bahadur held his breath, afraid a gigantic bee would zoom out from inside this man. He wanted to run away, but couldn't.

The sound ceased.

Almost immediately another took its place.

Bahadur found himself mimicking this sound, but he stopped himself.

The old man went on and on until he switched to a different drone. At some point he stopped droning and started singing.

It was like no other song Bahadur had heard before. It was like a rope you could hold onto and float free high among the clouds or dangle deep underwater, quite fearlessly, because no matter how freely you swung or turned cartwheels, the rope always held you.

At some time the darvesh in silk robes, whose name was Sheikh Jiu Sayyad Muhammad, came in quietly and sat down beside Bahadur.

They took no notice of each other.

At length the song was over and the singer opened his eyes.

'You have a pupil,' Sheikh Jiu said.

'Yes. He has been singing with me.'

'No, I haven't—' protested Bahadur.

'Not with your voice, but with your heart. That is how *dhrupad*[42] is sung. In the silence of the heart. But never mind that. We will begin in earnest tomorrow.'

Bahadur, bewildered, was about to refute this, when Sheikh Jiu placed a hand on his head. 'You will be happy here, Bahadur Shah.'

Bahadur caught his breath. 'Only the Sultân is Shah,' he said.

'That's right.'

'They call me Bahadur Khan.'

'That's right too.'

---

[42] *Dhrupad* [Hindi ... ध्रुपद] a meditative and spiritual form of music.

'I can't be both!'

'Not at the same time, no. With me, in my house, you are Bahadur Shah. When you're ready to leave my house you will be Bahadur Shah outside too.'

'Am I your prisoner, then?'

Both men burst out laughing.

The singer said, 'We are both His prisoners.'

'Whose?'

'Shankar. Allah. Gopal. You can give Him any name you want.'

'If I'm his prisoner, I'll call him bad names!'

'You can do that if you like, He'll still be listening to you.'

'And punish me, I suppose?'

'Of that I'm not sure.'

'Why not? I always get punished when I'm in trouble.'

'Who punishes you?'

'Everybody.'

'How does that make you feel?'

'Like a prisoner!'

'When you are Allah's prisoner,' said Sheikh Jiu, 'you're always free. Nobody can hurt you.'

'What about Shankar? And Gopal?'

'It is the same with them. If you stay with me, you'll be their prisoner too.'

'What? Of all three?'

'And many more. But nobody will punish you, and you'll soon make yourself free.'

'How?'

'Listen.'

The old man began to sing again, encouraging Bahadur to hold the note with him.

Gradually, Bahadur felt the buzz inside him recede. He rose abruptly and addressed Sheikh Jiu, 'I'll stay, but my friend must stay too.'

'Haridas?'

'How—'

'Never mind how. Haridas will also stay. It is arranged.'

'But his father's a pundit.'

'And a disciple of mine. Do not concern yourself with these differences. I will leave you now to sing *bhairav*[43] with Ustad Sayeeduddin.'

And so Bahadur stayed.

It wasn't all song and dance at Sheikh Jiu's, though there was plenty of both.

[43] *Bhairav* ... Sanskrit ... भैरव ... 'fearsome' A morning *raag*, often performed as an overture; Indian classicists believe it to be the first utterance of Lord Shiva. Bhairava is also one of Shiva's names, especially when he appears as a naked wandering ascetic with matted hair and ash-smeared body.

Haridas loved the studying, the debating, and the general arguments that went on through the day. Bahadur, having proved his dismal proficiency with the written word, was set to tasks instead. No task was too menial for him. He did whatever Sheikh Jiu ordered, but took orders from nobody else.

A year passed.

Then another.

Bahadur and Sheikh Jiu knew the peace would not last. When the roar beat up his blood to a froth not even the slow grave notes of bhairav could calm his chaos.

His principal passion was horses. They spoke to him as men and women could not.

At sixteen, his brother Sikandar had his own harem.

Did Bahadur notice her, or did she notice Bahadur?

The years had erased the moment, but eternal in her absence, she returned now. What set her apart from the hundred others abuzz around his brother like bees on a fig tree? Her beauty was noticed even then, for its remoteness. Her eyes were distant, always somewhere else. He imagined they too, awake or dreaming, sought what he did—the wind in his hair, the empty moonlit road. Now she rode with him, a shadow intent on his hurtling thoughts, understanding, consoling, knowing him before he could know himself.

He watched her at Sikandar's side, a spiral of smoke to his flame.

She had a silly name, Nazuk Leher. It was a name for the boudoir, but she did not belong in suffocating luxury. She woke him as tender fringes of green wake trees, and to him she was Nazuk Bahar.

He avoided Sikandar more than ever, to avoid her.

He broke into a sweat at the thought of her, he was ready to kill anyone who mentioned her name.

He concealed her, even from Haridas.

He would have her erased, wiped out, rendered invisible. He would hoard her.

As his secret, he would keep her safe.

'Would you like me to send you a girl?' his mother asked. 'You may have your own harem if you wish.'

'No. I don't wish. And don't talk of it to me again.'

Nevertheless, he was seduced.

If he refused the girl, Haridas cautioned, a procession of boys would knock at his door.

One evening [it was during Ramzan], as Sheikh Jiu reposed after breaking his fast, he summoned Bahadur, who as usual, was in the stables.

The hall was full. Disciples, passersby, travellers, all crowded together in the discipline of the khanquah.

It was the hour after *maghrib*, when each man may speak his thoughts before the qawwals began.

As Bahadur approached, the Sheikh invited him to sit beside him on the divan. 'I would like you to keep us close to your heart, Bahadur Shah,' he said. Then, raising his voice, he announced, 'Be loyal to your king. Sultân Bahadur Shah of Gujarat!'

There was a moment of stunned silence.

Then the audience rose as one man and queued up to pay obeisance to Sultân Bahadur Shah.

Bahadur welcomed each new loyalist with an affectionate embrace.

'Now go home,' advised the Sheikh, 'and think your thoughts, Bahadur!'

More pilgrims were expected next morning. He thought he would stick around to take a look at them. These weren't the usual visitors from Ajmer or *Dhai-din-ka-Jhonpra*[44] who came bearing gifts, but Dakshins who brought only arguments. He was not interested in their debates which could go on all day, he never could see the point. But he was curious about what manner of men walked a hundred miles and more on unsafe roads and through dense forest, just to exchange words that meant nothing.

Jogis who roamed naked, covered in ash, with matted hair and distant eyes, these were common enough. Awara Hindu, they were called in contempt. But they were dreaded too, fed, and sent away.

The khanquah was preparing to receive such men and he would stay to watch the fun.

'Take care of their horses,' said the Pir.

Horses? He had imagined them footsore pedestrians.

The Pīr turned away, but not before he had seen Bahadur's feet, shod this morning in a fine pair of boots. Bahadur flushed, but the Pir held his gaze, and he obeyed.

He took up his station at the gate as the pilgrims arrived, and in an hour he had learned to size up a man by his shoes.

Not all the shoes were of leather, which meant not all the pilgrims were Mussalman.

Was that how one told the difference between men? Whether they walked on slats of wood or on flayed hide?

He kept a pitcher of water at hand, and when they had taken off their shoes, he laved their feet.

Many of them stepped back indignantly. Some tolerated it with amusement. A few, those who were used to the attention, thanked him.

One pointed out, gently, that it was not a necessary courtesy. Only Brahmins expected it.

'Are Mussalmans meant to have dirty feet?' Bahadur asked.

Offended, the pilgrim turned away.

Qabil, the porter, caught the man's eye and chuckled. 'Leave the boy alone. He is a duom, he knows no better.'

---

44 Urdu … ڈھائی دن کا جھو نپڑا … 'a hut built in two-and-a-half days' is one of the oldest mosques in India, it was commissioned in 1192 CE/588 AH by Qutub-ud-din Aibak.

The strange word angered Bahadur. All the more because he guessed its meaning.

Qabil gave him a sly look but he said nothing.

The porter had once been an honoured guest at the khanquah, a man of Misr, full of strange stories, but that was before opium possessed him. Now he drifted from dream to dream, waking just long enough for an insolence or a curse. The Pir let Qabil stay because he never sent anyone away.

Bahadur sulked back to the stinking shoes and chappals. Some were so worn the leather had crumbled away. He could have sent for a cobbler and got them all replaced within the hour, but that wasn't the Pir's way. Here he must be humble, or, the Pir had made it clear, he could not stay.

The caked mud came off in scabs that got under his nails but after a while he found the rhythm soothing.

Ten pairs, twenty, fifty more. It occupied him all afternoon.

He would be needed when they wanted their shoes again.

He went into the kitchen, got himself rotla, *achaar*, a glass of buttermilk, and carried it all up to his usual perch on the terrace. Another reason why he liked the khanquah—food always tasted so much better here, and the cook had no surprises.

He was still chewing when he heard the cavalcade's approach.

Excited cries, flurried feet clearing the courtyard, none of that moved him.

Crouched where he was, he fought the usual sickening gripe of excitement and peeve he always felt when he thought of his father.

A shadow fell across his plate.

It was the Murid.[45]

He flinched instinctively. He loathed the fellow's knowing smile, and would have knocked it off his ugly face long ago if he weren't the Pir's son.

'Your father approaches, Huzoor. We would have been better prepared to receive him had you told us he was coming.'

He stared the man down.

'He is the Sultân. Our time is his to command.'

The Pir, he knew, would be at prayer. It was usual for him to meditate in solitude before *asar namaz*.[46] It would be wrong to intrude.

---

45 Among Sufis, a *murīd* [Farsi … مرید 'one who seeks'] is a novice committed to spiritual enlightenment under the guidance a of a *pīr* [Farsi … پیر 'elder'] a spiritual guide.
A *pīr* can also be called *Hazrat* or *Shaikh*.

46 *Namāz* [Farsi نماز] from Proto-Indo-Iranian námas [to bow, prostrate] is the word for Islamic prayer. In Arabic it is called *Salāt* or *Salāh* [سلاط]. According to the time of day there are five prayers:
Fajr [فجر] the prayer before dawn
Duhur or Zohr [ظہر] the prayer when the sun passes its zenith
Asar [عصر] the prayer in the late afternoon
Maghrib [مغرب] the prayer just after dusk
Isha [عشاء] the night prayer, between sunset and midnight.

Kings must wait on commoners occasionally, and Sultân Muzaffar would have no quarrel with that.

Still, this visit was a mystery.

They were coming up the stairs now.

He willed himself not to move, but he was at the stairwell before he realized.

The Sultân looked tired.

Was his father ill?

Bahadur panicked. What if something were to happen to him?

Bahadur had killed his first man in battle when he was fifteen. On the battlefield, the equation was simple, kill or be killed.

It was not so simple at home. There were frequent deaths in the palace. Duels, poisonings, quiet stranglings in the Rumi manner with a bowstring. People disappeared, and were quickly forgotten.

But his father—his father was king. If anything should happen to him—

The Sultân had not come alone. Sikandar had come too.

Even if he hadn't actually seen his brother a pace behind the Sultân, Bahadur would have guessed his presence from the faces of the others, pilgrims, students, servants, even the beggars who were sheltered there out of pity.

All of them looked amazed.

That's what happened to people who saw Sikandar for the first time. They simply couldn't look away.

They were perfectly justified.

Sikandar had the face of an angel. Lustrous eyes, the soft brown of a fawn's, their innocence belied by winged brows of intense black that seemed painted on his broad white forehead. His hair was hidden today by a turban of white silk adorned with a modest ornament of pearls. Thick curls clustered about his large diamond earrings. Their radiance set off the cruel delicacy of his lips which might otherwise have been overshadowed by the gallant moustache.

Sikandar's face was more than the sum of its parts. Its perfection fooled you into thinking the man behind it was perfect too.

Bahadur knew just how erroneous that was.

Sikandar's head would probably sound hollow if tapped. Certainly, it enclosed no brain. Bahadur admitted Sikandar had a kind of rash courage. He couldn't sustain it, though. He had fought a couple of duels, and his adversaries had been politic enough to get wounded early in safe places, and Sikandar had shown the mercy expected of a son of Muzaffar the Clement. He had never marched into battle yet.

When the Sultân was at war, Bahadur was the son he wanted by his side.

Not so at home.

The Sultân looked tired.

Just the heat, Bahadur told himself, and pushed away his terror. The truth was, he could not bear to think of what lay ahead.

The Sultân had eight sons, and only one fit to be heir—Bahadur.

Or so Bahadur thought.

It was a self-evident truth and he was surprised when his mother urged him to please the Sultân so that he might be favoured.

'Why would you have me do that?' demanded Bahadur. 'I don't need his favour. I'm his son.'

Lakham Bai sighed. 'And Sikandar is Rani Bibi's son.'

Bahadur roared with laughter. 'Even Rani Ma can't pull that off. Sikandar's never fought a battle in his life. His army will be made up of tailors and jewellers and pretty girls. If a cannon went off, he'll faint.'

'There's more to life than bloodshed.'

Somehow, he doubted that. The business of life was largely about death.

'I know your father,' Lakham Bai said. 'Your skin is not white enough for the throne.'

'What about his own? He's brown as a *supari*.'[47]

'He has to look to the future. To Gujarat's future. It is not enough that the Sultân should be Mussalman. He needs to look like one. Fair-skinned, like a foreigner, Afghan, Chaghtai, Rumi, so that his fidelity to the faith is never doubted.'

He shut his ears to that. His mother's cant tired him.

It made no sense. The people wanted a Sultân who looked like them—

'The people want Sikandar,' his mother said.

The Sultân's retinue fell back.

The Murid conducted the Sultân and his son to the Pir.

Bahadur jumped up and followed them. He heard his father say, 'Do not disturb his prayers. We will wait here. Leave us.'

The Murid bowed out.

Sikandar had caught sight of Bahadur. If his father heard his greeting, it went unacknowledged.

Presently, the Sheikh finished his devotions and opening his eyes, was about to make his obeisance to the king.

The Sultân stopped the Pir with a look—Bahadur had not yet heard him utter a word.

Still pinioning the Pir with his commanding eye, Muzaffar Shah reached out to his sons who stood behind him.

---

47 Betel nut [*Areca catechu*]

Bahadur grasped his hand.

His father's grip, strong, possessive and crushing his fingers, gladdened Bahadur.

Muzaffar Shah pressed his son's hand to his heart. His voice trembled as he said, 'Bless this dearest of my sons with glory, bless him that he may be Sultân of all Gujarat.'

Bahadur petrified, barely heard the Pir's murmured blessing.

When the prayer was ended, the Pir called out, 'May you follow in the footsteps of your glorious father, Bahadur Khan!'

Muzaffar Shah the Clement snarled.

His rage shook the khanquah like a tiger's roar.

He tore Bahadur's hand from his chest, but did not lose his hold, tightening his grip as he fought to control his anguish.

The Sultân's voice, icy and remote, pronounced, 'There has been a mistake. I was not aware Bahadur Khan was present. My heir is my oldest son, Sikandar Khan. Bless him, Pir Saheb, that he may reign with honour and glory as Sultân of Gujarat.'

Bahadur's hand was blue, the little finger crooked, almost twisted off at the knuckle. He stared at it as if it no longer belonged to him.

His father's voice had ceased.

The Pir was pronouncing the blessing.

For the second time he called out, 'May you follow in the footsteps of your glorious father—'

Before he could pronounce Sikandar's name, Bahadur caught his eye, and his voice faltered and fell silent.

The Pir shut his eyes.

'Your blessing is incomplete,' said the Sultân coldly.

The Pir replied, with great composure. 'Sikandar Khan, be a worthy son to your glorious father.'

Sikandar approached, and was blessed with the Pir's touch.

The Sultân relaxed. He sought the Pir's blessings on all his family by name.

The Pir smiled. 'I will not keep you here so long, Jahan-panah. Your family is numbered in millions, for are you not the father of your people?'

The king smiled too, and embraced Sikandar.

Bahadur stepped back, but the Pir's eye stopped him from leaving.

The Sultân took no further notice of Bahadur.

The Murid led the Sultân and Sikandar out to the courtyard where a divan had been hastily installed beneath an arbour of jasmine. Students had set out platters of halwa and fruit.

The Murid apologized for the rough fare.

Left alone with the Pir, Bahadur said, 'Your blessing is of no great value if it can be taken back and given to another in the same breath.'

'I took nothing back. My blessing for you, Bahadur Khan, is unchanged. You will have honour and glory as Sultân of Gujarat.'

'What of Sikandar, then?'

'He has my blessing too.'

Bahadur frowned. 'What is this you are so free with—blessing or prophecy?'

'A blessing believed is always prophecy. Go to your father now.'

'He does not want me.'

'You want him. That should be enough. Go.'

Lightened, Bahadur rode back with the cavalcade.

Sikandar, in good humour, challenged him to a race.

Sikandar's was the better horse, but Bahadur the better horseman. Bahadur shot past Sikandar like lightning, but espying his father's tight face, slackened his reins and let Sikandar win. They went indoors arm in arm.

Bibi Rani awaited them.

Ignoring Bahadur's greeting, she asked the Sultân. 'Is it done then? Sikandar has the Pir's blessing?'

The Sultân threw up his hands wearily. 'Yes, yes, it is done. But you should have seen how this little *qalandar*[48] boldly pushed forward and tried to take his older brother's place.'

Bibi Rani smiled the smile of exquisite sweetness that had sent so many of her seven thousand servants to unimaginable hell.

'Do not blame the boy. He is but his mother's son.'

Bahadur was silent. He believed his blessing. And that was prophecy.

It was the prophecy that kept him sane when the Sultân made the proclamation in his darbar, and anointed Sikandar his heir.

Life altered not an iota.

Bahadur had new dogs that year, Roosi hounds brought by two Kipchaks who expected the usual in return: silks, gems, geegaws. He cared nothing for such fripperies.

The dogs were worth much more. He took them out hunting. Within the hour they were one animal, dogs, horse, man. One animal. One purpose. One prey.

How strange, that final instant was, the hunt over, the nilgai wounded and run down.

The horse stopped of his own accord, forelock raised, head turned away.

The hounds whined and drew back. They disowned the dying beast, retreated to make room for him.

The nilgai ignored the others and looked at him. Its rolling eyes sought his in expectation. What was it pleading for? Mercy? Or death?

---

[48] From the Farsi ... قلندر [*qalandar*] ... 'a rough, unshaven, uncouth man.'

He granted both and dragged home the carcass.

What was he supposed to do now, eat it?

Cheated again.

Another evening, returning from the hunt, he had taken the carcass to the khanquah. He had dressed the deer, but would not stay to share the meal.

'He won't eat with us!' Qabil observed loudly. 'Why do you even ask? He is a duom, isn't he?'

Bahadur left in a red rage.

Duom. The word meant twin.

But that wasn't what Qabil had meant at all.

Two-headed. Divided. Split down the centre.

Treacherously double.

That's what Qabil meant by duom.

Divided between his Mussalman father and Hindu mother, Bahadur was an aberration.

Who could tell which way he would turn?

The word had him trapped between two syllables, his reason crushed, his spirit mangled.

Or, perhaps, it was just the devil in him that made him do it.

He laughed now at the memory and shuddered at his own laugh.

The next day he was at the khanquah as usual.

In the dead hour after lunch he walked through the stuporous halls and found Qabil drowsing in a darkened nook, smoke curling around him, lost in secret ecstasy.

Bahadur tied Qabil's wide pajamas tight around his ankles with a piece of string, then ran quietly down to the kitchen where the rat-traps waited. One of them had a prisoner, a fat, furry, yellow-fanged furious rat. It hurled itself against the bars when he lifted the cage.

Qabil stirred in his dreams, but made not a sound as Bahadur loosened the waistband of his pajamas and held it open as he sprang the trap. He knotted the string just as the maddened rat dived in.

Qabil still snored. Bahadur didn't wait around.

The next day, the Pir summoned him.

The khanquah was silent.

Suddenly, he was no longer student but prince.

The Murid took him to the chamber where Qabil was being nursed.

The Pir was at his bedside and on seeing Bahadur, wordlessly raised the sheet tented over the injuries. Qabil's skin was deathly white. A red gutter gaped between his legs.

The Pir replaced the sheet.

'Opium protects Qabil from pain,' he said. 'What will protect you, Bahadur Khan?'

'From what?'

'From your destiny.'

'My destiny? I am to be Sultân. Was that not your prophecy?'

'That was my blessing. I cannot take it away. But I give also my curse. Did you not make the village tremble with your Firangi dogs? You too will be torn by Firangi dogs when your time comes. Leave now, and return no more!'

Bahadur ran out, sprang onto his horse, and thundered away.

A few days later, there was a message from the Pir. Latifah, the cook, brought it, along with a small parcel of his favourite tidbits.

'He says your life is in danger here, better leave. I said when was Bahadur ever afraid of danger? Still, the Pir was insistent. You have his blessing, my son, whatever he may say. Listen to him, go away before it is too late.'

Bahadur laughed. 'Let me eat first, will you?'

7

Gujarat

He left at midnight. Alone.

Where would he go?

The road took him.

His horse, named Barq for his swiftness, had no need for reins. Even the pressure of Bahadur's shifting weight was redundant. Barq took direction from Bahadur's thoughts.

How else could he possibly know where to go?

The night pressed oblivion on Barq's eyelids as much as on his own. They might have been riding in their sleep, thundering into their dreams. Could they dream as one, boy and horse?

What was the country of sleep? It had no borders, no contours beyond those of the pillow—or were those the contours of his head? Where exactly did things happen, asleep or awake? It was a question that bothered him even when his head wasn't buzzing. The obvious answer, from everyone—things happened around oneself.

Not that he asked anybody except Hari. Not even the Pir whose name was a bleeding wound at present.

He asked Hari because that's where all his questions went. He hadn't really expected an answer, but Hari had taken the question very seriously.

'The world happens because you perceive it,' said Hari.

'I? I bring about the world?'

'Each one of us does.'

'So without me the world doesn't exist?'

'You wouldn't be able to tell, would you?'

'But I didn't create the world. Allah did.'

'And who created Allah? You did.'

That sounded perilously close to heresy. His father would have Hari flayed for it, so Bahadur stripped to the waist and wrestled his way out of that debate. He won, of course.

Breathless, they lay on the grass staring at the sky. Kites circled lazily, breaking the silence with their sharp whistles.

For all the peace around them, there was death in the air.

'They see us,' murmured Bahadur. 'They see everything.'

'Kites?'

'Hawks, too. My Shaheen sees for miles. She can land a deer at the very edge of the forest with Barq still miles away. I would like to see the country through her eyes. Imagine, Hari, it will be like looking down from a traveling mountain top!'

A travelling mountain top. That's what he needed when dawn cracked the night's carapace. It would show him this land. *His land.*

He was to be Sultân, was he?

Sultân of what?

What was this kingdom of his? What was Gujarat?

A Kutchi would say: Gujarat is a desert.

For the warriors in Champaner, Gujarat was rock—cliff and crag and steep hill face.

For the princes in Ahmadabad, Gujarat was fine fruit and soft green fields.

For the mallam in Khambat, Gujarat was pearls, corals and whatever else washed up from the sea.

What could it be to a duom?

In Qabil's country, duom was a tree.

So he had heard from a fellow student at the khanquah.

'What kind of tree?'

'A palm.'

'Coconut?'

'No. With branches.'

Bahadur laughed at the imbecility. Palm trees don't branch, any fool could tell you that!

The boy stuck to his stupidity. More, he said Bahadur could see for himself.

'What, trudge to the Zanj on the word of an idiot?'

The boy shrugged. Why go that far when it grew right here at home?

Here? In Batoh? In Ahmadabad?

In Diu.

Diu!

The very name sang of luxury.

It was the other name of Malik Ayaaz, slave, soldier, diplomat, all but Badshah of Diu.

Bahadur had seen him when he was fifteen, at his father's court in Mahmudabad. White, like a Firangi.

He was a Firangi, Haridas said.

As expected, Haridas knew his story.

Bahadur wasn't interested in the man's origins. He wanted to know about Malik Ayaaz's arsenal: his legendary guns and *huqqah* that startled the Rajputs out of the fortress of Champaner, and established Sultân Mahmud as Begada.

Bahadur didn't see any of those fireworks—Malik Ayaaz made a treaty of peace with the Rana he had been sent to subdue. The amirs whispered of treason. Malik Ayaaz had refused battle with an infidel. The man was a coward. A broker, not a soldier, the amirs said, and Muzaffar the Clement agreed.

Disgraced, Malik Ayaaz crept back to Diu.

Malik Ayaaz was dead now and Diu was with his son Ishaq.

If his father was Firangi, that made Ishaq a duom too. A duom among duoms.

To Diu, then!

The parched earth rang like stone beneath Barq's sharp swift hooves. Like stone? The ground was stone, wasn't it?

And stone? What was stone made of?

Blocks of sand, hardened to rock. Broken bits of palaces, forts, pleasure gardens. Grass seldom grew on battlefields. The soil was abrasive, a crumble that left crimson smears on the sole. Blood dust. Bone dust. Men. Horses. Wild animals. Shells. Rocks were made of these. With time [said Hari] the thought of rock shone out as gold and silver, veins secret with gems, iridescent. The thought of rock was older than our thoughts, yet it was no more than a wink in time.

And how old was time? Bahadur asked the question as a joke, but Hari had an answer for that too.

'Depends on the long and short of it.'

'The short of it, then! The shortest, quicker than the flash of my sword?'

'Oh a million times quicker. *Truti*— '[49]

'Truti?'

'It took you ten thousand truti to say the word.'

'Ah. The sparkle of a diamond, then? That brief?'

'I can't think so brief, Bahadur!'

'And the long?'

'One day of Brahma is a 1,000 Mahayugas, and each Mahayuga is 4 million years. We are in the last dark flash of our Mahayuga now, this is Kali, the time of evil.'

'You believe that?'

'The past always seems good, doesn't it? My father was a better man than I, and his before him, and so on. We fear the past, so we propitiate it.'

'Not me, I don't. So how old are the rocks. They're all evil Kali stuff, right?'

'No, much older. Anytime during this Mahayuga—'

'Oh never mind!'

When Bahadur set out from Batoh on the outskirts of Ahmadabad, Barq's hooves raised the dust over the granite heart of an ancient craton. That dust was the digest of volcanic events which had belched out the hills and rocks.

North of Bahadur's ride were the oldest rocks of Gujarat—a blood-soaked land known only by battles and murders. But who cared? The winds cleared away the detritus of blood and bone, and the landscape opened like a storybook.

In Modasa, a favourite retreat of his father's, thirty-five miles of schist lay exposed to the sun, dull brown bands of stone lit up with winks of mica or saturnine sulks of garnet.

---

[49] *Truṭi* [Sanskrit … त्रुटि] is a 'moment'—a unit of time equal to about 30 microseconds.

To the east, his grandfather's magnificent Champaner had rocks striped in light and dark bands. From a distance, to the lazy or exhausted eye, they resembled a petrified ocean, crest and trough arrested in motion.

All through his kingdom, Bahadur noticed massifs of granite. In Banaskantha, close to the holy Ambaji, Gabbar Hill rose up when Sati's flaming heart struck the earth. It must have! How else could you explain that hill?

His route took him south, and what better guide than the Sabarmati? Travellers both, rushing to reach the sea. The frothing river in its tumble was like Barq when he let him have his way, and today was such a day. The humpbacked river was no slouch and Barq had an inflamed eye on the twigs Bahadur tossed into the eddy and swirl.

Barq did not know he galloped over a doomed nursery. Gigantic eggs, perfect ovate boulders surfaced in the sleepy hamlets of Kheda. Haridas said they were Garuda's brothers scorched by the sun and frozen by time—but that was just a story.

'Why?' demanded Bahadur. 'Here is the evidence. These aren't stones. These are ancient eggs.'

'True, but no bird lays such enormous eggs. Besides, in the story, Garuda's brothers were snakes. Bahadur, have you seen a snake that lays eggs this big?'

And the riddle remained unanswered.

The eggs were sunk deep, very deep. Sometimes they turned up on the undersurface of quarried rock, beneath dense black blocks, encrusted in a yellow froth of limestone. Where did those black slabs come from?

Hari had an answer. '*Jwalamukhi.*'

Fire-mouth.

The Firangi recognized the term, and Hari said they agreed about the black rocks. There were jwalamukhi in Firangi lands too. *Vulcano* was their word for it, *masso vulcanico*.

Sometimes Haridas was so naïve, Bahadur didn't have the heart to contradict him, but this time he did. Really, the idea of a mountain belching out fire was too ridiculous!

Haridas, unfazed, stuck to the idea. Ambaji was a Shakti-peeth, wasn't it? And there was always a jwalamukhi close to a Shakti-peeth.

Bahadur groaned. More stories! That was the worst of punditry, he complained, the facts are all mixed up with stories.

Oh no, Haridas corrected him, the stories are simply forgotten facts. You have to drag them out of the story.

Good luck with that!

He, Bahadur, had better things to think about!

Like?

Like Khambat, for instance. Khambat the khazana of the Sultânate. That's where the Sabarmati was headed, and now, so was he.

Khambat was pure silt. River-ridden, what else could it be? The Sabarmati lingered here. Higher up it split the cliffs like a secret. Up there it was his river. Its power paced his pulse. Then it wavered, and changed course. Now the river, no longer fierce and solitary, strolled along, gossiping. The plain between the Sabarmati and the Mahi was noisy with the susurrus of sisters: Meswo, Vatrak, Khari, Shedhi, Mejan, Andheri, chattering scandal and silting family secrets all the way down to the sea.

And Khambat was full of rainbow stones.

Aqiqiyas were scarce in Ahmadabad, but every second man in Khambat was one. Many had migrated with their families from Ratanpur, where *aqiq*[50] lay everywhere. It surfaced in the grass along roadsides, treasured by little girls until scooped up by their greedy parents and sold. The stone was mined in Valia, in Ankleshwar, in Limodra, in Talora, but that meant nothing to the aqiqiya. He cared not where the stones came from, Khambat was his place. He simply sold them to the world.

For a long time, longer than anyone could remember, the world shopped at Khambat for aqiq. That was in the days when ships docked at Khambat, despite the tides. Grand ships, ships from lands nobody knew of—but Khambat was known in those lands and their sailors found their way here. Ahmad Shah, and then his glorious grandfather, had made Khambat—

Oh no, they didn't, interrupted Haridas. Khambat was in business when Misr was being built.

Huh? Where's the proof of that?

Under the water, on the ocean floor.

Who cared?

No ships called at Khambat now, not anymore.

That was because of the shifting sands, shoals that narrowed entry to the harbour. The Malaiki shoals, four of them, converged to the south. At ebb tide their banks, high and sharp were enough to deter even the most foolhardy sailor. All the channels to the Gulf had narrowed in his father's lifetime. Mahmud Begada had kept the channels cleared, but Sultân Muzaffar had spared no thought on them. And that was largely because by then Malik Ayaaz had built a bigger, safer, more accessible harbour for trade. He was headed there now, as were all the ships of the world, but still—

Khambat, with its rushing Bore, had its own stories to tell.

The Bore lurked unseen in the bend of the land, the nerve behind the elbow. And then—it would render the port useless, as a jarred nerve benumbs the hand.

Bahadur learned about it from a mallam, appointed to instruct him in the ways of the sea. Everyone said the Bore was generated by rocks that split the current in two, one arm for the Mahi in the east, the other for the Sabarmati. The mallam did not agree. He said the current was a live thing, a submerged streak of lightning, a noose whisked by the devil's hand. You could hear its clamour all the way down to Dholera creek, and how distant from the rocks was that?

Bahadur never did finish that bit of his education. He had been twelve, and some trifling fever sent his mother into a tizzy and she forbade any further excursions out to sea.

He would break that rule today if the mood took him. Barq whinnied a protest and Bahadur gave him a reassuring pat.

---

50 *Aqiq* [عقيق] is Arabic for quartz. Other names for it are agate, chalcedony, carnelian, onyx.
Prophet Muhammad wore a carnelian/aqiq ring set in silver to commemorate of the removal of idols from the Grand Mosque in Mecca in 630 CE.
Aqiqiya is a merchant who sells aqiq.

Not the sea, then, not this time!

The Bore rushed through the narrow channels with astonishing speed to well up against the Sabarmati just off Amli creek.

Not even the great ocean had tides like Khambat (the mallam said). With spring tides, the coast disappeared, and no surprise. The sea roared up from Diu, then after 13 kos Piram Island walled its path. It squeezed past, only to meet a narrower channel 18 kos further north.

The Bore on the east was the strongest, on full moon and new moon nights, the mallam said. The tide was as high as a two-storeyed house, and it rose that high in the time it took to say Ya'Allah. The Bore could be heard approaching like an army on the march, a sudden upwell of sound, an ambush, an invasion, heard the instant before the boat was lifted, tossed skyward, brought back face-down by that inexplicable force that grabs all that's airborne and draws it back to earth.

'Why does that force work on water?' Bahadur asked, 'I thought it only worked on land.'

The mallam chuckled. 'That's because there's land at the bottom of the sea.'

Bahadur laughed aloud at the memory. What a nation of storytellers! Nobody, it seemed, dared to speak a tangible truth.

Not today, then! He had no use for a dying port, an aged mallam, a malevolent current just now. He would take on those rocks another time, wrestle shoulder to shoulder with the tide.

Bahadur turned west, and taking the bridge at Shikari Mata he galloped towards Amli creek. Mid-morning now, time to forage. The creek was the right place. As he bid farewell to the river, the women at their washing stones looked up smiling over mounds of washed clothes, wrung and twisted, ready to be spread out on the sun-warmed rocks.

He picked up a twist of cloth and wrung it, draining a drizzle that drew appreciative laughs.

'We don't have your hands, dikro,' a matron called out.

'And I don't have yours, Ba! I can't make *rotli* to save my life.'

'Come on then, and let's see if my hands are as good as yours.'

It was fun not being a prince.

Barq followed the coastline. Bahadur spurred him through Gohilwada, mother country. He had no heart now for bards or their music. And none for this throne, which too might have been his by right, if his mother's words were true. If she lied, he knew it was from despair. She would see him king of *somewhere*. If not Gujarat, then Gohilwada. Would she have him become a second Mokhdaji, then?

He could have pointed out that Gohilwada had long been part of the Sultânate and earned himself a ringing slap for it. This was Lakham Bai's land, these were her people. Bahadur tried not to look at them as he thundered past Ghogha. It might not be so bad to be King of Piram! Just a jot of land, but Mokhdaji had used it to shake the Sultân of Dilli. Would he have lost his head without the treachery of a greedy merchant? He was one himself, wasn't he? They were all greedy, they were all merchants.

Still, he was glad he had Mokhdaji's blood in him.

He left the city by the south gate, his heart pounding angrily. He had neglected to pay his respects at the Baarwada Masjid, a place so holy that the Sheikh uttered its name like a prayer. Baarwada Masjid had been built during the lifetime of the Prophet himself. To visit it was to share the air He had breathed.

But he was done with masjid and khanquah, wasn't he? The Sheikh had told him the qibla here was not Makkah but Al-Quds.[51]

So what?

On he galloped, stopping late and starting early, seeking shelter with the humble, and camaraderie with none. He hunted and fished well enough, but there was Barq to think of, Barq to be fed and rubbed down and rested, sometimes against the horse's own will, for the space of half a day. Like his master, Barq was happiest on the road. Speed was everything, the wind in his mane, he seemed to leap over the stars as the ground fell away. Sparks danced like fireflies between his ringing hooves. Wings! Barq laughed at birds, but he envied Garuda, arched over the sun.

All along the road, the sea shimmered, a molten haze dotted with the occasional sail. For most of the day, a blur of blue and grey indistinguishable from the sky.

Bahadur thought fleetingly of the other side of the sea. There too he had ridden a similar road, breathing the sharp clean brine. Why had the land let in the sea? There was a point where the beach stopped, the shallows stopped, and a boat could ride out, as if the land had been punched in with a hammer to accommodate the sea.

Bahadur shuddered at the thought. The ocean frightened him. Not that he let that show, he was a strong swimmer. Only Hari knew. But then, Hari knew most things without being told. Perhaps for that very reason, Bahadur had ridden out without telling his friend.

The ocean seduced him on the last stretch. Sternly, he turned Barq away from the coast, walked him through the scrub and jungle till they got to Una. They returned to the coast at Ghogla and made for the beach.

And there it was, across the bridge of water, the land of the duom, Diu.

It was nearing *maghrib*. He followed a group of villagers, listening to their talk. They took no notice of the grimy lad leading a noble horse. A boy a little older than Bahadur fell in step.

'Where did you get him, then?'

'Get whom?'

'This raj kumar. The amir must be after you. Need a place to hide?'

Bahadur grinned.

'Come along, then.'

He expected the boy to lead him to a public stable, and there relieve him of Barq's rich trappings. Or else draw him into some dim lair of thievery in the forest. To his surprise, his guide kept to the road and strode quite jauntily, keeping up an incessant chatter with the crowd.

'Here, we are at the bridge now. If the guard stops you, tell him you're taking the horse to your master.'

---

[51] Arabic … القدس … 'The Holy.' It is the Arabic name of Jerusalem.

'I have no master!' The words were out before he could stop them.

'Sure, but why let the guard know that? Once in the city, you're safe. Nobody will question you. Go to the wharf and ask for Hamza. He is my friend. Tell him I sent you, you'll be safe. The auction is at eight—you should be there by six if you want to sell him.'

Bahadur caressed Barq's neck to calm him as he thanked the boy. They were at the bridge now. The guard paid no attention as they passed him, chatting.

Bahadur turned away from his companion to catch his first glimpse of the torchlit city.

There were flares everywhere. The air was balmy with the scent of roses. Excitement seized him. Mounting Barq, he sensed the horse's excitement too and gentled him to a trot.

'He is used to you already,' the boy observed.

'And I to him.'

Bahadur tossed the boy a gold coin. While he was staring at it in disbelief, Bahadur whispered in Barq's ear and the horse shot forward like lightning.

Now they were past the congested streets, past the flares, gaining on the dim outskirts, up a hillock, into a wooded cliff and then up on a promontory in full view of the ocean.

This was the ocean.

All he had seen before dwindled to a puddle, Khambat no more than a pond.

This was the ocean, southern limit of his land.

A shifting boundary, for the sea too was his father's kingdom.

His father's, and perhaps one day, his own.

Exhaustion overcame him. Too tired to eat, he let Barq munch on the rotla and dates in the saddle bag. He drank his fill of water, and finding a soft patch of grass for Barq, he spread a chādar on the rocks and lay down.

The moon was a chandelier lit with stars. The ocean tuned up, cleared its throat for alaap, the breeze brought a current of itr. He was in court with his father, fast asleep.

When Bahadur woke up, it was long past daybreak. Hunger compelled him. He turned his back on the ocean, and whistled for Barq who was nowhere to be seen. The horse answered with a soft neigh, but did not show himself. Irritated, Bahadur followed the sound. Barq had climbed the rocks over to the other side of the cliff. What had got him there? It was unusual, to say the least. Bahadur scampered nimbly over the rocks—and froze.

Barq neighed again, invitingly.

Arched over the horse was a palm tree split in two. A two-headed tād. A *doum*.

The tree was everywhere. It grew like hair, crowning the island with its tasseled heads, bearding its coast, outlining its startled hills, fringing its crystalline pools and curling with swagger over its greedy maw, the wharf feeding on the world.

All this, he would learn later.

Now, for Bahadur, there was just this tree. A young tree, perhaps the same age as he was. Bark pitted with last year's crop of pimples. One head turned east, the other west, two long gracile necks unconscious of each other, as if they ignored their common bole. And the parent bole itself equal in its division, endured the vaunted autonomy of each half, content in the knowledge that each of these would bifurcate and two would be four and four be eight and so on ,endlessly till some secret lock clamped down on their splitting. And two or sixteen or twenty-four, the many-headed tree would still be the one tree.

This young tree had only two heads as yet.

It was twice his height, though.

Looking at it was like staring into a mirror.

His skin concealed a tree just like this one.

He was this tree. His father's blood thudded alongside his mother's with every heartbeat.

Which was his tongue: Persian or Gurjari?

Which was his land: Gujarat or Rum?

Who were his ancestors: Rajput or Rumi?

How should he pray: with salaat or mantra?

To whom should he pray: Ishwar or Allah?

What was he? Man or horse?

Barq answered that last question by nuzzling him.

Bahadur laughed aloud.

Here was the duom, and only the duom, and always the duom. It had laughed all other trees off the island. What did it care about the darknesses of Misr and Zanj? It was here now. Those lands were for storytellers. *This* was home.

This was home.

Strange, he felt that too.

Bahadur walked away quickly.

He did not tarry on the island, he had quit it before noon, knowing he would return.

Always he would return.

Whenever home shut the door on him, he would find it here.

Diu.

8

1525

Bahadur had simple tastes when it came to food. His favourite meal was a *bajri rotla*[52] with a glass of buttermilk. But the rotla needed the tease of pickled mango. Sweet-sour *chhundo*[53] was his weakness. The grated mango, caramelized in the sun, sang of blinding light and cool shade, of gurgling streams beside the open road, of long rides with the wind on his back. It was just the thing he needed when he was cooped indoors on rainy days. So when a jar of chhundo came from Sikandar's kitchen, he commandeered it entire.

Rani Bibi was dead. Bahadur reminded himself of this a dozen times every day. Rani Bibi was dead, and with her had died the web of deceit and intrigue that held Bahadur captive. The very air felt safer. Since her death, Sikandar had made a few clumsy overtures of friendship.

Bahadur responded with warmth. He felt no animus towards Sikandar. The man was a fool, a pretty fool, but a fool all the same. Harmless.

His mother disagreed. Lakham Bai hadn't yet faced up to the fact of Rani Bibi's demise. Her terror of the Bhadar led her to mad extravagances. For instance, she appointed six tasters for Bahadur.

'Why do I need even one *bakawal*?'[54] he protested.

'It is the custom,' Lakham Bai said.

Nobody ever argued with custom, not even Bahadur.

'What's that you're about to eat?'

The generous dollop of chhundo on his plate glowed amber.

Lakham Bai summoned the first bakawal and handed him the plate.

'Enjoy! It is the best chhundo you'll ever taste.' Bahadur laughed.

The bakawal swallowed. A shudder seemed to pass through his entire frame. A jet of blood erupted from his pursed mouth and drenched Bahadur. The man buckled at the knees and fell forward, dead.

Bahadur did not argue over bakawals in his retinue after that.

---

52 A thick roti of millets, a Gujarati staple.

53 *Chhundo* [Gujarati … છૂંદો] literally, crushed. A sweet pickle of grated green mangoes.

54 *Bakawal* [بکاول … Urdu] Literally, *'He who tastes the first morsel.'* Such was the dread of being poisoned that no royal would eat a meal that the bakawal hadn't sampled first—and survived.

'I'm not Gohilwari for nothing,' said Lakham Bai. 'I can smell danger quicker than a hound. Heaven will defend you from swords and arrows, but to save yourself from poison, you need an honest cook.'

'How can you be sure these men are honest?' he teased his mother. 'Only one has died so far.'

'All the others will die too, and their families before them, if anything happens to you. I've assured them of that.'

For all her bravado, Lakham Bai was powerless. Bibi Rani's sway had been absolute, and now it appeared all loyalties had been transferred to her son. Within an hour of the bakawal's death, Lakham Bai had made arrangements for Bahadur to flee.

But Bahadur was going nowhere.

'The Sultân needs me.'

Lakham Bai, who would have slapped her son in exasperation, drew back at that. She turned away quickly, busying herself in arranging the pleats of her sumptuous *odhni*,[55] already perfectly aligned with a glittering clasp.

'Don't tell your father about this,' Lakham Bai pleaded in a fierce whisper. 'I'll tell him you're visiting friends. He won't question that.'

'He never questions any story about me, does he? This time, he's going to hear mine.'

Lakham Bai whirled around, her eyes hard and bitter like *sanchal*. They stared at each other, mirror images. Bahadur had his mother's amethyst eyes, brown, veined with purple, inward and bright, like crystals of black salt.

'Come and see me afterwards,' said Lakham Bai.

He nodded, reading the command for the challenge it was.

Sultân Muzaffar Shah was some time granting his second son an audience.

Bahadur was kept waiting for an hour, then one more. He did not notice the slight because he did not notice the wait. He paced the hall wondering what it would feel like to die.

He had killed his first man at fifteen, and many more in the four years that followed. That was in battle, that was what he was expected to do. If someone—anyone—wanted him dead, they could come and fight him.

Any weapon, any place, any time.

Anybody. Even Sikandar.

Sikandar was a poor swordsman. He couldn't wrestle with a chicken if he tried.

But Sikandar was never in any danger from Bahadur.

The more Bahadur considered it, the more certain he grew that when the point of his sword pricked Sikandar's milky skin, it would be powerless to advance. He would fling the weapon down, run to the stables and ride away.

Flight.

---

55 Originally worn over a dress as symbol of modesty, it now exists as a colourful accessory. The closest English equivalent is a scarf.

It was a simple solution to almost any problem, and he had perfected it with his stables. His horses were the best in the kingdom, swift, spirited and loyal to his command alone. He did not loan them out. He kept his stables as other princes kept their harems: jealously. And like a Sultân he rode them all in turn, out of duty, but trusted one alone.

Flight had not endeared him to the Sultân. Muzaffar Shah had reproved Bahadur more than once.

'Only the guilty flee,' he stated. 'When I hear of your departure, my son, I do not concern myself with your safety but only with that of my people. I ask myself—what's he done now?'

Silently, Bahadur had acknowledged the justice of that. His madcap scrapes were too numerous to defend.

This time, though, he was blameless.

The sight of his father chased away every thought but anxiety.

Muzaffar Shah had thought it fit to receive his son in bed, for it had become his custom, of late, to spend the afternoon hours in easy solitude.

The cavernous bed with its large ornate canopy was a well of darkness, his father's yellow face blurring in the lamp's flicker, the velvet haunch of bolster bruised and empurpled as carnage.

The Sultân was sucking on lemons. A dish of quartered preserves rested on the dome of his belly.

'Do you not find them sour?' asked Bahadur. 'They set my teeth on edge.'

'And mine. But they say this will cure me. For once, hakim and vaid agree.'

'Let me bring you some sweeter fruit.'

'No, nothing, son. Here, put this away.'

Bahadur took away the lemons and poured out some water from a surahi, but the Sultân declined it.

'So tell me, Bahadur, what made you think of me this afternoon? Isn't this the hour when you plan amusements for the evening with your friends? Or have you brought me a musician with a new *tarana*?'

'I've been here all morning—' began Bahadur.

'So have I, so have I. The difference between us is one of health. It is only proper the healthy must wait upon the sick. Let me waste no more of your time, precious as it is. Too precious to be squandered outside the stable, the kennel, and perhaps, the brothel. Don't answer, that was not my question. I do not question your activities, my son, but as your father I am aware of each and every one of them. Return to them, then, after saying what you have come here to say.'

Bahadur would have stormed out angrily, as he often did, but the memory of his mother's eyes made him stay. His own eyes burned with the bitterness he had seen in hers. He would see this through.

With some surprise he recognized the relaxing calm that brought a smile to his lips: it was the calm before battle.

Others had observed that Bahadur fought with a laugh on his lips, but he was unaware of that.

All he knew was the exhilaration he felt, the certainty that this was his place, this was what he was expected to do.

He had not expected that joyful ease here. But it had settled in him the moment he had decided to stay.

Bahadur drew out a velvet footstool and sat down.

'I do not recollect having invited you to take your ease here,' the Sultân admonished. 'State your business. If you have come to press your old demand, let me put you out of your misery. My answer's the same. Two jagirs are enough for you.'

Bahadur continued to sit and regard his father with calm attention.

'Indeed, I am content,' he murmured.

'Content? You?' The Sultân permitted himself a laugh. 'Do you even know what the word means? How can you, it is alien to your kind.'

'My kind? I am your kind.'

'I see no trace of that. You are your mother's kind.'

'There is no insult in that, sir, I trust you meant none.'

'See, that's what I meant. Just like your mother. You will not be drawn.'

Bahadur fell silent, tormented by an intense anguish he could not name. Yet, he found it difficult to depart.

'I am a sick man. I need my rest!' The Sultân's voice had turned querulous. 'Go about your business if you have nothing to say to me.'

'They tried to poison me today.'

'Really? And who may they be?'

'I was sent chhundo from Sikandar's kitchen.'

'And what made you suspect it might be poisoned? Or rather, who did? Your mother, I suppose? Like all her kind, she's suspicious. She has the mind of a snake.'

'No, she knew nothing about the chhundo, none of us suspected a thing till the taster fell dead within seconds.'

'Taster? You have a bakawal now? Your mother's idea, eh? See that the unfortunate man's family is looked after.'

'My mother has done that already.'

'Then there is no more to be said. You had a lucky escape.'

Bahadur felt again the deep calm that comes before delivering the death stroke.

Everything in him reverberated to the slow deliberate thud of his heart. His voice very gentle, he asked, 'What are you going to do about it?'

'I? What can I do? I'm a weak old man. When my blessed Begum died, my spirit went with her. The doctors tell me they'll cure me. How can they cure what is incurable? For no illness afflicts me. Only sorrow—sorrow and disappointment.'

'I am sorry if I have contributed to that.'

'Who am I to tell you? You are a grown man now. You should know, without my telling, whose wild ways and licentious life have brought me sorrow and disappointment. I have led a temperate life, I have been just.'

'And merciful. People call you Muzzafar the Clement.'

'Ah, that. They will have a different name for me when I am dead.'

'I pray that day is very distant yet.'

'Indeed you can see that it is not. My water is tainted yellow. My appetite has gone. I shall soon need a strong shoulder to lean upon. It takes me one hour to get dressed for the audience. No, Bahadur. Death is round the corner for me.'

'For both of us, it appears. Sikandar will not rest after one attempt.'

'No, indeed, he will not.'

'Will you not chastise him, then? Will you trust the country to a poisoner? Tell him to challenge me to a duel, to any test of skill, and I will welcome the chance to die in a fair fight.'

'But he won't.'

'True. What must I do then?'

'You are a soldier, Bahadur. Not a foot soldier, but a warrior. This is your war. Equip yourself to fight it.'

'Am I ill-equipped now?'

'Yes.'

'How should I equip myself?'

'You are not a child, Bahadur Khan! Go now, I need to rest.'

'I must leave the kingdom, then?'

'That might be wise, and wiser still not to tell me where you're headed. There is a boy I want you to take along. He will keep you safe.'

'What boy? Another taster? Another cook? No boy can keep me safe.'

'This one will, by taking the thorn out of your heart.'

'Then Sikandar has greater need for him.'

'You are mistaken. No such thorn troubles Sikandar's heart. Take the boy with you, keep him close. I brought him with me, he has been a great solace in my grief.'

'Ah, he is a musician, then.'

'Saraswati in boy's guise, not just any Gandharva. He is of your age. Be tender with him. He knows nothing of the world yet. Such knowledge will corrupt his music.'

'Why do you send him with me?'

Muzaffar Shah allowed himself a smile, but said nothing.

'I will take him with me. I'll look after him.'

'Do not wander too far, or too long. Let not your thirst for fortune make another Alam Khan of you.'

'What, is he back then?'

'He will be, in a day or two. He was noticed by Banjaras in the north.'

'I had thought he would be Emperor by now.'

They exchanged a smile.

'The man is a jackal running from camp to camp. The Lodis would have nothing to do with him, so I hear he ran north. The Chaghtai flung a shoe at him, and he's coming howling back.'

'What will you do?'

'I? Nothing.'

'You would not play him for Dilli?'

'What is Dilli to me, I who have Gujarat?'

'If Gujarat does not want Dilli, Dilli may want Gujarat.'

'Pah. Barbarians. Be on your way, then, Bahadur Khan.'

'Give me your blessing.'

'You have no need for it. Others, worthier than your father, have blessed you. Go.'

Bahadur bowed and made his salaam.

The Sultân responded with a stony silence that stayed Bahadur's hand that was extended to touch him.

At the door, Bahadur turned back. 'Where do I find this boy?' he asked.

'At Nagina. Go there at *maghrib*.'

Hauz-e-Qutub was still as lovely as Sultân Qutubuddin had intended when he built it more than fifty years ago, but nobody called it by its old name.

It was Bahadur's favourite haunt.

Long before *maghrib*, he left the city on foot through the Raipur gate. He was dressed like a commoner in a tunic of white muslin. His distaste for jewellery served him well on these excursions.

He had abjured his usual companions, fellows of small worth, sycophants, not friends. He kept them at arm's length. As long as they had costly presents and wine, they didn't complain.

The limestone lake—for it was excavated from the pure limestone that made up the city's foundation—was more than a mile in circumference. Seventy-two acres had been dug out as a thirty-four sided polygon.[56] Delicately chiseled steps ringed the circumference, leading down to the sweetest water in the city. There were six spokes to this wheel, six exquisite sloping sluices surmounted with chhatris, the channels embedded with garnet, jasper, cornelian and agate, and the chhatris lit with hundreds of tiny lamps.

Bahadur delighted in swimming in the dark, and usually finished a boisterous evening with several laps across the lake. Unlike Sikandar, he seldom visited Nagina Bāgh, but its white flowers scented the midnight air and made him wonder why he never noticed them by day.

This evening, though, Nagina was his destination.

The beauty of the twilit sky, the shadowy trees, the plaintive birdsong fading into the hush of night, all this would have moved him on any day but this.

Nothing touched him now.

Since leaving his father, everything seemed at an immense distance, separated from him by some hard substance of dazzling clarity so that he saw everything, but it let nothing through, and left him benumbed. He had agreed to the cooks, and now this musician.

He was still to take his leave of Sheikh Jiu at the khanquah—and what would the Sheikh burden him with?

Bahadur walked rapidly down the causeway, his mind intent on the things to be done by daybreak.

[56] The word polygon derives from the Greek and means 'many-angled.' Individual polygons are named according to the number of sides by combining a Greek-derived numeric with the suffix *-gon* added to it; e.g.; pentagon, hexagon, heptagon. A 34-sided polygon, the shape of Nagina Bāgh, is a triacontatetragon.

He had to see to his kennels. His dogs were trained to obey, but with him the older dogs had no more dignity than puppies, rolling on the ground, wanting him to tickle and wrestle with them. When he was away at Dungarpur last week, the dogs had been restless and morose, off their food, snarling without provocation. He would talk with them seriously tonight before going to check on—

Bahadur stopped, his thoughts arrested.

A note of music vibrated in the air.

A single note.

Plaintive to begin with, then slowly infusing joy as it swelled with richness, growing deeper, sweeter, and more resonant.

A single note of the veena.

The air fell silent again.

Night furled the trees into dark shapes.

Perhaps he had imagined it.

No, there it came again.

Just that one note.

A few minutes later, it had led him through the maze of *raat-ki-rani* to the centre of the garden.

Like its name, Nagina was a gem with flower beds set within a scrollwork of shrubs and trees. By day it dazzled with colour, but now, illuminated only by its flowers, it was a marvel of black and white. In its centre was a dial of flowers, its geometry reflecting the night sky. So accurate were its seasonal changes that astronomers could predict the celestial from this terrestrial display.

Bahadur, who had never seen this before, might have noticed it now if a young man had not manifested like a ghost, and startled him.

Bahadur acknowledged his salaam and looked around for the musician.

'It is I,' said the man.

'Who are you?'

The man answered with a swift phrase of music, exuberant, triumphant, liberating.

Nothing more was said.

He followed Bahadur in silence.

Later, Bahadur learnt his name: Bachchu.

Bachchu could not be commanded. He sang at will, but each song freed a struggling bird captive in Bahadur's heart.

9

Flight

Bahadur rode to Batoh while Haridas got everything in order.

Two hundred men, no more, Lakham Bai decided.

Bahadur ignored that.

Fifty men were more than enough.

Haridas compromised. He enlisted fifty, beyond their trusted band of twenty friends.

And then, there were cooks and tasters, grooms for horses and camels, trainers and kennel-keepers for the dogs, and a caravan of bullocks to carry rations.

Only Haridas and Bachchu would ride with Bahadur. The rest would follow a post behind.

It was well past *isha* when Bahadur reached the khanquah.

Sheikh Jiu awaited him at the gate.

'I was beginning to doubt myself,' he murmured as he laid his hand on Bahadur's head. 'Make haste. Ride back instantly and leave the city before dawn.'

'Haridas is making all the preparations.'

'Trust him with your life. And that fool Bachchu, who speaks with an angel's voice. All the rest you must doubt.'

'I'll leave them behind, if you say so.'

'No. They must go with you. Where will you go?'

'I don't know yet. North, I think.'

'North, for certain. There is a crown to be won!'

Bahadur laughed. 'I thought you said it was mine already.'

'Gujarat is yours. What more do you desire?'

'Chittor.'

The word had shot out of him. He had never coveted Chittor.

'Are you sure?' Sheikh Jiu asked thoughtfully.

He had said it, hadn't he?

'Yes, I'm sure.'

Sheikh Jiu shut his eyes. After a while he said, 'It will cost you dear. If you have Chittor you will lose everything else.'

'So be it.'

Sheikh Jiu looked at Bahadur with a sudden distance in his eyes. The change made Bahadur feel as if he were hurtling through the night sky, past dizzying banks of stars. He seemed to retreat further as he spoke again. 'Be good to us, Bahadur Shah.'

It was a command, but it sounded like a plea.

Sheikh Jiu knew his son's weaknesses.

Bahadur had already directed his income to be paid directly to the khanquah during his absence. Now he assured Sheikh Jiu that he had instructed his accountant to call at the khanquah every week for orders.

'I won't be here, Bahadur Shah,' Sheikh Jiu said.

'Are you making a pilgrimage, then?'

'Yes. The final hajj that will take me to Him. I have received the summons and will leave soon. This is the last time my earthly eyes will see you, but my spirit will guide you always.'

Tears dried on Bahadur's cheeks as he rode back. Something had clenched shut in him. He felt inexorable, adamantine.

His parting with Lakham Bai was swift and tearless.

They left at dawn. A hundred men in his entourage, the swiftest horses.

Leaving the Bhadar, Bahadur rode silently through Daryapur to Dilli Gate where Haridas, with his retinue, awaited him.

As they left the city, Haridas asked, 'Where to?'

'Chittorgarh.'

There! That name again.

'What compels me there?' He spoke his bewilderment aloud.

'That's easy! It is the kamarband.'

And, because Bahadur hadn't heard it before, because nothing is as pleasant as a story when you're awake in the small hours, Haridas began with ...

10

The Tale of the Kamarband

It has been called the belt, the cummerband, the jewelled zone; but none who have described it ever saw it.

The Firangi wrote of its value as:

Sixty crores ducats, or taking the ducat at fifty aspers, 30 million aspers.

To us such coins are of no value, so I'll tell you how it was made, and you can value it yourself.

It was of tenuous gold, fibrils finer than hair, meshed close enough to make it as much armour as ornament.

They say the jeweller Rohidas crafted it after seeing the comb of his dying daughter knotted with her fallen curls. He must have wept over it, for each one of the sixty thousand pores of that mesh had a diamond, a scintilla of such penetrant brightness, that, when worn, the lightest breath would blind like lightning. On this brilliant matrix was worked a creeper of entwined silver and gold.

Rohidas knew his fingers had done their work well when the belt attracted a cloud of confused butterflies into his workshop. Such butterflies crowded the window where his daughter lay dying. Her eyes lingered at the window, yearning for her garden, for the flowers she loved beyond all else. And in his prison, this belt was the garden he fashioned for her.

This vine had leaves of jade and olivine, picked out with emerald veins. There were cleverly fashioned flowers of Kashmir sapphire, fruit of Ceylon rubies, and tiny mangoes of the milk-and-honey chrysoberyl of Madurai.

These wondrous embellishments all paled before the beauty of the clasp.

Rohidas put that in much later.

By then his daughter was dead. By then he knew he had to sell the belt.

The clasp was fashioned like a lion's head. The mane was carved from amber and set with radiating whorls of topaz, carnelian, onyx, and rubies. The eyes were of ametrine, a shimmer of purple and gold. To meet that gaze was fatal: you could never look away.

This was the belt that was lost at Kapparbanj.

But before you hear that tale, perhaps you should ask how came the belt to Kapparbanj?

For that you must sing the glories of that most bloody monarch, the Butcher of Dilli, Alauddin Khilji, and his bloodier catamite Malik Kafur, the eunuch from Khambat, whose beauty was worth a thousand dinars. It is said that Malik Kafur's gratitude for the Sultân's love was as boundless as the ocean of treasure he poured at the Sultân's feet.

This ocean was a roaring tide of blood from the Dakshin kingdoms Malik Kafur looted, a crimson glissade of carnage gleaming with gold, iridescent with jewels.

From Kakinada, from Madurai, from the very strand where this land of Hindustan ends and the ocean begins, came the gems of the kamarband: diamonds, rubies, emeralds, pearls. The gold, even more precious, was melted from the murtis of the temples the eunuch in his ignorance thought he destroyed.

It was the eunuch who summoned the jeweller.

A belt for his beloved, Alauddin, a kamarband beyond compare. And he scattered diamonds, rubies, emeralds, sapphires by the fistful on the floor.

Rohidas declared himself unfit for work. His daughter was dying. His hands trembled, his eyes grew dim, the weight of grief oppressed his thoughts—how could he possibly cut the gems and filigree the gold with precision?

You'll find out how, the eunuch said.

He had Rohidas imprisoned in his own workshop with a caveat: let but the smallest detail seem copied from a familiar design, and he would lose his head.

So the jeweller invented this marvel, so airy and insubstantial, from the wealth of Kuber, the pot-bellied keeper of the earth's hidden treasures.

When the belt was made, Rohidas clamoured for liberty. But when he was freed, he found his captor dead, the city in confusion, his family fled.

He was a pauper, left holding this priceless treasure.

For a month he searched for his family.

He found them, hiding in abject misery, emaciated from grief and starvation.

He showed his wife the kamarband.

'Sell it!' she said.

Her words stung. Had the woman no eyes?

'None, for the belt has me bedazzled. If I could feast with my eyes, I would be beyond satiety. Can we eat gold? Chew upon diamonds? Digest pearls? We are reduced to that. The kamarband is worth all of Hindustan, but I'd sell it for a fistful of rice and a ladle of milk for our little one.'

With the Sultân dead and his favourite murdered, who in all Dilli would need the kamarband?

It is said that Rohidas ran from amir to amir holding out the kamarband in the sunlight, blinding them as much with its dazzle as with the despair in his eyes.

There were no buyers.

Confusion and chaos everywhere drove people to distraction.

At length, the jeweller found admittance to the royal harem. There he asked for an audience with that most tearful of women, Dewal Rani.[57]

O the story of Dewal and Khizr has been penned by the greatest of poets. Why should I, a mere dabbler in verse and story, presume to repeat it now?

Rohidas remembered Dewal Rani as the beautiful bride of Khizr Khan.

---

[57] Dewal Rani—The daughter of Raja Karna of Anhilwara. In 1296, Alauddin Khilji sent Aluf (Alp) Khan to invade Anhilwara. Rani Kamaldevi was captured and became the third wife of Alauddin Khilji, and very soon his favourite. Dewal Rani, her daughter, was brought to Dilli at her request a few years later, and married to Alauddin's son Khizr Khan. Following Alauddin Khilji's death, Mubarak Shah who succeeded him, had Khizr Khan blinded and murdered, and made Dewal Rani his queen. Mubarak Shah was soon murdered by his lover Khusro Khan, and Dewal Rani became, once again, the wife of a Sultân. Dewal Rani is the heroine of Amir Khusro's 14th century masterpiece *Ishquia*, and of Nandashankar Mehta's 1866 Gujarati classic *Karan Ghelo*.

Khizr Khan was dead now, and she was a bride again. Still beautiful, but with an adamantine radiance that proclaimed the endurance of extreme suffering.

The jeweller who had come to sell the kamarband surprised himself by saying, 'I have here a jewel fit for my daughter. My daughter being dead, I gift it to you.'

'I too am a dead daughter,' Dewal said. 'Take it away and gift it to the living.'

'Will you not see it first?'

And, unbidden, Rohidas took the kamarband from his turban, [he had concealed it in tatters for fear of ambush] and let it slip on to a patch of sunlight on the marble floor.

With a gasp, as if it were her last, Dewal Rani knelt down and extended trembling hands towards the object of beauty.

Almost immediately, a shadow plucked the jewels from Dewal's hand.

Rohidas was shocked to see who it was. A common *nautanki*[58] woman, dressed in cheap finery, mockingly dangled the prize before the cowering queen.

The impassioned jeweller sprang on the hussy and tried to wrest the kamarband from her grasp.

She gave a small push, the veriest nudge, but it was muscled enough to topple Rohidas on his back. She planted a foot, a heavy rough foot, on his chest.

'Let him go!' Rohidas heard Dewal Rani plead. 'He is a harmless tradesman.'

'Not so harmless that he trades with my wife!' the nautanki woman replied in a man's voice.

The nautanki-wali's breasts showed dark and bulbous beneath the thin pink silk of her baju.

Rohidas, who could not tear his eyes away, recognized them at last for large purple brinjals, of the sort much prized by cooks. They were stuffed into a harness that held them in place. Her long hair was plaited with strands of jasmine and strung with tassels of gemmed velvet. Besides, she had a fine mustache, curled and oiled, and eyebrows that knotted fiercely over her frown. The wretch raised her baju and wound the belt around her hairy expanse.

A faint cry escaped the suffocating jeweller.

He was rewarded promptly by a violent stomp from the nautanki-wali's foot.

Nautanki-wali?

What was he thinking?

This was the *Sultân.*

Shahenshah Mubarak Khilji.

But what was he doing dressed like this?

As if in answer, a soldier entered the room unannounced.

His daring should have cost the man his head. Instead, the Sultân took his foot off the jeweller's chest and sidled up to the newcomer, displaying his kamarband in a manner that might have seemed amorous had it not been so ridiculous.

Rohidas, despite his pain, permitted himself a laugh.

---

58 *Nautanki* ... [Urdu نوٹنکی] ... North Indian form of opera, generally an open-air performance.

Dewal Rani, who had been trembling but a moment earlier, now drew herself up in all her queenly dignity, and throwing a look of deep contempt at her husband, swept out of the room.

The jeweller, crippled by pain and a growing constriction in his chest, remained where he was.

Rohidas recognized the soldier. It was the rascally Patwari now known as Khusrow Khan. It was murmured that he was the king's favourite, but even the most salacious rumour could not match what Rohidas witnessed over the next few minutes.

The Sultân excelled in the fine art of seduction, striving with sweet blandishments to coax the brutish warrior out of his sulk. He displayed his charms teasingly, now letting the soft silk of his odhni float like a cloud over his lover, now cruelly ripping away the baju as if its weight were unendurable. With a sigh he shrugged off the harness and popped out the brinjals. Swiveling his hips he emerged from his voluminous skirt.

Rohidas now had the anguish of seeing his kamarband glitter and flash as the naked Sultân raced in mock terror before the determined pursuit of Khusrow Khan.

Try as he would, Rohidas could not look away from the kamarband as it twinkled in the crush of those heavy ungainly bodies, all but buried in sweaty folds of flesh.

Rohidas could not breathe. At first he thought he must be dead, then remembered the injury the Sultân's foot had inflicted on him. But that hardly hurt now. His pain was much deeper and impossible to locate. He had felt something like this when his daughter died. Something similar, but not as intense. The pain, he realized, was not in him, but in the kamarband. It cried out its anguish and he lay here paralyzed, unable to avenge its outrage.

He must have cried out, for he realized he was breathing again.

He heard the lovers whisper, speeding their transports towards climax. Perhaps he cried out again, for the Sultân asked, 'What's that sound?'

And Khusrow stopped his mouth with a kiss.

He must have cried out, for there was a terrific din: shouts, screams, wailing.

Now the Sultân, alarmed, threw off Khusrow Khan and rushed to the window.

Khusrow sprang on the Sultân and wrestled him to the floor, assuring him all the while in a high breathless voice that the noise was nothing more than a fracas in the bazaar.

The Sultân, no longer in the trance of passion, did his best to free himself, which, being the stronger man, he accomplished.

He ran to the door that led into the harem, but his long plait, so lavish with flowers, was his undoing.

Khusrow caught the Sultân by the tassels and dragged him to the window.

With one stroke of his khanda, Malik Khusrow sent the Sultân's head flying out of the window. Then he flung the khanda to the floor and left the room.

The headless body of the Sultân, shot out fountains of blood as it twitched.

Rohidas found he could stand up. He knew what he had to do.

The Sultân's corpse twitched in its last jactitation as Rohidas undid the kamarband.

'Give that to me.'

It seemed as though Rohidas had turned towards the speaker even before she spoke.

Dewal Rani did not spare a glance for the fallen Sultân.

As she took the kamarband from Rohidas, her hand closed around his and she drew him through the door into the harem.

'You are a dead man unless you flee,' she whispered.

'I was not noticed,' Rohidas gasped.

'But you will be, if you stay. I have no money to pay for your gift.'

Rohidas made a gesture of refusal and would have brushed past her to the stairs, but she restrained him with a look.

'I have no money. Instead, I burden you with a request. I accept your gift and beg you to deliver it to my father.'

'I have heard he is dead.'

'No. He is in hiding. I will arrange for your passage.'

'My wife and child are starving. I cannot abandon them.'

'Take them with you. My father will reward you well.'

'Khambat is a long way off.'

'Is it yes or no?'

'Yes.'

And that, my masters, is how the kamarband came to Gujarat.

ꝏ ꝏ ꝏ ꝏ

'What happened to Dewal Rani?' Bahadur asked.

'The villain Khusrow married her. He was slaughtered soon enough, and the Khilji line was replaced by the Tughlaq. As for the queen—'

'She is among the immortals in the sweet music of Amir Khusru,' Bachchu said.

'If you say so,' drawled Bahadur. 'I take it my ancestors plundered the unfortunate Raja and took the kamarband along with his kingdom? Now tell us what happened at Kapparbanj.'

ꝏ ꝏ ꝏ ꝏ

Kapparbanj?

The belt changed hands because of two Sheikhs and two elephants. And, of course, two kings.

But first, ask what the kamarband was doing on a battlefield?

I have no answer to that!

Why do kings travel into battle with their treasure?

To intimidate with wealth when valour fails them?

To bribe the enemy army into defecting?

To placate the conqueror and sue for truce?

Or, simply, for that magnificence which seems a necessary duty of kings?

Whatever the reason, that kamarband was among the camel-load of jewels that took up most of the space in the tent of Qutub Shah at Kapparbanj.

The enemy, Mahmud Khilji of Malwa, was the grandfather of the Mahmud, your father, praised be his memory, subdued. That earlier Mahmud, had travelled far from his kingdom of Malwa to Kapparbanj, which, as you know, is a day's ride from the Bhadar.

Malwa wanted Gujarat.

Gujarat, in the person of Qutub the Timid wanted to wait in a defensive crouch till the time was right. But the amirs were not of this mind. They beleaguered the Sultân till he agreed to war.

Mahmud had the blessings of Sheikh Kamaluddin.

Qutub had the blessings of Sheikh Burhanuddin.

Sheikh Kamal had recently died, at the height of his rivalry with Sheikh Burhan.

Qutub petitioned Burhan's son, Shah Alam, to accompany him into battle.

On the first day in camp, Shah Alam could not carry out his ablutions for lack of water.

A darwesh has no business beyond prayer, so he gave Qutub his blessings, and prepared to go home.

'Not so fast!' cried Qutub. 'Leave me your sword that it may lead me into victory.'

It was a childish thing to say—no man asks another for his sword, and Qutub, at fifty, was well advanced in years.

Shah Alam said as much, and sharply too, for a darwesh who minces his words is not worth his salt. But he did hand over his sword.

Naturally, it came with a warning.

'The moment you even think of injuring a Darwesh the sword will turn on you,' he pronounced.

Qutub protested his fealty to the Sheikh, and, buckling the sword, voiced another anxiety. 'Mahmud can be faced, but what can I do about Ghalib Jung?'

This Ghalib Jung was a famous elephant of Malwa. By feeding it some secret potion, its mahout maintained the elephant in a constant state of *musth*.[59] Ghalib Jung was more ferocious than a tiger. At the merest hint of the *ankush* he would go on a rampage, trampling men and horses as if they were ants. At the approach of his enormous shadow, roads emptied within seconds. The very birds fell silent. The sun hid behind any convenient cloud.

And Ghalib Jung, called the Butcher, was Mahmud Khilji's principal weapon. Qutub Shah had good reason to tremble

But Sheikh Shah Alam laughed at Qutub's anxiety. 'Call for Shiddati,' he ordered.

Shiddati was the youngest elephant in Qutub's stable. Shiddati had never faced battle before. A small timid creature, he blinked trustingly at the Sheikh when he was led in.

'Mind you, gore the guts out of Ghalib Jung,' the Sheikh said, patting the animal's trunk. And then, Shah Alam went home.

---

59 *Musth* … [Urdu مست] … Periodic (often seasonal) behavioural change in adult male elephants that makes them fierce and aggressive.

That evening, Mahmud sent a long poem of insult to Qutub.

Qutub answered with restraint, only reminding Mahmud that Malwa had been gifted to his fathers by the generosity of Qutub's ancestors.

The next day, they were arrayed for battle.

Mahmud on his elephant, sported a diamond-studded black canopy. Its glitter would have dazzled the enemy had Ghalib Jung's ponderosity not stood in the way.

Qutub, more modestly mounted, had chosen a green canopy that shone like a new leaf on a fallen tree.

Mahmud attacked Qutub's left flank and gained the field. But the rumour of treasure distracted his soldiers, and led by Muzaffar Khan, they plundered the royal tents.

It is said that Mahmud himself took charge of the *karmarband*, a priceless *bajuband,* and the crown, leaving Muzaffar Khan to load the rest of the treasure on his elephant.

Meanwhile, Mahmud's left flank was attacked by Qutub's right, and had almost folded when Ghalib Jung was unleashed by his mahout's goad.

It would have been all over if Qutub hadn't remembered Sheikh Alam's blessing and called for Shiddati to be brought out.

It was sublime, the idiocy of that moment!

The enraged mammoth staring down a small nervous calf.

Malwa must have roared with laughter.

At any rate, the face-off distracted them from a small group of Darwaziahs, our Dholkah braves, who sneaked through enemy ranks into the dark cavern beneath Ghalib Jung's pendant belly. At any moment the beast could have raised one of his feet and squashed their skulls. But their movements were disciplined and delicate. Four of them, at the same instant, plunged a clever and cruel blade into the tendon of each leg, and—Ghalib Jung, hamstrung, sank to the ground.

Did the Darwaziahs get out in the nick of time?

Or were they obliterated by the Butcher's plutonic weight?

The historian did not bother about such details. He was too busy noticing what happened next.

Shiddati, the little one, sank his brand new tusks deep in the belly of the groaning monster, and dragged out his entrails.

Mahmud fought singlehanded, astonishing the Gujaratis with his courage. They let him go and he galloped into the night shouting that he would be back at daybreak with eighty thousand more men.

Qutub was so relieved at the battle being over, it was some time before he noticed that his treasure was missing.

Muzaffar Khan was trapped and duly hanged.

Sheikh Shah Alam's prophecy was vindicated.

What more does a story need?

What?

Oh, the sword?

That was vindicated too.

Since you ask, it happened like this:

Qutub and Shah Alam fell out over, what else?—a woman.

Qutub urged his men to plunder the Sheikh's khanquah.

Out of respect for the darwesh, his men refused to obey.

The enraged Sultân rode around the village, slaughtering all who came in his way. In his fury the sword slipped from his hand and fell on his foot, and slashed it wide open.

The wound turned foul, and he died on the third day.

Or so the historian would have us believe.

Gossip tells us a different story.

One of Qutub's queens poisoned him.

Qutub's mother believed this version, for she sent the unfortunate Sultâna to her eunuchs, and they tore her to pieces with their bare hands.

And if that isn't a perfect ending to the tale, tell me, what is?

11

Chittorgarh

The kamarband was nowhere in Bahadur's thoughts when he reached Chittorgarh. From the moment he entered the fort, Bahadur was haunted by gloom. The warm welcome Rana Sangram Singh extended, the jovial challenges his cousins proposed, and the loving attentions of his aunt Rani Karnavati, these were all his heart could desire. There was nothing he could put a word to, yet he was filled with foreboding.

They had arrived late in the evening, and pleading exhaustion, Bahadur retired early only to lie awake through the small hours. Springing out of bed long before daybreak, he wandered out into the palace grounds.

It was cold. The sky wheeled close, churning out stars by the million.

A longing, intense and melancholic, slowed his step. He had come out with the thought of an early ride. That no longer seemed inviting. But for the tread of the guards, the night was silent.

Who could tell what the darkness concealed?

He too was invisible as he slid between shadows.

The fort with its armored guards seemed a prison, and he, incarcerated for the crime of innocence. He thought fleetingly of scaling the walls and eluding the guards. It would be a fine prank at this hour, but it would make the Rana look foolish by the light of day.

His oldest son was lately dead from a fever, and grief was a fresh wound on the Rana's battle-scarred face. Many thousands had perished by Rana Sanga's sword, yet in one's own home, Death was an unwelcome guest.

Kings, soldiers, heroes, murderers. That's what they were, every man of them, himself included—murder and darkness their element, secrecy and subterfuge their weapons, guilt their after-taste. The rest was just—duty.

Haridas had taught him well the duty of kings. Bahadur was unlikely to be king, but the thought allured him. Sikandar, he knew, wouldn't last long. The amirs would have him murdered. Death, at every step.

Death didn't frighten Bahadur. It puzzled him. How could everything simply stop like that?

A movement in the shadows.

His hand gripped the dagger at his waist. He held his breath.

It was a woman.

She left the palace and walked across the lawns, her step firm and intent.

A woman leaving the palace at this hour? A cheating wife or concubine. This one walked like a queen.

She carried no lamp, but the darkness made way for her. She passed through a crevice between trees, the stone walls seemed to dissolve around her.

He followed.

There was a door, of course.

It led into a long passage, very dimly lit by some chance glimmer of light. There were flagstones underfoot, the passage was arched like a tunnel. He realized the impregnable walls of Chittorgarh were hollow.

This could be a trap.

If so, he would brave it. Retreat was impossible now. The pale luminance fluttering ahead was nothing more than her odhni.

The darkness became absolute. She had disappeared.

Bahadur ran forward. If she had left the tunnel, the door might close behind her.

He was relieved to find the exit was open.

A short flight of stairs led up to—what?

Dagger at the ready, he emerged stealthily, but it was a wasted caution. The tunnel had brought him halfway down the hill, almost to the edge of the small town that bearded the rocks like fungus.

A small lane led into the town.

And there she was, at the end of the lane.

A commoner, then. A spy, perhaps?

He hurried, just in time to see her enter a small door set into a high wall.

He slid in a few paces behind her.

A courtyard, a flight of steps, a pillar with a pennant. The shikhar of a temple just visible above the steep stairs.

The woman skimmed up the stairs as if she were lofted weightlessly.

She went into the temple.

The pujari's wife? Daughter?

Or, had he got it upside down? The Rai's wife or daughter, keeping a tryst with a low-born lover?

It was a tryst alright.

She was talking even before she had reached her tryst, explaining in a low melodious voice why she was so late.

As she disappeared behind the marble screen, he overheard her words, disjointed, anxious, pleading, fearful.

Her lover was doing nothing to assuage her. He seemed a silent presence. Inexorable, though her voice was breaking with tears.

Her pain stung Bahadur like the swift slash of a scimitar, wounding close to the bone long before he felt the injury.

He heard her pleading, her helplessness evident in every syllable.

He could have cheerfully run his dagger through her lumpen lover.

What manner of stony heart could be unmoved by her voice, so full of tenderness and love?

No woman had ever spoken to him like this.

But the unseen lover must have reassured her in some way, for gradually, she grew tranquil, even joyous.

'Now we're together, nothing matters. Forget my reproaches, they mean nothing. I know I complain all the time, but you're the only one I can talk to. Then I ask myself why do I need to tell you? You know it all already, don't you?'

And she began to sing.

At first, in a murmur as private as thought, then, as if solving a puzzle, notes and phrases clarified into the line of a song.

Her tone, low, deep, vibrant, seemed to fill the darkness and lift a lid off his heart.

Her voice gained in clarity and strength as if she were singing for him, Bahadur, and not for that adamantine lover who refused her.

But had he refused her?

The song did not say so:

Sawariya, Mohaniya, Nagariya, mero Piya ...

Bahadur could contain himself no longer. He might die for it, but he would see her face.

The woman was alone.

Nobody in the temple but this lovely woman singing her soul out to the small murti of Krishna at the altar.

She stopped her song midway to resume the conversation.

'How much longer are you going to let them torment me?' she demanded. 'I'm tired of it, I tell you! I'm finished here.'

She wept bitterly, angry tears of humiliation.

Bahadur felt the indelicacy of his presence there, but he could not bring himself to leave.

She took up her song again.

Quite without realizing it, Bahadur joined in the refrain.

The woman took no notice of him till her song ended. Then, she said, 'Come here, child.'

She was older than him, certainly, but not so old that she should call him child.

Bahadur made his *pranam*, and with all the authority of a mother, she laid her hand lightly on his head.

'Sing with me.'

His voice followed hers, hesitantly at first, then with something of her own conviction.

Mero to Giridhar Gopal, doosaro na koi.

'I had to explain this to them, can you imagine?' she said scornfully. 'They wanted me to lie with the Rana on his pyre. Why should I, I asked them. Because I didn't lie with him when he was alive? Is this my punishment? He was a good man, yes, but he was not my husband. You understand, don't you, child? You know who my husband really is?'

'Yes.'

'Say his name.'

'Giridhar Gopal.'

'See! I didn't have to explain to you, did I? Why do I have to explain it to them? Over and over again?'

'Maybe, they should sing with you. You won't need to explain then.'

'Come with me. He wants me to show you something.'

She turned to the altar and addressed the murti. 'You wait here for me, I'll be back.'

And without further ado, she led Bahadur back into the tunnel.

When they emerged within the fort, she led him across the gardens to an isolated parterre.

'Look.'

She stood at the top of a staircase. The sky was pale with light now, just enough for him to discern a deep pit below.

'Come back and look at it again. He wants you to look at it. I want to tell you I will never enter it, never. Come by daylight and you will find the earth scorched. No woman has walked down these steps in a hundred years. But the time is at hand again.'

'What's down there?'

'Fire. This is where we women are sent when the enemy is at the gates. This is our Jauhar-kund.[60] We are supposed to choose fire over ignominy.'

'But you won't? Why?'

'Because it is evil. That is what he wants you to know. Life is a sacred thing.'

'I am a soldier. I have killed many men,' stated Bahadur. 'But I would not be responsible for a woman's death.'

'I am aware of that. That is why I brought you here. Killing yourself, or another, is an act of arrogance.'

'It is considered an act of honour.'

'If you are bound by such shackles, you will never see the light. Free yourself.'

'And how do I do that?'

'You'll know. My way is not your way, but you'll find out.'

She left him.

He watched her retrace her steps towards the tunnel.

He did not follow her.

He caught a glimpse of her, later in the day. She was talking with the Rana, laughter in every look and gesture.

'Find out who that is,' he murmured to Haridas.

---

60 *Jauhar* : Mass self-immolation of Rajput women in the face of certain military defeat.
The earliest accounts of jauhar come from Alexander of Macedon's assault on India's northwest in 327 BCE
Kund : Small lake.

'Oh, I know already. She is the Rana's eldest daughter-in-law, Mihira Devi.[61] Generally considered mad.'

Somehow, Bahadur thought her the sanest person he had ever met.

In the afternoon, he strolled over to the Jauhar-kund, watching in his mind's eye a fearful procession of women, urged and goaded into the roaring furnace below. He heard screams as their flesh charred, as their melting eyes fixed on him while everything lost meaning.

And stopped.

They were all drunk by afternoon, the princes and his men too. Bahadur slept the evening out, waking at moonrise just in time to bathe and dress for the night's revels.

His cousins had planned a lavish entertainment. Bachchu was all agog at the prospect of hearing the Rana's famous musicians.

'We have a famous musician too,' Bahadur pointed out.

'We do?' Bachchu was puzzled. 'Why didn't you bring him along?'

As usual, Bachchu's naïveté raised a roar of laughter which puzzled him still more.

'I have you, Bachchu,' said Bahadur gravely. 'That's quite enough music for me.'

'For you, maybe. But for Gujarat?'

'There's enough in you for Gujarat, and Mewar too.'

And, unthinkingly, Bahadur sang the song he had heard Mihira Devi sing.

'Where did you learn that?' Bachchu would not let him go till he had the story.

'I'm going there!' Bachchu shot off like a Firangi rocket.

'Bachchu, wait!' Bahadur called after him. 'She won't be there now,'

Bahadur knew if the lady kept away from the temple for a week, Bachchu would still be waiting there.

The evening slid into the usual enjoyable pace of such revels. The illuminations enchanted, the music enthralled, the food was delectable, the conversation was edgy but courteous until Firangi wine loosened the tongue. Bahadur, who had a headache, abstained from his usual indulgence.

The Rana's nephew, Veer Singh, remarked at this with a sneer. 'Saving up your strength for the night, are you? You will need it. Our women will tax your endurance.'

Bahadur disliked the fellow on sight, and refusing to be drawn, moved away with a smile.

'Watch your step with this man,' Haridas murmured in warning. 'Something about him makes my blood boil.'

---

61 *Mihira Devi* [*Meera Bai*], India's most popular and revered mystic, was a Rathore princess who married Rana Sanga's son Bhoj Raj in 1519. Widowed in 1521, Meera continued to live in the royal household. Following Rana Sanga's death after the Battle of Khanwa, she was constantly persecuted as a mad woman. She spent the rest of her life wandering the countryside in search of her beloved Krishna. Her last years were spent in Brindavan where she attained samadhi in 1547.

'Mine too.' Bahadur's hand brushed his sword, as if for reassurance. He was in full regalia tonight. The richly damascened scabbard at his girdle concealed a mean blade.

'Missing the famous kamarband, are we?' Haridas joked.

The Rajputs, resplendent in their finery, wore jewels that rivaled the kamarband presently in their custody, for Mahmud Khilji had surrendered all but his crown to them.

'Where is Mahmud?' asked Bahadur.

'In Mandu. But the kamarband is here, with the Rana.'

'I wish him joy of it,' Bahadur said.

As the night grew older, the music turned amorous, and the guests were led into the dance pavilion.

The dances were exquisite. Heroic compositions gave way to the languorous and the seductive. The dancers tantalized the smitten audience with their voluptuous movements and smouldering eyes.

One girl surpassed them all in beauty and grace. Her costume of ethereal blue silk billowed around her as she whirled, an apsara dancing in the skies.

Entranced, Bahadur moved a little closer to the dais.

Veer Singh clapped him familiarly on the shoulder and remarked loudly, 'Enchanting, isn't she? Surely, you recognize her?'

Bahadur held his tongue.

'No? I thought you might.' He burst into mocking laughter. 'She is the daughter, the only daughter, of the Qazi of Ahmadnagar.'

Bahadur froze.

'The Qazi! Such a stupid old man! Begging me to kill him and spare his daughter! Spare her? Bahadur Khan, I enjoyed her right there before his eyes! The last thing he saw was his daughter's shame. And then, I cut his neck.'

His next peal of laughter was louder than the music, louder than the roar inside Bahadur, louder than the furious pounding of his heart.

Veer Singh's laugh rose in a wild guffaw and then broke off abruptly into a gurgle.

Bahadur heard the gurgle.

He heard the sudden silence in the pavilion.

He watched Veer Singh's torso lurch forward and part from his hips. Incredibly, his legs staggered another step before they crashed to the floor.

Bahadur saw this. What he did not see was his sword complete the arc of its swing and return ready to be sheathed again.

Everybody had moved away.

The dancers had fled.

The shocked audience retreated.

Backs to the wall, they watched—fearful, anticipant.

Bahadur stood alone in the centre of the pavilion, the dead man at his feet.

He raised his eyes and scanned the room, measuring each man's gaze.

Most looked away.

The moment swelled like a blood drop—tense, bright, portentous.

Five men stepped forward and ringed Bahadur.

They were all princes of blood. It was their right to avenge their brother.

Bahadur, hand still on the hilt, felt the familiar ease of confrontation.

His muscles limbered up, his eyes grew keen. Death was furthest from his thoughts. He was here to win.

Something whispered in his brain, told him he didn't stand a chance. They would pinion him. Go for his knees, his hands. They would not kill him quickly.

It didn't matter.

He could feel their hot breath on his face. They smelt feral. The steam of violence rose off their scented skin, fecal and putrid.

With great delicacy, the tallest of them reached out and relieved Bahadur of his sword.

Oh well, he still had his hands.

Now began the game of feinting at him with their swords, making him dodge each thrust.

They would make a spectacle of him, kill him with ridicule before the merciful end.

He resolved not to dodge.

At the next thrust he grasped the blade, and with superhuman effort, had twisted it out of his enemy's grasp before even he realized what he had done.

Armed again, he prepared to cut his way out.

A glance told him Haridas and two of his men awaited his command at the exit.

Bahadur moved like lightning, bewildering his captors, attacking in all directions while avoiding every thrust.

'Halt!'

The command, imperious and calm, jolted them all into stillness.

Rani Karnavati advanced towards the circle of combat. She held something close to her neck. It was a small vicious poignard.

Pushing her way past the Rajput princes, she took Bahadur's hand.

'Look well, you men of honour,' she spoke in a quiet voice of absolute command. 'This is my son. My son Bahadur Khan. My left hand holds him. My right holds this dagger. Touch but a hair of my son's head and this dagger sinks into my neck. See, the injury you have caused him, has already drawn blood.'

A spurt of blood followed her hand as she lifted the dagger off her neck to reveal a small cut.

'And as for this beast,' the Rani put out her dainty foot and kicked the dead man's leg. 'He has been cut down like the animal he was.'

Rana Sanga walked up to Bahadur. 'If you had not been so quick with your sword, I would have used mine. I have no ill will towards you, Bahadur Khan. This man was dishonourable. You gave him an honourable death.'

The five princes retreated, their eyes full of thunder.

Bahadur's sword was restored to him.

The audience melted away.

The Rana and his wife did not linger.

'What now?' asked Haridas.

They did not stay long.

The Rana did his best to simulate warmth and friendship, but the fracture was undeniable.

Bahadur surprised a small greedy flame of hate in the old man's eyes. Humbly he thanked the Rani for her kindness, and she replied with an empty smile.

It was time to leave.

Bahadur looked out for Mihira, but he did not see her again.

It was a silent cavalcade that departed the gates of Chittorgarh.

Soon Bahadur was met by a convoy sent by Hassan Khan Mewati.

'Another kingdom in need of a king?' murmured Haridas.

'What do you mean?'

'Isn't that what this is all about? Aren't you a king in search of a kingdom?'

'I'm no king, Haridas.'

'No. Not now. But you could be.'

'And, of what kingdom?'

'Hindustan.'

12

Dilli

The road to Dilli could well be the road to Hindustan.

Hindustan—a foreigner's word. It constricted the land into the invader's map, its boundaries shifting with each conquest. Sapta Sindhu, the land of the mighty river and its seven tributaries became Sindhustan, Hindustan, and all the people the invader met became *Hindu*.

'That can't be right,' Bahadur objected when Haridas explained this. 'You are Hindu by faith.'

'By the *geography* of the invader, I am Hindu, and you are too, Bahadur. My faith is not Hindu.'

'What is it then? You're telling me something impossible. I'm half Hindu myself.'

'Our faith has no name, though it has been called this or that. It isn't a written religion like yours. Yes, we have the Vedas, the Upanishads, more scripture than Islam, more gods, more prayers, more—everything. And everything is diverse and plural. From time to time one voice overrides the rest, *rishi, sanyasi, jogi, sant* or *acharya*. Each gets a few thousand followers. But they are all echoes of the old faith.'

'Not Mahavir.'

'Mahavir, certainly, Gautama also. Mohammad too.'

'You could lose your head for that, Hari.'

'I'll be sure to remind you when you are Sultân.'

Dilli was Lodi now. What would it be tomorrow? Would Alam Khan prevail? Perhaps even now he was secretly collecting an army.

'My father calls Alam Khan a jackal,' Bahadur mused aloud.

Muzzafar Shah, when still Khalil Khan, had first met the jackal at his father's court. 'Tell me about Alam Khan, Hari. About my grandfather and Alam Khan.'

Haridas began:

Sultân Mahmud, a man of rapacious appetites had been vastly pleased with the gifts Alam Khan had brought him: salted sides of leopard and lion, a caged bear with its young. He was less pleased with Alam Khan's petition.

Alam Khan wanted to wage war against the newly crowned Sultân of Dilli, his brother Sikandar Lodi.

Bahlol Lodi, the wily Afghan who had usurped the throne of Dilli from the dissolute Sayyids, was a man Mahmud Shah respected, and Sikandar was his chosen heir.

'The grandson of a goldsmith! His mother is common as dirt,' Alam Khan spat angrily. 'What right has he to the throne?'

'Thrones are inherited by capability,' Sultân Mahmud murmured into his famous moustachios. 'Do you consider yourself more capable than Sikandar? Or is it merely the matter of the gold-smelting grandfather?'

'Both,' Alam Khan sputtered angrily.

'In that case, let me state my mind. You have yet to prove your capabilities. And your grandfather, besides being an agent between Farsi merchants and Hindu ones, is a complete mystery. Sultâns are forced to invent convincing genealogies, but to the best of my knowledge, your father never bothered. He was too busy ruling his kingdom.'

'Which is mine by right. A right I mean to assert, and for which I need your assistance.'

Sultân Mahmud kept Alam Khan hoping till the big cats were eaten, the bear exhibited at several thrilling exhibitions, and then let loose into the forest for shikar.

Very soon after that, before they could pine for their parent, the bear cubs were roasted entire and presented gilded with silver and gold at a magnificent entertainment given by the Sultân in farewell to his dear friend Alam Khan.

Alas, the treasury could not now sustain the expense of another war, and Alam Khan must seek an army elsewhere. Several camel-loads of gifts were given to him, richly inlaid trinkets, damascened suits of armour, bales of silk and cotton, worked with silver and gold.

To speed him on his way, the Sultân ordered luxurious receptions at different stages of the journey, a contingent of cooks, musicians and dancing girls being sent a day ahead, to anticipate the disappointed Afghan.

When Prince Khalil Khan ascended the throne of Gujarat as Muzaffar Shah, he kept close track of Sikandar Lodi's court. Even more than his military feats, Sikandar's canny management of family malcontents impressed Muzaffar Shah. Sikandar had subdued each of his rebellious brothers in battle and then appeased them with positions of power. Alam Khan had been given Etawah—

'And what's this argument with my father?' Bahadur asked. 'My father seems to think he is certain to return.'

'Oh the story goes back a while ...'

The Gujarat court heard no more from Alam Khan until Sikandar's death. Alam Khan felt the time was now ripe to overthrow his nephew Ibrahim. He assured Muzaffar Shah that everybody in Dilli loathed the new Sultân. He lacked respect for family, for nobility, and was a man of low intelligence. Alam Khan, on the other hand, was universally beloved. But for the lack of a few crores of rupees, he would be Sultân by now. It was best to delay no further. The Chaghtai was knocking at the gates.

Muzaffar Shah was swayed by this last argument.

Muzaffar gave Alam Khan money and horses enough to make a grand entrance.

The arena was bloody.

Ibrahim Lodi had recently assassinated his rebellious brother, Julal who, just a month ago, had crowned himself as Sultân Jalaluddin in Jaunpur. His other brothers—Ismael,

Hussain, Mahmood and Azim Humayun were rounded up and imprisoned in the dungeons of Hansi.

All this happened three years ago.[62]

Meanwhile, Alam Khan mustered his forces.

From Muzaffar Shah's court at Mahmudabad, he had gone straight to Kabul. There he had met the Chaghtai, and, styling himself Prince Alauddin, announced his claim to the throne of Hindostan. Perhaps the Chaghtai laughed—we don't know, but we do know that Alam Khan now looked elsewhere for an ally.

He sounded out the disgruntled Afghan nobles, many of whom were in hiding. Daulat Khan Lodi of Lahore had already taken the extreme step of asking the Chaghtai to invade Dilli, but on the advent of Prince Alauddin, Daulat Khan turned his back on Babar, and joined Alauddin.

'And so he gathered an army?' Bahadur was surprised. Even on slight acquaintance, Alam Khan was not the sort of man who inspired confidence.

'Forty thousand horses,' Haridas said tersely. 'And I learned of the battle in Chittorgarh.'

'How?'

'The Rana's pigeons. They fly in at sundown from—everywhere. The Rana's readers needed a bit of help. I was around.'

'So what happened?'

Ibrahim advanced to meet the rebels.

He made camp at nightfall, when Alauddin was still twelve miles away.

Ibrahim's camp was ambushed at midnight. While the king fought like a man possessed, the fleeing enemy seemed to swell in numbers.

Daylight explained that anomaly. Most of his soldiers had deserted to the enemy.

Ibrahim turned to face a small anxious group of faithfuls, all that remained of a detachment twice the size of Alauddin's.

Whether it was resignation or hope that he read in their faces, Ibrahim felt compelled to hurry to the watchtower.

The sun came up.

As Ibrahim watched, small hamlets that had scarcely yawned awake exploded into smoke as Alam Khan's army streamed into them. Screams and shouts of victory mingled in a strange cacophony that drew circles of predators into the sooty sky.

Ibrahim hurried back to his men. 'Get the elephants!' he ordered, and hurling himself on his charger, galloped off without looking back to see if his army followed.

The shrill trumpeting of Digvijay, his favourite elephant, put his doubts to rest.

For the next two hours, Ibrahim sought his uncle through a growing red mist. The chill smog trapped the arterial spray of slaughter. By noon the air was a rusty haze, metallic and feral. Ibrahim wandered through the dead, turning them over with his foot, searching faces.

But Prince Alauddin had disappeared as dramatically as he had erupted.

---

[62] 929 AH; 1523 CE

Bahadur was silent.

His father was right. Alam Khan would be back, asking for more. That was how a jackal behaved, slavering, while still licking its chops from its last meal of offal.

Muffazar the Clement had compared his son Bahadur to Alam Khan. The memory sank into Bahadur like slow venom that maims and cripples before it kills.

13

Lodi Bãgh, 1526

The graves were all occupied. All around him, slept kings and queens. Within their sandstone encasements, their lives, like their persons, were imprisoned for perpetuity. Such remembrance was worse than anonymity. When remembered at all, they would be remembered by their graves. He didn't want to join them here. He probably wouldn't. His body would not be kindly lifted and brought home on grieving shoulders. There would be no grief for him. That caused him no dismay. He regretted nothing. He anticipated nothing. There was only this moment. Now.

Ibrahim had been king for twenty years. His father for twenty-eight, his grandfather for thirty-eight. A diminishing scale. They had died in bed. His grandfather of the usual infirmities of age, his father of quinsy, as if they had made peace with a lifetime of war, and that very peace had slain them. Ibrahim lacked patience enough for that. He would risk everything at daybreak, and let what may come its bloody way.

As if in agreement, a kite shrieked overhead.

Ibrahim stepped out from the dargah and searched the pallid sky. This was not the vibrant whistle of a circling bird. This was the outraged shriek of a predator robbed of prey.

The sky was an empty haze of mist. The bird shrieked again.

Angrily, he whirled around, instinctively grasping his dagger. The gesture drew a rueful laugh. Had it come to this? To be suspicious of a bird because it mocked him?

One cannot stab a bird. It must be trapped first.

What should he do with the captive?

Strangle it?

No, that was a trick of the seraglio.

It must be blinded and its wings clipped close, the bones sawn off at the shoulders.

How it would fight! It would draw blood as it bled, a fit end for its kind.

There! He saw it now, atop a naked tree. His trophy tree. The gnarled branches made the tree look like an aged hand tortuous with veins and raised in protest. He had seen that often enough on the battlefield—one hand clawing the air in voiceless protest as his sword flashed like a comet and sent the other winging. The fountain of blood hid his enemy's face, but all his anguish was in that protesting hand. Others counted heads, skulls drying on the battlements, one on every merlon, but Ibrahim's trophy was that intact hand grasping at emptiness as life ebbed away.

This tree stood there among the mausoleums as his trophy. He had never seen a leaf on it. Birds shunned it.

Not today.

The angry bird was not the only one on the tree. Balanced on the topmost twig it spread its wings and raising its beak, shrieked again.

The tree was full of birds today. Fifty or more. Except for this one, all silent and motionless.

He noticed for the first time that the shape of the tree, the shape of the protesting hand, was the shape of the decorative tree of life. That tree was everywhere: on trellises, tiles, rugs, carpets, its waving branches lofting birds, flowers and fruit, fantastic and colourful.

The kilim he had been kneeling on a few minutes ago, a kilim blessed by a Pir, had the very same tree unfurling in rich hues of scarlet, blue and gold.

And here it was again, on the horizon, mocking him, the tree of immortality,[63] his trophy tree, filling up, crowding with shapes of death, black intaglios of certainty stamped against a sky as empty as eternity.

He dismissed the thought as superstitious.

His enemy was superstitious. Babar had set fire to the main bazaar in Lahore when he entered in triumph last year.

Slaughter, Ibrahim could understand. His Khans and Indian chieftains had been Babar's first victims—Behari, Bhikun, Mubarak had all fallen within minutes, their blood commingling with that of the infidels.

That was only right. But why torch the bazaar?

When Ibrahim had wondered aloud, his advisers had told him it was an old Chaghtai custom.

'Those customs won't work here, in Agra or in Dilli,' Ibrahim replied curtly, without reason. No, he had no use for superstitions.

The kite had fallen silent.

Ibrahim took one last look at the tree. The birds were black effigies welded onto iron. Immutable. Indestructible.

Then, at some silent signal, they flew away.

He laughed in relief. One more, the tree of life, his tree, his trophy tree, raised its gnarled hand in protest, clawing the void.

Ibrahim's laughter, loud and triumphant, stilled the air. In that silence he realized how many voices had ceased: the chatter of squirrels, the seductive cooing of mating doves, a koel suddenly bereft—

Here it came now, the chirp he was waiting for.

The little brown bird hopped up to him.

---

63 Farsi … شجرة الخلود … *shajrat-ul-khuluud.*

He had no idea where it came from, but it waited for him at this spot every evening. As usual, it cocked its crested head in enquiry.

Ibrahim bent down and held out his hand.

It was a game they played.

The bird flew up, perched on his wrist, and waited for him to open his fist.

He took his time uncurling his fingers.

The bird shifted and chirped impatiently. Once she saw the crumbs, she fluttered up, hovering as he walked.

A few seconds of this courtesy, and she returned to her perch to peck and gobble till her crop was full. Her meal lasted till he reached the end of the path. She would hover again for a few steps before taking off.

This evening, as he felt the light taps of her beak on his palm, Ibrahim wondered if he would ever see her again. Strange. If he were to die tomorrow, all he would regret in a lifetime of fifty-one years was one small hungry bird.

Do the dead feel regret?

He doubted it.

But the living do, and his disappearance would distress the bird.

The thought of her hovering hopefully evening after evening, was unbearable. He wished he hadn't been so stingy with those crumbs today. She was almost done, just a few more pecks to go.

Swiftly, his right hand trapped her, thumb and index finger tightening in an iron circle enclosing her neck. She barely struggled. He flung the loosening tassel of fluff into the hedge and, without breaking stride, walked away.

The relief was enormous.

How could such a small bird be such burden?

Well, he was rid of her now!

He had a few more things to do before dark fell. Last light was still half an hour away.

He walked past the Maqbara[64] of Mohammad Shah, the last of the Sayyids—no, not the last. Allauddin, who had built this tomb, was the last. He had handed over the throne to Ibrahim's grandfather without bloodshed, begging only to be left alone among his orchards in Badaun. What kind of man did that?

The kind of man who had to deal with Bahlol Lodi, Ibrahim chuckled.

It had rained earlier in the afternoon, a passing shower, a benison between the twin curses of intense cold and intense heat.

The hillock and its maqbara were reflected in a puddle. A pale swirl of mud made the reflection as misty as the original, the grassy hillock a brief but solid interlude between two mirages.

It was that reflection that had decided the matter of his father's maqbara.

---

64 Urdu ... مقبرہ ... Mausoleum.

The loft of the octagonal monument of Sayyid Mohammad Shah was magnificent—some thought too grandiose for so forgettable a monarch. People thought Sikandar Lodi, being the greater monarch, deserved a grander tomb, but Ibrahim, seeing the reflection in the puddle, made up his mind.

It reminded him of the mirage on the march to Agra from Hunwantgar.

The heat was unimaginable, the goatskins empty. They strained towards the horizon magnetized by the inviting sheen of water that retreated at their approach.

A cry of despair broke out. It was stifled quickly by a whip.

A stillness overcame the army. They made camp, unable to trudge any further. Bullock after bullock, dead in harness, dragged the convoy to a standstill.

As the King walked through the camp, a soldier sprang at him and seized the gourd of water at his belt. Ibrahim, furious at the insolence was about to strike him down when his father's hand stopped him.

'Drink!'

The command was gracious, but the rascal laughed, the bottle raised high.

'You're unlikely to be thirsty, huzoor,' he mocked.

'And why do you say so?' enquired the King.

'You are drunk on blood. You won't feel the heat either, having robbed so many temples of their shade.'

Nobody stopped him. The carnage at Hunwantgar was on every man's mind, and every man's eye was on the King.

The man drank deep from the flask and spat on Sikandar Lodi.

This time his father didn't stay Ibrahim's hand.

The next morning they counted 800 dead, and left behind twice as many to die as the army dragged itself towards Dilli.

Ibrahim remembered the mirage only because he cherished the memory of his father that day. He admired his aloofness. He designed his father's tomb on the same lines as Mohammad Shah's but made a few concessions to his own tastes. He enclosed the tomb in a garden. The walls were closely guarded. Nobody was allowed entrance but him.

There was one other—of necessity—for gardens must be tended. This one, lawns bordered with flowers of every colour, festive with birds and butterflies, soon became Ibrahim's refuge.

He seldom entered the mausoleum.

The four stately trees, *neem*[65] they were called, were old already when the maqbara was built. Now their shade made the lawn a place of prayer.

A parrot chased its lover from one tree to another. A squirrel chattered. The scent of roses drifted and was lost in smells of cut grass and wet earth.

On a seat, as usual, a flower awaited him. This evening it was a blood red blossom.

---

65 *Neem* [Urdu … نیم] [Farsi … ازاد درخت]—*Azadirachta indica*, the 'free tree' *azad darakht* of India.

The carmine petals wounded his palm. He set it down hastily.

'It does not please you, huzoor?'

'It cannot please a man who is readying for battle. I fight the Chaghtai at dawn.'

'It is his flower.'

'His flower? It is not a flower of his country.'

'No, but he has met it here in ours. He has an eye for flowers, they say.'

'Who says?'

'The Lahori.'

'Has he been planting gardens in Lahore after burning the market place?'

'No, I heard nothing of that.'

'You wish me well then, if you give me his flower?'

'I do.'

'If I return, I will see your face.'

The gardener did not answer. He must have left, as usual, without salutation.

Ibrahim wondered idly if their conversations would continue after he beheld the man. Probably not.

It was a peculiar friendship. It had begun curiously enough, five years ago, when he noticed a change in the garden. The desultory pink and yellow blossoms had given way to a riot of colour. The lawn was clear of leaves, the seat covered with a cotton shawl. He had lifted off the shawl with the tip of his cane, demanding to know who had placed it there.

'I put it there to keep off the dust, huzoor,' someone answered.

'Who are you?'

'Mali.'

'What is your name?'

'Gopal, huzoor.'

'What are you doing here, Gopal? This holy ground is no place for a kafir. Go home and attend to your idols.'

Gopal, yet unseen, fell silent.

'Do you hear me?'

'Ji, huzoor.'

'Why do you linger?'

'The plants will die without me.'

'I can get better gardeners.'

'No doubt, you will, huzoor. But these are my plants.'

'You are arrogant. This land is mine.'

'But these plants are mine.'

'It won't please my father to have a kafir tend his maqbara.'

'But the flowers please him, don't they?'

'They please me.'

'Then let them live, and let me stay.'

'Out of sight, then. If I set eyes on you, you are a dead man.'

Ibrahim did enter the maqbara this evening. He stood for a moment marveling, as the scarlet flare of sunset filtered in through jaali and crevice. It cast a reticulum of red on the chill floor, pulsatile like a live thing. He wondered if it would disturb his father's rest.

'Do you think he's here under these stones, then?' Gopal had asked one day.

'Don't you?'

'I know he isn't.'

'You know no better because you burn your dead. Tell me, did you torch your father's body, watch his skull explode?'

'I did.'

'And it did not pain you to cause him that hurt?'

'He was beyond pain. That was just his cast-off clothing. His body, just waste.'

'And where do you think he is now?'

'I don't know.'

'A handful of ash, I suppose.'

'A little more than that, he was a hefty man.'

'Do you not worry, Gopal? All your days will end in a handful of ash.'

'And how will yours end, huzoor? In another maqbara, lying beneath another mountain of stone.'

No, he thought not.

Ibrahim left the *rauza*.[66]

The gurgling stream was full of clamouring birds—ducks, geese, cormorants.

The paths were shadowed now. Soon there would be torchlight drenching the walls, turning the sandstone blood red.

He walked quicker, towards the Bada Gumbad. There was something he sought. It had never failed him yet. There it was, a pinpoint of light.

In the lintel of a pillar a small lamp glowed. Someone lit it every evening. It was tucked away on the inside curve of the verandah. You couldn't see it unless you were looking for it.

He hurried, compelled by the need to assure himself the sooty lintel with its two stone flowers and six-petal jasmine still held a lamp, that the lamp had oil enough and wick enough to last the night.

He had never felt any such compulsion before, and couldn't explain it now.

It was there.

There was oil enough for the brave small flame, no bigger than his thumbnail.

---

66 Urdu … روضة … shrine or tomb.

He cupped the flame in his palms. Its heat was gentle and lingering as a kiss, and like a kiss, it inflamed him.

A shadow moved in the arch beyond.

'Stay!'

He stepped forward to cut off retreat, dagger at the ready.

But it was only a woman, a common creature, eyes wide with fear, the cup of oil spilling now over her mean clothes.

'So it is you who lights this lamp every evening?'

Her silence was answer enough.

'Why?'

'It is usual, huzoor.'

'It pleases me.'

Her eyes met his briefly.

'You please me.'

He took the cup from her and wiped her oily fingers with his scented kerchief.

In the lamp's shimmer her beauty was like that of stone, enduring, unpretending, true. Her lips were tender against his, her small fingers clever in their caress. Melding limb to limb they moved swiftly into the shadows, her fallen skirt spread at their feet like a bloodstain. Her hair had the scent of leaves, her skin the softness of the little brown bird, her eyes the steady light of the lamp. She was pliant as water, balm to his burn, scabbard to his sabre.

The sound of footsteps forced them apart.

For a moment she clung to him, terrified.

He put her away gently and throwing the skirt on her, strode out into the light.

It was Nehal, his mother's favourite eunuch.

In his father's time, Nehal had been sent as peacemaker from a Raja, bearing five horse-loads of treasure. The treasure had been accepted, but Nehal was sent back, having disgraced himself in the zenana. Ibrahim never discovered the details, but Nehal was received back in royal favour when Sikandar Lodi fell ill, and over the years had become indispensable to the queen.

Nehal bowed and stepped aside.

Ibrahim was surprised to see his mother.

His own emotion caught him off guard, but the very next instant his joy was baffled by her words.

'No, I'm not here to give you my blessing. May fortune go with the righteous, my son. I am here for her.'

'For whom?'

He hoped the woman would have gone by now.

His mother did not deign to answer.

Within minutes her guards appeared, dragging the woman. They had been stationed at the rear, and the poor girl had run right into them.

'Nehal, strangle her!'

The command, given in a voice of exquisite sweetness, the queen mother turned away.

'Leave her alone,' said Ibrahim.

'Yes! Leave her alone!' A voice echoed his. 'She isn't yours to kill!'

A man stepped out of the darkness and reached for the woman.

Ibrahim stopped him with an imperious gesture. 'Who are you?'

'He is my husband.' The woman shook herself free of the guards and glared at the company.

'Nehal, put her eyes out!' the queen mother commanded.

Nehal gestured to the guards who closed in on the woman a second time.

'Free her!' Ibrahim ordered.

'If I go home with him he will kill me!' the woman shrieked.

The queen mother turned away. Nehal and the retinue followed.

The guards stepped back.

The woman stood sobbing, ignoring her husband. 'Don't let him take me,' she wept.

'Come home with me, girl,' a short oldish man appeared at a run, all out of breath. 'Come along, let's go.'

'And who are you?' Ibrahim demanded.

'I? You don't know me, huzoor? I am Gopal.'

'Gopal!'

'Ji, huzoor.'

'And this is your daughter?'

'Ji, huzoor.'

It was a moment when Ibrahim Lodi felt very like his father. It was the feeling that had made him state on his first day as King that a King had no family and no friends, no loves and no desires, and no loyalties except to the throne.

'The law is on your side,' he told the husband. 'No law can stand between a man and his wife.'

'Then I will kill her,' the man answered calmly.

'If you do, I shall have you hanged for murder.'

'If she goes to her father I will kill her anyway.'

'And I will have you hanged anyway.'

'Will no one ask me what I want?' the woman cried.

The three men looked at her in surprise.

'It is my life you are bartering, don't I have a say in it?'

Ibrahim Lodi looked at the tubby old man who grew such beautiful flowers.

'I warned you to keep out of my sight, Gopal,' he said. 'You should have left when I asked you to. That would have been best for everybody.'

'I suppose you will keep your word now, huzoor?'

'Do you doubt it?'

Ibrahim Lodi summoned the guard and gave the order almost lazily. 'Hang this man.'

The woman shrieked a curse at him.

Ibrahim, who had begun to walk away, stopped and gave the guards a final instruction.

'When you're done hanging him, strangle the whore.'

14

The Khanquah of Nizamuddin Auliya

The khanquah of Hazrat Nizamuddin[67] was very different from Sheikh Jiu's in Batoh.

Richer, bigger, noisier.

Bahadur was ill at ease. He was well received, his retinue shown every kindness, accommodated with every comfort, and yet that affectionate warmth he had expected was lacking.

He put it down to his own shyness, for he found it difficult to set aside his reserve. This made him stiff and reticent, an attitude easily mistaken for arrogance.

The Murid gently refused his offer to take up the task he had been accustomed to at Sheikh Jiu's khanquah.

Bahadur's job was to collect the filthy and worn footwear, clean and restore them to their owners when they took their leave. He offered to do the same here, careful to explain this was a duty expected of him at Sheikh Jiu's khanquah, and he would be happy to fulfill it here.

The Murid rejected his offer with a smile.

Bahadur felt his scorn, but responded by saying he was in the habit of making himself useful when in a khanquah, and would be happy to perform any other task the Murid might think proper.

The answer this earned was, 'I will think on it.'

Then he discovered that some of the Sheikh's disciples had raised a hue and cry about Bacchu's presence in his retinue.

'There is no place for infidels in our midst!' the Murid said. 'Your pundits are better accommodated among their own kind.'

'I am used to a refuge that doesn't differentiate between men,' Bahadur answered stiffly. 'Debates with jogis[68] were common events in Shaikh Jiu's khanquah.'

---

67 *Hazrat Nizamuddin Auliya* [1238 – 1325] — The most revered Sufi saint of India. He founded the Chishti *silsila* [order]. Among his more ardent disciples was the poet Amir Khusro. Today, Hazrat Nizamuddin's khanquah in Dilli lends its name to the District.
Wali [Arabic … ولی]; plural *Auliya* [Arabic … اولیاء] — variously translated 'master,' 'authority,' the word is most commonly used by Muslims to indicate an Islamic saint.

68 Urdu … جوگی … Hindi … जोगी … A wandering mendicant who has renounced the worldly life.

'That does the Sheikh great credit. But our ways are different here.'

Bahadur sent for Bacchu, but Haridas answered instead. Bacchu was in the basti, he said, giving no other explanation.

'Perhaps all of us move should in there with him,' said Bahadur.

'I will go,' Haridas answered. 'And as for you, Huzoor, an emissary waits at the door.'

'Send him in. I need to behead someone, urgently.'

'You'll have to wait. Get yourself a kingdom before you act like a Sultân.'

'You'll delay that, I'm sure.'

'If I can. Knowing my head will be the first to roll.'

'Send the fellow in, Hari. Then let's escape and find Bacchu.'

'Once you see him, there's no getting away. You're trapped.'

'Send him away, then.'

'That would not be politic.'

'I can't always be politic!'

'You can never be politic. That's why I'm here with you.'

Haridas dodged the cushion Bahadur flung at him and left.

But he was back almost immediately.

'It seems you have to choose. There are two messengers outside. Which one shall I send in?'

'Who are they?'

'One is from the Sultân, the other from the Sultân's harem.'

'Which is more important?'

'The eunuch, I think. He is quite a personage.'

'Then he can wait. I will see the Sultân's emissary.'

The Sultân's emissary was preceded by a factotum who commenced announcing his master's many titles.

Bahadur was beginning to tire of this recital when the man himself came in, and with a very courteous salutation, conveyed the Sultân's pleasure at learning his beloved friend and ally, the Sultân of Gujarat, had trusted his son Bahadur Khan to his care, and could barely contain his impatience to see him. If it suited his honoured guest, Sultân Ibrahim would be happy to see him in court this evening. The hour before *maghrib* was exceedingly pleasant in the palace gardens. Might he expect Bahadur Khan today?

'Tell your master we will be there,' Bahadur answered, his frank smile compensating for his lack of ceremony.

The second messenger took his time coming in.

The delay was easily explained by the size of the man. Over six feet in height, he was dwarfed by his own rotundity. His gorgeous gem-encrusted clothes must have taken up a mile of velvet and silk. He was further impeded by a train of pure white silk closely embroidered with pearls. So artfully was this crafted that a swathe of moonlight seemed to swing from his shoulders. Making his salaam, he waited in silence for Bahadur to recover.

Bahadur too waited for the stranger to introduce himself.

The impasse might have gone on forever if Haridas had not intervened.

'His Excellency, Nazir Nehal,' Haridas announced.

'Ah.' Bahadur's response was just ambiguous enough for Nehal to take it for awe.

'The Queen Mother commands your presence,' he said.

'At what hour?'

'An hour before *maghrib*.'

'I am engaged at that hour, unfortunately.'

'Then you must send your regrets to the person who engages you at that hour,' Nehal said in a conversational tone. Despite his grandeur, there was very little formality about him.

Bahadur took the bait. 'That's impossible. The Sultân expects me.'

A smile passed quickly over the Nazir's fleshy features. 'The Sultân is accustomed to wait.'

'You will convey my thanks to your gracious lady for thinking of me, and also my regret that the hour makes my attendance on her impossible.'

Nehal smiled. 'You are new to our court. I would advise you to reconsider.'

'I am not used to advice.'

'As your Highness commands,' Nehal sneered and bowed out.

'That was ill done,' declared Haridas as the door shut behind Nehal.

'It is done now.'

Haridas shook his head. 'I will be very surprised if the matter is done. Best stay here indoors till *asar*.'

'Why?'

'I expect the Nazir to return.'

Haridas was not wrong.

An hour later, Nehal presented himself again.

This time he came bearing gifts.

Two men preceded him with baskets of fruit.

Nehal himself carried a tray of gold. On a cushion of green velvet lay a small dagger, the jade sheath exquisitely inlaid with gems. The ivory handle was inscribed.

'The Queen Mother begs you will accept this small token of affection and equally honour the sentiment inscribed on it.'

Bahadur frowned. Taking the dagger from the cushion he handed it to Haridas.

'Beware of beauty,' Haridas read the inscription..

Bahadur turned the dagger over in his palm. 'It is beautiful, but its wisdom is directed more at the enemy.'

'Not so,' cautioned Haridas. 'Do not unsheathe the dagger.'

Bahadur laughed.

'Tell your lady that her message is understood.'

'She will be pleased to hear it from your own lips, huzoor. The Mallika Jahan awaits you in her *palki*.'[69]

'She is here?'

'A small distance away. May I lead the way?'

'Certainly.'

Bahadur was curious to discover what manner of woman would send him a poisoned dagger to sue for peace. He tossed the dagger to Haridas and swaggered out.

The Queen Mother's palki could have been mistaken for a commoner's conveyance. Bahadur did not think much of her planning. If she wanted to travel incognito, she should have left Nehal behind, along with her silks and satins.

He changed his mind the instant he saw her.

'You have received my gift, I think,' she said, after they had exchanged courtesies. Her voice was low and melodious. She had exquisite hands. Behind the gauze veil, her eyes were shards of glass.

Bahadur bowed.

'You heeded my warning.'

'I value my life. I did not unsheathe the dagger.'

'That was clever of you. Are you clever enough to understand my message?'

'Oh, I understand it. I'm not certain I'll abide by it.'

'You said you valued your life.'

'I value it more than a bauble, certainly.'

'A crown is just another bauble, especially on another's brow.'

'What would you have me do?'

'Go home. This isn't your fight, Bahadur Khan.'

'But it is yours.'

'Not mine, not mine.' She lost her composure. Her hands flew up to clutch her hair. 'Listen, child! There is a room for me at Hansi. A dark room with no windows, and two grim women at the door. A corridor away, three of my sons languish in similar rooms. We will stay there till death releases us. My fight is to stay out of that room. Do you understand?'

'I understand enough to tell you that a home awaits you in my father's kingdom. My mother will welcome you as a sister.'

'Kind words, and deeply felt. Here, I charge you to give this to my sister. Ask her to wear it for me.' She unclasped a bracelet from her wrist and held it out. Then picking up the gold-topped cane next to her, she tapped the roof of the palki.

The palki set off at a run. Nehal mounted his horse and followed.

---

69 Urdu ... پالکی ... palanquin.

'What a relief to find you still alive,' Bahadur teased, for Haridas was still weighing the dagger thoughtfully. 'Come, give it to me.'

'Not on your life! You'll unsheathe it thoughtlessly, that poisoned spur will spring out, and Gujarat will have lost its king.'

'First, I do nothing thoughtlessly. Second, we don't know it has a poisoned spur. Third, I am not the king.'

'Wrong, on all three counts.'

Haridas would have kept the dagger if he hadn't been distracted by a sound outside. He was back soon enough.

'It is nothing—' He was about to reassure Bahadur.

The words died on his lips.

Bahadur—and the dagger—were gone.

15

Maghrib

In the palace gardens, the hour before *maghrib* was really very pleasant, and so was Sultân Ibrahim Lodi.

He dispensed with formalities quickly, and walked Bahadur through the delightful gardens, not omitting to introduce him to his pack of hunting dogs.

'They are as eager for the hunt as I am,' he said, dropping guard. 'I'm tired of waiting for the Chaghtai. I've driven him back five times, but he prowls like a man-eater. You know what he's like. You've heard the stories. Towers of skulls. The soil is so blood-soaked nothing will grow for years. And now, as if that isn't enough, Dowlat Khan and my renegade uncle—but you know about that affair.'

Bahadur feigned ignorance, and Ibrahim enjoyed going over that last battle which had ended so victoriously.

'Where is the Chaghtai now?'

'At Panipat. That's 40 kos away.'

'Why there?'

'He comes and goes.'

'And you?'

'I wait.'

Ibrahim smiled, showing long yellow teeth that rendered him suddenly vulpine.'I live in a nest of serpents,' he said. 'These smiling faces that throng me will go over to the Chaghtai any moment. They are here only for gold. Who is the greediest? How can I tell?'

'Oh that's easy.'

'You know a way?'

'Watch.'

Bahadur walked away from the Sultân to join a group of nobles. He greeted them with great respect.

As expected, they made much of him.

After a few minutes of exchanging compliments, Bahadur excused himself, claiming an urgent need that could not be denied.

As he made a hasty exit, the Queen Mother's dagger slipped from his tunic.

Whether Ibrahim Lodi witnessed what happened next, Bahadur never learned, but he certainly did, from his vantage in the shadows of the outhouse.

The group he had been speaking with broke up, the nobles wandered off to listen to the musicians or to sample the dainties so artfully displayed..

One figure slid back furtively to the spot where the dagger had fallen.

Bahadur watched him conceal the dagger in his vest.

Bahadur strolled up to Ibrahim Lodi and pointed out the man who had picked up the dagger. 'There is your greediest Baig!'

'Why do you say so?'

'Summon him, and you'll know.'

'Let us go to him instead.'

The noble greeted the Sultân with an insolent stare.

'This gentleman has my dagger,' said Bahadur. 'The one I spoke about just now.'

'I have no dagger of yours!' the man retorted angrily.

'Pardon my error, I spoke hastily,' said Bahadur. 'Since I gave it to you, it can no longer be mine. I beg that you show it to his Majesty, particularly the inscription on its blade.'

A little shamefaced, the noble removed the dagger from his vest.

'You see how he values it? He wears it so close to his heart.' Bahadur laughed. 'Yes, it is a pretty thing. But that's merely the scabbard. Show us the blade, good sir!'

The noble, now perfectly at ease, unsheathed the dagger.

Bahadur held his breath.

Was it a swindle? That poisoned spur?

The blade was almost out—

Almost—

But something snagged at the last inch.

The man tugged impatiently. The blade flashed. He fell face down in the grass, writhing in convulsions, turning blue as his breath sputtered into stillness.

The inevitability of his act closed in on Bahadur. He wondered if, in her luxurious mahal, the Queen Mother felt any such qualm.

16

The Basti

The Basti of Hazrat Nizamuddin was a mean lane behind the khanquah. Bahadur found his way there next morning, shortly after *fajr*.

Haridas, as promised, had quit the khanquah the previous day.

The Murid had expressed his displeasure, saying the infidel had been true to his base nature by filling his stomach for a week at the Sheikh's expense and then slinking out without a goodbye. A prince of Bahadur's stature should know better than to associate with men of that ilk.

Taking a small bag from his belt, Bahadur flung it down on the floor between them.

It burst, scattering gems and gold coins in all directions.

The scattered gold was picked up quickly by the boys who had been at study in the corridor.

'I trust that will meet your expenses,' said Bahadur. 'The Sultân's men will be here presently to move my effects. Do not obstruct them.'

'The Sheikh will be grieved by this.'

Bahadur made no answer.

The Murid continued, with some satisfaction. 'Yes, the Sheikh will be grieved, but not surprised. Your fame reached his ears long before you did us the honour of your presence. Think, before you act.'

'You should have thought too, before you insulted my friends.'

'They are infidels. They cannot be your friends. They are enemies of Islam.'

'Look around you, Murid. This is a country of infidels. To them, we, you and I, we are the infidels. It is a dirty word, but it has a simple meaning. It only means they have a different faith.'

'They worship images of stone.'

'If you believe that, you are a greater fool than I thought, and I won't waste my breath on you.'

The revulsion he felt was past bearing. Mastering his rage, Bahadur stepped out of the khanquah.

The Basti sucked him in. What had seemed like a short cul de sac was a meandering lane that branched promiscuously, roofed by the overhang of balconies.

Nothing set Bahadur apart from the crowd. He was dressed in his usual simple suit of white. The cut of his tunic betrayed him as a stranger, but his dark skin and lack of ornaments marked him for a commoner. He was bareheaded. A tailor may have noticed the texture of his clothing as uncommonly luxurious. A cobbler may have discerned the tooled leather of his shoes as quite unlike any other pedestrian's. A cutler might have calculated to a nicety the thickness of the sword the swing of his right arm might accommodate. But these, you'll agree, weren't common observers, and Bahadur passed unnoticed.

Doorsteps, windows, balconies, shopfronts, terraces, lanes, all beaded with a sweat of people. And where in this roil was he to look for Bacchu or Haridas?

There was some kind of tamasha ahead on the street.

The crowd slowed and coalesced.

Bahadur jostled his way forward.

It was a monkey show. The Bandarwala was urging his reluctant stars to stick to the script, but the animal in a balding velvet coat ignored his companion so seductively veiled in pink gauze. The song turned plaintive: Radha implored, Kanha stayed obdurate.

The Bandarwala's discordant voice imposed a lewd innuendo on the simple lyric. Perhaps his tone irritated Radha, or it might have been Kanha's insolence—he was calmly eating a banana—but Radha decided she had had enough. With one quick swipe she pulled off her pink veil and tore it to shreds.

The Bandarwala abandoned his song and got at her with his stick.

The crowd roared encouragement at Radha. Kanha was awarded another banana.

The hoots and jeers of the crowd and the contrapunctal wails of the Bandarwala made a deafening cacophony.

Bahadur, trapped in this clangour, was overtaken by a sudden bout of faintness. He was blacking out when a breath of cool air revived him.

Around him, the crowd too had paused to take in that reviving breath which seemed to have stolen in from some perfumed inselberg hidden in the clouds.

Everybody seemed to know where it came from, for every face was turned that way.

Bahadur followed their eyes.

It was no breeze that had stilled the crowd, but the sweet melody that issued from a window.

The singer was in gloom, but Bahadur had no difficulty in recognizing Bacchu.

Each pleading phrase followed a cadenza of yearning notes, growing sweeter and lower till it ended in a vibrato of anguish.

Everybody had forgotten the monkeys till someone gasped and then everybody forgot the song.

Radha was now luring Kanha in tune with the melody. She approached him with shining eyes and languorous hips, and Kanha flung aside his banana superbly and allowed himself to be seduced.

As Bacchu's song quickened in tempo, the lovers embraced ardently. When Kanha tired, Radha teased him to begin again.

Bacchu kept singing and Bahadur marvelled at the crowd.

The sight of animals mating generally provoked crude comments. Loud bets were placed on performance, and it wasn't long before each man hurried away to test his own competence. Women giggled shyly, eyes avid behind the *ghunghat*, taking notes.

There was none of that today. It was as if the music had bewitched every man and woman. Each one of them was transported into a very private delight. Their faces betrayed what their clothes concealed.

Bahadur broke his own trance and raced up the stairs to Bacchu's window.

Bacchu had stopped singing. His eyes were closed. He was humming to himself, lazily fingering the tanpura.

'I tried to stop him,' said Haridas. 'But I'm not Bahadur Khan.'

Bahadur threw up his hands in exasperation. 'Stop him? Why try? It sings when it wants to, it is the nature of the beast.'

'The court is always on the lookout for a fresh supply of *ghilman*.[70] These lanes are full of agents. Near the dwellings of the great, no son or daughter is safe. And Bacchu's voice would have reached the Chaghtai's ears by now, so swift are his spies. This time he won't stop at the Doab, he will fight his way through to Dilli for Bacchu.'

'He is at Panipat already. Don't frighten Bacchu, Haridas.'

'Oh I don't think I have, more's the pity. He's a complete innocent.'

'Hide him, then. Bacchu, be silent.'

'Later.'

'No. Now! Be silent now.'

'You can't order me to be silent. No man can.'

'Right. Fight me.'

'What?'

'You heard. Fight me. Give him a sword, Haridas. Fight me and let me kill you and you'll be silent forever.'

'You'd do that? You'd kill me?'

'Of course I would, if I had to. Be silent or the Sultân's court will have you.'

'Why? If they want to hear me sing, I shall.'

'I wonder what *raag* you'd sing when they cut off your balls.'

'Am I so *besura*? Is that how they punish their singers here? Are the ustads very formidable? I have heard of none that are good here. The qawwals at the khanquah irritated me. Their ears can only hear their own voices, never the music. In Jaunpur, now—Bahạdur Khan, let us go to Jaunpur! There is real music there. Listen—'

Bahadur seized Bacchu and clamped his mouth with a steely hand.

---

70 From the Arabic [غلمان] and its singular *ghulam* [غـلام]. *Ghilmān* were slaves-soldiers/mercenaries in armies of Islamic nations, they were taken as prisoners of war from conquered regions and commanded high prices for their services.

When he let him go, Bacchu staggered, and fell against Haridas. He buried his face in Haridas' shoulder, and clung to him.

Bahadur gathered them in his embrace, tears breaking past his rage, at last.

Haridas freed himself and led Bahadur to a divan. Bacchu hurriedly spread his shawl on the filthy mattress.

Bahadur, unconscious of these attentions, gave himself up to the relief of tears, not knowing what he wept for.

'I have a remedy for your pain,' said a voice.

Bahadur sprang up, his hand at his belt, reaching for the sword that was not there. His furious eyes, still blurry with tears, focused slowly on the fantastic figure that emerged from the shadows.

He was the tallest man Bahadur had ever seen. His skin was dead white. In contrast, his reddened eyes glowed like embers. His hair, matted with filth, and piled high in a knot, announced his status.

'Here.' He held out a glowing *chillum.*

Bahadur struck it from his hand.

'Pick it up, Prince!' the jogi said. 'You are all heart now, all nerve and fire. Jai Bhole! It is not your musician but you who are innocent. Bacchu will come to wisdom through music, Hari through his learning. What is your path, Prince? Battle? Power? Ah. I see it is so. Will it bring you wisdom?'

'Will your *charas* do that?'

'No. Many will assure you that it will, but take my word for it. It won't. But it will help you acquire wisdom by freeing your mind from pain.'

'No. It will undermine my strength. It will make me short of breath. I can endure pain but not weakness.'

'Very well. Here is something sweet. Try it.' He placed a small brown pastille before Bahadur.

'What is it?'

'Majoon.[71] It will relieve your sadness and clear your brain. You'll sleep well and wake up refreshed. Try it. If it helps you I will make up a stock of it.'

'No,' Hari intervened. 'Don't take it, Bahadur Khan.'

He could have bitten off his tongue as he uttered the words. Predictably, Bahadur put the pastille in his mouth.

'Delicious. Give me more.'

'Not now. That is enough for now. Hari, watch him.'

And the man melted into the shadows again.

Hari shrugged. 'Very well, I hear the Sultân has need of amusement.'

---

71 Arabic … معجون … is an electuary, a cannabis edible in the form of a jam, a fudge, or a pastry. Originally from either Egypt or Morocco, it can contain honey, nuts, dried fruits and various drugs.

'Would you make a laughingstock of me?'

'Not I! Spit it out, Bahadur.'

'Spit what out? There's nothing in my mouth. Look!'

'Good strong teeth, and sorry, no universe in there. You are a plain mortal, Bahadur Khan.'

'Find me a Gopi, and I'll prove you wrong. Hey Bacchu, give us a song!'

'I won't sing for you.'

'Did you say won't? Will not? Never mind, then, I'll dance without music—'

It got him late.

It was past *maghrib* when he woke.

His eyes lit on Hari, gloomily crouched at his feet.

They stared at each other.

Hari looked as if he had been weeping.

Across the room, Bachhu was the very picture of misery.

They were his baggage, as were the others, the horses, the camels. Barq.

'Is that *charsi*[72] still in this room?' asked Bahadur. 'I'm going to sleep for a little while more. If he's still here when I wake up, I'll kill him.'

'He's long gone.'

'Then what are we waiting for?' Bahadur bounded up. 'Hustle, lads, the Sultân awaits us!'

And so, they were lodged for a pleasant week in the palace.

Bahadur kept Bacchu close to himself, and when he was with the Sultân, Haridas had the care of him.

That was a mistake.

Haridas, who took his scholarship seriously, undertook to educate Bacchu and they very nearly came to blows over the alphabet.

The cook brought Bacchu a parrot to console him. And Bacchu, keeping his promise to be silent, taught the parrot to sing.

On the third day, Bahadur received a summons from the Sheikh.

'It would be wise to go,' said Haridas.

'In that case, I won't.'

'Why did you leave?'

'Because you did.'

'I can't expect a welcome in any khanquah, Bahadur.'

---

72 Urdu … چرسی … drug addict.

'Why not? Sheikh Jiu loved you.'

'To him I was Haridas. To this Sheikh I'm a Hindu.'

'Kafir!'

'Likewise!'

'When will this stupidity end, Hari?'

'End? It's just begun. Come with me to Kashi. Come as my Mussalman friend, not as Bahadur Khan, and let us find out how welcome you are in the temple there.'

'It takes two oxen to plough a field, Hari.'

'What king, Sultân or raja, has ever believed that?'

'In Jaunpur they do.' Bacchu piped up suddenly. 'I have heard ustads.'

They laughed, but it soon appeared Bacchu was not the only one who wanted Bahadur to go to Jaunpur.

17

The Lodi Camp

The following afternoon, Bahadur accepted an invitation to ride north to inspect the camp of Agarwal Mandi in the Doab. His companions, adherents of the Sultân, spoke freely of the crisis in which they found themselves.

Ibrahim had proved his mettle in routing Alam Khan, but the Chaghtai was a horse of different colour. Now the Chaghtai had decided to wait, and Ibrahim's patience was wearing thin.

'Will it not tire out the army, to wait till the enemy makes the first move?' Bahadur asked.

The nobles, middle-aged men, many battles old, laughed at his naïveté.

Still, Bahadur found signs of discontent everywhere in the camp.

Sipahis lounged about. Horses grazed unsaddled. Elephants shifted uneasily on their great feet, a malignant glint in their angry eyes.

A small detachment had ventured into the village and was riding back with booty that was greeted with hearty cheers—two young girls in a cart of sugarcane, cowering within the blanket used to capture them.

Bahadur felt a pulse hammer at his temples.

Haridas laid a cautionary hand on his shoulder.

Bahadur shook him off impatiently and plunged in the direction of the cart.

At that, the Khan accompanying them, mistaking Bahadur's intentions, called out to the cheering men. 'We have a guest here, a royal guest! Be hospitable.'

The men backed away from the cart, muttering.

Haridas, in a quandary, waited for Bahadur's next move. Around him, Bahadur's contingent gripped their swords. Was it to be Chittorgarh all over again?

But Bahadur stopped short of the cart, alerted by a sound he recognized all too well—the neigh of a startled horse.

Barq pointed north.

Bahadur gave the horse free rein, his men galloping close behind.

Their puzzled hosts followed at a canter, reaching the camp gates just in time to see their guards being dragged feet forward in the dust, lashed to the horses of Babar's marauding party.

Bahadur turned towards the Afghans, his eyes full of question,

They stared back, sullen and undecided.

With a cry Bahadur lunged forward.

His retinue fanned out, urging their steeds.

Barq was a thunderbolt in a cloud of dust. Bahadur standing in the stirrups, engaged the rearmost Chaghtai, grabbed the reins, and toppled him off the horse. His sword flashed once to cut the prisoner free and leaving his men to take care of the injured man, he thundered ahead.

The next few minutes were pure joy. Gone was the malaise that had consumed him this past week. He was all nerve, all muscle, all brain. With instinct quicker than thought he parried and lunged, fighting five men singlehanded till his company caught up.

'Don't hurt the horses!'

Bahadur's soldiers knew that would be his only command.

For the rest, he expected them to think like him.

They returned to the camp with the freed guards riding the captured horses.

Bahadur, exhilarated by the adventure, laughed off the praise the Afghans lavished on him.

'Your prize awaits,' the older Khan smiled, indicating the cart of sugarcane.

This time the men cheered.

Bahadur laughed.

It was a new laugh, one Haridas was learning to dread.

'And who was the brave who threw the sack over the girls?'

A *sipahi*[73] swaggered out of the ranks.

'I can capture many more fine birds for Huzoor,' he leered.

'Let him go, Bahadur,' Haridas implored.

'Get me a good strong length of rope,' Bahadur ordered.

A flutter of interest quickened the crowd.

The man returned with the rope.

Bahadur rode up to the cart.

The two girls, clutching each other in terror, huddled deeper into the sack.

'Come here, sisters.' Bahadur spoke softly, making no move to dismount.

The terrified girls approached, whimpering.

'Follow me.'

Bahadur rode back to the crowd. The two girls hesitated behind him.

He called the sipahi and asked him to name a friend who had helped him.

A thin lad blustered forward.

Bahadur cut the rope in two, made a noose of each and handed them to the girls.

'Here are the men who captured you. Now, they are your prey. Put a noose around each man's neck, if you wish for justice. Nobody will harm you. My men will take you home.'

The Afghans made a sound of protest.

Bahadur's hand flew to his sword.

Emboldened, one of the girls stepped forward with the noose.

The other shuddered and refused it.

'Take them home!' ordered Bahadur. 'I will hang them myself.'

---

73 Urdu ... سپاہی ... soldier.

'Leave off, Bahadur,' Haridas begged.

'Why? Why should I leave off? Because these are farm girls, and not princesses? I don't remember you stopping me in Chittor.'

'You were too quick for me then.'

'And too slow for you now? That's easily remedied!'

And quick as lightning he slipped the noose over the sipahi and whispered in Barq's ear.

The horse darted forward, jolted the man off his feet, and snapped his neck.

Bahadur threw down the second noose and grabbed the younger man by the neck.

Haridas shut his eyes.

Bahadur let the boy go.

Wheeling Barq around, he galloped away, leaving Haridas to make his apologies to the Afghans.

Late that night, Haridas received a visit from two Afghans, Husain Khan Lohani from Raberi and Qutub Khan from Etawah.

Courtesies past, Haridas held his tongue through the long silence that followed.

Finally Qutub Khan spoke. 'Today's story is all about the palace.'

Bahadur's groom had led the captured horses to the Sultân with a courteous note Haridas had written. It apologized for Bahadur's absence, and pleaded a headache after his exertions.

This resulted, of course, in a procession of hakims bearing potions, ointments, plasters, powders and the inevitable pastille of majoon. Bahadur snored through it all.

'The horses pleased Ibrahim,' said Qutub Khan.

Haridas bowed.

'I need not remind a pundit like you of the fickleness of kings. Ibrahim Lodi has the blood of his brother on his hands.'

'Kingship knows no kinship,' Haridas intoned this old chestnut with an air of omniscience.

'True. Which is why we, the Sultân's kin, have need of Bahadur Khan. We hear he is not for his father's throne. Is that true?'

'The Sultân's first-born Sikandar Khan is the heir apparent.'

'Bahadur Khan is not a man who will take second place.'

'No, indeed.'

'He has the qualities of a king.'

'True.'

'More. He has the qualities of a general.'

'True.'

'He is young. Twenty?'

'Not that yet.'

'The right age to think of building an empire.'

'True.'

'Dilli has no heart for empire. That's why the Sultân's father of revered memory, the great Sikandar Lodi, established the throne at Jaunpur.'

'You may have heard of the shameful assassination of Jalaluddin. Now Jaunpur is in the tyrant's grip. Bahadur Khan can free Jaunpur.'

'Jaunpur, Dilli, Malwa, Chittor.'

'Bengal, Orissa, Gujarat.'

'Why not? Already the islands of Balaghat belong to Bahadur Khan.'

'To his father, the Sultân,' Haridas interrupted..

'Empire is a family matter—from there, the Dakkan is easily managed. After that what small raja can withstand the mighty army surging south? Bahadur will reign as no Sultân of Hindustan has ever ruled before. Gold, jewels, land, luxuries, fame—'

'And from his triumph over infidel lands he will be revered as Ghazi.'

'And all this—for what?' asked Haridas bluntly.

'We merely ask him to assume the throne of Jaunpur.'

'Surely there are many great Afghans—'

'True. I will be frank with you. We are westerners, but our eastern cousins have our support. This is not generally known.'

'It will be my secret.'

'We see you are a man of honour. A pundit does not break his word. Our western brothers here would see Mahmud Lodi on the throne.'

'The Sultân's brother? Is he not in prison?'

'Prisons can be opened.'

'But you are not in favour of this.'

'It will be a massacre. His brothers can't stand up to Ibrahim.'

'Bahadur Khan will be welcomed in Jaunpur.'

'We are for Doab before daybreak. There, we will await Bahadur Khan's decision.'

'You leave now? The lines of battle are drawn at Panipat.'

'We wait at Bãghpat.'

'We rely on you, pundit. Jaunpur will not be without advantages for you, for I think you will not be separated from your prince.'

'You will make a good wazir. Jaunpur has always had a pundit as wazir.'

'I am not an ambitious man. I aspire only to education.'

'Then Jaunpur is the place for you. A library on every street!'

'Really?'

'We hear, also, that Bahadur Khan is devoted to Sheikh Jiu of Batoh.'

'We are both his saliks.'

'You too? Then in Jaunpur you will be doubly welcome. The Shattari silsila has Hindavi ways that we Afghans find strange, but to each his own.'

'What is your view, pundit? Will Bahadur Khan come to Jaunpur?'

'He is the guest of Sultân Ibrahim, and after today the Sultân will bind him closer to his heart.'

'If he has such an organ, yes. You are a wise man, pundit. Rely on your wisdom, not on your expectations.'

'Sound advice.' Haridas bowed them out. He stood silent in the darkened room, and then he went to wake up Bahadur.

'Treason,' Bahadur frowned. 'You should have thrown them out, Haridas. We had better tell the Sultân about the plot in the morning.'

'Of course, and have your head sent home in a bag, and mine thrown to the jackals. And Bachhu left bleeding by the roadside after every Afghan from the Sultân down has fucked him to a frazzle. Sure. You go ahead and tell the Sultân, Bahadur Khan.'

'What a morbid mind you have, Hari. Ibrahim will thank me and have me lead his army against the Chaghtai.'

'Then there will be another poisoned dagger for you.'

'I won't fall for that trick twice. Do you think me a fool?'

'You must be, if you think she will use the same trick again.'

'She's a noble lady, Hari.'

'They're all noble, ladies and gentlemen. They murder and rape and thieve and still remain noble.'

'What would you have me do?'

'Meet the Sultân as usual. Say nothing.'

'And Jaunpur?'

'Listen, Bahadur. These Afghans will use you. They will have you fight Ibrahim Lodi and then they will murder you.'

'I agree. First, they will make me a murderer, and then, they'll murder me. But only after I have fought the Chaghtai. I dearly want to do that, Hari! I think the Sultân will ask me to. I'm sure of it. After yesterday, he should know the Chaghtai is our common foe.'

The Sultan's tepid welcome next morning disconcerted Bahadur—he was riding to Panipat, and did not invite Bahadur to accompany him. His advisors looked worried.

Bahadur's day was taken up in sports of skill. He won each competition with ease, and finished with a swim in the Jamuna.

Exhausted, he retired early.

He was half asleep when the cook burst in, crying murder.

On their journey from Ahmadabad, they had acquired four Marwar camels at Dhanduka. Females, swift, ill tempered and ungainly. Bahadur would not let them be loaded, and bought a couple of mules only to carry their feed. Nobody dared question him, but they were all puzzled, all except the cook. *This* cook. He took charge of the beasts. When they crossed the desert, he brought around cups of frothy camel milk and earned Bahadur's respect.

This cook, the camel-milker, was the man who burst in on Bahadur, jabbering about scents.

Bahadur threw a cup of water at him.

'Huzoor, it is a matter of scent.' The man summoned up nerve. He spoke with grave urgency, but very calmly. 'It is purely a matter of scent.'

'What is a matter of scent?'

'Death.'

'Whose death? Yours or mine?'

'Forgive me, huzoor. Yours.'

'And what is this scent?'

'A flavouring in the pulao. A most delicate pulao, cooked in the milk of almonds, with an aroma so enticing, no man can resist it.'

'How do you know all this?'

'I cooked it, huzoor. I was given a poison to flavour the almond milk. I am to bring it to you in an hour. You sent word you would eat in your apartments tonight.'

'So you were in my brother's pay all along? Why do you confide in me now?'

'I am your servant, huzoor. Kill me if you wish, but do not dishonour me with suspicion. This is a Dilli matter. The Sultân himself watched me cook the dish.'

'I hope he paid you well.'

For answer the cook revealed a laceration on his neck. A bruise was developing around it. It was the mark a poignard makes when kept pressed with gentle but definite intent.

'It is the scent, huzoor,' the man repeated. 'The moment I lift the lid the scent will overpower you.'

'Why then, you too must die with me, for we will breathe the same air.'

'Not so. I will serve you with my face swathed in muslin so that this slave's unpleasant breath may not taint your enjoyment.'

Bahadur laughed.

'I beg you to believe me, huzoor.' The cook was in tears now. 'I have come here at great peril, if I'm not back in the kitchen, I will be suspected.'

'Oh, I do believe you. Go now, and bring in the meal.'

'What will you do, huzoor?'

'You'll see.'

The meal was brought in.

Bahadur asked the cook to tell Sultân Ibrahim Lodi he had watched Bahadur lift the lid and inhale. That would be enough.

The alarm would not be given till daybreak when Bahadur would fail to show up for namāz. That gave them six hours.

One by one the men in his retinue left the palace, by different gates. The cook drugged the guards at the stables with a dish of *kheer*.[74]

---

[74] Urdu … کھیر … a delectable dessert made essentially from rice and milk. There are various versions where cardamom and saffron, almonds and pistachios are used as enhancements.

Bahadur led the horses out into the darkness, walking them for the first mile. Then he mounted Barq.

'Jaunpur!'

His men followed without question, without rations, without baggage.

To Jaunpur it was, then—but not because of the cook.

Was it perhaps because of Alam Khan?

In the silence of the forest, soothed by Barq's leisurely amble, his father's taunts returned to wound anew with fresh venom. 'Take care you don't become another Alam Khan in your wanderings!'

18

Bãghpat

They had been on the road since dawn, Barq and he. The first four hours were flight. They passed an endless blur of hamlets startled out of sleep. His thighs were moulded to the horse's flanks with that tender lightness that passed for language between them. The reins were slack and Bahadur rode barefoot, shoes dangling from his belt. They breathed as one, they fed and rested as one, now man, now horse, now wind, the silver tail a chancy flash in the mist.

Jaunpur, then!

What would he find there? Who cared? It was a place, a name, a destination, something others would read as purpose to his purposeless flight.

The road vanished. The air slowed. Branches parted at their approach. For the first time in days, he breathed easy. The sunlit womb of green and gold, the forest floor a springy carpet for Barq's slow canter, and somewhere above a peek-a-boo sun—this was happiness.

It couldn't last.

Barq neighed, his ears prickled, a hot sour stink came off his coat. In response, Bahadur's sword leapt in a bright arc.

What lay ahead? Another message from Ibrahim Lodi, one swifter than a poisoned dish of meat? Or was it the Turkish death warrant, so popular among the Afghans? The near invisible horsehair strung taut in the rider's path that decapitated neater than a sword?

He felt Barq relax.

Whatever the alarm, it had passed now.

Bahadur laughed at what awaited him at the clearing. A low brick wall, dilapidated, but with a grand portal, a trellised lime-washed façade with a scalloped arch. The interior was a mosaic of coloured tiles salvaged from the rubble of broken monuments.

It was practically an industry, this royal obligation to smash and build.

Dilli was replete with cracking old dargahs and palaces waiting for the Chaghtai's axe. That he would arrive, Bahadur had no doubt. Babar simply cut his way through.

Of course, at home in Gujarat, it was mostly the rubble of temples that materialized as door stops, niches, whatnots, pretty carvings, here a lotus, there a breast, a leg and a bunch of arms, you used what you could.

Rajas, Hindu or Jaina, had smashed each others' temples before the Mussalman took over the job. Eventually, it all crumbled to dust beneath the hooves as you thundered through time. All it ever was, all it would become, was dust.

The gate opened to an Idgah of fair proportions. The buildings beyond suggested a khanquah. Bahadur felt led from one khanquah to another, as if these white buildings were dots and only by connecting them could he follow his line of destiny.

The thought irritated him.

He hesitated to break cover more from hubris than from any apprehension of danger.

Barq prickled with excitement.

He heard voices.

A line of men appeared at the gate. Their leader was middle-aged, the others were very young—mere boys some of them.

Bringing up the rear was the cause of Barq's excitement, a lovely chestnut mare with a mane that looked like churned cream.

Bahadur was about to approach them when he heard a rustle behind him.

He knew that step, even before he heard Barq's soft snort of welcome.

Krishna, Hari's horse.

A dog had joined the men at the gate now, a bowlegged bitch, a kitchen dog fattened on scraps.

Haridas, puzzled at Bahadur's hesitation, motioned the others to keep back.

Bahadur dismounted, and leaving a discomfited Barq behind, walked out. He was followed by Haridas, also on foot.

The men at the gate surged forward.

Greetings passed.

The leader spoke. 'Which of you is the Sultân of Gujarat?'

Whatever else Bahadur had been expecting, it wasn't this blunt demand.

Haridas restrained him with a gentle touch, and answered, 'Neither of us is the Sultân.'

'One of you must definitely be the Sultân. So we were informed.'

'By whom?' asked Bahadur.

'By the holy Hazrat Shaikh Sharfuddin Panipati. Everything we do here is directed by him.'

'What has he directed you to do for the Sultân of Gujarat?'

'Why, to provide him with rest and good cheer until—'

'Until what?'

'Until the wishes of Hazrat Sheikh are revealed. Meanwhile we are to provide him with the best horse in our stables and the best sword in our armoury, for he will have need of both. I am answerable to the Sultân himself. For sure he is one of you young men.'

'I am Bahadur Khan. My father is the Sultân of Gujarat. Take me to Hazrat Shaikh Sharfuddin so I might seek his blessings.'

The Shaikh, Bahadur discovered very soon, reposed in a small garden beyond the Idgah. His modest tomb was surrounded by yellow jasmine and red oleander. The hot air entrapped the delicious scent, stirring up tendrils of perfume with every zephyr.

'His Excellency Pa'indah Khan will wait upon your Highness when it pleases you,' the man whispered in his ear.

Bahadur drew back as if stung.

'Pa'indah Khan?'

'Of Jaunpur.'

'Ah. Where is he stationed?'

'Across the fields, beyond the bend, at Tatiri. But you need not trouble yourself about that, he will find his way here.'

'I accept your invitation to rest and refresh ourselves. When I am rested, I will ride out to meet Pa'indah Khan. I trust you will make my friends welcome.'

The boys were already showing the visitors around. Bahadur relaxed.

They seemed simple folk. Haridas would find out what their needs were and make a suitable endowment. The horse and the sword had probably been provided by Pa'indah Khan. The mare might do for Barq, but the sword was better left sheathed.

'I go alone,' said Bahadur, when Haridas prepared to leave with him. 'If I don't return by sundown, leave the moment darkness falls.'

Haridas frowned. 'And if the Afghan—'

'You will hunt him down and kill him for me.'

'Of course. Khuda hafiz.'

Haridas turned away, but Bahadur, moved by an impulse he could not explain, called him back and embraced him.

Moments later, in a streak of silver, he disappeared around the bend.

Barq's initial spurt of speed eased off at Bahadur's command. Hidden now from the khanquah, Bahadur sought a hiatus of solitude.

The pretty story of the Hazrat providing horse and sword was fit for storytellers. Haridas would enthrall them with it one of these nights, in the cold of the Rann perhaps, while passing round a cup of Firangi wine.

Just a story!

What was the truth?

This Pa'indah Khan, whoever he was, was here to pull him into Jaunpur. Once he got there—what then?

Fields lay ahead. Had he been riding hard, he wouldn't have noticed them as fields but as a four-coloured carpet suspended in thin air. Smoky scrub hovered over the sandy ground; above this a wall of mustard stalks sprang up in jubilant green to hold aloft a cloudbank of brilliant yellow.

A wayside eatery had its *choolah*[75] lit. A vat of dal simmered beneath a fragrant cloud of ginger and jeera.

He could have done with a bowl of that, and a roti or two rolled out of the waiting pillow of dough.

The episode of the poisoned meat had left him shaken but he was frantic with hunger now. He called out, but the cook was nowhere around.

Carts laden with sugarcane passed him. The oxen stepped at a regal pace, as if their burden of sweetness demanded such ceremonious slowness. The drivers dozed, trusting the intelligence of their steers. Bahadur restrained himself from reaching out for a cane.

Two things prevented him—the suspicion that dislodging a single cane would bring the piled cartload crashing down, and the fact that he wasn't at home.

---

[75] Urdu ... چولھا ... a clay oven.

In Gujarat, his pranks were tolerated like any other teenager's. Here in the north, he was a prince. Hunger, he was beginning to see, might be a frequent punishment for being a prince.

The mustard field appeared impassable. Rather than injure the tender crop still a month away from harvest, Bahadur resolved to keep to the road and ride around the field.

Small dwellings dotted the wayside. Like the khanquah, they also had souvenirs salvaged from demolished mansions and monuments: a patch of marble trellis in a brick wall, a carved lintel, the broken threshold of a temple upended to display lotus and chakra.

Many houses were coloured with green and blue lime, courtesy of some distant *sabz mahal* ground to dust. Elsewhere the pink of sandstone lent blush to pedestrian whitewash.

He passed a courtyard where two girls, avid with secrets, stood gossiping. They were scarcely older than the two he had sent home from Panipat. Their red shalwars were grimy with use, but their shawls were resplendent, cast-offs from some Dilli harem.

And so it turned, the wheel of circumstance. Men and women died faceless and unsung, but the accumulations of their lives, their detritus and waste, washed up on beaches far and unknown.

Three children at play stopped to watch him. The oldest, not yet of the age of reason, glared at him with unconcealed animosity.

Bahadur wondered what event in the child's brief experience had made him so wary of strangers, and summoned him, not really expecting a response. But he came willingly enough.

'What is this place called?'

'Hamidabad.'

Bahadur pointed to the courtyard where two tethered cows jostled against a hillock of bagasse left out to dry. 'Is that yours?'

The boy picked up a twig and brandished it at Bahadur.

'They're my father's cows. If you touch them, I'll hit you.'

'No, I don't want your father's cows. I'm here to give him something.' He would have tossed the customary coin, but the child's eyes compelled him to dismount and explain. 'Be sure to tell him I was passing by.'

The boy made no attempt to take the coin from Bahadur.

'What's your name?'

'Bahadur. What's yours?'

'Guddu.'

'Give this to your father, Guddu. It is his. I'm only returning it.'

The boy shut his palm like a trap over the shiny gold coin. Then the three children turned abruptly and scampered away.

Bahadur passed a clearing where *upla*[76] was being patted out from a stinking mound of cow dung. Presumably, the boys' mother had been interrupted in her task.

---

[76] *Upla* ... Urdu ... اپلا .. Hindi ... उपला ... Dung cakes used as fuel.

At the far end upla had been stacked fancifully to make a small fortification. Confronting this was a very realistic stockade of twigs. Certainly, Guddu's handiwork.

Bahadur's delight was anguished with bewilderment. Where would Guddu's fortune lead him? Would he stay home to grow sugarcane and farm cows, or would he risk his wits in battle? The child had a soldier's heart, fearless and alert. Who would notice? Tired parents who laboured all day to eke out enough for a meal?

Buffaloes behind a crumbling wall looked up briefly at Barq's approach and dismissed him with an insolent stare.

The heavy tread of oxen approached. The mirror on his ring revealed a cart crammed with young men standing packed against each other in a solid cube of human flesh, like slaves on their way to auction.

But they weren't slaves. They were neither tough enough, nor pretty enough, for either of the two uses of a slave.

'Where are you off to?' Bahadur asked the driver as the cart drew abreast.

'Panipat! To kill the Chaghtai! You must be on your way there too. Huzoor, your horse is champing for battle.'

'I'll find my way there. Khuda hafiz.'

'Khuda hafiz!'

So were they all, all of Hindustan, in the hands of Khuda.

Call him Allah or Shankar or Hari, whatever his name, he was having a good laugh at all Hindustan crowding Panipat to keep out the Chaghtai.

The Chaghtai would scatter them and shatter the battlefront like glass.

Bahadur's arm tingled for his sword.

But it wasn't his fight.

He had decided that long before the Queen Mother's warning.

It was definitely not his fight.

What was?

It was all that he was good at. The battlefield was the only place where he was never faulted.

'You're living in the wrong age, Bahadur,' Hari often remarked. 'You belong in the *Mahabharat*.'

'Were those battles different?'

'Who knows? The poet says they were battles of honour.'

'Ours aren't. These are battles of greed, battles for treasure and land.'

'So they seem to us. Who knows how poets will remember them afterwards?'

Afterwards?

A soldier had no afterwards. He had only now.

And what, or where, was his now?

Was he condemned to ride his days out as he had been riding for the past hour? A soldier in search of a battle? Or, a prince in search of a crown?

Another hamlet lay ahead. He had circumscribed the fields, so this must be Tatiri, the refuge of the Lodi rebel, Pa'indah Khan.

Here too, cartloads of rubble had been emptied in lots. Broken tiles and bricks. Planks. Ladders. Bamboo for scaffolding. Very soon the dust heaps of Dilli would be resurrected as mansions for the lords of Hamidabad and Tatiri.

Not that this little village didn't have a past.

There were crumbling houses here too, humbler ones of brick and plaster, wattle and daub, clinging just as grimly to the memory of a vanished time. Terraces and balconies were bearded with peepal and weeds.

Bahadur sensed instinctively that these places would never be tenanted again. They would stay on as hollows of decay haunted by forgotten griefs. Some had been invaded, opportunistically, by trade.

On the ledge of a broken balcony two stories above, a tailor sat cross-legged, darning a tattered coat. His head was swaddled in a turban, a pair of spectacles wobbled on his nose, his forehead was a nest of wrinkles. He strained at the inch of cloth he was mending. From the rapid flash of his needle, Bahadur guessed that the stitches would be near invisible against the coat's faded weave.

There was a pool of shade just a foot away from him, but the tailor had disdained it for the glare that permitted his precise stitches.

Why did the man labour so over a mere inch of cloth?

The owner of the coat would pay his coin and walk away pleased that the darned patch did not show.

The very invisibility of the stitches that made up the tailor's triumph erased his labour, the purpose of his craft was to render his life purposeless.

The tailor's labour had distracted Bahadur from the bustle around him. Tatiri was gearing up for excitement.

Distant music, drums in a teasing antic beat, suggested amusement of some sort.

A laughing crowd of young people erupted from a crevice in the street's brick façade. Their joyous cries and clouds of the *gulal* they flung in the air made a festival of the moment.

The drum grew louder, and the piping gave way to serious music. A very determined sawing at a *surbahar* served as introduction.

The crowd parted, and the dancers came into view.

The man dressed as Mahadev had a black rope around his neck to represent the *naag*[77] and a shard of mirror in his hair as a mock moon. A startlingly realistic eye was painted in the centre of his forehead.

Kamadev, a young man with a bow covered with roses made a feint of aiming arrows at Mahadev while Parvati danced, singing heartbreak.

Mahadev ignored her, kept his two good eyes shut, and glared at the world through his painted one.

Kamadev now made a lucky hit. One of his floral arrows grazed Mahadev's shoulder.

With a yowl of pure outrage, Mahadev opened both eyes. This sent a tremor of dread through the crowd. They all backed off hastily, clearing space for a most spirited tandav.

Kamadev reeled about drunkenly, and pitched forward into a column of smoke energetically wafted at him from a small brazier.

---

[77] *Naag* ... Sanskrit [नाग] ... cobra.

Mahadev resumed his magisterial calm, just in time for a fourth dancer to make her appearance.

This was seductive Rati, rolling her eyes and her hips to great encouragement from the crowd, as she petitioned for her husband.

Mahadev ignored her too, but Parvati, returning now in a veil of pink and gold, proved much harder to resist.

Flinging his *naag* to the ground, Mahadev fell in step. Kamadev burst out of a second installment of smoke and whirled Rati about.

That was the signal for the crowd to go wild, singing and stamping their feet.

'What festival is this?' Bahadur asked a relatively sober bystander.

'What festival can there be after Shiv Ratri? This is just entertainment for the nobles.'

'Who are these nobles?'

'*Ram jaane*. They're staying at the haveli, but they are at the temple most of the time. These people are coming straight from Pura Mahadev where they danced all morning.'

'Is it an old temple, this Pura Mahadev?'

'Older than history. You must see it if you're passing through.'

Bahadur lead Barq carefully through the excited swarm towards the gap in the street.

A narrow path tiled with featureless stone unfurled before him. Equally featureless were the brick walls on either side, converging at a gate nearly half a mile away.

An ideal cul de sac for an ambush!

The tall gate-posts were bright with the popular pigments of blue and green.

The heavy iron gates were shut. There seemed to be no other aditus.

A twenty-foot wall painted bright yellow cut off the interior.

Although no guards were visible, the gates swung open when Bahadur was yet a hundred yards away.

A curious spectacle greeted Bahadur. So fantastical was it that he stopped to reconsider.

Two low-branched trees diverged like a giant pair of thighs. Between them a monstrous white cunt was birthing something dark that twitched and squirmed.

Was this a delayed effect of yesterday's majoon? He moved forward in a trance.

He felt a complete idiot as his hallucination settled into banality.

The white cunt was a gigantic canvas sack of bagasse being loaded on a cart. The angry camel twitching in its harness was the monster being birthed.

Two men on ladders were busily lashing the sack to the cart. A third, from the very summit, shouted a question at Bahadur.

'I'm looking for Pa'indah Khan,' he answered.

'You'll find him on the riverbank behind Pura Mahadev. He's generally there at this hour.'

The man pointed out the egress and Bahadur found himself at the temple in no time.

If it was an ancient temple, it was equally ancient in neglect. It had defied four centuries of determined iconoclasts, but very shabbily. The walls were discoloured. The small chattri was encrusted with bird-droppings.

Another laughing field of mustard undulated in ripples of yellow and green.

At the far end was a line of young poplars. From this distance the leafless trees looked like twigs, fragile and defenseless. Beyond them was the dark canopy of mango trees, and past that, the river.

Always, the river.

The fortune of this kingdom was bound between its two rivers.

Back home, rivers were for sustenance.

For battles, there was the sea.

Maybe that's what he should heed, Bahadur thought. He would build himself a navy.

The haze lifted.

A cheery brightness now shone all around.

The sun had also stirred up smells. The choking pungency of mustard, the overpowering grassy odour of *gobar*.

Barq picked his way delicately along the borders, careful not to tread on the crop.

The picket of trees gave way to a field of flat green.

Spinach.

Barq's nostrils twitched at the succulent emerald leaves. Bahadur restrained him with a gentle touch.

Beyond this clearing ran the river.

The path was curious. Three sinuous furrows had been blistered into the grass between fields. They paralleled each other, rising and falling with perfect synchrony on the hump-backed land, like the three stripes on a squirrel's arched back.

Bahadur caught sight of a figure pacing beyond the trees ahead.

Pa'indah Khan.

Bahadur urged Barq forward, then reined him back, checked by an unexpected sound.

The man was singing.

His voice, a magnificent baritone, rose and fell like turbulent waters.

The words were simple.

When will you come? When will you come to end my torment?

The notes, though, recited an entire history of wonder, expectation, yearning.

Bahadur, swept up in the torrent of sound, dismounted and led Barq quietly to the trees.

Up close, the poplars were far from fragile. Their gracile branches interlocked to form an advance guard of cavalry.

The singer had stopped pacing. He sat leaning against a tree, arms uplifted by the quickening tempo of the *raag*. His voice had the sweetness of *gur*, the sting of ginger, and the perfume of roses.

Bahadur was suddenly overcome by a vision of his father.

The singer's voice rose in a powerful crescendo and, as he followed the *raag*, Bahadur saw his father's face transformed in ecstasy.

The tears that blurred Bahadur's eyes were those that ran down the Sultân's careworn face.

Any singer who drew tears from the Sultân was honoured by him as his guru. He had given Bacchu to Bahadur's care with just such a notion. Fiercely, Bahadur swore to himself that nothing would part him from Bacchu.

This singer was nowhere as sweet as Bacchu. But then Bacchu was a gandharva, and this man?

This man was of the earth, earthy.

Bahadur, unwilling to break the song, stayed very still. But Barq's impatient snort gave him away.

In an instant the singer had leapt up and whirled around, dagger in hand.

Bahadur threw up his hands in truce.

'Why do you need a dagger, Pa'indah Khan? Your voice is your weapon of conquest, and Bahadur is your slave.'

Pa'indah Khan hesitated, his face betrayed his chagrin at Bahadur's cheeky introduction. But Bahadur's laughing frankness was hard to resist.

Pa'indah Khan bowed. 'I'm happy my music has pleased your honour.'

'What do you call it? I have not heard this *raag* before, nor your style of singing.'

'They are pleased to call it Jaunpuri. My grandfather, Sultân Hussain Sharqui composed it, and we try to preserve his style. He called it *khayal*.'[78]

'Sharqui. Then you're not Afghan?'

'Indeed not. I'm as Jaunpuri as this *raag*. And for that reason alone, deputed to introduce you to Jaunpur.'

'There is one among us who will relish the introduction you gave me.'

'Perhaps that is why he joins us so impatiently.'

Bahadur frowned.

The man's ears were sharper than his own.

Now that he mentioned it, Bahadur heard horses in the distance.

Bahadur's pulse quickened.

Haridas' Krishna was unmistakable even at this remove.

What urgency had brought Haridas here?

78 *Khayal* [Urdu … خیال] — thought, imagination.
A syncretic musical form developed from Indian and Persian music, the Khayal is an imaginative exploration of melodic patterns based on ragas.
Though it began in the early centuries of the Dilli Sultânate, it took its present form in the 14th and 15th centuries when the Sharqui rulers of Jaunpur, themselves accomplished musicians, patronized this art form.
Today it is the very soul of the Hindustani classical mode of musical performance.

19

Hokka for Hire!

Hari's eyes were blank.

Whatever the news, it demanded privacy.

Bahadur turned to make his excuses to Pa'indah Khan, but the man had already retreated courteously. He was leaning against a tree, staring at the river in studied disinterest.

Bahadur lingered. The moment in all its eerie stillness, its wild beauty, the river a ripple of grey silk, the blank sky, the stranger avoiding his eyes—every little thing burnt into him. Something told him he would live this instant over and over again through all his remaining days.

Barq twitched impatiently. Bahadur reined him in. He waited in the forlorn hope the delay might erase what had not been written, silence what had not been said.

Then Barq, breaking discipline, wheeled around abruptly and trotted up to Haridas.

News of this kind never needed words.

'When?' Bahadur rasped.

'More than a month ago'.

A month!? Had he lived a whole month since that moment and never felt a tremor? Baffled, he tried to recall that month. It was all a blank. The faces around him, strange or familiar, were all blank as Hari's eyes had been, wiped clean of purpose, emotion, even, it seemed of politeness, for they gazed back at him as equals. Only Hari hung his head as though his neck awaited the sword.

The silence screamed: *Muzaffar Shah of Gujarat is dead!*

What did that make him, Bahadur?

Barq grew tensile, weightless, buoying him up.

Did Bahadur's sword leap into his hand, or was it there already, spinning a bright blur that bedazzled his companions?

Warning, possession, stratagem, the sword was all of them, and none of them.

He felt Hari's hand on his shoulder and let himself be guided back to the khanquah.

On Hari's command, he was left alone. Hari sat across the threshold, sleepless, while Bahadur paced about restlessly, unable to comprehend a world without his father. And on the throne—Sikandar. How was he supposed to live with that?

'What news?' he barked. 'What's happening at home?'

'We should hear something by dawn.'

'You're always ready with wisdom, why so silent now?'

'I've nothing to say, but I mourn with you.'

'You? Why? You had no great love for the Sultân.'

'True.'

'Why pretend then?'

'It isn't for him I mourn. It is for you.'

'Me? Why? I'm not dead.'

'Not yet. But you will be, unless you calm your wits.'

'Pah.'

But sometime before dawn, he did fall asleep.

It was noon when he woke. Hot with shame, he hurried out to the well and bathed. He noticed that the boys scattered at his appearance. Hari was nowhere to be seen.

'Huzoor.' The Sheikh in person.

Bahadur accepted the robe he held out, and walked with him back into the house.

A meal had been laid out for him. Fruit on an earthen platter. Buttermilk. Roti with dabs of melting butter. Honey.

He shook his head, and would have turned away, but the Sheikh had torn a roti and dipping it in honey, held it already at his lips. It would be churlish to refuse such tenderness.

As he finished his meal, Bahadur heard Barq's soft neigh. The horse, led out from the stables by one of the boys, awaited him.

None of his own men were visible.

'There is some news,' the Sheikh said. 'Nothing definite as yet. Haridas set out with the rest to the next post. The messenger has collapsed there. We should hear soon. Meanwhile, a ride before namāz?'

The man was courteous, but it was an order nonetheless.

Bahadur decided to humour him. There was little else to do. His brain was numbed with a relentless hammer-stroke. It had no words, no thought, no feeling. It swelled within his skull, pounding for release.

Barq understood. He rode the wind, the landscape a smudge of green and brown beneath the blue wheeling sky. Bahadur let the horse take him where it would.

Barq left the countryside and thundered into the highway, retracing yesterday's ride. Back to Dilli? Never! Bahadur's protest only made the horse gallop faster.

Bahadur felt the familiar madness seize him. What did it matter where? As long as he stayed on the road, everything was safe. His world was safe. And how could that be? The centre of his world was gone.

Barq stopped at a barn, an old rundown shelter. Barq's ear twitched and Bahadur heard a distant neigh. Krishna. As always, Barq knew the way.

Hari appeared at the doorway and ran out, seeing Bahadur. Their embrace said everything words and tears could not. Haridas extricated himself and said, 'He won't last long. The others have scattered in search of a vaid or hakeem. His words falter, his tongue grows blue. Not long now.'

The messenger on the pallet was little more than a boy, sixteen perhaps. Hari knelt by him. 'Kanu wake up, Bahadur Khan is here.'

'Water.'

The boy drank thirstily. His eyes focussed slowly on Bahadur. 'Sikandar Khan is Sultân!' he gasped. 'But they'll kill him.'

'Who will kill him?'

'All of them.' The boy's eyes glazed as if he had seen a ghost. His lips gibbered soundlessly. A pale light skimmed his features. A breath, a sigh; so ended his small and troubled life.

'He said more,' Haridas whispered. 'Sikandar is to be crowned soon. Bahadur you must hurry.'

'For what?'

They rode back in silence.

The day passed. Then another, and another, and still Bahadur had not spoken. He stayed indoors.

Though Barq neighed at the window, he would not be moved. Haridas was banished for talking. Only Bacchu was permitted to look in when he wished.

It seemed to Bahadur that Bacchu's voice sang his thoughts, but he could put no words to them.

On the fourth day Haridas was summoned. For all this time, Haridas was but a step away. Yet it seemed to Bahadur as though his friend had returned after a long separation.

'Where have you been hiding?' he demanded.

'In plain sight.'

'You'll never be a courtier, Hari.'

'You'll never have a court, Bahadur, if you don't move your arse.'

'You won't dare talk to me like that if I were Sultân.'

'Become one first, find out later.'

'I'll have you beheaded.'

'Coward. Unsheathe your sword if you want a fight.'

That was impossible to resist. They fenced their way out of the house into the clearing. If Bahadur was quick, his foe was cleverer. Soon every boy and man in the place had joined the breathless ring of onlookers.

The air tightened with the smell of blood and no blood as yet had been shed.

As Bahadur's sword flew down on Hari, his wrist was stayed by the lightest touch of his friend. Hari's fingers encircled Bahadur's hand and pulled him down to the ground beside him. Both Bahadur and Hari were laughing and oblivious to the audience.

Except for the Sheikh, the rest shuffled away.

'Are your quarrels always resolved like this?' the Sheikh asked.

'This was no quarrel,' said Bahadur.

'Perhaps not, but what will you do Huzoor, when your friend's hand is not there to stop yours?'

'An unnecessary question.' Bahadur rose, dusted his clothes. 'Hari's hand will always be in mine.'

The Sheikh bowed, ironically it seemed to Bahadur,.

'Why, do you doubt his loyalty?' he demanded.

'The Sheikh doesn't doubt my loyalty,' Hari said. 'He doubts the kindness of destiny.'

'Don't we all? Look Sheikh Sahab, we have a visitor.'

Bahadur had recognized the man at the distant gate.

It was Pa'indah Khan.

'Hari, make my excuses. Tell him to wait for me by the river, and we will ride out to him at *asar*.' The words had formed themselves before he knew. He had given no thought as yet to Pa'indah Khan, but he would have to, now.

Sultân or Padshah, what was it to be?

'Consider the Chaghtai,' Hari implored. 'We have been away from home for three months now, and two of those have gone staring at the Chaghtai.'

'You fear him.'

'Yes. I fear for my people, my land.'

'Dilli is not your land.'

'The Chaghtai's land is the world. That includes our land.'

'He won't dare.'

'He will dare, Bahadur.'

'This isn't my fight.'

'You gave your word to the lady. To the Sultân's mother.'

'No I didn't. I promised nothing.'

'Well, then.'

'They are brutes.'

'All soldiers are. You and me too.'

'Not you.'

'If you only knew. But this is not about us, Bahadur. This is bigger than us. Bigger than you.'

'Of course it is. I'm only a wandering prince.'

'That's all you'll ever be if you think so about yourself.'

'How else should think of myself, O pundit?'

'As a king in search of a kingdom.'

Hari's words startled Bahadur. He hadn't really thought of himself in that manner.

Of course he had.

It was all he had thought of since he left home.

They were all bidding for him: Lodi, Sharqui, Rajput.

And here he was, a hokka for hire.

20

At the River

Pa'indah Khan waited for him by the river, but they could have been at court, so formal was his manner, as if Bahadur had gained overnight the stature of a king. There was no song today to loft the air above the oppression of duty and grief. Both commingled in the restraint the two men felt. Words, Bahadur understood, would have to be carefully measured or else not spoken at all.

'I had hoped this meeting would be a happy one,' Pa'indah Khan began cautiously, 'but the sun is in eclipse in these days of mourning.'

Bahadur acknowledged the courtesy and Pa'indah Khan continued, 'We have news from your country, but I hesitate to voice it for fear it may be inaccurate or untrue.'

'I would like to hear it all the same.'

'Rumours, mere rumours. It is said that your brother Sikandar Khan has become Sultân.'

'That is only expected. He is the legitimate heir.'

'More given to the darbar[79] than to the battlefield, they tell me.'

'My kingdom is a peaceful one, and a king who does not war will keep it so.'

'Well said, huzoor, for who wouldn't wish for peace? In Jaunpur we long for peace—not just for Jaunpur, but for all Hindustan.'

'You are ambitious to take on the care of Hindustan.'

'The option is unbearable. We cannot allow Hindustan to take on the care of Jaunpur.'

'I understand your masters do not agree with Sultân Ibrahim.'

'I will speak frankly. Sultân Ibrahim is of no consequence. Even as we speak, the Chaghtai may have murdered him. If he lives past the day, his nobles will strangle him as he sleeps. This is the deciding hour for Hindustan. This is *your* deciding hour, Bahadur Khan.'

'You would have *me* face the Chaghtai in Panipat? Sultân Ibrahim has not asked my help. This is not a matter on which I may speak freely, but believe me, he does not wish me well.'

'That is but natural.'

'Why? I'm no threat to him.'

Pa'indah Khan's granite features underwent a change. Bahadur realized the man was smiling.

'You are amused?'

[79] Farsi … دربار … *darbār* … a king's court or a formal meeting where the king discussed matters of state.

'Forgive me. I smile at Sultân Ibrahim's arrogance in thinking you an ordinary foe.'

'Ill will hurts all of us.'

'Only the ill wisher. Allah has protected you for a purpose, Bahadur Khan. Ibrahim will die, if he isn't dead already. What then? Do we gift Hindustan to the Chaghtai?'

'I have no army.'

'Within a day you shall have one to command.'

'I? I am young, Khan Sahab. Barely six or seven battles old. A skirmish, yes, but I don't need to tell a seasoned soldier like you—'

'Men older than me will accept your command.'

'I am wanted at home.'

'That isn't what I hear.'

'All the more reason for me to be there.'

'Pardon me, huzoor, if my words touch a nerve. But the reason that compelled you to leave Gujarat has grown stronger now.'

Bahadur's face darkened.

Pa'indah Khan's reminder scathed like an insult. With it came a fear he could not immediately explain. His mother's face flashed, brief as a blink, on the edge of that terror. She had promised to be safe with her people in Sorath, but how long could she stay away? Her home was in the Bhadar.[80] Now, with a new Sultân, she had all the more reason to resume her rightful place. No, Lakham Bai would not wait for Bahadur's permission to return home. What then?

His father had scorned her. Lakham Bai had faced his insults with a stony dignity that had impressed even Bibi Rani. For the first time, Bahadur conceded his father's cruelty. Hate froze him. Everything receded: his years at home, his journey, Dilli, even this worried man at river's edge, all of it was a blur. An emerging clarity dazzled, keen as a sword.

It was his battle, win or lose!

'Which is it to be, Bahadur Khan? Our generals must know today. The Chaghtai will not wait much longer. With you, or without you, we must move. It will be better with you.'

'Yes, I would not wish to hold you back.' Bahadur met Pa'indah Khan's eyes. They were grave and calm, preparing, as he was, for an inevitable destiny.

Hari and the others waited beyond the poplars. He had left Barq behind too, unsaddled, for an hour of frolic with Krishna in the fields.

Hari would see the damage was paid for.

Without Barq, his mind was incomplete.

'Come, Khan Sahab.' Bahadur hurried past the others, to the edge of the highway.

'Today is the fifth of Rajab,' Pa'indah Khan said.

---

80 *Bhadar*—In 1411, Ahmad Shah, the First, built his new capital at the site of the historic city of Asaval and named it Ahmadabad. The citadel he built was named after the old citadel of Patan, Bhadra, later familiarized as Bhadar. Its magnificent architecture highlights Indo-Saracenic design at its most delicate and aesthetic best. For the next two centuries it was the showpiece of the Gujarat Sultânate. Sultân Mahmud Begada made it the centre of Gujarat's traditional crafts as well.

'What of it?'

'Our Jaunpuri pundits predict the Chaghtai will attack on the 8th.'

'Why? Does he consult the stars too?'

'Perhaps. But our pundits have their news from more terrestrial sources. The tanners of Panipat have been celebrating. Their stores of hide are all emptied—for the promise of great wealth. They have sent for hides from all neighbouring villages, but who will part with goods for no payment?'

'Only the terrorized.'

'When the Chaghtai needs hides, if he cannot get them off cattle, he will get them off people's backs.'

'What's the hide for? They cannot be making armour at this hour?'

'They have a huge collection of carts too—*araba*. The neighbouring villages have lost all their bullocks.'

'What is this new manner of battle?'

Pa'indah Khan did not answer.

Across the road, more fields wheeled into the distance. The highway spanned the green expanse like a torpid snake.

To the east was Jaunpur.

To the north Panipat.

Westward, home.

'It is a long march from Jaunpur to Dilli,' Bahadur mused. 'Three hundred kos.'

'A long ride for our amirs. The army is cooling its heels in the bylanes of Dilli and Agra already, faithful to a man.'

'Faithful to whom?'

'To the king we hope to crown in Jaunpur.'

'I am thankful for your offer, Pa'indah Khan.'

Bahadur felt his words more deeply than his voice betrayed. The Jaunpuri Lodis had trusted what Muzaffar Shah had rejected. His father had valued a small jagir more than his son, and here were strangers offering him a crown. He would be a fool to refuse.

He glanced over his shoulder. Hari was too far off for his features to be read, but his bearing seemed readied for battle.

But he would not heed Hari in this.

'The fortune of Hindustan is in your hands.' Pa'indah Khan said. 'Think well before you decide to let the foreigner in.'

'Hindustan is full of foreigners. Your Lodis are foreigners. My own father's court was filled with men of many colours.'

'True. The throne of Jaunpur was founded by a Habshi. The Lodis are Afghans. But you and I, Bahadur Khan, we are the colour of Ganga mud, where all the colours of the world abide.'

'Are we? I wish I could believe that.'

'Who has told you different, son? If anybody, anybody at all, has doubted your worthiness, Bahadur Khan, you must silence them, no matter how close or how revered.'

'What do you mean?'

Pa'indah Khan shrugged. 'There is a time when a man's loyalty should be only to himself. Everything passes: youth, beauty, love, land, wealth, this creed or that. In the end, you have only yourself. That is the ultimate loyalty.'

They fell silent.

Bahadur whistled a low note.

Barq trotted up and nuzzled him.

Bahadur walked up to the road.

The horse followed.

Bahadur saddled him and stepped back.

Barq neighed impatiently.

Bahadur mounted him and flung the reins over his neck. His legs swung clear of the horse's flanks.

No word or touch or gesture passed between man and horse, even Pa'indah Khan could see that.

Bahadur turned to Pa'indah Khan.

'I go where the horse decides,' he said.

With an impatient neigh, Barq tossed his mane and turned west.

Bahadur cupped a hand over Barq's ear, and the horse shot forward, a bolt of sliver lightning in the brown malodorous air.

And so he lost Hindustan.

21

14 February 1537 [Part ii]

Diu

Bahadur opened his eyes at a sound resentfully, unwilling to be roused from his reverie.

A crow—nothing more. It flapped its wings, cawed and stared until he shooed it away. The crow came back.

Bahadur shut his eyes again but found it impossible to recapture ease under the bird's baleful scrutiny.

The heat sustained the cloud of scent from the roses and tulsi. The hokkas knit their heads together as they nodded in puzzlement.

What had he done?

Had Hindustan ever been his to lose?

Part Two

22

The Road Home

To the Chaghtai, Dilli was Hindustan.

He could have stopped the Chaghtai. He said so to Haridas on the road out of Bãghpat.

'What's dragging you home then?' Haridas demanded.

'Destiny,' he hazarded.

Haridas, the pundit, laughed. 'We make our own destiny.'

'Maybe I'm just sick of these strangers, their food and their language—'

'But their music is good,' Bacchu reproved. 'We should have stayed.'

Three days on the road, nights camped out in the open. Haridas sat vigil all night, fearing for Bahadur. There was no arguing with him—every stir of shadow was an assassin.

At daylight Bahadur strapped him on Krishna's rolling back with his *pagdi*, twenty yards of silk, surer than steel. As Krishna galloped, Haridas slept like a baby.

Speed!

Barq was faster than the wind, not nearly as fast his namesake lightning. Bahadur felt the pull of something incalculably immense compelling him. It glittered cruelly, a diamond wall, dazzling, inscrutable, receding like the horizon he panted after.

They had split into bands of four. Bahadur had with him Haridas, Bacchu, and a groom, all of them in common travel-stained clothing that should have disguised them.

The horses gave them away.

The groom was an elderly man, taciturn and humourless. They endured him for his skills. There was no sickness in a horse he couldn't fix.

On the fourth day, from the heat perhaps, the groom fell ill, and they were forced to stop.

Haridas said a day's rest would heal him, and they went into a village for shelter. It was a small hamlet, impoverished and nearly empty.

The Patwari, a surly man, refused them entry, turning away from Haridas' gold.

Bahadur's hand flew to his sword.

'No matter, we will be lodged in the shade of your peepal,' Haridas placated. 'As you see, our friend is ill with fever.'

'We have no food, no water, no vaid, no hakim,' the villager argued. 'What's here to help him?'

'We have water enough to last us a day, and enough food. I'm a vaid myself. You cannot deny us shade.'

'Go to the forest, then. Plenty of shade there.'

'No,' Bahadur said quietly, sword in hand. 'We have decided to stay here,'

The Patwari laughed. 'Put your sword away if you want to stay alive. If they see your sword they will murder you.'

'Who will?'

'The women. They have sworn to kill every soldier they see.'

'We are jogis then,' Bahadur smiled, putting away his sword.

'Braves like you? Hah. Princes more likely, but I'll settle for merchants.'

There was no need to ask why the women were so vengeful. This was the only man left in the village.

'They curse the Chaghtai with every breath, but they curse their own men more for their stupidity,' said the Patwari. 'Stay here. Beyond our hamlet, the next six are empty too. Our boys went out in bullock carts, cheering. Children ran after them for a mile. The highways were full that week, cart after cart after cart rattled by, from dawn to nightfall, crammed with men who shouted as if they had won the war already. Every man was a hero. Where are those braves now? Two men stayed back, one being lame, the other being a dimwit. They have gone to Panipat to bring back the dead. I sent them out as soon as the bird arrived. None of us could read the letter it carried. Also, there is no one who can read in the next village too. I sent these men, because it was my duty. Tell me, what will they find when they reach the battlefield? Death makes us all the same. Who can tell brother from enemy, Hindu from Mussalman, or even Chaghtai from Lodi?'

Bacchu, having settled the sick man in the tree's shade, settled himself too, in comfort enough to sing.

His voice was no louder than the rustle of the peepal in the hot breeze. He kept to the *taal* of the breeze, rising and falling in its cadence, drawing together the staccato leaf-notes in harmony with a growing melody.

The villager backed away and disappeared into a hut.

In a while he returned with a pot of water and a stack of roti. The roti was stale and cracked like leather.

'It is all we have.'

'If we eat this, what's left for you?'

'They've decided on starving to death, anyway. Nobody has lit a *choolah* since the bird came. Now I can starve with them too.'

'What about the children?'

'They are sleeping.'

'Sleeping? At this hour?'

'Afim. They will die peacefully this way.'

'We'll fetch food. Keep watch over our friend.'

Bahadur was silent as they rode out into the forest. Still silent as they brought down a deer, a nilgai large enough to feed the village for a day. They shot another to use as barter at the next village. It bought them rice and flour.

Bahadur acquired a cow at knife point.

It was afternoon by the time they returned.

The village was a different place now.

Bacchu was surrounded by a huddle of sleeping children. Their mothers watched from doorways. Bacchu's *raag* had a low sobbing as contrapunct. Bahadur wondered if the mothers expected Bacchu's music to ease the children into death.

When they saw the supplies, first one woman, then another, and then a crowd of them came forward to rouse the children. Some sat up, befuddled. Others slept on, perhaps never to wake again.

Bahadur unsheathed his sword.

'There will be no more afim. No more murder. No child or woman must die.'

'We are dead already,' a woman barked back. 'You think we're scared of your sword?'

'Come and fight me, then.'

'You are a coward to fight a woman.'

'And you're a coward to murder your child.'

'What's there in this world for her? Who will feed her, clothe her, keep her? Who will marry her? She will end up a whore.'

'Then that's her destiny. You cannot change it. But she can.'

'What a fool you are. Who can change destiny?'

'My friend here is a pundit. He'll tell you. I'm just his guard.'

'Then shut up and give us the food, and maybe we'll let you have some too.'

'No, thanks, my stomach is full already.'

Not a morsel passed his lips that day although every fibre of him screamed out in hunger. He brooded morosely, listening to Bacchu.

In every hut, weeping, wailing, shouting out their pain and bitterness, all of them were listening to Bacchu.

After sundown, their host returned with a young woman. She glared at them with a stony face.

'This is Maina. Her husband sent the bird. She has the letter. If punditji could read it?'

'Will you let us read it, Maina?'

Maina held on to the small packet in her hand. 'What for? To learn that my husband was a coward? I know that already. Why would he send me a letter? Of what use is it to me?'

'He sent you his love because he couldn't come home to be with you,' Haridas said with guile.

'Really? He was no use to me before.'

'Then you are free of him,' Bahadur said. 'And we are free to read what he wanted you to know. Read, Hari.'

'And if I let you read that, what will you give me?'

'What do you wish for?'

'A husband.'

The sick man raised himself on an elbow.

'Here he is.'

'You? Another sick man? No thanks.'

'A passing fever,' Haridas assured her. 'He has the strength of a lion usually.'

'How do you know? You are no woman. And you? How strong are you?'

'He is a pundit,' Bahadur said.

'You, then.'

'Me?'

'Yes, you.'

'I am sworn already.'

'Sworn, but not married. And what's an extra wife or two?'

'I cannot break my word.'

'Why do a bunch of milksops like you want to read my letter?'

The groom sat up hurriedly. 'The night air is bad for my lungs. Now if I had a roof over my head, I could use my breath to better advantage. Give us the letter, lass, and we'll see who rides the swifter—you tonight or I tomorrow.'

Maina looked him over carefully.

Then she held out the letter to Haridas, and sat down to listen.

To my beloved Maina, these last words of her slave Puranram, written by the kindness of Sadasukh Munshi. Do not forget to give thanks for his generosity. I bless him with my last breath, wishing him prosperity and bliss.

Chatur has done his duty if you are holding this letter, my Maina. I know you have no great love for him, but I beg that you will save him a few grains for my sake. Indeed, he has been more a child to me than a pet—

'Yes, the pigeon was a clever bird,' the Patwari interrupted.

'What's that to you?' Maina sneered.

'I trust you will be able to keep it,' Haridas said. 'If not, I will gladly buy it.'

'Too late,' the Patwari sighed. 'Maina wrung its neck the moment she freed the letter.'

'Of what use was it to me?' cried Maina. 'I don't remember you complaining when you ate it.'

Here I am on the last day of my life, bleeding from my wounds. I have been cut in the legs and by good fortune, the right is bound up whole, but the left is lost below the knee. Do not grieve, Munshiji has a hakim at hand who will give me a powerful draught to ease the pain, once this letter is written.

I will now give you news of the battle and the fates of those known to me, but above all, I write to tell you how fortune favoured this humble villager and placed him by the side of a great Sultân.

This morning, before daybreak, we were roused to march towards the enemy. The enemy was but small in numbers, and therefore we imagined him insignificant. This was our first mistake.

We thought to swarm them like ants, for so the order was given.

We marched left, towards the right of the enemy. The reason was that our barids had brought news that the Chaghtai Prince Humayun, a lad of eighteen was in charge there, and we thought he would be easily overcome. This was our second mistake.

Our third was fatal: we did not heed our barids. They brought news that carts, the type we call araba, were being amassed, and we had not asked why.

Alas, as we marched closer, we realized the point of those carts.

Each cart was bound to the next—

'The hide,' Bahadur cried out. 'Oh fools, not to have seen why he wanted the hide! Pa'indah Khan told me the Chaghtai had bought up entire tanneries. He needed thongs to lash the araba together.'

—each cart was bound to the other with raw hide, and between them was placed a barricade. Together this array formed an impenetrable wall, protection for the matchlockmen who fired from behind. It is a sneaky way of

combat, unworthy of us Hindustanis, but these are Chaghtai and know no honour. And so in marching forward, we were baffled by araba, and our men continued to fall without breaking that barrier. In the confusion, we failed to observe that like a vulture spreading its wings before it swoops down on prey—

Bahadur groaned.

'Tulghuma! Tulghuma! What general could have failed to see it?'

'He spread out his flanks to turn them inwards and envelop the enemy from the rear. Ibrahim was ignorant of the Mahabharat, but the Chaghtai seems to have read it.' Hari chuckled.

'One doesn't need the Mahabharat to know this,' Bahadur retorted angrily, 'anyone with an ounce of sense can anticipate it. Continue, Hari.'

—like a vulture spreading its wings before swooping down on prey, the enemy on right and left curved in on us, so that our mighty army was completely enclosed by a few thousand men. The confusion was indescribable. No man dared use his sword for fear of running through his neighbour, so close were we huddled to shelter from the unceasing rain of arrows. And then the enemy was among us and it was each man for himself. I marvelled at my courage, for I had none before. I was engaged to play the trumpet, but not a note did I blow. Instead, my khanjar[81] worked with a madness that makes me fear for my soul. I, who feared to squash an ant all my days, have today killed many men. Chitragupt[82] will soon tell me where I stand. War is an evil thing, and we who think it glorious must be very evil too.

At this juncture, I was not yet wounded. I was fighting shoulder to shoulder with a brave man, an amir by his armour. His arm was tireless, indeed he seemed to have four arms like a god, for he struck in every direction. I finished off a soldier he had wounded, and noticing me, he asked my name. I told it, and the next moment, I was smothered by his arm that came down like an iron bar between me and an arrow. It pierced him deep, but he pulled it out, careless of the gush of blood that followed, and continued to strike out until the sword slipped from his hand and his arm dangled uselessly by his side. There was some relief to my right, but I could not leave this man who had risked his life to save mine.

He fell before me, and the next moment, I had fallen too. I sheltered him as best I could from the stampede, but it was too late for both of us. My eyes darkened. I heard Yamraj's buffalo, but I made him wait so that I could solace the last moments of my friend. I saw now the rich emblem on his armour. On his scabbard I read his name.

Maina, my beloved, it was the Sultân.

And so he died, in the arms of an ignorant pigeon-fancier, Sultân Ibrahim Lodi, may the gods be kind to his soul.

Now I died too, but awoke to a great silence. It seemed the battle was done. The sun blinded me. Pain shattered my bones when I tried to move. One leg was missing. I was wedged in by the dead. I lay there thinking of you, my Maina, cursing myself for not having made you happy. Never mind, you will find your happiness soon now, and I will not grudge it. I loved you with every breath I took, and that was my misfortune. It made you cruel, and me abject. We should have had the courage to part the moment we met. Instead, we have each destroyed the other.

---

81 From the Arabic … خنجر … a curved double-edged dagger.

82 In Hindu mythology, Chitragupta is Yama's accountant. He trails the God of Death, pen and palm leaf in hand, keeping an account of the good and evil in every soul ensnared by Yama's noose.

I expected to die there, if not from my wounds, then by the enemy's scouts as they came to strip the bodies of treasure.

I heard voices.

The scouts were here, but they were not after treasure.

I shut my eyes and waited for the worst.

'Here!' a man sang out. A young voice, not much older than mine. I opened my eyes to a chink.

'Tahir Tibri! What have you found?' another shouted.

Tahir Tibri had found the Sultân.

Planting a foot on me for better purchase, he propped up the limp form of Sultân Ibrahim Lodi against the piled up dead, and cut off the head.

'A Sultân's head is worth a pargana or two,' he laughed.

I do not know when he eased his weight off me, for nothing eased my pain. But I was still alive. I determined somehow to get out, thinking of Chatur waiting in his cage, trusting me for a few morsels of grain. The Chaghtai had left. The wounded were left to die in the pitiless sun, and I among them. Somehow I crawled to the edge of the field where the frightened villagers had gathered to render what help they could to the wounded.

And there Munshi Sadasukh rescued me. I refused hakim or vaid knowing their potions to staunch my pain would merely make for a quick and easy exit. I begged him to find Chatur, and such was his kindness, he went immediately to the rude shelter where I had left the bird, and returned at a run, cage in hand.

Alas, I had nothing to give my Chatur as he pecked my extended hand.

Munshiji writes this at my request, and I wish I had all the gold in the world to reward him, but having none, I gift him my prayers for his peace and increase.

All the men of our village were scattered through the ranks, but I have seen many of them among the dead. I have left word with Munshiji of all the names I recollect, and he will look for them among the wounded.

To you, my beloved, your slave Puranram makes his farewell, begging forgiveness for his many faults. To our kinsmen and friends, my loving remembrance.

The letter ended with a postscript:

The brave soldier Puranram left this world on finishing his letter. It seems as though he had made Yamraj wait at the threshold so that he could speak his thoughts. I am fortunate to have been with him at his last moments. May his soul be at peace.
— Sadasukh Munshi

In the silence that followed, Maina held out her hand to the groom and drew him into her hut.

23

Rana Sanga

Rana Sanga's message reached them at Tonk. He wrote:

> *I would be honoured if you await your brothers as my guests at Chittorgarh. I have news that will demand a Sultân's heart and a soldier's nerve. You have both already, but you need rest to recover the strength to act. If you ride to Chittorgarh on receiving this, you will have a peaceful week in which to prepare yourself by the time your brothers arrive.*

'Now what could that be, but news of Sikandar?' asked Bahadur..

'Or of the Mughal. Nobody calls him the Chaghtai since Panipat,' said Haridas.

'The Rana wants to know why I didn't fight.'

'Perhaps he wants to know if you will fight.'

'The Rana is for battle, you think?'

'Like you, Bahadur, he has thought of little else.'

That was true. The Rana was a walking war museum. He reminisced about his battles by counting his scars. He had traded body parts for victories, and in victory he had consistently shown mercy and justice. Bahadur could not overcome his shame that his father Muzaffar Shah had once merited the Rana's mercy—as he himself had, during his last visit to Chittorgarh.

'That place makes me uneasy, but I suppose we must go?'

'You need the Rana on your side, Bahadur.'

'Against whom?'

Haridas did not answer.

They arrived late at night, and were conducted to their luxurious chambers.

Haridas startled Bahadur by settling down for the night on a couple of cushions, his back against the door.

As usual, Hari was deaf to his protests.

As usual too, Bahadur demanded a story, but Hari was already asleep.

The next morning, the Rana waited on Bahadur, condoling his loss. His embrace was warm, but Bahadur sensed a wariness in the old warrior's muscles. He was definitely on guard. This nettled Bahadur. Perhaps he had been foolish to come unarmed. He had thought it impolite to even wear the short khanjar—more ornament than weapon—in the Rana's presence.

'I'm eager to hear your news,' Bahadur said after the preliminary compliments had been exchanged.

'All in good time. First, let's see what the day brings us.' The Rana led the way out into his garden. At a look from Bahadur, Haridas stayed behind.

The Rana made pleasant conversation, again, cause for unease. He was not a sociable man. Bahadur enquired about Rani Karnavati. The Rana said she was away, visiting an ailing aunt.

'We are all getting old.' He smiled. 'The world is for men like you now, Bahadur.'

'You are my uncle, sir,' replied Bahadur. 'You've carried me on your shoulders to show me the world.'

'Then you must see farther than I can. What do you see, Bahadur?'

'Gujarat.'

'Is that enough for you?'

'Is it not covetous enough to have my eye on a kingdom not my own?'

'You must know this: your brothers have asked for protection.'

'My brothers are riding here for refuge from Sikandar?'

'For refuge from you.'

'I don't understand.'

'Sikandar Shah's days are numbered. Your brother Latif Khan has mustered an army.'

'Then it is Latif they must hide from, not me.'

'The people want you. The amirs want you.'

'Why me?'

'Because you have the heart of a Sultân and the nerve of a soldier.'

'As you said in your letter. Are these good attributes?'

'What do you think?'

'I would rather have the heart of a soldier and the nerve of a Sultân.'

'Why?'

'A soldier's heart is open because of its daily brush with death. It doesn't have time for secrets. A Sultân has the nerve to be decisive. His decisions make victory—or defeat. So I would like to have an open heart and a decisive brain.'

'Come then, and let us find out if you have such gifts.'

The dovecote was surrounded by an exquisite marble jaali embedded with gems and generously bespattered with guano.

The Rana took a small parcel from the groom. Unwrapping it, he slid out a slip of fine silk covered with writing. After reading it carefully, he handed it to Bahadur who refused it saying, 'My old ailment persists. I still can't read.'

'No matter. You have Haridas. Keep him with you, Bahadur.'

'Always.'

'The letter tells me your brothers are a day's ride away. I think it would be better if I let them know you are here.'

'No. I will go to meet them. If they have sought your protection, and you mean to give it, they should come here unafraid. If it is me they fear, it is up to me to resolve that. I cannot put that burden on you.'

'Very well. I have a trusted man at the city gates. He will place his house at your disposal. He will bring your brothers to you.'

Bahadur agreed, though he had no intention of waiting for his brothers to discover him. He would go out and meet them on the road.

The letter put away, the Rana said he wanted to show Bahadur his roses. As there were no roses in bloom, Bahadur strolled silently, waiting for the Rana to speak his mind.

'You did well to keep away from Panipat,' he said.

'You really think so? I regret it now.'

'Why? Do you think you could have driven away the Mughal?'

'I am certain of it.'

'You are an arrogant fellow, aren't you?' The Rana laughed.

'No, merely an honest one.'

'Which is more than the Mughal is. And now he has let me know I broke my word. I, Sangram Singh, whose word is feared more than his sword.'

'Do you know him then? This Zahiruddin Babar? What kind of man is he?'

'What kind? Is he not named Babar? Why do you not ask why Rana Sanga did not fight at Panipat?'

'On whose side?'

The Rana stopped short and skewered Bahadur with a stare. 'So you knew all the while!'

'Of course. I know you made a deal with him, but I don't know what the deal was.'

'I begin to see there's more to you than a quick sword.'

'Everybody, but everybody, wanted Ibrahim Lodi's head, even his own mother.'

'Particularly his mother; as he imprisoned his brothers and would have imprisoned her too, if he weren't so afraid of her. It is a good thing, really, to fear one's mother and father.'

'To respect, not to fear.'

'Did you not fear your father?'

'I did. It would have been better if I hadn't.'

'I will tell you what my deal with the Chaghtai was. If he would move against Ibrahim Lodi, he could have Agra, and I would keep Dilli.'

'But you did not send in your army. Is that his reproach?'

'Yes.'

'And you did not because—'

The Rana stared him down silently. After a while he said, 'I miscalculated. I thought he would go back. He won't. He wants it all. He wants all Hindustan.'

Rana Sanga baffled Bahadur. Did he think Babar was a wolf like Taimur? Had he not noticed how he disciplined his army? How battle was a science to him, not a religion?

The Rana was a far better and more experienced soldier than he, Bahadur. He could only conclude the Rana had been stricken with shame at having invited the Mughal into the country. It had paralyzed his will. It would be some time before Rana Sanga fought again. He wondered if the noble Karnavati had turned her back on her husband when she learned the truth.

'You have always been a man of action.'

'Yes, and now it appears to you I'm not. I'm waiting, and I don't know for what. You refused Panipat, and so you're here with me, and not across the battlefield. If you must claim your kingdom, do so because it deserves you, and not because you deserve it.'

'How can Gujarat deserve a thoughtless boy of nineteen?'

'Everybody starts young. You can start by not being thoughtless. Knowing you, I expect you'll ride out to meet your brothers unarmed.'

'I am unarmed as I speak with you.'

'I accept the rebuke. But I am not competing with you for the throne of Gujarat.'

'You think Chand and Ibrahim are?'

'They only lack the nerve and skill. Chand is coming to me not for shelter but for an army.'

'Which you may or may not provide?'

'Which I can or cannot provide, depending on my priorities and commitments.'

'I understand. I am grateful to you for that confidence.'

'I am unarmed too, Bahadur, my son. There are still places on this withered tree where a knife or an arrow might find lodging.'

'But I have no such weapon either on my person or in my armoury, even if your army fights for Chand Khan. With my father gone, you fill his place in my heart.'

The next morning, Bahadur and Haridas rode into the town that frilled the base of Chittorgarh. Their host, Afzal Khan had a small but comfortable house prepared for them. He commended the central hall for its coolness and suggested it would be the ideal meeting place.

'We are outdoor men,' Bahadur laughed. 'This is not a darbar, my friend. I am here to meet my brothers.'

'And yet you are armed, Huzoor.'

Bahadur regarded the man thoughtfully. 'He looks like a conspirator, doesn't he, Hari?'

'A small and stupid one, but yes, I agree.'

'What shall we do with you, Afzal Khan? What shall we do with the two men you have stationed on either side of your famously cool hall? What shall we do with this surahi that you have temptingly placed upon this table?'

'This is our famous sharbat, Huzoor.'

'Then oblige me by drinking a glass.'

Afzal Khan gibbered helplessly as Bahadur thrust the glass at him. He dashed it on the floor with a contemptuous laugh.

'We will not be needing your roof, Afzal Khan.'

They rode out into the noonday sun. The road gleamed bald in the shimmer of heat.

An hour later, they heard hoofbeats.

Bahadur dismounted and unbuckled his sword. He walked out into the middle of the road, and strolled towards the approaching horses.

The riders reined in.

Haridas, his heart thumping painfully, clutched at his bow. At his side Barq neighed in alarm.

Bahadur stood his ground.

The vanguard gave way to Chand Khan.

Bahadur opened his arms.

Chand Khan dismounted and embraced him.

Ibrahim followed.

Instead of walking into Bahadur's embrace, Ibrahim bowed to him.

'Sikandar is dead,' he said. 'Bahadur is Shah of Gujarat.'

Bahadur shook his head.

Haridas came forward.

Ibrahim repeated his words.

'What happened to Sikandar?' Bahadur asked.

24

At Mahmudabad

The lamp of beauty needs a mirror for the wavering light of its flame.

Sikandar Shah of Gujarat, on the 28th day of Jamadi-ul-ākhir, the third day of his ascension to the throne of his ancestors, ordered a mirror to be placed at the foot of his bed.

This was his chamber of adoration, where even the most celebrated beauty of his harem, Nazuk Bahar, was refused admission.

Here Sikandar was free to gaze upon his perfection. He lost himself in the depth of his limpid eyes, he traced with a trembling fingertip the exquisite line of his lip. He settled his chin in the roseate cup of his palm and drank deep of himself until passion exhausted him.

This was the sole purpose of kingship, this solitary enjoyment of his perfection.

For the rest, he had done the right thing–opened the treasury and the stables to his amirs, making every amir his friend for life.

He had gifted away one thousand seven hundred horses to his loyals.

Of course there were murmurs. There were always some malcontents.

But he had no time for such distractions.

His brothers demanded all his attention.

Khush Qadam, his mother's slave, had nagged him to remove Khudaband Khan, but he had silenced him, hadn't he?

Khudaband Khan stayed. His father's wazir must be his too.

Sikandar, dazzled by his own beauty, dazzled the world with gold. But a queen's favour is deeper far than any Sultân's treasury, and Imad ul Mulk had enjoyed the queen's greatest indulgences. Sikandar's gold was small change. Imad ul Mulk used it to buy himself a small army.

Did Sikandar know? The only army he knew about marched far away from Mahmudabad. His brother Latif Khan had drummed up an army in Nandurbar. The Raja of Munka had lent his savages, and Latif was marching in fine fettle towards the throne.

Sikandar did not read Latif's impetuous revolt as animus. They were all bound to hate him, now that he had the throne. Every brother was a threat. He was rid of Bahadur. Yes, that was an intensely personal animus. That cost energy. None of his other brothers tired Sikandar out so much. They were all threats, Latif, Chand, Ibrahim, even the infant Nazir. Them he could buy, subdue or erase. His sisters Ruqaiyya and Radiya had made good marriages. They were too distant for their husbands to covet his throne. But they might have ambitious sons. By then his own pleasant exertions on a legitimate wife or two should have paid off with princes enough.

Still, Sikandar conceded, Latif Khan would have to be suppressed.

So Sikandar had sent Sharzah Khan, after buying his loyalty with more than usual generosity. Sharzah Khan's cronies, all men of adventure with a heart for battle signed up eagerly. There was little danger of defection.

The impecunious Latif had nothing to offer. His ragged army of Bhils and Dangs lived off rodents and other foul creatures of the undergrowth. The hills were treacherously inclement. Men dropped dead after a few hours in the sun.

From bare and empty slopes, from crags and precipices, and from bald rocks, arrows rained down on Sharzah Khan and his braves. Visible but for an instant, men sprang out of arid ravines to claw at a throat. In a blink they were gone, victim and captor absorbed into anthracene rock.

One thousand seven hundred men died that afternoon without lifting a bow or a sabre. As many men as the horses he had gifted.

But Sikandar was a man of persistence. Within the hour he deputed Khizar Khan to go the way of Sharzah with twice as big an army.

And then he went out to play *chaugan*.[83]

He chose the hour when the market was crowded, when the streets seethed with life, when bored children looked out of school windows, when, the day's cooking done, women came out into the balconies for a bit of breeze.

True, the sun was fierce at eleven, but he scarcely felt it under his muslin canopy. The canopy was lined with the pink pearls of Basra, a delicate attention to his companion's beauty, for Nazuk Bahar rode with him. Her face unveiled in defiance of custom, he let the world admire this most prized of his many priceless possessions. Once a month was more than enough for these jaunts, or she would be getting ideas next and before he knew, demand to be queen.

Is that the sun abroad with the moon, his tame poets would wonder at court this evening. That metaphor was getting really stale. They had better come up with something more original if they wanted to keep their heads.

Sikandar giggled inwardly at the thought of himself striking off a poet's head for a bad line.

A king could do a thing like that.

A king should do a thing like that, if he wished to be remembered.

Oh, he would do better–he would menace, and then the poets would have to petition in verse for mercy, and what wonders may a poet not compose to save his neck? And so he, Sikandar, described in the chronogram of verse, would be immortalized.

That day, the game of chaugan had gone on longer than he expected. When he returned to the palace, he had no heart for an afternoon of dalliance. The sun had given him a headache. He called for a cooling sharbat of khus and chandan. He had them bathe his temples in the delicate oil of roses his father used to receive every month from the gardens of Malik Ayaaz in Div.

And then they were all gone, leaving him alone.

---

83 From the Farsi … چوگان … a team sport played on horseback by aristocrats in ancient Iran. It begat the polo of today.

Ranas had metal mirrors.

The Dakshin Rajas had obsidian mirrors.

The Qizilbashis had mirrors of glass, true, but these were flawed and made a monster of the most delicate face.

But he, Sikandar Shah of Gujarat, he had purchased at the value of three elephants, a Firangi mirror that reflected not just his features, but every flicker of muscle beneath his taut opalescent skin. Too fatigued today, another time, he would measure his rampant nakedness against the mirror. For now the beauty of his limpid eyes was sufficient to drug him into a swoon of pleasure.

And yet, something kept him from surrendering to pleasure. The memory of his nightmare still rankled.

A week ago, was it?

More.

But he had woken up every night since, at the same time.

That night the ghariyal was striking when he woke in a chill exudation of fear.

One. Two. Three.

He was still dreaming, surely?

They crowded him, their Reverences, the Syeds of Batoh. Qutub-al-Qutab. Shah Alam. Sheikh Jiu. And with them was his father in full court regalia, Sultân Muzaffar Shah.

They spoke with one voice: *Descend!*

And Sikandar had become aware that he was seated on the throne. His buttocks pressed not against the delightful yield of velvet cushions, but on something as cold and hard as a maqbara.

Descend!

And by the power of their voices he was pitched headlong to the floor.

He woke thus, face down, choking in the moist fuzz of the khus mat.

The ghariyal struck.

One. Two. Three.

Darya Khan came to dress him for court at seven. To him Sikandar confided his nightmare. 'I dreamed my days are numbered. Is Bahadur Khan come?' And he related every detail of his terrible dream.

But that was a week ago.

And now it was not Bahadur, but Latif who was on the march, and that he had dealt with hadn't he?

Tonight he would sleep.

When the lamps were lit he would drink in the beauty in the mirror again.

Now in the gently filtered light of afternoon, in the shimmer of muslin, his face was a mask of pearl.

By night, in the golden dazzle of lamplight, it would gleam like polished ivory, like the portrait the world would remember.

He had sent for a painter from Venice.

The Firangi were great artists. One of the qizilbashi had shown him a small portrait, a nude, the breasts so real, he had to stay his fingertip from dimpling the skin.

He would be painted like that, naked, sprawled on tiger skin, the skin of a white tiger from the Mughal mountains, none of your common Bengal black and orange trumpery.

White tiger skin, and white plumes plucked from the tall African birds.

White would be his colour.

They would call him *Safed.*[84]

Sikandar slept.

Shadows.

Voices.

A cast of light.

In a dream he heard whispers.

'He is asleep.'

'Look in the mirror.'

Were they speaking to him? He was still looking in the mirror wasn't he?

There he was, skin of pearl, eyes of onyx, pillow swarmed by curls clustering close as bees.

There he was.

Out in the street, the bazaar fell silent.

Everything withdrew into the sharp short shadows of early afternoon, yet nobody let down the shutters for a nap. Many forgot they had not eaten. Children stayed indoors, fearful of the sudden hush.

Nothing had happened.

Nothing yet.

An hour ago a cavalcade had clattered grimly past.

The tall broad figure of Imad ul Mulk was too well known to be mistaken. Everybody who saw his face that afternoon shuddered and shrank back.

His company was equally grave and intent.

No more than an hour earlier the young Sultân had flashed past like a comet leaving a trail of brightness in the air. Who could help noticing his companion? The women were enchanted by her clothes, the men by what hid beneath.

Now like a curse, like an eclipse, like a creeping fungus that will soon corrode, came this cavalcade of severity, so punitive and exacting it had wrung the air of brightness and arrested all thought.

Everything waited.

And nothing had happened as yet.

Sikandar, asleep, heard nothing. Imad ul Mulk entered despite the protesting door keeper. He swept past the chessboard Sikandar's friends were frowning over. Chessmen clattered. Imad ul

---

[84] Urdu … سفيد … white.

Mulk stepped through the vestibule into the bedchamber. The players reset the fallen pieces, and waited.

Through his dreaming, Sikandar felt a shift of light–and woke.

There he was in the mirror, a little tousled and befuddled–but what shadow overcast his alabaster forehead?

Imad ul Mulk's face floated up from the gloom–Why was he dreaming of him?

Or maybe it wasn't a dream. The old fellow was here on some state matter.

'What is it now?' Sikandar asked wearily, 'Can't it wait till I'm awake?'

As if in answer, a brilliance dazzled him.

And then, darkness.

Before the *azaan* had sounded for *asar*, the palace gates gaped open.

No guard was in sight.

The cavalcade reappeared, Imad ul Mulk in the lead, his stony face inscrutable.

And when the last horseman had passed, there followed a common cart such as is used to transport firewood.

A *thela*, drawn by a slave wretched in appearance, as though resurrected hastily from some dungeon.

The street was momentarily solaced.

What else could so mean a carriage transport but refuse?

But why did it take this royal route, ignoring the decency of a less public exit?

What was it carrying?

Was that a cot?

Yes, it was a cot.

A plain, even rude piece of furniture, too crude to have emerged from the palace.

A man lay asleep on the cot.

A tall man.

His legs stuck out.

His legs were encased in the finest muslin.

His slippers were of velvet, their gemmed edges flashed in the sun.

The rest of him was covered with a glistening mantle of scarlet that drew down a black canopy of flies.

His face was bared so all may know him.

They had gazed on its beauty but an hour ago.

Sikandar Khan, Shah no longer of Gujarat.

25

Plans

'Latif will prevail,' Ibrahim concluded. 'But it is you the people want, Bahadur Khan.'

'Taj Khan says the same.' Haridas read the letter the princes had handed Bahadur. 'The amirs are for you too, I suppose?'

'You doubt that?' asked Chand Khan.

'Very much. They are divided in loyalty. Each man has a different price. It depends on what Bahadur Khan will pay.'

'You are cynical, Haridas.'

'No, Chand Khan, I am truthful. Bahadur Khan can never, must never, depend upon his nobles if he wants the throne.'

'Some of the amirs are good fellows, Hari.'

'Very good fellows, but not of this land. They are from Roos, and Rum and Misr; from Khorasan, from Isfahan; from Firangi lands we haven't even heard of. Every man of account is either Afghani or Habshi. Every man of learning either Arab, Farsi or Yahudi. How many men can you count at court, Chand Khan, with the colour of your skin? How many have fathers born in this land?'

'Foreigners were the pride of our father's court,' Chand Khan said angrily.

'As they will be of Bahadur's court when he has one,' Haridas responded unperturbed. 'Ornaments, but not functionaries. Loyalty to the king is commanded by loyalty to the land.'

'So you think Dilli will be disloyal to the Chaghtai?' Bahadur asked with sudden interest.

'My observation doesn't apply to Dilli. For centuries now, Dilli's loyalty has been bought by terror. I will think very highly of the Chaghtai if he deals a different coin.'

'You are wrong, Haridas. The Chaghtai are known for their cruelty.'

'You speak as if cruelty is unknown in our court, Ibrahim.'

'Kings have to be cruel if they wish to remain kings.'

'If you say so.'

'What would you have Bahadur do, dismiss these great amirs and rule with a pack of ignorant barbarians?'

'If he did that, your great amirs would stay back to learn from the very barbarians you despise. Why do you think they stay here? For the Sultân's gold, yes, but what of the men of learning?'

'Admiration, I suppose. They get our respect.'

'True. Their learning gets our respect. The learning they have learnt from us ignorant barbarians.'

'Ha.'

'You, Chand Khan, were dazzled by the Firangi who made a musical clock for your father. But he only made the clock after he learnt the science of numbers here, in your father's court.'

'Who taught him? Your father?'

'Actually, yes. But anyone who knows the Meru Prastara could have, and practically every pundit knows it.'

'Do you?'

'A cow gives birth to a calf every year. The calves begin giving birth to calves when they are three years old. Tell me, O learned man, the number of progeny produced during twenty years by one cow.'

'That's a riddle—'

'Shut up Hari! Chand, I am illiterate myself, and yes, Hari is right. I cannot depend on amirs, but I'm not going to rid myself of them either.' Bahadur spoke in a cold voice none of them had heard before. 'The people are for me, you say, Ibrahim. What about you?'

'I am for you.'

'Chand Khan?'

'I am for you too, but I will not bear arms against my brother. If I face Latif Khan, it must be as a brother, not an enemy.'

'Then you must wait until I have dealt with him,' Bahadur said.

'You'll fight him then?'

'No. Not unless he attacks me. The throne belongs to none of us. It belongs to the people.'

It was a grand thing to say. Bahadur almost believed it.

But who *were* the people? City-folk, village folk, sailors, farmers, merchants, soldiers. Surely, he could get them on his side?

'Sikandar's murder was foretold by Shaikh Jiu,' Ibrahim said. 'He took his seat on the throne without paying his respects.'

'I have lived with Shaikh Jiu. He is not a vindictive man,' Bahadur objected.

'No, but his son is,' said Chand. 'Asked why he didn't go to pay his respects, Sikandar replied "*Pir mud, murid jogi,* the father's dead and the son's a wanderer—to whom should I pay my respects?" When Sheikh Badah heard of it, he said, "The Pir is not really dead. Nor am I a wanderer. It is your crown, O Sultân, which is a delusion."

Ibrahim shrugged. 'Such stories will crop up everywhere now.'

'Don't dismiss them,' said Haridas. 'They knew of these events in Bãghpat, long before Taj Khan sent us the news of the Sultân's death.'

'They did?' Bahadur was startled. 'But that was surely the saint's prescience?'

Haridas laughed. 'Bahadur, give those saints some credit. Their divine spark is just a very excellent spy network.'

'Spies? They are men of God, Hari. They can't have spies in their employ?'

'They don't, for every one of them is a spy.'

'Nazir Khan will have to be rescued from Imad ul Mulk.'

Haridas did not reply.

Within the hour, having trusted Chand Khan to convey his gratitude to Rana Sanga, Bahadur rode out to meet his destiny.

26

Sultân

On the ride, Bahadur's silence was obdurate. He noticed that it made even Hari circumspect of his next move, and that saddened him. Still, he found it impossible to let a word spill. Hari must take things as they happened. Bahadur thought neither of Chand Khan nor of Ibrahim, who now rode with them. Neither of Latif Khan nor the imp Nazir who, perhaps by now, had been crowned Sultân. He thought of none of them. When the time came, he would know what to do.

There was only one thought, only one name that beat in his brain since he had left that miserable hamlet. Humayun. Humayun.

Humayun, a little younger than him, had the command of his father's army.

Humayun, at eighteen, had been entrusted with quelling a rebellion.

Humayun, having won the battle at Panipat, he heard, had been sent on to Agra to deal with the angry and defiant populace. His father had trusted him to do all that.

What was he like, this Humayun?

Bahadur couldn't allow himself to ask this question. In time, stories would unroll like carpets, their embellishments familiar designs. He did not want such fantasies. He wanted to see this boy, to look him in the face, to cross swords with him and understand what he had that made his father love him so.

Sikandar had his beauty. Nobody could resist that.

What did Humayun have?

Bahadur did not realize he had spoken aloud until Hari answered him with two words, 'The diamond.'

'What diamond?'

'The only diamond in the world. Beside it, all the rest are paltry bits of glass.'

'Really? And how came he by this wonderful diamond?'

'You are not in a mood for hearing stories, I think.'

'And you not in a mood for telling them.'

And so they rode on in silence.

At Dungarpur, there was news. Raja Udai Singh had intercepted a letter Imad ul Mulk had written to Babar Padshah [as the Chaghtai was now being called] with the offer of a kror[85] of tankahs and the port of Diu in exchange for an army.

Bahadur said nothing.

Rage suffocated him.

Latif Khan had ridden into Dandukah to enlist Taj Khan's help against the new Sultân—for Nazir had been crowned as Sultân Mahmud but a day ago.

Taj Khan had declared his loyalty to Bahadur's cause and advised Latif Khan to do the same.

Bahadur smiled. Latif would not be dissuaded. He would attack before Bahadur got to Ahmadabad. To waylay and ambush was his style.

Onward, then!

At Kapparbanj, he found friends who had been in hiding from the wrath of Imad ul Mulk and had secretly journeyed to join him.

Modasa. Harsol. Sagargaon.

His retinue grew from town to town.

He still rode in silence.

Hari endured him, doing all the talking needed, making bargains, offering rewards, keeping importunities at bay. By now everybody knew there was no bypassing Haridas.

How would he reward Haridas when he had the throne?

On the 26th day of Ramzan, at the height of noon, Bahadur rode into the city of Nahrwala, the capital city of his ancestors, the home of Gohilwara.

Taj Khan and his loyals had made the journey from Ahmadabad to welcome him.

Bahadur did not tarry.

He was in Ahmadabad well ahead of time, making a triumphal entry through the Kalupurah Gate the very next day, riding straight to the royal cemetery at Manik Chowk. After reciting the *fateha*, he rode into the Bhadar.

Lakham Bai greeted her son with her customary dignity, but when they were private, she embraced him with a tenderness that confused Bahadur. He felt his mother tremble. Her eyes, so like his own, were dilated with fear.

'What will you do now, son?' she whispered.

'I will be Sultân.'

'Gujarat has a Sultân.'

'A child of six.'

'And there is Latif.'

---

85 *Kror*, spelt today as 'crore' is a unit of measure. It equals ten million.

'And Chand. And Ibrahim.'

'You will do what a king must.'

'And what is that?'

'Let nothing, let nobody, come between you and the people.'

'Not even my brothers?'

'Not even your brothers.'

'I cannot hurt them.'

'All men are your brothers when they stand by you. Your brother is your enemy when he opposes you.'

'Rana Sanga said something of the same sort.'

'You should heed his words. He is a great hero.'

'He means to fight the Chaghtai.'

'A fight my son is itching for. That is not your fight, Bahadur.'

'I have heard that from Ibrahim Lodi's mother.'

'Ah. Her fight is not over yet, I hear.'

'Why, what's been happening?'

'Nothing. As yet. The Chaghtai is being very kind. He has given her a lavish jagir.'

'After having taken away her kingdom.'

'Others do worse. Sultâns and Rajas fight battles. Their wives and mothers notice both the conquered and the conqueror.'

'You speak in riddles.'

'The diamond is gone, I hear.'

'What is this diamond I keep hearing about?'

'Never mind that diamond. Recover the kamarband. That belongs to us.'

'Who has it now?'

'Malwa has been a vassal long enough. So it must be Chittor. Rana Sanga has it. I heard about your rashness. That was a bloody business, son. What made you trust yourself to Chittorgarh a second time?'

'I was treated with honour.'

'Honour be damned. It is just subterfuge. The truth in the *Mahabharat* comes after the battle, when the blind king and his queen treat the victors with honour.'

'Bheem would have been crushed by the king's embrace if Krishna had not substituted an iron column for him. A chink in the queen's blindfold was enough to cinder Dharmaputra's little toe. '

'Remember that story.'

'It seems as though every story ends in bloodshed. Everything ends in murder.'

'That is your dharma. You are born to fight. A soldier has no other duty.'

'But I do. I, Bahadur.'

'For you, my Bahadur, there is no *I* anymore. There is only Gujarat.'

There was only Gujarat.

On Eid, at a darbar that would be talked about till the end of time, Bahadur became Gujarat.

He rode towards Mahmudabad where the pretender, a frightened child of six, cowered on the throne.

Halol first, to the grave of Sikandar Khan.

He recalled Sikandar's laugh, beheld again his brother's incredible beauty.

But he felt no grief.

He was getting used to silence. It was a fine place to hide.

This was a bloody business, and growing bloodier by the minute.

Taj Khan reported that Imad ul Mulk had laughed when his friends urged him to flee. 'Why should Bahadur Khan punish me?' he asked. 'Have I not cleared his way to the throne?'

Murder.

More murder to avenge murder.

Every day awash in blood.

The traitors were killed. The child Mahmud Shah was returned to his nursery, Prince Nazir Khan once more.

Latif Khan rebelled again, this time accompanying Raja Bhim of Pal and his brother in a cruel raid on Sultânpur, burning villages and plundering the poor like a common dacoit.

At Bahadur's behest, Ghazi Khan pursued the rebels. The Raja and his brother died in battle, and Latif Khan was severely wounded.

Bahadur sent an ambulance of hakims and vaids post haste, but Latif Khan died before they could minister to him. He was buried in Murgh-dira, the mean hamlet where he had breathed his last.

Bahadur had the body shifted to Halol, and interred opposite Sikandar's grave.

That same week, Nazir Khan died, and Ibrahim soon after.

Both had been ill from a fever that was sweeping the city. Despite that, rumour was quick to accuse Bahadur.

'Poison,' said Haridas. 'They'll say you either poisoned or strangled them.'

'They? The street?'

'Rumour becomes history, Bahadur.'

So he would be remembered, if at all, as a fratricide.

'Chand Khan cowers behind Rana Sanga.' Bahadur sneered. 'Perhaps I had better poison him as well.'

Famine broke out.

He opened the treasury and deputed his amirs to go to the poorest villages.

The army mutinied.

He learned the soldiers had not been paid since the last year of his father's reign.

His compensation was munificent, but he knew, even without that, their loyalty was his.

Murder. Rebellion. Peace.

And the first year of his reign had flashed past.

Dilli also echoed the rumour that tormented Bahadur. But Dilli being Dilli, it wasn't rumour but fact.

'This is how it went,' Haridas said:

27

Pizzles, Please!

Emperors have large appetites. Zahiruddin Babar's appetite was rather more finicky. His palate was delicate, and he enjoyed savouring the flavours of his new conquest.

He sent for the sixty Lodi cooks--savage unbelievers to a man–and ordered them to produce a repast fit for the conqueror of the world.

As the cooks made their salaam and prepared to carry out the royal order, Babar observed, 'I understand there is no fine dining in Hindustan. Still, if your late master ate your fare, you must have learned how to cook for a king.'

A shudder rippled through the assembled cooks.

'We have cooked for kings,' the head cook replied very carefully. 'Many kings. Many, many kings.'

'Many many many kings,' the second-in-command added.

'And yet you're not so very old as to have cooked for so many kings,' the emperor mused. 'Is that the way of cooks?'

'No, sire. It is the way of kings.'

The repast was cooked.

The Padshah relished every dish and summoned the cooks again. 'You can continue in my kitchen,' he decreed. 'The four chief fellows can stay. I am pleased with your dishes. What are these delicious green meats?'

'Vegetables, Majesty.'

'Really? And where to they come from? There are no gardens in Hindustan.'

'From Jahanpanah's native Kabul, where the finest gardens of the world are. So I have heard. I am only an ignorant cook, I only buy the provisions.'

'Aha. I thought I recognized the taste of the sweet waters of Kabul.'

'Your Majesty is wise in all things.'

'And the fragrance in the food, appetizing and comforting at the same time, what perfume is that? For everybody knows there are no perfumes in Hindustan.'

'Your Majesty is omniscient. The fragrance comes to us by way of Hormuz and Aden.'

'I am also delighted with the silken cloths on which I was served, and the gold and silver vessels. Indeed I have never seen both metals used together in this exquisite way. They tell me it is a local art.'

'But one which your humble slaves were taught by the mastercraftsmen of Samarqand.'

'Ah! Samarqand, the name is music to my ears! And music–I was enchanted by the music so like the melody of a waterfall. But when I sent for the performer, he was a naked savage, with no more than a thin wrapping for his shame. Tell me, what manner of man is that? Why has he no fine robes gifted for his talents?'

'He will be grateful for your Majesty's concern.'

'We shall see if a fine suit of silk does not produce a better tune. Are these Hindustani tunes?'

'Pardon my ignorance, Majesty. I know little beyond my art.'

'Art? You consider cooking an art?'

'It is believed so, Majesty.'

'Very well. I have just one rule. You must be the first to taste the food you have cooked.'

'With respect, Majesty, one cannot cook for oneself. The food is rendered impure if I look upon it with appetite. I cannot offer your Majesty tainted food.'

'I understand. Then set out my dishes first and from each dish try a little only to ensure that it is fit for a king. Is that not acceptable? Is there not a story among you unbelievers of an ignorant old crone tasting a fruit to decide if it was sweet enough to offer the best among men? I have heard that story from my own scholars who can read your pagan books.'

'Your Majesty's knowledge is indeed boundless. Yes, that is allowed. We will do that.'

And so, rewarded with a coin or two, the cooks were permitted to feed the emperor.

'He is a barbarian,' the others told the head cook.

'True, but an informed one.'

'So well informed that he believed your lies.'

'Those were not lies. He was testing us, so I gave him all the right answers.'

'If he thinks us so low, why does he stay? Let him go back to his wonderfully cultured country and gorge on stinking cheese and those foul strips of dry meat his amirs suck all day.'

'On goats' eyeballs ...'

'... cooked in the steaming urine of rabid wolves.'

'Which gives me an idea ...'

You can be certain the cooks vied with each other in conjuring up the rarest meats, the wittiest vegetables, the most succulent fruit and such rice and dal as only their own mothers knew how to make. Of sweets they invented marvels: honey and fruit juices trapped within evanescent floss, creams of such delicacy they vanished even as you looked. And all this with the rich sear of ghee so aromatic it commanded perpetual allegiance to the cow.

Between meals the emperor was kept humoured with crisp savories so ethereal they melted like snowflakes on the tongue.

For his thirst there was nectar distilled from a thousand fruits.

He chose buttermilk and curds that tasted of Brindavan, but came, no doubt, from Badakhshan. And then there were wines, wines in a country that didn't make wine. These too came from the emperor's ancestral Takla Makaan.

On days when the Emperor prepared for battle, the wise and sagacious Chef sent in heroic roasts, gargantuan carcasses stuffed with smaller carcasses stuffed with still smaller ones stuffed with even smaller ones stuffed with song birds choked with conserves reduced to a crystalline absolute so fragrant it scented the breath all day.

On an evening when Babar called for music and gazed long and dark with luminous eyes at the pretty boy with the lute, the Chef sent him stalks of asparagus dripping melting butter. Served on a dish of amethyst inlaid with gold, these stalks of asparagus alternated with stalks of similar length, but these were of lucent lilac, knobbed a deeper purple, and wonderfully barbed. Only a very great fool would mistake them for vegetables, but what creature grew so wondrous a pizzle? With a burst of laughter, the Padshah lifted one by the knob and felt the frisson of the first spiral of barbs against his eager lip.

So immediate was the reward that the laughter was knocked out of him.

His pupils dilated, his alabaster forehead was pearled with sweat. His eyes, burning sweet fire, singed the eyelashes of the beautiful young man who immediately dropped his lute.

The Padshah staggered to his feet, scattering the astonished company, and grabbing the boy with one hand, and the dish of barbed pizzles with the other, darted like a thunderbolt into the nearest pavilion.

The next morning the chief Hakim visited the kitchen and demanded to know the name of the animal that had provided the Padshah a long night of enjoyment.

'Lion,' said the cook.

It was a thoughtless answer.

'I expected no less,' the Hakim said. 'Even though they were smaller than expected.'

'A certain degree of shrinkage ...'

'True, true. But there were seven penises in the dish. Who is the hero who killed seven lions? Why was His Majesty not told about the hunt?'

The Chef, unperturbed, answered with great elan. 'The lion in question is not in the Padshah's domain. In the wilds of Rajputana there is a species of lion that has anything from seven to ten penises, depending on the season. When one such lion is killed, there is great jubilation. My brother, who cooks for the Rana, sent the organs as a gift.'

'Why send it here? Why not serve them to his master?'

'His master has the testicles.'

The Hakim forced to be content with this, left, munching on dal-moth.

'Now this is a very big lie,' the second cook said. 'For this we lose our heads.'

Just then a shadow, an enormous bulge of a shadow fell on the kitchen floor.

'Well well well, if it isn't our old Bakasur! Got your old job back, Ahmad?'

The huge man smiled happily. 'They don't cook like you in Etawah, Gopichand. What have you for the Padshah today?'

'Nightingale tongues in honey.'

'Too finicky for me. Give me a plate of dal chawal, and I'll lick up that morsel later.'

Like the cooks, Ahmad, the bakawal, had been part of the Lodi kitchen. There was little that got past Ahmad then--or now.

'So you've been feeding the Padshah lion's pizzle. But I notice also the sudden ubiquity of rat traps.'

'Yes, can't afford to have rats in the emperor's kitchen, can we?'

'Absolutely. Which is why we keep cats, eh? But the cats, where are they, Gopichand? All our noble caterwauling, randy gentlemen cats, where are they? Dead of shame. How can they live when their best parts now fuel the emperor?'

'Here is your dal chawal, Bakasur. Eat, and stop your bak-bak.'

'You shouldn't have lied to the Hakim,' the second cook whimpered. 'Now we're all lost.'

'I did not lie,' Gopichand retorted with dignity. 'A lion is a kind of cat, and I have served him the seven lions of my kitchen.'

'And what will you do if he asks for the hide of this remarkable lion?' the bakawal asked.

'We'll see then. But tell me, Bakasur, how did you get your job back?'

'By the kindness of Nehal.'

'Then be careful. Be very careful.'

Gopichand was astute, but he had one weakness. He could never resist a pretty face. And the slave girl who approached him next day for an ounce of honey had the prettiest face imaginable. So Gopichand fussed about finding the right honey, and measuring it out into the right cup and mislaying the lid for another ten minutes, all the time making the pretty girl's dimples come and go with his banter.

'Now what?' he snapped when the second cook interrupted this delightful exchange.

'The emperor fancies a hare today, and there's not even a rabbit in sight.'

'No matter. I will provide one.'

'Are you a magician then?' the girl giggled.

'Let me know any time you feel like a bit of magic.'

'I'll send you a message through Ahmad then,' she laughed as she fled brushing past the mountainous bakawal.

'Arre Bakasur, you always come in at the wrong moment. Round up the rat traps would you, I have a hare to prepare.'

The rat traps yielded dozens of infuriated bandicoots, and the three other cooks flayed them with dexterity. Salting tender bits of flesh, they rubbed them with garlic before dropping them into a vat of curds whipped with saffron. Ghee hissed in the cauldron. In slid bayleaf, cinnamon, cloves and cardamom.

'Dhaniya!' yelled the Chef.

And in went handfuls of cracked coriander seed.

'Jeera,' he whispered in an undertone, and the fourth cook scattered cumin atop the mound of roasting spices, keeping it just warm enough to impart wit.

'Careful,' the Chef warned. 'Cool it or it'll reek like an amir's armpit.'

Not a hint of anything harsh, or irritant, tainted the balsamic vapour.

The Chef stopped the third cook standing at the ready with peppercorns bruised just enough to smart.

'But we always use pepper for hare,' the third cook protested.

'This is not hare, even if we're cooking hare. GingergingergingerGINGER!'

Now the air sang with all the seven notes of spice.

Pink and white wheels of onion went spinning into the cauldron, losing their sting as they hit the fragrant lava, rendering their syrup as they stiffened into crunchy filigrees of gold.

Time now for fistfuls of the Chef's masala, a dark crumble that trapped a whole forest of flavours. A quick swirl, and in toppled the vat of marinade.

Sweet, tenderized morsels of meat bobbed up eagerly soaking in the essence of the gravy, while the curd settled in a creamy emulsion commandeering every vagrant molecule of flavour.

And there it was, steaming in the Padshah's ganga-jamni bowl, a luxurious khargosh qorma,[86] palpitating beneath a shower of rose petals, veined with apricot slivers and canopied with whipped cream.

'I'll get the carrots done,' the second cook said. 'And today they really are from Kabul. Talk of pizzles, I'd like to know what kind of animal grows these ugly things.'

Crimson, grey, black, stubby, pitted, rugose and indented, the pile of carrots looked better suited to whet the emperor's appetites than the tom cats' slender and barbed arsenal.

'Raghuvir, what are you mumbling about?' the Chef snapped.

Cook number three had lost his voice. He opened and shut his mouth like a fish, miming alarm, pointing to the bakawal's back.

Ahmad's back was behaving most peculiarly. It convulsed in its encasement of grey silk like an earthquake trapped in a bowl of cooling nihari.

'What is it Ahmad? Speak up, what's got into you, man?'

Ahmad turned around slowly and held out a folded piece of paper.

'What's this?'

'Some kind of powder.'

Gopichand froze.

There was no need for questions.

His decision was awaited. The bakawal simply wanted to hear him say--

'No.'

'No?'

'The Padshah's salt runs in my blood. No.'

'A little while ago, Ibrahim Sultân's salt circulated in you.'

'Then too, if you remember, I said no.'

'That was understandable. Bahadur Khan was a mere boy. He never meant us harm. It was a caprice of the Sultân. He forced it on Bahadur's own cook.'

---

86 *Khargosh* ... خر گوش [Urdu] ... rabbit.

Qorma ... قور ما [Urdu] ... a spiced meat dish [originally from Turkey] with a luxurious gravy. The term is generic and the ingredients and flavours differ by region.

'Who was lucky he had a master who protected him. Whom do I have?'

'The queen.'

'With respect, she is now a widowed lady with a small property allowed her by the Padshah.'

'Padshah! He is a barbarian.'

'And what are you, Ahmad? What am I?'

'Mortal, like him.'

'Who gave you this powder?'

'The charmer you were flirting with.'

'The queen's slave–'

'Hush, here she comes again. No it is another.'

A second girl even prettier than the first sidled up to Ahmad and whispered, then darting a bright glance at Gopichand, swayed seductively away.

'You'll have to do it Gopichand,' Ahmad said. 'The queen has your children.'

'No!'

'Yes, that's what the girl just said. She's had them brought to her garden. They're playing there beneath the mango tree. Here's the complete message: There's a rope at the foot of the tree.'

Gopichand cried out in anguish and banged his forehead against the hot cauldron, branded before he had sinned. 'If I have to trust in the mercy of one or the other, I choose the emperor,' Gopichand said, suddenly calm. 'Move over, Raghuvir–the rest of you take the day off. Show yourselves in the palace. Let it be known I'm just beginning to cook a delicacy so rare, I sent you home that you may not witness the making of the masala. Now, Ahmad, what will you eat? Let us share a meal, my friend, for certain neither of us will ever eat again.'

'Oh don't be such a pessimist. The queen has an army.'

'Such an army that it can fight the Chaghtai.'

'The Rana has promised to help.'

'Promises, promises.'

'The queen has Nehal.'

'Yes, that's something to look forward to. Take your choice, the emperor's sword or Nehal's buggery. For our last meal, I have your usual dal chawal. Will that do?'

'Let's eat then. Give me a lick of pickle, the hot lime one, do!'

And so they ate.

'Now I must keep my promise,' Gopichand said. Taking the packet from Ahmad he poured a little of the white crystalline powder on his palm.

'What if it kills you at once,' Ahmad protested.

'No, I think I know this poison,' Gopichand said, swallowing a large pinch of powder. 'It is a common sort of *sendha namak*.[87] Look–'

He dropped a pinch into the stove.

It flared up with an intense white flame.

---

[87] Himalayan rock salt

'Yes, I know the stuff. It will make me retch, give me gripes and then one big trumpeting stool, and it is out of my system. But that's just one pinch. A lethal dose will have to be much larger.'

He got busy with the next dish. Fluffy *malpua*[88] with crisp gold frills, but today, instead of soaking them in syrup, he dredged them in powdered sugar.

After a moment's consideration, Gopichand arranged the malpua in an octagonal network on the royal platter. Over this he sprinkled a little of the poison. Then he poured in the ethereal foam of almonds he had ready. Over this glistening cumulus he balanced fritters of apple, peach and mango, Between them were flowers of golden rabri, flavoured with the essence of champa, each blossom resting between dark green sprigs of tulsi. This confection he concealed within a cage of sugar floss, and studded it with tiny crimson roses crystallized whole.

'The best thing I've ever done,' he sighed--then ran to the garden to retch his heart out.

That Friday, duhr took longer than usual. Babar was famished. The heat was trying, and he was short of sleep. He desired nothing more than a simple meal and a nap. He recollected having asked for a hare at lunch. The thought disgusted him. He sent for the Chef.

Trembling inwardly, Gopichand made his salaam to the Padshah.

'What is the yellow rice you serve called?' the Padshah demanded.

'Dal chawal, Jahanpanah.'

'It is a most excellent dish. Of Isfahan, I imagine. Or Istanbul.'

'If your Majesty so pleases.'

'Well, which is it?'

'With respect, sire, it is Hindustani.'

'No doubt a most royal dish?'

'Again with respect, sire, it is a most humble dish, served in the poorest households.'

'It is fitting for a Padshah to taste the food of the humble now and then. I recollect having asked for hare.'

'It awaits your Majesty's appetite.'

'Well, I have very little of it today. I will indeed taste the hare as you have prepared it, but bring me some dal chawal too.'

Gopichand's heart sank. Dal chawal would restore the Padshah's digestion. Without the soporific richness of the khargosh to numb its keen edge, the Padshah's appetite would make him pounce on the poisoned dish and lick it clean. There was no time to prepare anything else, so he bowed and retreated in abject misery.

He took cheer as he remembered that he had used only a little of the poison, and that he had sprinkled it in such a way that most of it fell between the malpua, not on them.

'Chalo, Ahmad, our time is come,' he said. He broke off one petal of a champa of rabri from the king's dish, and sampled it, tears streaming down his careworn cheeks.

88 *Malpua* ... مالپوا ... a north Indian fritter made from wheat flour, jaggery or sugar, and spiced with cardamom.

As the Padshah sat down for his meal, he noticed that Gopichand was there in person to serve him.

The Chef was freshly bathed, a tilak of chandan and kumkum blazed like a wound on his forehead, and he was dressed formally in a fine black achkan.

'With Jahanpanah's permission,' he mumbled, advancing with a bowl of dal chawal.

'Why do you serve me today?' demanded Babar.

'I have brought you my mother's dal chawal, Majesty. It restores the appetite immediately.'

The Padshah swallowed a mouthful, then emptied the entire bowl.

His companions, all of them Mughal, sucked thoughtfully on strips of dried meat. A foul miasma of putrefaction floated over the dish of qaaq.[89]

Gopichand wrinkled his nose.

'The aroma displeases you?' Babar enquired.

'With respect, Majesty, the bad air of Hindustan does not agree with the superior meats of Kabul.'

There was general agreement. The Padshah stated the strips he had eaten yesterday definitely stank. The cloth was hurriedly cleared of dried meat.

Gopichand poured a sharbat of ginger and honey to cleanse the palate, and uncovered the hare.

The Padshah's companions swooned from sheer pleasure as they inhaled the aroma.

'Good,' agreed the Padshah. 'But nowhere as good as the dal chawal.'

The emperor tasted the hare, declared it excellent and passed it on to the company. It was the veriest morsel he tasted, Gopichand calculated, no more than half a rat.

It was all up to Raghuvir's carrots now. They had been stewed whole and floated plump and succulent in pomegranate juice flavoured with cloves.

The Padshah shot an astute look at Gopichand. 'It appears the lion of Rajputana is a mere cat compared to the carrots of Kabul,' he remarked casually.

Pale with agitation, Gopichand served the dessert.

The Padshah was much taken by the beauty of the sugar cage. He broke off the crimson rosebuds and distributed them among his favourites. Then he carefully lifted off the champa flowers with their greenery and laid them aside to be enjoyed later.

There was complete silence as the Padshah ate.

Fritter after fritter alternated with the champa flowers.

He nibbled on the tulsi to refresh himself before returning to the assault.

The malpuas had drawn in the powdered sugar–and the poison–and had retained their marvelous texture. The Padshah bit happily into the crunchy frills till they filled his mouth with sugary softness.

Gopichand stared at his feet.

The plate was nearly empty–it was meant to feed all his eight favourites too, but the Padshah had eaten it all.

---

[89] Urdu … قاق … jerky—trimmed meat cut into strips and dried to prevent spoilage. The word *jerky* itself derives from the Quechua word *ch'arki* meaning 'dried, salted meat.'

'Finish it!' Babar pushed the plate away with sudden petulance.

His brow darkened.

He lurched forward, and quickly steadied himself.

He drank some water.

He demanded the dish of qaaq to be brought back.

Then he rose abruptly and bolted to the water closet.

The sound of his retching filled the hall. In sympathy, the eight favourites began retching too.

Guards closed in on Gopichand and Ahmad.

In the dungeon, Gopichand waited for news of his children. Nehal may have strangled them already. Perhaps the Lodi queen had strung them up from the mango tree. He prayed their deaths had been quick and merciful.

The queen, having learned that the powder was no poison, would have vented her fury on the nearest victims. He imagined the moment. No tremor would betray her agitation.

She might not even look up from her book or her embroidery as she gave the order: 'Kill them!'

Order? It would be a murmur gentle as a sigh. Later, she would weep for the children and consider herself kind.

In his anguish Gopichand had travelled far beyond tears. He felt nothing now. Perhaps he was dead already.

'Your children are with me,' a quiet voice said.

It was too dark to see, but there was no mistaking the voice.

'Mercy,' the Chef croaked.

'Oh, don't plead for mercy. The dog will decide.'

'What dog?'

'The dog I fed my vomit. All the hakims and vaids are observing him.'

'He won't die.'

'Neither, it appears, will I. I knew as soon as I felt sick that you were responsible.'

'Naturally. I'm your cook.'

'A cook with no desire to poison me.'

'But I did poison you.'

'First, you knew the poison. Second, you used only very little–that told me someone had given you the poison. My men found the packet you had discarded. There was still quite a lot of powder in it. My chemists are having it analyzed.'

'It is a common salt, it burns with a white flash.'

'I was correct in my first deduction, and correct also in the second. Why did you poison me? The answer was obvious. You were threatened. A man's life may be of no account to him, but threaten his children and that man is your abject slave. So all I had to do was find your children, and I would have found the murderer. I have found your children, I have them now.'

'I am grateful for your mercy.'

'I have shown no mercy yet. Your children are with me, but not necessarily safe.'

'My life is yours,' Gopichand said desperately, knowing it was no use.

'Obviously. There will be a trial on Monday. You will be condemned. The nobles will decide the punishment. Obviously, you will die.'

'Obviously.'

'The amirs are cruel men. They will enjoy the spectacle.'

'That is their tragedy.'

'And not yours? How so?'

'My pain will end as theirs begins.'

'You have an answer for everything.'

'I am going to die. We might as well converse as men and not as master and slave.'

'In that case, I shall inform them you are being tortured right now. Excuse me, my bowels are still unpredictable.'

Babar's bowels continued unpredictable over the weekend.

On Saturday the royal stools were examined by a learned body of hakims.

The dog which had fed on the vomit lazed in its cage all day. Vaids and hakims were divided on the state of its digestion.

The vaids predicted it would pass wind.

The hakims argued in favour of hard stool.

The royal observers shied stones at the dog, and when it did not snarl or yelp, it was pronounced incurable.

The dog, disgusted by its last meal, only wanted to sleep it off. Around midday, it shook off its ennui and went for a walk.

The Hakims reported the Padshah's stool contained parched bile. He had miraculously voided every last trace of poison from his system. Sweets were distributed through the royal household, and plans made for a truly exciting trial on Monday.

The Padshah drank a bowl of milk on Sunday, and another on Monday morning.

Thereafter he was dosed twelve-year aged theriac[90] containing 55 herbs mixed with the flesh of vipers and squills dissolved in cow's urine and Attic honey. The news of a successful purge was broadcast by late afternoon, and he made his appearance in court looking a little pale, but otherwise in high humour.

When the court assembled for the trial, Gopichand's confession, extracted under torture, was read out.

The two slave girls were produced, and despite his own suffering, Gopichand could not but weep for them. Ahmad loomed, dwarfing the Padshah.

'Do you have anything to say for yourself?' Gopichand was asked.

'Only that I commend my children to Jahanpanah's mercy.'

The Padshah inclined his head ever so slightly and Gopichand contented himself with that–

---

[90] From Greek *thēriakē* ... 'antidote against venom' [*thērion* 'wild beast'] ... a medicinal concoction used as an antidote to snake venom and other poisons.

Haridas stopped.

Bahadur hurled a cushion at him. 'So what happened then?'

Ahmad, the bakawal, was neatly cut in four.

The first slave girl was trampled by the Padshah's elephant.

The second slave girl was shot.

The dog went free.

As for Gopichand, the Padshah found it curious that so many bandicoot pelts were recovered from the kitchen, and so he had the Chef flayed.

What could be more just than that?

'But the Padshah wasn't poisoned,' Bahadur protested. 'He wasn't even sick. And it wasn't even poison.'

'But the intent was clear.'

'The Lodi queen's intent was clear. The cook only wanted to save the Padshah.'

'That's not how history will remember it.'

'How do you know?'

'The Padshah is a bookish man. His version will make history.'

'And our historians, Haridas? What will they write of me?'

'That remains to be read. But history takes time. Meanwhile, we have our bards. They sing of Khanua already, I hear.'

28

Mulgaon, 1536

There is an empty patch of land, my masters, where the soil burns red. No pyre needed there, save your sandalwood! The embers on the ground will turn your feet to ash.

Only one shadow bisects this land. When the sun is at zenith it falls like a scythe, like the wingspread of a vulture, like the bat of eternal night.

Everything is silent here. Nothing whispers in the heat. But by moonlight, when the shadow cleaves the silvered ground, it begins to speak.

Listen.

Listen. From the tangle of a thousand tongues, words emerge as one.

Where have we heard them before?

In the sighing wind of Samarqand!

How many heads today?

How many heads did he bring home today?

For the shining sword has passed this way.

What casts this shadow? you ask me.

Tower? Tree? Pillory?

It is a tower, Shastikars.

A tower taller than any tree.

Don't strain your eyes, it is too dark to see.

But you can smell, my brothers.

Fill your lungs with the stench and rush to the bushes to retch your stomachs out.

We know now it is a tower of heads, rotting like melons in the heat.

Will our heads join it too?

Fear not, Shashtikars, the sword is sheathed now.

It trusts to your intelligence, once it has shown what it can do.

Where is this tower?

At Khanua.

Where was Hindustan lost?

At Khanua.

Where did Hindustan gain an emperor?

At Khanua.

Where did Hindustan lose an emperor?

Again at Khanua.

Weep for Sangram Singh, bravest of the brave.

Weep for the nameless soldier, bravest of the brave.

And when you have done weeping, come with me to watch the battle.

By the Padshah's reckoning, it is the 9th day of Jamadi-ul-akhir, of the year 933.

By yours, Shastikars, 855 Shaka, on the first day of Chaitra.

And because some of you will carry my tale to the Firangi be it known by his own time also. 16 March, 1527.

The sun is half way to the zenith, my masters, and what do we see?

The army on the march. Six miles to the enemy.

Two miles into the march, a halt.

Perhaps it is so that we may look closer and learn their faces?

Look then, look well on Zahiruddin, sometime Chaghtai, now Padshah of Dilli.

He walks among his men, as if he would read each man's soul in his eyes.

Why this halt? you persist in asking.

Very well. I will tell you. It is his way.

He makes a note of each man and learns with that one swift glance, what to expect of him.

An army is only a collection of men, but a good army is a collection of like-minded men.

And this is what Zahiruddin is trying to decide. How many of his 10,000 think alike?

Their loyalty is but two days old.

Two days ago, abject in defeat, deserted by braves, decimated by death, the army slunk back from Bayana, retreat in every breath.

The King's jyotish cried a warning.

Mangal, risen like a fireball in the west, glowered every night. Marching towards him betokened certain death—*Retreat!*

You can see, my brahman masters, well versed as you are in celestial things, you can see the man was a fool, for is it not certain that Mangal blesses every enterprise, big or small, with certain success?

Do not blame him, O Pandits, he is but an import from Samarqand, and who knows how Mangal behaves in that sky?

For certain the army believed him, for every man breathed—*Retreat!*

The word could not be spoken, lest it render the army speechless to a man.

With a flash of that sword the Padshah might thunder away, leaving his army standing motionless.

The horizon would hold him by the time they toppled, rank by rank, every man enrobed in scarlet as he gave up his head.

No, for certain one could not say—*Retreat!*

But who's to stop a man from thinking?

And ten thousand men thought just one word—*Retreat!*

And the Chaghtai, Zahiruddin Babar, he heard that thought.

And what then did he do?

Did his sword flash?

Did their heads topple?

No my masters, that is not the way of Kings.

This King, who has a garden full of apsaras and houris with hair of pure zari, has also a tank in his garden with a bit of poetry on it.

How do I know? Have I been in Ferghana, in Badakshan, in Samarqand, in Kabul?

You know the truth. I have not even crossed the river out of Shashti Pranth. But the Amir who passed by last week, the angry one who drew his sword at the Firangi, he was here hot-heeled from Kabul, and it is in that city that the King has a garden full of apsaras. And this very Amir has often been their guest. This short cross-eyed foul mouthed Amir has even dallied with zari-haired houris! Do I believe him? Yes! For how else would he know of such pleasures, my masters! My ears burned as I listened to the Amir. Such things, he assured me, such things are common in Kabul.

What things?

You expect me, a Brahman, to tell you?

I cannot. But this I can say. Imagine what you have never imagined before, and then dare a thousand times worse, and you will be still many miles away from what these apsaras can do.

In that garden of apsaras and houris, there is a fountain of golden sweet-scented wine. It bubbles with laughter day and night. And on the edge of that fountain the King has inscribed a poem. Listen, Shastikars, to know the man this Zahiruddin was before Khanua.

Give me but wine and blooming maids
All other joys I freely spurn
Enjoy them, Babar, while you may
For youth once spent will ne'er return

And this bhogi, this rajbhogi, what did he do with his discontented army?

Did he buy them with wine as the Firangi do?

Not he!

He came out of his tent, wine cup in hand, and before the amazed army, he threw it down and stamped on it, grinding it to dust.

And he swore the solemn oath of kings. Never again would he touch a drop of wine, my masters!

On the instant the man became a sanyasi.

He declared this would be no common battle, but a holy war it being their duty to fight unbelievers and barbarians.

For the enemy consisted of both, Hindu unbelievers and Afghan barbarians.

Remember, to him we are a nation of unbelievers and barbarians.

We think him no different, so why argue?

And the army raised a cheer, and rose full of resolve, Victory in every breath—

But that was two days ago.

The Padshah stopped his march to give the uncertain a chance to desert.

He stationed his guards at all exits, but he himself waited, sword in hand at the fence after dark.

The camp slept deep. The Padshah's blade waited. Dawn found it unstained.

The next night, the Padshah did the same thing.

Two miles into the march, he camped on the banks of the Banganga at Khanua.

Scarcely had he pitched his tents when the enemy, impatient to meet him, was sighted in the distance.

And then, my masters, it was war!

The Padshah was everywhere. In the thick of battle, among the humblest soldiers and the loftiest generals he moved like lightning, a sword in each hand, smiting swift and sure and strong till there were enough heads, both Rajput and Afghan, to build a tower and turn the soil red.

Who fled?

Rajput and Afghan both.

And Rana Sangram Singh? That's another story, my brothers, another round of toddy.

What, is the pot empty?

Then it must be the pot of the Qalandar of Hindustan, for that is how the Padshah is styled in Kabul.

And do you know why? Because he has impoverished himself, generous man, to turn the beggars of Dilli into rich Amirs. They still starve, I hear. But the treasury filled with their taxes has made every man, woman and child in Kabul rich! Imagine, each man, woman and child in Kabul has received, by order of the Padshah, one silver sharrukh!

Here is a Padshah, here is a Qalandar, whose hands, like Karna's are always open and generous. As long as he gives, does it matter if what he gifts is not his own?

A fine nation is Hindustan, with a Qalandar for Padshah, and beggars for Amirs!

So fill that pot, Shashtikars, for the toddy is your own, and let us be amirs together tonight before the Firangi makes beggars of us all.

Tonight the moon is bright, brothers, so must my story be.

Brighter than any told before, and like the moon, it must dissolve into ink.

There are among you Shastikars, people from the sun and the moon. You are suryavanshi, he is chandravanshi, I am something in between, Trishanku is my constellation, and who among us does not know that tale?

O you bright ones, condemned to darkness, you will hang me at dawn.

Before daybreak will I escape, my masters, to the great bazaars beyond, to a land full of stories where yatriks come and go, and treasures are cheaper than they are at Shaniwar Bazaar.

In that land, brothers, no man is Brahman or Shudra, none Mussalman or Hindu, none Isa, Yahudi, Baudh or Jain. Nor is man, man nor woman, woman. This tattered dhoti that covers my shame too will lift from me in story land, for I will become story.

We are but essence and perfume and notes of music, points of light perhaps—who knows?

O you bright ones who look to your ancestors, do you gaze on the sun and the moon and imagine them there?

Why, every fool knows the sun is a ball of fire, the moon a ball of ice, so what are your relatives doing incinerated or frozen up there?

Maybe instead, they have gone the other way, to *patala.*

Atala vitala talatala whatever the places they pass through, finally, will they meet a bejeweled snake with ten hoods, will they?

You are privileged persons, so maybe you will see all these wonders, but I, ignorant Brahman, teller of tales, I must take to the air and vanish into story—

But listen, before I go, to one more tale.

You crept away from Khanua, shuddering. Trembling in fear you left the battlefield. But brothers, you were not alone. Another shadow followed yours.

In the darkness you could not see his face.

But had the moon shone as it does tonight, you would have seen a short but sturdy man limping painfully. Look closer and you will notice he has but one arm. His face is a nest of scars, lit by one eye that glares like Mahadeo's third.

You will see all this and ask—what was this cripple doing on the battlefield?

Don't make me laugh.

The man was the battle itself.

One-armed, one-legged, one-eyed, he held eighty thousand horse, five hundred elephants, one hundred and fifty chieftains, five Rajas and fifty Raos in his command.

Where are they now?

Some in that tower have left their heads, but others are deep in bargain with the Padshah.

Betrayed by the jackal Silhadi, and then all the rest, Rana Sangram Singh, slunk into obscurity at daybreak, like the moon itself.

Like the moon itself, he was consumed by growing betrayals in the months to come.

Everybody left him, but his own light gathered strength.

Would he have won the next battle?

What do you think, my brothers?

In Dilli, the Padshah paced sleepless, wondering when Rana Sanga would return. He bought or killed all Rana Sanga's allies.

Babar's time was wholly taken up in preparing for Rana Sanga.

Rana Sanga's time was wholly taken up preparing for the Mughal.

It was too much for Rana Sanga's people to bear.

The stubborn old man—he was only forty-five—would go back to the battlefield unless they stopped him.

And so they did, my masters.

They gave him wine, but he asked for a cup of milk.

He was in hiding. He had not tasted milk in months.

It was brought to him. A silver cup of milk.

'I shall sleep deep tonight,' the Rana said, and never woke again.

So I ask you, Shashtikars, who was the enemy?

Was it the Padshah? Was it his family? Was it his own greed?

For what is battle but greed?

Greed for another's goods, land, cattle.

War has no glory but the decaying corpse, no loyalty but greed.

The Mughal says he fights the unbeliever, the Firangi says he fights the pagan, the Hindu says he fights them mlecchas both.

All lie.

Their saddlebags lie, their coffers lie.

Look at the battlefield, brothers, you can look at it for it is far away.

You can smell death in its air

You can't see the battlefield we live in, though, can you?

You can't smell the death in our air?

Look among ourselves, locked in little prisons of faith and caste and language, condemned to choke. No matter how foul our own air, we refuse to breathe another's.

The Firangi is here now.

He pretends he is our friend.

He will take our wealth, our fields, our children, the very tongues from our mouths so that he can save our souls.

He has burnt every masjid and smashed every temple, and he tells us it is for his god.

He lies.

It is not his god but his greed that compels him as it compels Sultân and Padshah and Rana and Raja.

Who wins?
The fellow with the quicker horse, better aim, louder gun.
Who loses?
No matter whose side we prefer, the losers always are you and I.
We don't need them, my brothers, we don't need Padshah and Raja and Rana.
We don't need our huge platoon of gods, nor Mohammad, nor Issa.
Do they feed us? Do they cure our ills? Do they nurture our children?
Not they!
Who does, brothers?
We do.
With no help from any of these unseen and unknown benefactors, we do.
To them we are unseen and unknown.
But to us they are unseen and unknown too.
Can we not live without these evils?
When will we learn that?

Instead we cut each other's throats for gods and kings and rules and laws made by who knows what idiots in some long forgotten time.

For this is the truth of Khanua.
It is the truth of Kali, the Yuga that began when we turned on each other.
It is the truth, not of Dilli, but of us Mulgaonkars of Shashti Pranth.
The battle is within us.
We betray our own selves.

What—here already?
Set up the gallows, though it is not yet dawn.
And the rest of you are in a hurry to go?
No matter, I'm in a hurry myself.
I'm done with your stories, and in a hurry to discover my own.

29

14 February 1537 [Part iii]

Diu

The day had moved quicker than he expected. Had he fallen asleep? Perhaps so, for he was crowded with old faces, old events. The surge of pain they induced was actually welcome. He was so tired of the numbness that enveloped him.

It was a strange disease, this numbness.

He knew the exact second when it began.

At that instant it had been a numbness of the fingertips. They were free and disconnected from his body, they moved of their own free will, quicker than thought. And having acted, left him burdened with what they had done.

Only the fingertips at first. Then his arms, his legs, the entire cavity of a man that packs the machinery of life, all that fell numb. His face followed, his eyes.

Now all that remained sentient was thought. And that he sought to numb with drink.

The Firangi evidently thought him a charsi as well. But he had never touched the stuff. The Firangi mistook a man's pain for folly, and yes, he had been foolish.

Humayun. Humayun. All his follies, save only one, had been because of Humayun.

But there was plenty of time. He would set things right. He would drive the Mughals out of Hindustan. He could do that. He had lost his nerve earlier, listening to this fool or that. He was different now. Older. He could live with the pain in his head.

Thirty—thirty-one—a man had seventy years gifted him. There were forty years ahead. He could afford one lazy afternoon, surely?

The fans of hokka overhead made a pleasant shade. The ocean murmured its lullaby.

Bahadur slept.

Why did that memory anger him so?

Through the chill hour of the announcement of his father's death, he had felt bereft of will, and in the days that followed, bereft of thought as well. His words were forced, his actions mechanical. Distanced from himself, robbed of grounding force, he was in free-fall.

But now, the memory of those frozen days angered him. They returned barbed with words and sprung with thoughts he could never have uttered then, nor acknowledged without feeling their whiplash.

In the afternoon silence now, those thoughts returned. Fanged and clawed, they tore mercilessly into his mind.

The truth was still too shameful to be uttered aloud, but he could think it now, the thought that had been the constant refrain in all his days of wandering.

I'll show him!

When he reached Dilli, the refrain had lengthened:

I can't have Gujarat? Very well, I'll get Hindustan!
I'll show him!
I'll show him by driving out the Chaghtai!
I'll show him by displacing the Lodhi!
I'll show him!

What then?

He had played the dream out in his brain so many times he had it down to the last detail.

Bahadur's dream always began with a flash, incandescent, blinding, searing his eyes with the tearless burn of dozens of sleepless nights. And then the brightness would come into slow focus. He would see with great distinctness a crystal tear tremble on the stubble of his father's weatherbeaten cheek. A tear glittering brighter than the diamonds in his earrings that flashed rainbows when he turned his head.

At this point, Bahadur's own eyes would feel the coolth of tears as his father's voice said: *My son.*

Those were the only words Muzaffar Shah Haleem uttered in Bahadur's wild imaginings.

Those two words completed his dream. They meant he had Hindustan and Gujarat and who knows what other land and its people. He watched it all, all of it unrolling like one magnificent carpet at his father's feet. He himself stood at the far end, and yet, magically, he could see that tear tremble as his father said: *My son.*

Bahadur whispered those words now.

The gentle rustle of hokka fans absorbed them and they became the caressing sound of the tree.

But he had never heard them said, had he?

Those words had never been spoken by his father, who always addressed him as Bahadur Khan. And that was never pronounced as a name but as a snarl, an insult, a jibe, a sneer, an epithet. Something that dangled from his neck—a proclamation of failure.

The more he won, the more he failed in the eyes of Sultân Muzaffar.

My son.

He couldn't dream those words any longer, but in those days they clung to his nineteen-year-old brain like cobwebs.

He hadn't left home because of Sikandar's attempt to murder him. He would have stayed and faced that, but Muzaffar Shah had been glad to see him go.

He could not then see past the courtesy of kings.

He saw his father now as he saw other kings: men like himself paraded about in luxury, but beneath that crust of gold and gems half-finished and empty, for what were they without majesty? What quality distinguished them from the meanest of their subjects?

He shrivelled with disgust. It was second nature to him now, this disgust. He felt it too often, towards too many, but principally towards himself. At such moments, the roar within him became unbearable till it settled into a deeper numbness. He called it a headache for want of a better word.

What would Muzaffar Shah think of him now?

That was all too clear, painfully clear. More painfully, it didn't matter anymore.

He recalled now the narrow twisting alleys of Dilli, sweating people at every pore. The Chaghtai would tax them and bleed them as the Lodhi, the Tughlaq, the Khilji had.

Dilli never had a king of its people. The bards sang of earlier kings, unbelievers all, like the crowding populace, so how could they matter? They were nullities. It was the duty of a true believer to erase them—or so he had been led to believe.

What was this thing called belief?

Its only purpose was to set man against man.

More disgust.

His empty stomach growled its disapproval. It was being purified by fasting through this holy month. There must be something to that. It made him calmer, stronger. Victorious.

'Exalted,' he heard Hari say. 'Hunger gives us that feeling of being superhuman. Look at our sanyasis. They fast for months, and the whole world trembles before them.'

That was true too.

The king who stained his sword with the blood of a sanyasi was dead within the week.

What was that story about Feroz Tughlaq? A Dilli story, but it could have happened anywhere.

Still, Bahadur conceded, Dilli was not just anywhere. It was the heart of kingship. A place where the ruler distanced himself from the ruled. That distance was bridged by the flow of money. Coins, gold, silver, jewels, land, money. Relentless as a river rushing towards the ocean, everything flowed towards the ruler. Dilli was that tight power-mongering coterie in court, speaking the twinned language of barter and murder.

He knew it all.

Why then did he covet Dilli?

Because Dilli was Hindustan.

He laughed from joy at the memory of crossing the border of his father's kingdom. It was exhilarating, a moment of sheer abandon. He had never since felt so free. Everything was foreign—land, language, trees, people, even the weather, and that foreign-ness was freedom.

Did Bābar Padshah feel that too? Is that why he chose to stay and not just carry away tonnes of treasure like Ghazni, Ghori, Sabuktagin, Sikandar?

Freedom or treasure?

He was far richer than any Padshah could be. Then, as now, even with Humayun having plundered his treasury.

Once a thief, always a thief …

Bahadur stopped the ungenerous thought.

Had he himself been any better?

He had never coveted treasure. He simply loved its beauty, content that it might be his to gift, not own.

Except the belt.

That he had coveted, lusted for, as he had never lusted for any woman.

And it was his now.

In perpetuity.

No, Dilli was not about treasure.

What then?

My son.

Hari had called him a king in search of a kingdom.

Hari was, as usual, right.

But he was still outside Bahadur's dream. Bahadur had not meant to keep it secret. He merely assumed that Hari, who knew everything about him, knew this too.

He had told Barq. And the horse, hearing the wordless thought, held his head higher before breaking into gallop that rivalled the wind.

Ah Barq!

Ah Hari!

It was all Hari's fault.

Everything was.

If Hari hadn't deserted him, would he have turned to Humayun?

But Hari had not yet deserted him then. He had merely refused to advise. 'You will know what to do when the time comes, but it must be no man's knowledge but yours.'

Whenever Hari took that lofty tone all you could do was address him as Pundit for a whole day or challenge him to a fight. Either way, his opinion never changed.

Bahadur had evaded murder in Dilli. It was neither the first time, nor the last. Death on the battlefield was different from betrayal. He would have no rancour against the man who ran a sword through his heart. But poison? That rankled.

Would he have fought at Panipat if Ibrahim Lodi hadn't sought to poison him?

No. Poison had not determined his choice. He sought revenge for that murderous act knowing the crafty Sultân would meet his end in the battlefield. He felt no rancour against the Sultân's mother either. Why had she said that it was not his fight?

Of course, she was afraid the Jaunpuris would claim him.

By the time he was on the road to Baghpat he felt like a piece of carrion fought over by crows. As always, he said nothing, leaving it to Barq and Hari to divine his thoughts.

They had both deserted him now.

But he still had the tree.

The hokka nodded, reading his thoughts.

Yes, he wanted Hindustan. He still did, impossible though the thought, he admitted it grudgingly. If he could rid himself of the Firangi and fight Humayun on his own ground—

Treachery.

He had picked his way out of the maze of murder in Dilli, but he was trapped in it within his own court. There was no knowing the ambitions of men, nor the depths of their vengeance.

He did not set much store by vengeance. After all, it was his one act of vengeance that had devastated his life.

Hari had said so too. 'People don't remember glorious victories. They wait for a misstep, a shame they can recall till the end of time.'

Hari did not name it, but Bahadur knew the misstep he meant. Qabil. It was that deed that condemned him as a cruel man. It had made him a murderer. Everywhere he was talked about as the murderer of his brothers.

Latif had died in battle. Ibrahim and little Nasir of the fever that ravaged Ahmadabad that year. Chand, exiled for his many perfidies, still alive, was reputedly poisoned.

All this was fact.

But rumour was very different.

No matter where they began, the stories came back to him.

Latif lay bleeding and unattended till Bahadur delivered the death stroke. He had choked little Nasir in the presence of Ibrahim and Chand and had them blinded and thrown in prison when they protested. He had killed each one of them in new ways, with new tortures every week.

He did not protest. Not only because stopping a rumour was as impossible as stilling the wind, but the truth was, he would not have protested even if he could.

False as it was, the rumour was just. By his one act of vengeance he had deserved it.

And what had he tried to avenge?

Qabil had spoken nothing but the truth. Duom was what he was.

The tree nodded, cooling him with its gentle breath of assent.

But none of these thoughts had troubled him at Baghpat.

Even before he heard of his father's passing, he had felt suddenly older. Dilli had done that, within a day, within hours. He was no longer flattered by the respect of older men; older not just in age, but in battle. He took his place among them as an equal. Already, he was alert, knowing death was but a hairsbreadth away from a smile. Already primed, for Hindustan.

Pai'ndah Khan had understood him. He had gauged Bahadur's hesitation correctly. Bahadur would not accept a crown without a fight. He knew too that Bahadur was certain of victory.

How empty that boast rang now! But at nineteen, it was no boast but belief. Once victorious, Bahadur would shake off the Afghan yoke. Would he rule from

Jaunpur—or from Dilli? That was the question in Bahadur's mind, and there was no answer forthcoming.

Now he knew why he had left it to Barq.

He hadn't then, and then not for years.

Haridas mentioned it just once. 'You've always trusted Barq's instincts quicker than your own.'

That was both true and untrue.

Barq always perceived quicker, but Bahadur had acted quicker than perception.

He understood now that he had left it to Barq knowing fully that Barq would point west, towards home. He knew with fatal certainty that Dilli meant—death.

He had been prepared to risk that.

I'll show him.

He would not die in battle, but by mean trickery—poison or ambush or strangled in his sleep. That was the Dilli way.

He had been ready to dare that—not just to face the Chaghtai, but to wring from Sultân Muzaffar's bitter lips those magic words:

My son.

But Sultân Muzaffar had betrayed Bahadur once more. He had died before Bahadur could *show him,* and where was the point in risking his life after that?

Yes, he would win the battle and drive out the Chaghtai, Bahadur was very sure of that.

And it would be a victory to treasure.

But for what?

To serve the Afghans till they tired of him? What would he do, in ruling Hindustan? What did he know of its people?

It would be lonely as hell in Dilli, even with Hari at his side, and Bacchu never far away.

He wasn't sure he would like it.

Through all his emptiness and grief he hungered for welcome.

They knew him back home.

They knew his wildness, but they also knew his face.

He would go home and if he ever needed a kingdom, it waited there for him.

His decision was made already.

But he decided, for once, to be politic. He played the the madcap cavalier they expected him to be. He threw the reins down, leapt on the saddle, and left it all to Barq.

He woke with the feeling of being watched—his hand had closed on his dagger even before he woke. A polite cough announced the presence of a friend. In the shade of an enormous banyan beyond the dargah was Malik Toghan's palki.

It never failed to surprise Bahadur that any palki could possibly contain the Malik, and that men strong enough to carry it could be found at a whistle.

Malik Toghan usually rode on his camel Farida, as famous for her cussedness as she was for the sapphire worn around her neck. Nobody had ever seen Malik Toghan walking outdoors. Within his magnificent mansion he sometimes used a wheeled chair. Yet here he was, wedged inside this enormous palki.

'No, don't get out,' Bahadur said hastily. Packing Malik Toghan in again might be problematic.

'Come in then, huzoor, there is plenty of place.'

There was, indeed, to Bahadur's surprise. It was the most luxuriously appointed palki he had ever seen.

'So what brings you out in the sun? I thought you would be blissfully asleep.'

'The Firangi have sent word their Governor is ill. The reason, sire, being the venison.'

'They accuse me of poison, do they?'

'Far from it. It was all eaten, as Noor Mohammad told us. But I have news of what came before the deer was cooked.'

'What?'

'Your message was given to their necromancers.'

'What message? I only sent them the antelope.'

'The meat was the message. The carcass had been dressed and cut in thirds. They thought it meant they too would be flayed and butchered.'

'Are they mad? It was just game!'

'And then I had my men prepare the loin, raising off the silver sheath to leave the meat tender. You know these barbarians! They will stew the meat till—'

'Spare me your recipes, Toghan. What of the loin?'

'They have a physician, very renowned in Europe, but not so successful here, our hakims and vaids frequently make game of him. Joao Roderigues.'

'Why, I know the name. I saw him put to shame by their own pandit, Martim Affonso Sousa's friend.'

'Da Orta, yes. He is a different cut from these lumpens. I have sent him cuttings from my rose garden. But this Roderigues—'

'Yes, yes,' he urged.

'Seeing the loin unsheathed, this worthy pronounced the meat poisoned. He said the sheath had been removed so that the poison could be rubbed deep into the meat, and he warned them not to touch it.'

'And yet they ate it.'

'Can you stop hungry men? So their necromancers came up with a second story. A gift you sent them a week ago—'

'The brace of partridges? Yes?'

'—changed overnight into a basket of skinny fowl, all with their heads cut off. The necromancers swore they had seen this happen.'

'Now I am a magician?'

'Worse. They fear you with the terror a child has for the dark or a woman has for a lizard.'

'Yes, but why is this relevant now?'

Toghan's face saddened.

'Wait—don't tell me! This Governor has refused your invitation. He will not dine with us tonight.'

'He sends his regrets. He is taken ill with an ague.'

'I am puzzled by their game,' Bahadur admitted after a silence. 'What do you think, Toghan?'

'They won't be satisfied till they have everything.'

'They control the port. What more do they want?'

'They want you.'

Bahadur thought and then spoke. 'I'll get Firangi Khan to write to my friend Martim Affonso. A private letter.'

'He is not popular at the moment.'

'Then do this for me, Toghan.'

'Command me.'

'Invite that doctor as my guest. Arrange for all the scholars in the kingdom to come here to Diu. Hakims, vaids, men of science, and we will have a grand exchange of learning. And then we will learn their intent.'

'I doubt if the doctor will have any idea of that.'

'Pah. Doctors know everything, they notice everything. Then you will do it?'

'It is done already.'

'About tonight—you will miss the Governor true, but may we not feast without him?'

Toghan brightened at that. He lived for these junkets.

'Now I hope you will come home with me and rest in comfort till *iftar*.'

Bahadur shook his head. 'I've left Barq out there. I'll ride over in an hour or so. I like it here, in the shade of the hokka. My gardeners tell me you won't give them the seed. I told them it grows nowhere but here and in the Sahel.'

'You are right. It can't grow in your garden.'

'Why not?'

'If it did, what would bring you to Diu?'

Bahadur smiled. 'You will, Malik Toghan. Or have you forgotten the day we met?'

How long ago was it?

After Khanua.

30

Khanua, 1527

There was news from Malwa. From Agra. From Jaunpur. From Dilli.

His spies brought news, but no embassies arrived with invitations.

'You are excluded, it appears,' Haridas laughed.

Bahadur, nettled, turned quarrelsome. 'What's so funny about that?'

Haridas laughed harder.

'They have enough without me I suppose. Enough men, horses, elephants.'

'Indeed they do,' Haridas turned grave. 'Such an army is unheard of. But—'

'But what?'

'They have an army, but no plan. They are huge and slow. The Chaghtai is small and swift. Elephant against horse. It will be Panipat all over again.'

'Not if they have Rana Sanga.'

'The Rana will sustain the fight, but they need a forerunner to advance and provoke.'

'Who do the Mughals have?'

Haridas did not answer.

Bahadur caught his breath.

Humayun.

Humayun had been summoned back to Dilli.

That was the first tremor of intent.

Babar wanted his son at his side even though the battle was still far off.

Muzaffar Shah had wanted his son far off, even though he had fought hard and often. Muzaffar Shah had never acknowledged Bahadur's courage or nerve on the battlefield. He had silently appropriated all Bahadur's victories. He gave the orders. Bahadur obeyed, but not always. He obeyed instinct first, an instinct that led him to certain victory. He won but felt no pleasure, only the dread of reprimand.

Humayun had been summoned back to Dilli from the east.

The east by this time was full of Jaunpuri Afghans. After Bahadur refused their cause, they had manifested a certain coolness. Pa'indah Khan had sent congratulatory gifts, but they came from the man, not his masters.

Bahadur was glad he had refused Jaunpur. They were rallying about the dead Sultân's brother Mahmud. He had been proclaimed Sultân. They had mustered an army, and when Haridas said, 'The Mughal has sent his son east to quiet the Afghans,' Bahadur did not ask which son. As far as he was concerned, Babar only had one.

It was not arrogance, that quiet voice that spoke in his skull: *You could have won Khanua.*

He could have won Khanua, won Dilli, driven out Babar—and none of this would have happened.

Humayun wouldn't have stolen his kingdom.

He would have had Gujarat and Hindustan, both.

He would have ruled Dilli from Mahmudabad—and why not?

But he did not fight at Khanua.

It was Rajput against Mughal, and he was Rajput enough, wasn't he?

Bahadur's spies had brought him news nearly a month before the battle.

He knew also the Padshah's strategy.

He could have told Rana Sanga—what?

He had seen fewer battles than the Rana.

But the truth was that he knew, in some inexplicable way, the mind of the Chaghtai—the Mughal, as he was now called everywhere. He could predict each move, but he usually hid that knowledge, even from Hari. How could he face the question that was sure to follow: *Why then did you run away from Panipat?*

Lakham Bai had said something that startled him, and left him feeling dizzy and ill for days.

She said, 'Now is your time to ally with the Mughal.'

'The Rana considers me his son.'

'The Rana's blood runs in your veins, but to be a great king you must be more Mussalman.'

'And break temples like Sikandar Lodi?'

'Your father broke temples. Your beloved grandfather did. How do you think he got his two forts? Do you think yourself a better man? Your father's mother was as much Rajput as I am.'

When Bahadur repeated this conversation to Haridas, he was answered with a stony silence.

'I am not letting you go till you tell me what you think.'

At length, Haridas said, 'Bahadur must side with the Rana and the Sultân of Gujarat must side with the Padshah.'

That's how it always ended. He was a man divided.

'The Rana did you a great kindness,' said Haridas, 'in not asking for your help.'

'You aren't suggesting he thinks I would choose the other side?'

'He must be praying you won't. In your place, that's what *he* would have done.'

Haridas watched him closely for a few minutes. 'Tell me what the Mughal is planning.'

'What? Am I a spy now?'

'Yes. The exact kind of spy this battle needs. A spy inside the skull of Zahiruddin Babar. You know exactly how he thinks.'

'I never said that.'

'Ah. But I know exactly how you think. Agra first,' Haridas prompted.

'I would block the roads first. Malwa's to the south, Rana Sanga's to the east. That's Dholpur, Gwalior, Bayana. Three battles for three forts.'

'Wasteful,' remarked Hari. 'Why not try bribery, Firangi style?'

'Meaning?'

'The benevolent master of the universe sends you his love, and with this priceless gift, swears eternal friendship. Only in the Mughal's case it is likely to be a truly priceless gift, the heirloom of some minor baig or raja whose head is rotting in a basket. Quite unlike the Firangi's porcelain urinal.'

'Spittoon.'

'Urinal. They captured a Chinese *nau* back in 1509, and they are still gifting cracked crockery. As I said, why not bribery? Love me back or I'll flatten you.'

'Depends on the mettle of those chiefs.'

'Hah. Depends on religion.'

'All three are Mussalman, but I wouldn't count on that. Say one of them would capitulate. That is still two battles. I would wait. I would send a detachment half way, and wait for an answer. It could turn either way.'

The news arrived at sundown. Gwalior and Dholpur were the Mughal's now. Nizam Khan of Bayana was undecided.

'Which means the Rana has a better offer,' said Haridas..

'Or Nizam has the better spirit,' Bahadur retorted. 'The Chaghtai can't see that. He doesn't know us yet.'

'What? We are smarter than him now, are we?'

'Battles are never about that. When you fight to keep something, you fight harder.'

'Then why did the Lodi lose at Panipat?'

'Ibrahim Sultân couldn't see beyond the tip of his nose.'

'And Rana Sanga has a longer nose?'

Bayana gave battle to Babar's detachment—and routed them. The news was dismal. The Mughal camp, in disarray, was all for retreat or mutiny.

Meanwhile, Rana Sanga had gathered his forces.

Mahmud Lodi, Sultân without a kingdom, nonetheless brought 10,000 loyals. The Rana's army had many Mussalmans, including Hassan Mewati, with his 12,000 men. Every Rajput Raja was there. Raja Shiladitya, Silhadi as the Mussalmans called him, brought Chanderi into the battle.

Skirmish followed skirmish in the weeks ahead, but battle was still a murmur away.

For a long time the Rana played the waiting game.

'What happens when your wait is crucial to the outcome?' asked Hari. 'What do lazy men do? They quarrel. The Rana's army will quarrel.'

'And Babar's won't?'

'That depends on the Mughal. He has them, a ragbag of rejects, with no loyalty, no cause; he has them now from terror or ransom. He cannot keep them unless he gives them a cause.'

'They have a cause. They are fighting for Hindustan.'

'Which they shortsightedly believe is limited to the Doab. Too many kings have passed this way for people to feel any loyalty to the king. And they are too diverse an army, sourced from here there everywhere, to feel any loyalty to the land. But—'

'But there is always religion.' Bahadur sighed.

'You will use it some day yourself.'

Bahadur shot a cold look at Hari. He never could bear this difference between them.

The story would be told over and over again. Of how the Padshah rallied his broken army by exhorting them to fight the pagans and infidels. It was no longer a war for domination, but for faith, and on the instant each man became a ghazi. It was a simple ruse, it worked every time, that belief in divine privilege. It killed Mussalman and Hindu with equal ruthlessness.

Tuesday.

Mangal was propitious for battle, even if the Padshah's soothsayer told him just the opposite. Hari was reading the spy's missive aloud.

The enemy was sighted early on Tuesday morning while they were about to make camp. Rana Sanga had decided to advance.

They met at Khanua.

Then followed a detailed inventory of placements and personages that Hari seemed to delight in. Bahadur heard only one sentence:

On the right wing was the exalted son, honourable and fortunate, the befriended of Destiny, the Star of the Sign of sovereignty and success, Sun of the Sphere of the Khalifate, lauded of slave and free, Muhammad Humayun Bahadur.

'Don't tell me the Rana brought his elephants,' Bahadur said wearily. 'Don't tell me they didn't know about the mortars, the matchlockmen, the noise of it all. Any decent elephant would have run crazy.'

Hari was silent.

Bahudur's voice rose in rage. 'How could they be so blind and so stupid! Don't tell me they advanced straight into the Mughal. They did? It must have ended right then. Tulghuma! How could they not anticipate tulghuma?'

Hari read out the roster of the dead:

Hasan Khan Mewati. Rawal Deo. Charndar Bhan. Manikchand Chauhan. Karn Singh Rajput.

Princes all.

'And Rana Sanga?'

'Disappeared.'

'To fight another day. We should send for him, Hari. Perhaps he is wounded. He should rest here. We have better vaids and hakims than Chittorgarh.'

'He will never go towards Chittorgarh.'

'Yes, he'll be watched for.'

'And not only by the Mughal.'

'What do you mean?'

'Send for the Rana, Bahadur. I have a feeling he will trust Gujarat more than Chittorgarh.'

Bahadur, puzzled by Hari's words, nonetheless sent out feelers in all directions for Rana Sanga.

But the Rana had vanished. The arid landscape that nurtured his early years had absorbed him back once again.

'Leave off!' Lakham Bai commanded her son. 'Too much zeal in that direction will earn you an enemy you can't afford right now.'

Bahadur frowned at that.

'Ah, that doesn't sit well with my son. Very well, you can save him from the Mughal. You can save him from his crafty Rais. But can you save him from Karnavati?'

'What do you mean?'

'There are some women, my son, who think they hold up the sky. She is one of them. She knows no right or wrong, only duty. She is like a gun. Watch her point, and death lies that way. She wants to bargain. The Rana wants to fight. Who do you think will win?'

'The Rana without question.'

Lakham Bai's disbelieving laugh pursued Bahadur through his nightmares. He kept up the search, losing heart each day.

When news arrived at last, it was bitter.

The Rana was dead, poisoned by his own nobles.

No king had shown such valour, no soldier such intelligence, and no conqueror as much grace as Rana Sangram Singh. And this man had become an inconvenience to those he had considered his own.

How long before he, Bahadur, became one too?

Soon after Rana Sangram Singh's death, Rani Karnavati sent an emissary to Babar. She offered the famous belt as tribute, in return for Bayana.

Babar, responded with great courtesy and offered another jagir instead of Bayana.

Karnavati kept the belt.

After Khanua, came Diu.

Unlike his father, Bahadur was clear about one thing: Diu was Diu because of Malik Ayaaz. During his lifetime, Malik Ayaaz had handled the Portuguese with great skill. They had their spies, and they had Malik Gopi.

Malik Gopi was too rich to be in the pay of the Firangi whose idea of luxury was pissing in a porcelain urinal. But he wanted Diu: he wanted the control Malik Ayaaz had over the counting houses, the port, the customs. And he was prepared to give the Firangi room to trade. If they won Diu by force, they would need Malik Gopi more than ever. Accordingly, he introduced his Firangi friends into the court of Muzaffar Shah.

Malik Ayaaz had driven out the Firangi in the heroic battle of Chaul. The son of the Firangi Viceroy had fought with great bravery and his father wrote to Malik Ayaaz: *He that has eaten the cockerel must eat the rooster.*

The following year saw Malik Ayaaz humbled at Diu. His Egyptian friends turned tail and fled at the first cannonade.

All that was *before* the Firangi snatched Goa through three days of unending slaughter. The streets choked with corpses putrefying in the heat. Mussalmans were herded into masjids and set ablaze. That was hearsay: he was a child of three when that happened. At fifteen he had been surprised to learn that Goa was not really Firangistan.

Haridas had told him the Firangi of Goa, Afonso de Albuquerque had decided all he needed to keep the whole of Hindustan was to secure four ports: Aden, Basra, Goa and Diu.

'This Dalbu must be a very great fool.' Bahadur laughed. 'Even I know Basra and Aden are not in Hindustan.'

'You are the great fool, not him,' Hari retorted. 'You think of Hindustan as land.'

'Isn't it? How do the Firangi think of it then?'

'As an ocean. It is their road. It is their highway. All the shores are theirs. They go wherever their ships take them, and when they make port they claim the land.'

'As if people would let them!'

'They have guns.'

That was the unanswerable argument, always. The Firangi had bigger and better guns.

After they got Goa, Diu was of little interest to them.

Malik Ayaaz's military skills had won Champaner for his patron Sultân Mahmud Begada Diu was his reward. But Muzaffar Shah, falling in with the counsel of his envious amirs, had accused Malik Ayaaz of treachery and banished him.

Malik Ayaaz was dead, and his son awaited Bahadur at Khambat.

Khambat was a dying port now. All the trade was through Diu. Malik Ayaaz had tolerated the Firangi presence there, but he still held the reins. Now that he was dead, what would happen to Diu?

As he awaited the Malik's son Iliyas, Bahadur reproached himself for not having asked this question earlier.

Malik Ayaaz had three sons: Iliyas, Ishaq and Toghan.

Ishaq was a troublemaker, Haridas had identified that the first time they had met the three brothers.

Iliyas was of no account, a weak man who contented himself with siding with the strongest.

Toghan was a man of luxury. He lacked his father's military skills, but had inherited his genius for strategy.

Now Iliyas brought the news that Ishaq had married a Rajput woman and was plotting with the Ranas to kill every Mussalman in Diu and set fire to the city.

Bahadur interpreted the message for what it was: a request from Malik Toghan to rid him of a troublesome foe.

Haridas had warned him, in the very first week of his reign, of the blanket immunity of faith. 'You can use your devotion to Islam to justify just about any enormity you commit.'

'I won't be using it,' Bahadur retorted.

'If you don't, your historians will.'

'If I commit enormities, I will be responsible for them.'

'That won't make you a great king, only a cruel one.'

'You sound like my mother.'

'She is the mother of a Sultân now.'

There it came again—

Bahadur's blood raced as he rode towards Diu.

31

The Rann

He never got there.

He can't afford to think of that journey now.

Not today.

Shutting his eyes in determination, Bahadur, wide awake, returns to the moment.

He leaves the road to Diu at Junagadh and thunders towards the Rann. There are no stops, except an hour for Barq to recover. One solitary hour in 100 kos. There is no night, no noon, no pain. There is no time. There only is here. And there.

Now there is here.

Where?

Where in this blankness will he find Haridas?

He is blinded by whiteness.

The air is mist. Heat slams his skin, burns his lungs, chars his lips. The ground is crushed glass.

He dismounts.

Barq neighs, but he is past the horse already, stumbling in this curious shimmer that betrays at every step.

Not a breath stirs.

Not a track betrays a path.

Too slow, too slow, emptiness roars in reproach.

A shadow stains the whiteness. A cry is torn from him but the next moment kills hope. It is the tracker. The man has pursued him despite Bahadur's order.

'I will have your head for this,' he snarls.

'Certainly, huzoor. But afterwards.'

This is the tracker's kingdom, here even the Sultân must be a follower.

How does he know where to go?

He halts abruptly and turns to face Bahadur.

'It is too far off. We need a camel.'

Bahadur nods, the words mean nothing.

'One kos further.'

He hurries, but the guide is faster. How does he know where to go?

There are no Kos Minars here. This is the Rann.

The black dots on the horizon become a waiting camel, a man with a skinful of water.

Bahadur refuses water, refuses to mount the camel.

'I'll walk.'

'You cannot keep up, huzoor, once my Rani begins to run,' the guide rasps and before Bahadur knows, they have lifted him between them. Protest dies on his lips. These are grim men, as coarse and dry as the salt underfoot. The desert is theirs. Obey or die.

'Hold tight. A camel is not a horse.'

He is up in the air now, but the farther he sees, the whiter it grows.

Rani begins to run.

He is jolted out of fear, out of melancholy, out of grief into a kind of wonder he cannot grasp. He tries to hold on to it, but it passes through him like air, incandescent with heat, desiccating him into crags and cliffs. No longer skin and bone and muscle, he is crystalline within; blood and tears a crush of glass, every breath abrasion.

Perhaps Hari feels this, he thinks. Hari is dead and so am I, but how will I find him in this mist?

Speed gathers up the ground, lowers the sky. There's just enough space for the camel to tunnel through.

Suddenly, sound explodes in his skull.

The air is shrill with kites.

'Here,' the man growls and Rani lurches to a halt, kneels and shakes them off like irritants.

Bahadur breaks into a run.

He's led now by Hari's laugh, challenging, mocking, daring him in a childhood game—

A sated vulture is hunched over bones he recognizes at first glimpse—how?

They belong to a body as familiar as his own, though they carry not a trace of the man.

Brother. Friend. Guru. Beloved companion of every road he had ever taken.

Haridas. This is Haridas.

This is what Haridas has left him. His castoffs. His bones.

They are calcined already, abraded between sun and salt.

Nevertheless he does what must be done.

No prayer stains his lips as the fire burns.

A fistful of embers crumbles to a fine ash in his grasp.

He opens his fist and Hari is lost in the wind.

Bahadur sat up abruptly, his head spinning.

He spat out the bitterness.

He would seek out Bacchu now. Yes, Bacchu would have something to make him whole again.

But he stopped himself.

Bacchu would know his pain and draw tears out of him. He couldn't afford that now.

He would sit here for a while more and consider the Firangi.

Part Three

32

The Mirror of Sikandar bin Manjhu

I, Sikandar ...

I, Sikandar, in this mirror set forth the kings of Gujarat, their deeds and their memorials, that the reader might view what manner of men they were, mortal and fallible and thoroughly unfit to hold the threads of destiny of people, Hindu and Mussalman alike.

Gnashing his teeth, Sikandar continued:

Greedy, bloodthirsty, ignorant, bestial in their perversions: these arrogant Sultâns never flinched from committing the most dastardly deeds, be it rape, murder, lechery, buggery, fratricide or parricide. They were surrounded by ambitious men whose devious stratagems and foolhardy advice spurred them on to unspeakable enormities and monumental follies.

He set down his qalam with a sigh.

It wouldn't do. It wouldn't do at all.

It was the truth, yes, but it was his opinion. And there is no such thing as an honest opinion. Bias is the nature of the beast.

Tomes of dead kings surrounded him. He didn't believe a word they said.

Tarikh-e-Muzaffar Shahi. Tarikh-e-Ahmad Shahi, *Tarikh-e-Bahadur Shahi*—all written by court historians in the lifetime of these kings—were no more than pretty stories meant to titillate the ruler's ego. Of *Tarikh-e-Mahmud Shahi,* he was less critical. Mahmud Shah Begada was dead by the time the historian had finished his notes, so he managed to retain some of the better stories.

Sikandar thought these tomes might be read as notes. But with each reading the writing became a complicated jaali designed to occlude and confuse. He had to strain beyond it to glimpse the shapes of truth. When he had discerned them, they appeared to be great events moved by paltry men. On the chessboard of Time, Sultâns were lowly pawns, crowned through circumstance, always restricted or compelled by an intelligence other than their own.

What were these men like when they were alone? What were their thoughts and motivations?

The more Sikandar considered this, the more inexplicable these monarchs grew.

Sikandar was not a man of faith, but he was, like his father, a political animal. Both had their goals clearly defined very early in life, and they never swerved from them.

Sikandar bin Manjhu was approaching sixty.

Manjhu had died doing the only thing he did—reading.

The spectacles had slipped from his venerable nose, but his forehead was still corrugated in concentration when Sikandar found his body. Sikandar had some trouble prising the precious manuscript from Manjhu's fingers. Manjhu's grasp had grown greedier in death, true, but not very much. Through his monotonous life his grasp had avariciously retained every scrap of paper, vellum or palm leaf that floated his way. His library was filled with books he had bought, demanded, wangled, or pinched from passing scholars. Court and khanquah were equal poaching grounds for Manjhu. He stuck to the Syeds knowing they shuffled Sultâns, conjured them up or erased them. He cared for neither Syed nor Sultân, but was prepared to swear by either, provided it got him a book.

The manuscript he had died reading was an illuminated *Shiva Puran*. Sikandar stowed it away hurriedly before they had company. It would never do for the Syeds to hear of Manjhu's last heresy.

The Syeds mattered to Sikandar. They paid his bills, now that the monarchy was so dodgy.

'Monarchy is always dodgy,' his father had remarked—how long ago?

He, Sikandar must have been twenty, twenty-five?

Twenty-five. It was after that shabby affair of the—

Oh, never mind. Twenty-five.

That's right, he was twenty-five.

And his father, had been about his age now, nearly sixty.

It was a conversation that changed Sikandar's life.

The Conversation

Manjhu

Monarchy is always dodgy, I'll tell you how I came here—

Sikandar bin Manjhu

To Mahmudabad?

Manjhu

No, no. Here. To Gujarat.

Sikandar bin Manjhu

Where were you before that? I thought our ancestors belonged here.

Manjhu

Ancestors? I don't even know who my father was. My mother was not as honest a woman as yours. I grew up in the basti of the blessed Nizamuddin—

Sikandar bin Manjhu

In Dilli?

Manjhu

Where else? Where else can the dregs find their way into the king's wine cup?

The Mughal was new to Dilli when I caught his eye.

Lucky for me I was ill-favoured, eh? Or it might have been his bed and not his library.

Cross-eyed, scarred, one-legged. Doesn't get worse than that.

The Mughal was a bookish man, see, better read than some of his scholars. But I, not yet sixteen, was better read than him.

Two obscure lines of a manuscript that puzzled his scholars were like sips of clear cold water to me. I drank in the rest of the manuscript thirstily and asked for more.

You may be sure I did this in a dim garret, and not in his splendid court.

And how came I by the manuscript?

And how did the story of my skills travel to his small red ears?

[What? I've seen them boy, that's how! He had small red ears like a rat's, but the rest of him was comely enough.]

There's a certain bookseller—no doubt he's still there, or his son, or his grandson. I swept his shop and swindled his customers and falsified his accounts, just so that I could read the merchandize. The bookseller's wife had her own entertainments upstairs, so grandees from the court occasionally trod the creaking staircase. One such left his belongings in my care so that he could be unhampered in his amorous exercises.

Naturally, I opened the parcel. He was an old customer, so there definitely would be a book or two inside. If worth it, I would negotiate a price. I was deep in it when he returned, all smiles, tucking in his kamarband.

He was taken up short when he saw me. Straight away he dragged me with him, into the Royal Presence.

I was certain I was about to be hanged or beheaded or flayed or tickled by any of the other amusing royal caprices that make such uproarious reading.

But it turned out very differently.

'Read!' commanded the Padshah.

I read.

His scholars crowded around, exclaiming.

Just then a boy of my own age, a handsome fellow, this scented exquisite, entered, and the scholars backed off, bowing.

All their talk passed over my befuddled head. My neck burned in expectation of the sword's incandescence.

'Come with me,' the boy said.

Did I hesitate?

I was out of that darbar in a twinkling, hurrying towards some rat-infested dungeon or another.

But no—

'Come,' the boy repeated.

And—I entered Paradise.

In truth, if it is my lot to attain it, the Paradise of eternity will not compare with Humayun's library.

'Get a bath and some decent clothes,' the boy said. 'I would have you read that *masnavi*[91] with me, but your stink is more than I can bear.'

'Yours would be too, if you lacked water and food,' I had said before I could stop myself.

The boy's hand flew to his sword.

'Feed the child!' the Padshah's voice ordered behind me. 'Let us see if he is still quarrelsome on a full stomach.'

And so I stayed.

Sikandar bin Manjhu

That's not how I've heard Humayun described. I've heard he was wise, gentle, noble.

---

91 Farsi ... مثنوی معنوی ... *Masnavi-e-Ma'navi,* The Spiritual Couplets, is the compilation of about 25, 000 verses by Jalal al-Din Muhammad Balkhi better known as Rumi. The cardinal compilation of Sufi thought, it interprets stories and anecdotes derived from the the Qur'an, from the Hadith, and from daily life into a *vade mecum* of a moral existence.

Manjhu

Yeah, right. That was after he was dead.

Sikandar bin Manjhu

What about the diamond, then?

Manjhu

What about it? Kept it in his kamarband all his life, till he gave it to Shah Tahmasp—

Sikandar bin Manjhu

Shah Tahmasp of Persia? That's not what I heard. Humayun gave it to his father as soon as he received it.

Manjhu

Yes, that's true. That was dutifully done. In a country besotted with its parents, it makes a great story. Of course everybody overlooks the obvious. The diamond was never Humayun's to give away.

Sikandar bin Manjhu

Whose was it?

Manjhu

I've often wondered. The man who mined a diamond worth two days' food for the entire world had probably never tasted a square meal. I can assure you the very day he came up with this prize, he went to bed with his stomach growling for a ladle of kanji.

The Dakshin Raja whose property it became was looted by the Rajput Mahlak Deo of Malwa.

When Alauddin Khilji approached Ujjain, the Raja appeased him with the diamond.

When Alauddin killed his own uncle, he paid off his Rajput Tomar with the diamond for services rendered.

When Ibrahim Lodi befriended Rana Vikramjit Tomar of Gwalior, he took custody of the gem, but he had to hide it from his brothers. So he left it with Vikramjit's family, and they guarded the diamond from Ibrahim's acquisitive family.

Ibrahim fell at Panipat. So did Vikramjit.

Babar hastened to seal off the treasury in Dilli, and sent Humayun to do the same in Agra.

Sikandar bin Manjhu

Wasn't Humayun merciful to the Rana's widow? Grant him at least that.

Manjhu

Merciful? Allah, what kind of idiot have I nurtured! The poor woman and her children were trying to flee when they were caught and brought before him. The treasury was sealed already. She had to think fast. What else could buy her children freedom? She took the diamond from her waist and handed it to Humayun. So much for mercy!

Sikandar bin Manjhu

Did you ever see it?

Manjhu

Oh yes, very often. Humayun used to play with it in the Library, and scatter rainbows over the walls. I wore an eyeshade. Its brilliance nearly blinded me.

Sikandar bin Manjhu

But Humayun gave it to his father—

Manjhu

Who gave it back to him. It was a pretty exchange, poets drooled over it.

It didn't change the fortunes of Dilli. Nor the fortunes of Humayun. But, if you ask me, that diamond is what controlled Gujarat's destiny.

Sikandar bin Manjhu

Gujarat? How so?

Manjhu

Ah, to tell you that story, I'll need a glass of Firangi wine.

Sikandar bin Manjhu

You are not a drinking man.

Manjhu

Agreed. But this story needs either wine or opium. I foreswore opium the day I first saw Humayun high on it. And I learned the truth from Sultân Bahadur when he was in his cups. This is his story, isn't it? Fetch that wine!

Although I met Mohammad Hussam, the amir who was writing the *Tarikh-e-Bahadur Shahi* only in the eighth year of the Sultân's reign, I had met the Sultân long ago. At the same bookseller's in Dilli.

Sikandar bin Manjhu

Ha. Bahadur was illiterate. What was he doing at a bookseller's?

Manjhu

Did I say he came there to read? No, he came there for his friend, Haridas Pundit.

We were all the same age—Bahadur, Haridas Pundit, Humayun and myself.

Sometimes I wonder what a happy life we could have led as a band of friends if we hadn't been born so differently.

Bahadur and Haridas were of one soul, I could see that at a glance. And yet they were different as oil and water. Haridas loved books almost—almost as much as I did, and Bahadur, as you know, couldn't read a line.

For a fortnight, Haridas was a regular visitor. He would read all morning—and when he discovered I read too, we had some fun together till my master kicked me out with a curse.

Bahadur came in, and took in the scene at a glance.

That's all he needed, just that instant.

His sword flashed, blinding me with terror, for I thought he had certainly beheaded the bookseller.

But he had merely struck off the old man's cap and sent it spinning across the shop.

Nothing more was necessary to make my master treat me with grudging respect—of course it helped that Bahadur bought all the books his friend read.

I often returned to this incident in later years. That was Bahadur's genius—speed. It was his strategy, his strength.

Later, it was called his downfall.

He was seen as arrogant and headstrong. He was none of these, but he did not think like other men. Some say, in derision, his principal advisor was his horse. For certain, Bahadur's response to a crisis, any crisis, was flight.

Towards or away from the crisis?

I don't think he even noticed. Before you could ask that question, he had galloped away.

Why, the day I met Hussam Gujarati, Bahadur had just fled—but I'll arrive at that point later.

I found Hussam Gujarati in Bahadur's camp because I sought him out. Humayun's guards brought him to me in shackles.

For a moment I could not believe that my simple request, 'See if you can find Hussam Gujarati, the scholar' had resulted in such mindless obedience—I had never before given an order.

Apologizing for the rudeness, I had him freed and lodged him in my own tent.

From him I learned the events which are by now, well known, but lack all understanding of the Sultân's personality. This I learned from Hussam Gujarati who had observed the Sultân from his early boyhood, and so was able to confide in me the submerged history of this strange man.

I will begin, therefore, from the first year of his reign, and arrive at the singular collusion of tragedy and desire that was to advise all Bahadur's actions till the very end.

Bahadur Khan became Sultân of Gujarat, and Babar, Padshah of Dilli, in the same year. Having refused the fight at Panipat, Bahadur was eager for details.

It was noted that his questions always related to Humayun. Babar's confidence in his eldest son was a matter of great interest to Bahadur, and he questioned all visitors from Dilli on the appearance and demeanour of the prince.

At the battle of Khanua, Humayun fought alongside his father. From that fight, too, Bahadur kept away.

It could be argued that there were more pressing worries in his own kingdom. The army mutinied. Famine broke out. His brothers died with embarrassing convenience. In Dilli he was spoken of as a murderer.

There was trouble in Diu. He heard of it in Khambat. He was there, as usual with his Khan-e-khanan, his old friend Haridas. He was planning a sailing expedition when the news arrived that Ishaq, the son of Malik Ayaaz was stirring up revolt.

By then it had become a phrase—*Bahaduri*. 'To do a Bahadur' meant to ride fast and furious into the dusk, to disappear into the night and emerge fresh and renewed with the new sun.

And so the Sultân did a *Bahaduri*.[92]

Mateli. Gondi. Dhanduka. Ranpur. Jasdun. Bansawar. Deoli.

At the old fort of Deoli came the news that Ishaq, taking fright at Bahadur's approach, had fled to the Rann.

Bahadur was all for pursuit, but Haridas counseled him otherwise. Bahadur's presence would command peace at Diu. He pointed out that the Firangi were still slavering after Diu. And as for Ishaq, he would deal with the rascal. So Haridas rode into the Rann.

Sikandar bin Manjhu

What's that? A bookworm on the battlefield?

Manjhu

Bookworm? Yes, we are all of us bookworms, but Haridas Pundit could fight too. He had fought alongside the Sultân in many battles, and he was as fearless as Bahadur.

And so he died, transfixed by an arrow from Malik Ishaq.

The news arrived at midnight.

They say Bahadur shot through the night like a thunderbolt on his silver horse Barq, covering 50 kos before dawn.

Nothing more is known of that journey of Bahadur's.

When he returned, the horse collapsed from exhaustion. Bahadur's hands were burned raw. Hakims and vaids buzzed around him even though he wasn't carrion yet. Ten days, and not a word did the Sultân utter. On the eleventh he set out towards Diu, and there he stayed a month. He would return to the island every year after this.

---

92 An act of bravery.

Sikandar bin Manjhu

To lick his wounds?

Manjhu

You can be flippant, you're no Sultân yourself. But you might have been one.

Sikandar bin Manjhu

What do you mean?

Manjhu

Time now to hear the secret of your birth. When were you born?

Sikandar bin Manjhu

The year Muhammad Shah was murdered. He was killed on the 12th day of Rabi-ul-Awwal, in the year 961.

Manjhu

Who murdered him?

Sikandar bin Manjhu

The usual faction, but what does that have to do with me?

Manjhu

Listen, fool, or I will be thinking you are as foolish as your father—

Sikandar bin Manjhu

Why abuse yourself?

Manjhu

Sikandar, Sikandar! Have you looked in the mirror? Are you cross-eyed like me? Dwarfed like me?

Sikandar bin Manjhu

I take after my mother.

Manjhu

That you do, my child.

Sikandar bin Manjhu

I weep for her every day, but you have been father and mother to me, Abbu.

Manjhu

I thank you for those kind words, my son, but I am neither father nor mother to you. You were thrust in my arms—a stinking howling bundle—by Itimad Khan.

Sikandar bin Manjhu

Abbu!

Manjhu

Know that the throne was ruled by a child for years after Bahadur's death. That child grew up to be Mahmud Shah, the worst Sultân Gujarat has ever known. This Sultân was murdered at the very instant your mother gave birth in the royal stables. She was hidden there by her tirewoman, for the Sultân's order was to kill all his pregnant wives and concubines. He was afraid of having sons who might displace him, so he never slept with a woman without first providing her with a potion for abortion. Your mother was one of the houris of Deer Park. Ah, the Deer Park!

Sikandar bin Manjhu

I don't want to hear about the Deer Park. Tell me about my mother!

Manjhu

That's what I am doing.

The Deer Park was big as a battlefield, and cultivated like a forest, but with the most exquisite flower beds.

The Sultân thought bare tree trunks most vulgar, and he had them draped with silks and velvets and the branches were hung with pretty trinkets.

By lamplight—all his frolic took place at night—by lamplight it looked as if the galaxies hovered, their stars dangling like ripe fruit.

Every labyrinth in that bosky forest had a bazaar, and every shop had a houri selling every imaginable pleasure—from delectable sweets and ethereal perfumes to her own generous charms.

Music enchanted the air.

At a signal, nilgai and deer were set loose from their cages and the king and his retinue hunted them by the moon.

Your mother, dear son, was one of the king's houris, and she was with him on the day when he surprised Burhan—

Sikandar bin Manjhu

Who is this Burhan?

Manjhu

Is it possible you've remained so ignorant despite all your reading?

I don't blame you. No book mentions the name of Burhan. But I will!

This Burhan, the son of a stable-hand called Pyare, was a beautiful youth. Naturally, no beautiful boy or maiden escaped the Sultân. So Burhan was appointed the Sultân's valet in no time.

Burhan was ambitious—and promiscuous. Also, he drank, and often with the Sultân.

Now, understand that the Sultân was a holy man, a sheikh-zada, surrounded by holy men who despised the unholy acts of others. So the nobles thought it only prudent to inform the naïve young Sultân that this beautiful youth was a catamite, and a drunken one too.

Naturally, these vices were insupportable to the noble Sultân who needed two hours of maalish every afternoon to recover from his drunken revels with Burhan.

So he called for Burhan to be walled up in the palace.

As the wall was being built, Burhan's grief-stricken parents begged for mercy.

The story goes that the Sultân relented, and became famous for his benevolence.

The truth is a little more murky.

Apparently, the masons who were building the pillar around Burhan got as far as his neck, and then packed up and went home. The next day was a holiday, and the day after that too, so it was on the third day that they got back to the job.

By then, the Sultân had already entered the palace with his retinue. As he passed the half-built pillar, Burhan raised his eyes in reproach. The Sultân, stricken to the soul, immediately ordered Burhan's release.

Because the boy was half dead from exhaustion, the Sultân had him encased in cottonwool and nursed in the royal bedchamber. Vaids and hakims hung around till he recovered.

Burhan got his old job back, and no more was said about drunkenness or promiscuity.

But one evening in the Deer Park, Burhan wandered off arm-in-arm with a sweet-voiced boy. On the usual hunt, the Sultân, in pursuit of some hapless beast, burst into that very moonlit grove where Burhan and his lover were entwined in the throes of ungovernable passion.

Although he was famous for his fits of jealous rage, the noble Sultân did nothing. Perhaps the presence of your noble mother at his side consoled him.

Months passed.

One afternoon at the height of summer, complaining of a headache, Sultân Mahmud Shah asked for sharbat. Sipping the sweet refreshment, he was overtaken by nausea. He cried out, 'Burhan, you have poisoned me!'

Burhan, with his usual blandishments, assured him it was just the heat, worries of the state, his poor digestion. Nothing that couldn't be fixed with a pastille of this sweet majoon.

The trusting Sultân accepted the majoon, and lay down drowsily, his long hair trailing over the head-rest. The young brute lavished a lover's caresses on the Sultân's perfumed mane, and then deftly knotted it round the chair.

There lay Mahmud Shah, deeply drugged, neck extended on offer to the lightning sword.

Burhan was no common criminal. This was not going to be a crime of passion.

He slit the Sultân's throat with a small clever knife, and staunched the boiling geyser of blood with the Sultân's own turban. Those twenty yards of Dhaka muslin compacted into a brick of congealing gore.

Then, locking the bedchamber, Burhan sent for the Bagh Mar.

Ah, you won't know them. They were disbanded by Itimad Khan.

The Bagh Mar were the Sultân's most trusted men, twelve hundred of them, and each had killed a tiger with his bare hands. Wazirs had no power over them. They answered only to the Sultân.

Because they knew—who didn't?—that the Sultân's catamite was his closest confidante, they came at once when Burhan summoned them.

Burhan told them the Sultân was resting, shocked by the discovery that his trusted amirs had hatched a plot to assassinate him. He commanded the Bagh Mar to stand guard in the antechamber.

They should know the Sultân had already issued an urgent summons to these rascally nobles—his wazir led the list. As each noble entered the antechamber, the Sultân relied on his Bagh Mars to strike instantly.

The Bagh Mars' fidelity to the Sultân was absolute.

The amirs' sense of duty towards their Sultân was equally strong.

One by one the amirs entered the antechamber.

Each was despatched on the instant, to heaven or hell, as the case may be.

It was then, even as whispers rustled like dry leaves at every window, it was at that villainous hour that Itimad Khan burst into my humble study—and before I could rise from my desk, he had dropped a stinking bloodstained bundle into my lap.

You!

And you burst into such a wail of helplessness and despair, what else could I do but comfort you?

You burrowed into my crooked wickerwork chest, searching for a breast.

'Keep him!' Itimad Khan said tersely.

From his very terseness, I understood. You were his child.

Sikandar bin Manjhu

Impossible! Everybody knows Itimad Khan was a eunuch.

Manjhu

Yes, the story of Itimad Khan's balls is universally known.

He grew up with his scrotum encased in a velvet purse of camphor. The fragrant vapours singed his testicles and shriveled them into peanuts. And so, the pretty youth had been sold in the slave market as a eunuch.

The credulous Sultân gave him charge of the harem. The ladies delighted in the aura of camphor that enveloped Itimad Khan. I am told it made them swoon with a delicious coolness on sultry afternoons.

Your mother, poor woman, was one of the many, and she died giving birth to you.

She had to be concealed from spies who reported immediately to the Sultân any sign of morning sickness or increasing girth. The harem's rations were checked daily for the presence of tart green fruit—mango, lemon, amla, tamarind.

I don't know how Itimad Khan managed to dodge such vigilance and hide her in the stables.

Sikandar bin Manjhu

But the Pīr says Sultân Mahmud Shah was a holy man.

Manjhu

Well, wouldn't he? The Sheikhs had the poor man by the short and curlies. Look at the things they made him do. They got him to war against the Hindus—the Grassias, the Rajputs. He looted their land, and had every one of them branded like cattle.

No Hindu was allowed within Mahmudabad unless he wore a red-and-white badge that denounced him as a kafir. This, by a Tank Sultân, in the land of Tank and Khatri!

And who are these Sheikhs? They are all men who have no allegiance to Gujarat. Men of Bukhara, Afghanistan, Rum, Abyssinia. Yes, they have allegiance to the Sultânate—but not to the people. Sultâns come and go, but the people make up the permanence of a land. It is their memory that survives.

Sikandar bin Manjhu

Oh, I won't agree there. History is about kings and their conquests, also about their follies. And the people? They are unsung, like you and I.

Manjhu

I will die unsung, but my son, that is not what I wish for you. Write your history any way you will. I will tell you all I know, but make of it what you wish.

††††

Sikandar excused himself. His tumult was too private even for his father's loving eyes.

This ugly wizened old librarian was his only family, and today even that relationship had been erased.

A cold rage stilled him.

Manjhu [he would never think of him as Abbu again] had kept with the Syeds out of expedience, and had encouraged him to do the same. Now it appeared Manjhu had no loyalties: neither to Humayun, nor to Bahadur Shah, nor to the holy Pīr Syed Mubarak or his fauladis, and definitely not to the dissolute Mahmud Shah, nor to the eunuch wazir Itimad Khan—What was he saying?—*nor to his* father, *Itimad Khan.*

The observer in Sikandar pointed out that it made Manjhu the ideal historian, but Sikandar still kept a few loyalties. To whom? The stupid Sultân, Ahmad Shah? To Syed Mubarak and his son, who were even now, capitulating to the Mughal? To the land and its people, Hindu and Mussalman alike?

That last was Manjhu's only loyalty, one Sikandar didn't share in the least.

His only loyalty was to the faith.

He would write a just history. He would judge these Sultâns by the faith they were meant to uphold.

But he would not be telling Manjhu that.

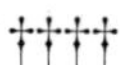

Sikandar bin Manjhu

Please continue, I will take notes as you speak.

Manjhu

You are grieved, my son.

Sikandar bin Manjhu

I am not your son. Speak!

Tell me, what did Humayun's diamond have to do with the fortunes of Gujarat?

Manjhu

You must understand that I was an eyewitness.

For the two years I spent as his librarian, Humayun's pattern of life had become mine too. I was part of his luggage. The only thing genuine about Humayun was his love of books, and for that, I loved him. But he was indolent, and never waited long enough to absorb what he read. Ask him about it two days later, and he would be clueless. Still, I wasn't complaining. I had clean clothes, two meals a day, and as many books as I wished to read—or as many as I could read, for my wishes truly exceeded my cranial capacity.

This is how Humayun became Padshah.

In the month of Zul-Hijjah, on its 9th day, in the year 935.[93]

Humayun and his train left Qila-e-Zafar at Badakhshan without a firman from the Padshah. It was, indeed, an ignoble act, irresponsible and irrational. It left the town exposed to invasion from the Auzbegs. Without a unifying head, the Qila couldn't possibly defend itself, so they sent for Saeed Khan of Kashgar, inviting him to march into Badakhshan with his army.

The following month, the Kashgaris marched towards Badakhshan. They halted when they found that Humayun had already sent his younger brother Hindal Mirza to take his place at Qila-e-Zafar.

Now this Hindal was at that time, just ten years of age. Only Humayun's arrogance could imagine that even as a figurehead a ten year old could reconcile those fierce hotheaded chiefs.

Meanwhile, the Kashgaris, now unable to advance for fear of provoking Babar's wrath, found themselves stranded in the snow. Neighboring towns and villages refused them entry. The Pamir routes soon closed for winter, and the Kashgaris, left to starve, took to plundering innocents.

You can imagine what this did to Babar when the news reached him. Humayun's idiocy had antagonized the entire lot of tribal chiefs Babar had worked so hard to subdue.

---

93 26 August 1529 A.D.

When we reached Dilli, the Padshah expressed his displeasure and Humayun was ordered to his *subah*[94] at Sambhal. We cooled our heels there while Babar had to go in person to settle the northwest.

Maham Begum, Humayun's mother, was terrified lest the Padshah pass over Humayun and instead choose his son-in-law, Mohammad Zaman Mirza, as successor.

Luckily for Humayun, he fell ill.

At first it was a fever. Then a jaundice, for he was already much given to drink. Then the fever returned, this time smouldering in his bones like a slow fire. His mind began to wander.

The hakims and vaids of Sambhal soon washed their hands of him, so we put him on a bier and transported him on the Jamuna to Agra. I went with him, for my job was to keep his waking hours amused with stories of Sinbad.

The queen Maham Begam met the barge at Mathura. She brought with her a famous vaid of that town who took one quick look at the prince and said his life could only be saved by great sacrifice.

Now that is the kind of prescription a doctor offers when he wants to save his own neck.

Later, at Agra, when several venerable hakims echoed the vaid's opinion, the Padshah took it literally.

He sent for all his scholars [this humble librarian was among them] and asked us to explicate on the words 'great sacrifice.'

One must give up an object of great value for the common good, he was told.

Sikandar bin Manjhu

Give up to whose safekeeping?

Manjhu

Why the Almighty's! And his representatives on earth, the Ulema were swift to reply.

An object of great value, they stressed. So valuable that, converted into money, it might feed all the people in the world for two whole days.

This, as you know, being the accepted value of Humayun's Diamond, it was quite clear what the Ulema considered a worthy sacrifice.

They went further. They reminded the Padshah that the Diamond came from an infidel and was very likely accursed. It would have to be exorcised of all its demonic uncleanness.

'Really?' the Padshah remarked thoughtfully. 'Do you really think the diamond is Humayun's most valuable possession?'

I could have told those beards what was coming, but they were so full of flatulence, they simply chorussed, 'The diamond! The diamond!'

'So you set the value of a paltry bit of glass higher than—myself?'

The assembly was nonplussed.

---

94 Urdu … صوبہ … province.

A senior cleric ventured the opinion that Jahan-panah was not, strictly speaking, an object, and so he could not be properly considered a possession.

Besides, suggested a second, the Padshah's value was incalculable.

'Precisely,' Babar responded. 'I am, indeed, the most valuable of Humayun's possessions, and I, therefore, offer myself.'

Hazrat Walida cried out, 'What matters Humayun's life to you? You are a king! You have other sons. But I—I have just this one—'

[It smote me to see how her words extinguished the light in Princess Gulbadan's eyes. You may not know that Maham Begam had recently adopted these children, Gulbadan Begam and Hindal Mirza, as her own.]

The Padshah answered her calmly, but with great sternness and dignity. 'Maham! Although I have other sons, I love none as I love your Humayun. I crave that this cherished child may have his heart's desire and live long, and I desire the kingdom for him and not for the others, because he has not his equal in distinction.'

Straightaway he hurried to Humayun's bedchamber, and there consecrated his life to the Almighty, praying that his sacrifice might be accepted and his son's life spared.

And so, as we all know, it came to pass.

Humayun kept the diamond and got the throne.

Sikandar bin Manjhu

But what does that have to do—

Manjhu

—with Gujarat? Patience, lad.

When Bahadur Shah heard the story, he had his jewellers calculate the value of the diamond and his accountants compared it against the value of the jagir he had been refused by his father. He would repeat Babar Padshah's words (for by then they were common knowledge) in wonderment, and question Hussam Gujarati closely about Humayun's attributes.

Now here came Bahadur's second pitfall. Hussam Gujarati had no personal acquaintance with the Mughals, so Bahadur looked out for someone who did. And that's how he found that rascal who caused his downfall.

Sikandar bin Manjhu

Mulla Mohammad Munshi?

Manjhu

That is a name that is as good as no name. Anybody can be a Mulla Mohammad Munshi.

Sikandar bin Manjhu

Who was he?

Manjhu

Aha! He was a munshi in Humayun's court. More than that, I don't know. After a certain incident, anonymity became his best defense.

There are dozens of such scribes—accountants, letter writers—sitting with little desks at the ready to inscribe the whims of state. Letters, accounts, firman, and verse, always verse! Terrible poetry, sentimental trash.

Dilli amirs get the poetic urge without notice, the way old men get bowel movements and young men get erections.

One afternoon, the young Padshah felt a verse coming on and sent for this Munshi.

The royal summons waylaid the Munshi on his way to the water-closet. It was his first pilgrimage in that direction in three days, but the emperor's poem would brook no delay. So, now he sat in a clench, qalam in hand, praying the Padshah's inspiration be immediate and very brief.

Of course, it wasn't.

And as the Padshah dithered over a rhyme, sweat rained from the unfortunate Munshi's brow. His usually brown skin turned crimson. His pupils were black pools of terror.

The Clench was no longer sufficient to hold back the excrement.

'Have you written that?' Humayun asked.

The Munshi's attention was all on his bowels, and he heard not the Padshah's question.

His health and his dignity hinged not so much on relief, but on the manner of it. On its physical state, so to speak.

True, the solids were in rapid advance under the surge of deep currents. What if he took the wind out of their sails? That would leave them in the doldrums, torpid and inert, at least for the length of the Padshah's poem.

That called for some expert maneuvering of the nether parts. How was he to manage this under the royal gaze?

With the greatest delicacy, he raised his left buttock. For fine tuning, a certain degree of tightening was essential. He had almost accomplished it all, when the Padshah repeated his question.

With an imperious gesture, the Munshi silenced the emperor and completed his delicate adjustments.

'Wretch! Is this how you address your Padshah?' thundered Humayun.

In answer, out issued an equally thunderous volley of farts.

Sulfurous, stinking, scandalous.

Roseate with relief, the Munshi sang out, joyously, 'Ah sire! You may be the Padshah, but this humble Munshi is the true Shah of Paạd!'[95]

Sikandar bin Manjhu

You made up that story!

---

[95] Urdu … پاد … fart.

Manjhu

Take it or leave it.

Bahadur Shah guffawed with laughter when he heard it. It was his first laugh since the death of his friend. And seeing that, some well-meaning halfwit, thinking this filthy fellow might as well be the Sultân's clown, sent a messenger to bring him to Gujarat.

The Munshi was in hiding, as you can imagine, and the messenger had a hard time locating him. But he came willingly enough, only too glad to escape Humayun's wrath.

Hussam Gujarati says he was a man of low taste, quarrelsome, and of ribald wit. However he managed to insinuate himself into the Sultân's good graces.

In court this Munshi was the very soul of courtesy, and from him Bahadur got all his information about Humayun.

About this time Hussam Gujarati accompanied Bahadur to Malwa, where they camped in a village called Sambalia, awaiting Sultân Mahmud Khilji.

Now the Khilji had his throne by the grace of Bahadur's father, but he was reluctant to meet Bahadur.

After two days, Sultân Mahmud Khilji sent an excuse. He had broken his arm, which prevented him from travelling.

Insults of this sort never bothered Bahadur. He merely asked the envoy to speak the truth. The envoy said Sultân Mahmud prevaricated because he feared Bahadur might demand of him the handover of Prince Chand Khan, Bahadur's brother, who had taken refuge in Malwa.

Bahadur had no such design, and was grieved by the suspicion cast on him. He sent back a message saying he would come to Mandu himself, as the Sultân of Malwa could not travel.

And then, of course, he took Mandu.

Soon after, another event occurred which changed him overnight.

Without his friend Haridas, Bahadur's fits of anger and melancholy became frequent. He isolated himself by riding out in fury. His beloved horse Barq had never recovered from that terrible ride into the desert. It died soon after that, wounded in a small skirmish. Its son, Kuchak Barq became the Sultân's mount, and showed great bravery on the battlefield at Mandu. That horse now was the closest Bahadur had to a friend.

But there was someone else too.

When Bahadur inherited Sikandar Shah's throne, he also inherited his harem. All the women he sent home with gifts or dower—save one.

Nazuk Bahar.

Bahadur's mother had readied a harem full of beauties for the Sultân, but the only one he ever visited was Nazuk Bahar.

I have the story from one of the eunuchs. I got him drunk so that I could learn the truth.

This girl was beautiful, of course, and like all her kind, a gilded butterfly. She ruled Bahadur with a miser's grasp. He could deny her nothing, and she took everything. The old Bahadur hadn't noticed her silly talk and her venal and selfish ways, but they irked him now.

The eunuch reported that very often Bahadur's visits were limited to the making of peace offerings with silks and jewels. Nazuk Bahar had her own palace, her own army of cooks, maids, slaves—and, I've heard, she had mirrors everywhere.

Soon after he took Mandu, he was all for building her a luxurious palace there, but the girl refused to move out of Mahmudabad.

Bahadur was besotted. No matter how far his adventures took him, he would ride back at the first opportunity to spend an hour with her.

Had the girl been ambitious, Bahadur's amirs would have had her poisoned, but she was just a greedy little fool, poor thing!

And then she overplayed her hand.

It was her game to strip Bahadur of all his finery at each visit and send him back in a simple white kurta pajama. And, of course, it delighted Bahadur.

But there was one jewel he would not part with—the ring Haridas had given him at his coronation— a fine emerald, encircled with diamonds.

One evening she demanded it for the thousandth time, and he, for the thousandth time, refused.

As usual, in recompense, he lavished more gifts, more treasure, more gold on her.

It was unusual for him to stay the night, but he did, that evening.

He woke, startled, in the small hours.

A vise gripped his hand—or so he thought, but only after his other hand had found his dagger.

The blade gleamed in the moonlight, and then dimmed as his vision dimmed, slammed by a sharp jet of blood.

His hand was still imprisoned, tighter now, impossible to free.

He cried out and this eunuch came running, lamp in hand.

What a sight the light revealed!

Bahadur's hand was in the grip of Nazuk Bahar, her slender fingers tight around his emerald ring.

His blade had caught her with deadly precision, across the neck.

She died before she had even sensed that he was awake.

Her face [said the eunuch] was intent and wary, still absorbed in the task that death had interrupted.

Bahadur was crazed with grief.

The eunuch managed, somehow, to free the dagger from his grasp, afraid he might do himself an injury.

Bahadur would let nobody touch the dead girl. He bathed the body himself, dressed it in finery, and on a flaccid finger he placed that coveted ring.

Then he rushed to his horse and galloped away.

Sikandar bin Manjhu

To Diu, I imagine, to lick his wounds?

Manjhu

You may imagine what you wish, but these are the facts. From then on, his generosity and his weakness for luxuries and beautiful things became even more marked. He kept buying fine things and jewels as if Nazuk Bahar were still greedy for them. He would gift them away to anyone who approached him.

Talking of jewels, it was around this time that he regained the famous belt.

Sikandar bin Manjhu

What? The belt that was lost at Kapparbanj?

Manjhu

The very same. And this is how it happened.

On the fourth day of Shawwal, 938,[96] the fortress of Raisina became a charnel house. Bahadur, as always, offered safe conduct to women and children trapped inside the surrounded fortress, but what can be more bitter than such charity?

Silhadi, the Rajput, had been in Bahadur's custody for a year. During this time, he had turned Mussalman. He was a man of great wealth, and greater luxury, almost as decadent as the famous Malik Gopi of Muzaffar Shah's court. His son, Bhupat Rai was loyal to Bahadur to the very end. Silhadi was one of the great Rajput lords, and his fortress of Raisina was in the care of his brother Lakshman Dev.

When Raisina was surrounded, Lakshman Dev and his nobles came out to acknowledge Bahadur. He told Bahadur that Silhadi's harem, of more than 800 women, was in the fort. Bahadur asked him to bring them all out and move them to safety.

But Rani Durgawati, Silhadi's principal wife and the mother of Bhupat, kicked up a fuss. She refused to budge unless her husband came in person to escort her.

And so Silhadi was sent into the fort, along with Malik Ali Sher.

Silhadi's intent was to bring them all out to safety.

After having entered the fort, he was assailed by the bitter reproaches of Durgawati. Malik Ali Sher watched him disappear into a big crowd of elders. Their angry voices rang out, but the Malik was saved the trouble of eavesdropping, for soon Silhadi conducted him right into his harem. There were more than a thousand women there. Ali Sher would say later he had never seen so much beauty at one glance before or after.

And, before Ali Sher's disbelieving eyes, the slaughter began.

Sikandar bin Manjhu

Slaughter? I thought they burnt themselves.

Manjhu

And is that not slaughter?

But that was later.

Sihaldi cut the throats of his women to save them from the pain of being burnt alive.

Sikandar bin Manjhu

Some of the women may have been Mussalman.

---

[96] 10 May 1532

Manjhu

Of course they were. What difference does that make? Are there no Hindu women in the harems of Sultâns?

Sikandar bin Manjhu

It is the Sultân's duty to rescue Mussalman women in distress.

Manjhu

You can say so in your history if you like, I can't stop you.

Bahadur tried to intervene and stop them from such dastardly murder, but Silhadi was bent upon it, and sent out a message through Ali Sher defying Bahadur to do his worst.

And Bahadur did.

It was a battle, wasn't it? What did you expect him to do, flee?

Sikandar bin Manjhu

The blood of all those women is on his soul.

Manjhu

I don't agree. He gave them safe conduct, and he was never known to break his word. Save that for the Mughal! The women killed themselves because they had been brought up in the belief that it is the honourable thing to do.

Sikandar bin Manjhu

And you don't think it was?

Manjhu

No, I do not. Life is precious and sacred and we must deal with what it gives us. I say that, I, born to ugliness and rejection and loneliness. Even I say that.

Sikandar bin Manjhu

I disagree. Bahadur was a murderer.

Manjhu

You are the historian!

When Bahadur entered the fort, smoke blinded him.

The huge pit of fire, the *jauhar-kund* writhed with bodies fighting to flee the heat. Many of the women were still alive.

Piteous voices cried out to him through the haze of smoke.

An arm, a face, a leg flashed before exploding into cindery flames.

When the fire died down—it burnt all night—Bahadur descended into that pit. While the ashes were still smoking he raked them with his fingers.

The onlookers thought he had gone mad.

They stepped back, wary, watchful.

He was in there a long while.

When he climbed out his cloak was filled with jewels he had picked from the ashes.

He held out his cloak to Burhan-ul-Mulk, and that worthy accepted it, much to general disgust.

Later, I learned that he had understood Bahadur's intent better than others did.

That treasure was given to the poor and the starving.

And Silhadi's luxurious ladies, who had never known a moment of discomfort in their pampered lives, provided dal and rotla to the famished of Raisina.

Sikandar bin Manjhu

He could have fed them out of his own pocket, couldn't he?

Manjhu

If you are determined to despise Bahadur Shah, you can say so in your history. *I* will stick to facts.

Sikandar bin Manjhu

I thought you were telling me about the famous belt. Or did that cost Bahadur one more *jauhar?*

Manjhu

Not then. That was yet to come.

But following the *jauhar* at Raisina, Bahadur became distanced from everybody. At the same time, he was more energetic than ever. He drove out the Firangi from Diu—and there too he met the man who would destroy him.

Sikandar bin Manjhu

I thought he had met him already, that farting Mullah.

Manjhu

The mullah merely started the affair. This man lost Bahadur his crown. Rumi Khan—like Mohammad Mullah Munshi—another non-name.

But Rumi Khan was not of Rum. He was of Roos, I think. He was a master of guns. He had brought with him Laila and Majnun, two huge cannons that Bahadur had conveyed all the way to Champaner. Rumi Khan trained the army in cannonade, and Bahadur was the first among the Khan's students.

At this time, while preparing the army at Mahmudabad, Bahadur married the daughter of Jam Firoz of Sindh.

Sikandar bin Manjhu

Ah.

Manjhu

What does that mean?

Sikandar bin Manjhu

A Sultân's duty is to produce heirs. I hear he did not do his duty very well.

Manjhu

You are very well informed, considering you were born a decade after the death of the Sultân.

Do you, or do you not, want to hear about the damned belt?

Sikandar bin Manjhu

Continue, please.

Manjhu

The army was for Chittorgarh.

Sikandar bin Manjhu

Rana Sanga was dead by now, right?

Manjhu

And his son Ratan Singh too. The new Rana now was his nephew Vikramjit, a fool, sadly named Vikramaditya! Weak, quarrelsome, malicious.

Sikandar bin Manjhu

You would say that. He was the enemy—

Manjhu

The Rajputs said that too. The nobles loathed him, but that was not Bahadur's concern.

Vikramjit had sent his army to Raisina—beaten back, of course, but still that made him the enemy. Besides, he had been making small vicious attacks on Malwa.

If you remember my telling you, Bahadur coveted Chittor. It was an impossible goal as long as Rana Sanga was alive.

Sikandar bin Manjhu

What about Rana Sanga's wife, the Rani who saved Bahadur's life? Was she dead too?

Manjhu

Rani Karnavati? No, she wasn't dead. She was the real power behind Vikramjit and the nobles when Bahadur marched with an army of a million or more to Chittorgarh.

Let me tell you how he did that.

First, he sent the guns and artillery to Mandu. Hussam Gujarati went with them, and he told me such an arsenal had never been seen anywhere before.

Bahadur had modeled his artillery on Firangi lines. The Firangi Dalbukhidki had such an arsenal in Goa and he had shown it to Malik Ayaaz, but that was twenty years ago. When the guns reached Mandu, Bahadur rode out from Mahmudabad, making the journey in just 3 days. What a horse that Kuchak Barq was! What a man was the Sultân!

Sikandar bin Manjhu

Enough praise. Give me facts.

Manjhu

Facts, then.

When the advance guard (Hussam Gujarati among them) reached Mandsor—ah Mandsor! The name drives a stake in my heart—

Sikandar bin Manjhu

Why? You weren't there, were you?

Manjhu

Patience, son—

Sikandar bin Manjhu

I am not your son. Continue.

Manjhu

At Mandsor, Hussam Gujarati read out to the amirs a message from Chittor. It begged for reconciliation, as abject a surrender as can be imagined.

It was sent by pigeon post to the Sultân—who laughed it off.

Quite rightly, too. He did not believe a line of it.

Tatar Khan, the son of Alam Khan, [sometime Sultân Alauddin Lodi] was in command, and when the pigeon flapped back from Mandsor, off he marched to Chittor.

Chittorgarh has seven gates, and Tatar Khan had opened two of them, but not a whimper out of the Rajputs as yet. They were simply not willing to fight. By then the guns and artillery had arrived, and, with them, Rumi Khan.

Sikandar bin Manjhu

The Russian?

Manjhu

The same. They surrounded the hill of Chittorgarh, and the Sultân, riding 100 kos in a night—

Sikandar bin Manjhu

That's simply not possible.

Manjhu

I was going to say a night and half a day, but how can I speak the truth if you keep interrupting? Hussam Gujarati said Bahadur rested for a day, sleeping like a baby while the army waited below, and the Rajputs worried above.

That night, though, Bahadur moved the guns. He worked like a common soldier, shoulder to shoulder with the meanest of them, clad like them, covered in mud, sharing their rations, so that many of them did not recognize him as they took orders from Rumi Khan.

The great guns, Laila and Majnun were hauled uphill and loaded.

The battery began.

With each cannonade, a portion of the hill seemed to crumble and fall away.

Meanwhile, a segment of the army was sent to ravage the fields in the lowland.

Without a single life being lost on either side, Chittorgarh was surrounded.

And still, despite the roar of guns, and the quaking hilltop, the Rajputs would not give battle.

The generals were puzzled.

Rumi Khan was all for mining the walls, but Bahadur stopped him with a smile.

People are quick to condemn Bahadur as impulsive, but his great strength in battle was his patience.

Sure enough, the envoy brought a second missive, this time from Rani Karnavati, offering to restitute the usurped territory of Malwa, and, I quote the exact words of her letter, as recorded by Hussam Gujarati —

... the golden girdle and the jeweled crown and cap which belonged to Sultân Mahmud, and the value of which jewellers are unable to estimate, and which were won on the day of our victory over that Sultân.

The girdle stolen at Kapparbanj from Sultân Qutbuddin—the girdle that was nobody's, that had been Dewal Rani's for an instant, but which belonged really to the dead daughter of the jeweller who crafted it. That girdle, was now offered to Bahadur Shah.

He accepted the terms of surrender.

Hussam Gujarati said when he finally beheld the girdle, the Bahadur's face lost its usual mask of grief.

Perhaps it was the flash of its many gems that animated his features.

He did not send it to his treasury at Mahmudabad.

It remained, from the moment he received it, always in his possession. I will return to it later.

Time now for me to recall the stinking Mullah—

Sikandar bin Manjhu

Ah. Now you must tell the story from your vantage. Where were you when Bahadur was grabbing—

Manjhu

—*extending his kingdom* is the term you are looking for.

We were doing the same, at the Mughal court. I say we, because Humayun never travelled without his library.

When Humayun ascended the throne, his empire was bounded in the northwest by the Amu Darya. Badakhshan, Nalkh, Qunduz, Kabul, Qandahar, Ghazni, they were all Mughal before the victory at Panipat. Punjab and Multan were almost completely his. South of Multan, Sindh was Arghun territory. The Jamuna at Allahabad formed the boundary in the east. But the Doab was all Mughal. To the west, Dilli and Agra. To the east, Allahabad, Chunar, Benaras. North of the Ganga, Sambhal, Bahraich, Lucknow. Ayodhya, Gorakhpur, Ballia. Oh, it was an empire, alright, all of Hindustan![97]

Not all of Hindustan, not yet. Argun, Bengal, Chittor and the Afghans, always the Afghans, still held out. And of course, Gujarat.

Humayun did not see himself as a conqueror like his father. But he wasn't complacent either. In the first year as Padshah he captured the fort of Kalinjar, almost as inaccessible as Chittorgarh. This was an opportune victory as it allowed Humayun to assume the title of Ghazi for having conquered an infidel Raja. There followed other successes: he won a battle at Dadrah against the Afghans, and, more importantly, he won over Sher Khan.

Meanwhile, news of Bahadur's exploits was a constant buzz in the Dilli court. It was not as though Humayun was particularly interested—but the amirs and baigs were. In the first two years of his reign, not only had Bahadur won over all the dissidents in Gujarat, but he had acquired the fabulous kingdom of Malwa as well. Then came the Dakkan. All those

---

97 *Hindustan/Hindostan:* From the Farsi هندوستان … The land of the river *Sindhu* [Indus] became the toponym for the subcontinent from its western limit at the Sutlej to Varanasi in the east. The sound change for *s* to *h* in Proto-Iranian occurred in mid 9th century BCE. By the time of Alexander's invasion, *Hindu* applied to Sindh and the lands east of it. From the beginning of the Common Era, *-stan* was suffixed, as an indicative of place.

little Sultânates were vassals by now. Twice he had chased away the firang. Egypt and Istanbul formed a ring of protection around his eighty-seven ports.

Oh yes, Bahadur was Shah of more than Gujarat, the richest kingdom in Hindustan. And for all the camaraderie the Rajputs pretended with the Mughals, they were, all of them, Bahadur's cousins, so there was no telling how the wind might turn!

The Hazra Walida Maham Begam could not stand this. So she compelled Humayun to hold lavish festivities that would dazzle the world with their magnificence. Under pain of death the starvelings of Agra were forced to decorate their homes with flags and flowers—and pay for these frivolities too. Illuminations from Cheen, musicians and dancers who were surely on loan from paradise, and the sweet scents of flowers made the nights all too short for the follies they began. The gifts Humayun made were without compare: 12,000 khilats with gold buttons were given to the amirs. How much more would it take to keep them loyal to Humayun?

And then came Humayun's splendid plan, one that deeply involved me—the foundation of a new city.

The Lodis were bloody kings, and the Tughlaqs were even worse. Push further back, and you have the murderous Alauddin Khilji.

Humayun wanted a city that would not carry this bloodstained past. A capital for the exchange of thought and knowledge. The idea came to him when he was at Gwalior—around the time that Bahadur Shah was getting ready to storm Chittor. He went to Gwalior for another round of public festivities, just in case Bahadur had failed to notice the Dilli extravaganza.

At Gwalior, Humayun was weighed against coin, a practice in Hindustan since the beginning of time. He weighed 15,000 tankas, and the money was distributed among the people.

We hurried back to Agra at the news of Maham Begam's illness. After her death, Humayun concentrated on his plan for a new city.

He chose Indrapath, telling his Hindu subjects that the ancient capital of the Pandavas once more had a just and wise ruler. The arrogance of kings is something only another king can understand—you can bet Sadhuram and his wife had a hearty laugh in their hovel.

The Pandavas had certainly chosen intelligently. The Aravalli hills formed a bow and the Jamuna the bowstring. Within this, lay the arc of power.

Look at the older Dillis—Qila Rai Pithaura, Siri, Jahanpanah, Firuzabad.

None of them is planned like Deenpanah.

Deenpanah is simply—magnificent.

And, can you believe, the city was built in just nine months!

In Mohurram of the year 940[98] Humayun consulted his jyotish—he was a great student of both astrology and astronomy. At the chosen hour, he laid the foundation stone. It was completed in Shawwal of the same year.

The Library was designed by me, but I never saw it built. I had expected to be allowed to remain as Librarian, but I soon saw that Humayun had more exalted ideas.

---

[98] July 1533

With his customary grace he bestowed on me a new title—that of Traveling Librarian.

I was stuck in this miserable rut for life. I lost interest in Deenpanah. I made plans to abscond, but a one-eyed dwarf is soon found, and my ugly head would be staring out from the spikes of Lal Darwaza, stinking in the sun.

So I stayed.

There were festivities, more magnificent than those at Agra or Gwalior.

Bahadur Shah of Gujarat sent a graceful letter of congratulation, and Humayun wrote back with equal warmth. This was their first exchange.

Just around this time, Mohammad Zaman Mirza, Humayun's brother-in-law, on whom had been settled several jagirs in Bihar, allied with his brother and nephews and began organizing a rebellion against the throne. Small fry, really. I don't blame Humayun for thinking they could be easily dealt with. He had them captured and thrown in prison, and of course, being the ocean of mercy that he was, he would not have them hanged or trampled by elephants, but only blinded.

But Zaman Mirza, a youth of some charm, managed to subvert his jailer. He escaped with his eyes intact, and found his way to Gujarat.

Now Bahadur Shah had decided that his court must rival Deenpanah, and he was far more generous and less exacting than Humayun. Scholars, artists, musicians were made welcome and maintained with rich gifts and much appreciation. But there were others too—travellers, renegade mercenaries, mystics, craftsmen, jewellers and political refugees. Of these, Zaman Mirza and the former Alauddin Lodi, now Alam Khan, were both Humayun's enemies.

Alam Khan had escaped from his prison in Qila Zafar in Badakhshan and returned to his old refuge, the Gujarat court. Bahadur had no great respect for this jackal, but Alam Khan's son, who was of the same age as Bahadur, was a different man. Tatar Khan was a skilled warrior and very soon proved himself in Bahadur's army. He sought Bahadur's help in organizing an assault on Agra in a bid to restore his father to the throne. Bahadur was not ready for that, but he did like the idea.

Humayun was at Kalpi on his way to dealing with the Afghans when he heard that both his enemies had been given sanctuary in Gujarat. Bahadur might use these two renegades to organize an assault on Dilli. Shaken, Humayun returned to Agra.

And none too soon. Tatar Khan was knocking at the door. Bahadur Shah had sent him out with orders to keep the campaign defensive, but Tatar Khan was no strategist.

Already, with an army of 40,000 men, Tatar Khan had taken Bayana.

Humayun sent his brothers Hindal and Askari Mirza to rout Tatar Khan. Bayana was recovered, and Tatar Khan's army, seeing the determination of the Mughal charge, deserted almost to a man.

Bahadur had planned this as a diversion—his actual target was Chittorgarh. The belt had only bought a temporary truce. The fool Vikramjit spent all his time in the company of wrestlers, and the disgusted Sisodias had washed their hands of him. The promise of restoring Bahadur's territory was ignored. A second assault seemed in order, and, with the Rajput fraternizing with the Mughals, Bahadur needed Humayun to be looking the other way.

Hindal Mirza, with an army of 5,000, pursued Tatar Khan into Mandrael. Tatar Khan had a few thousand men left—no match against the Mughal killing machine. But he flung himself, Rajput like, at the enemy—and died.

Both Humayun and Bahadur chose to ignore this skirmish. Humayun never claimed Bahadur had a role in Tatar Khan's attack, and Bahadur never acknowledged any. It ended Alam Khan Lodi's pretensions too.

But sheltering Zaman Mirza was quite another thing. Humayun's first response was to march to Gwalior. He considered that should be warning enough for Bahadur.

The letter writing began.

Humayun expressed his displeasure at Bahadur's hospitality towards Zaman Mirza.

Bahadur replied avowing total ignorance of any enmity between Humayun and the Mirza, hastening to assure Humayun of his friendship.

But he did nothing to extradite Zaman Mirza.

This made Humayun angry. He wrote back, ominously, '*The most helpless man is he who had a friend, but has managed to lose him.*'

So it went, back and forth, till the rascally Mullah wrote the last letter. Hussam Gujarati only heard of it afterwards.

The mullah read the letter out to Bahadur and his amirs late at night when they were all far gone with Firangi wine, and by daybreak, it was on its way to Humayun.

A cold water shower and a sharp rebuke from his wazir made Bahadur panic, and he sent a courier after the letter-bearer. He should have ridden out himself, the only horseman fast enough to overtake the royal *dakiya*.[99] But the letter reached its mark.

Sikandar bin Manjhu

Why, what did it say?

Manjhu

One jibe after another, witless insults.

I remember the moment when it was read by the Padshah. He simply dropped it to the floor and walked away.

I followed him, knowing he would not resent my presence in his refuge.

When I reached the Library, I did not reveal myself. Humayun was weeping. Not tears of rage, but bitter tears of sorrow, as one sheds when a friend has proved a traitor.

But Humayun's nobility never lasted very long.

Sikandar bin Manjhu

What did the letter say?

---

[99] Urdu … ڈاکیا … postman.

Manjhu

If thy sword hast no tongue [to speak of your valour],
Do not trouble the sword of thy tongue by mere boast.
If thy sword hast no lustre, my son,
Do not brag of thy father's noble descent.
If thou art short-statured, do not tie wooden legs to thy feet,
To look tall in children's eyes.
By the grace of God, so long as I am ruler of this country,
No king dare challenge my army.
Why do you, who have so far only faced a few Afghans, give yourself the trouble?
It is advisable, that acting on the proverb, 'Let not Satan mislead you,' you drive away vanity from your head.

And that's just a sample. The rascal dared to add a verse of Hāfiz to round it off:

The ascetic asked for the nectar of Paradise
Hāfiz for the cup
Which of the two God prefers, remains yet to be seen.

Sikandar bin Manjhu

And what was Humayun's answer?

Manjhu

O thou that are Chittor's foe
How art thou occupied in seizing infidels?
A king has arrived at thy head
And thou seated in hope of seizing Chittor.

To which Bahadur replied in a verse written by his court hack in equally vile poetry:

I that am foe to the city of Chittor
Am seizing the infidels by force
He who succours Chittor
Thou shalt see how I seize him too.

Sikandar bin Manjhu

Didn't Rani Karnawati appeal to Humayun by sending him a *raksha bandhan*?

Manjhu

No, that is just a pretty story.

Humayun could have aided Chittor anyway, but his advisors were against it.

Sikandar bin Manjhu

Why?

Manjhu

Oh, a Ghazi may not make war on a Mussalman who is fighting an infidel, that is the first tenet of brotherhood among kings. No doubt Bahadur's advisors told him the same, so he was sanguine he could blast Chittor to smithereens. which he did. Or rather, Rumi Khan did, but I don't know the details of that battle, not being there myself.

Sikandar bin Manjhu

What about Hussam Gujarati? Why is he so silent about it?

Manjhu

He is not. But I will be. The matter ended badly, very badly for Bahadur, although he was the victor.

On the third day of Ramzan[100], twelve thousand women jumped into the *jauhar-kund,* led by Karnavati.

Sikandar bin Manjhu

Murderer!

Manjhu

If you say so.

Now Bahadur made his worst mistake. He made a bitter enemy of Rumi Khan.

Earlier he had promised Rumi Khan Ranthambore. He reneged on that, and gave it instead to a Gujarati amir, Malik Nassan. Now this Malik was the rightful incumbent—these are inherited appointments and the worst thing to do would be to hand over the fort to a foreigner. The battle was over, now wounds would have to be healed.

Sikandar bin Manjhu

How do you heal the suicide of twelve thousand women?

Manjhu

Bahadur had done that already—by the suicide of his soul.

He was a man benumbed, going about his duties with a manic mechanical precision.

The damaged fortifications were rebuilt. The fort was provisioned.

---

100 8 March 1535

Bahadur took stock of his position. As Hussam Gujarati puts it, the light was struck from his face.

Bahadur had one question though, and he asked everyone. He was looking for a woman. Hussam Gujarati didn't know what connection Bahadur had with this woman, but when he learned she had not perished in the *jauhar*, he gave thanks to Allah.

And more, this woman was believed to be mad.

Her name was Mihira Devi.

Meanwhile we were not idle in the Mughal camp. We had marched to Ujjain, and each day received Rais and Ranas we had never even heard of. Our men were under strict orders to treat the locals with great courtesy and to extend help whenever needed.

For once Humayun employed his father's principles in disciplining the army. Usually, he celebrated his triumphs with his brutish amirs, in a daze of fine wine and opium, spending days in his own private paradise. I loathed him at these times. It killed me to think of the country in the hands of such a fool.

The army, of course, just waited for these moments to run wild—plundering, pillaging, raping.

Sikandar bin Manjhu

All soldiers do that.

Manjhu

Not if their leader can command loyalty.

Bahadur's men would fight like devils just for him—and they did, without food, without pay. They would follow him—

Sikandar bin Manjhu

—all the way to hell, I suppose? So what did Humayun's march to Ujjain have to do with Bahadur?

Manjhu

I've just told you. Naturally, the Rajput were eager to befriend Humayun after Chittorgarh. Everywhere we halted, the army was provisioned afresh, the horses were watered and shod.

Bahadur had a march of nearly 100 kos to Mahmudabad. Much of that is Rajput country. Even at knife point, no villager would give him water or grain.

His best option was a quick march—not quite possible with tired men made to haul heavy guns, and a sulking and discontented general.

I suffered from boils. Every summer I was enveloped in pustules. They were ugly to behold, and the remedies were uglier still. My face was painted with a foul green paste and I sought the Padshah's indulgence for a week—the boils generally took that long to heal.

Humayun however, was not going to let me off easily.

'You are excused from my presence, but I will ask you to carry out a task of immense importance. As you are aware, while at Gwalior, I had asked Ghyasuddin bin Humam-al-din[101] to write our history. Yesterday he confessed he has completed it. What, in so short a time? I asked. He presented me with the manuscript. In general he is a truthful man, but one may not know how far this honesty extends in writing a history, and I will leave you to judge that.

I replied that I would be glad to read the manuscript. Of course Humayun was having none of that.

I must hear the man himself, Khwandamir as he was styled, go over each line with all his allusions and references, that I may write a suitable commentary.

'I shall expect it by the time we conquer Gujarat,' Humayun concluded.

Never before had I prayed for Bahadur Shah's victory, but at the thought of wading through that sycophant's syrupy effusions, I wished him strength and glory.

Sikandar bin Manjhu

I have not read this history.

Manjhu

Do so without delay, if only to catalogue the Padshah's wardrobe.

Sikandar bin Manjhu

Was it so very grand?

Manjhu

Oh, the man was ruled by the planets! Listen to Khwandamir:

As Saturday is the day of Saturn, and the colour of Saturn, according to the astronomers, is said to be black, the ever-successful King, dressed his royal body on this day in a black habit; and his face, which resembled the Sun, appeared to the people like the planet Jupiter, which shines in the darkness of the night.

Sikandar bin Manjhu

Spare me Ab—

Manjhu

Ah! The word sticks in your throat, does it?

No matter, address me as nothing, I am become a null to you.

---

101 *Ghyasuddin bin Humam-al-din,* [c1475—c1535 CE] Persian historian. He is best known for his universal history *Habib al-Siyar fi Akhbār afrād al-Bashar* [حبيب السير في اخبار افراد البشر] *The Beloved Report on the Multitudes of People* and *Qanun-e-Humayuni* قانون همایونی, *The Edicts of Humayun.*
He is buried in Delhi in the dargah of the Sufi saint Hazrat Nizamuddin.

Sikandar bin Manjhu

What does Khwandamir say of Bahadur Shah?

Manjhu

He did not notice him at all!

He noticed nothing but the Padshah sitting on his gold embroidered solar patch in the sixth circle of mirth.

Sikandar bin Manjhu

What's that?

Manjhu

One more of Humayun's caprices.

Bisāt-e-Nishdt, the circle of mirth, was a carpet made of different coloured threads, to resemble planets and elements.

The first circle was white, like crystalline ether.

The second was blue.

The third, the circle of Saturn, was black. Humayun made certain his Hindu nobles occupied this, as it matched the colour of their skin.

The fourth circle, dedicated to Jupiter, was the colour of sandalwood, and the wise Syeds were seated on this.

The fifth, that of Mars, was red.

The sixth, the one the Padshah occupied, was golden, like the sun.

The seventh, the circle of Venus, was bright green.

And the eighth, violet, was devoted to Mercury.

The ninth, of the Moon was white—

Sikandar bin Manjhu

Why do you tell me all this rubbish?

Manjhu

So that you may understand the nature of the man.

But you are impatient to return to the battle, I see. Well, here goes, then.

We marched to Mandsaur, and planted ourselves right in Bahadur's path.

Hussam Gujarati told me that Bahadur's wazir and other senior amirs advised him to attack. They could have broken right through Humayun's forces, the soldiers' morale was high, the Sultân being among them.

But Bahadur hung back.

Rumi Khan advised him not to attempt the attack. Now this was a disgruntled man, angry and forced to suppress his discontent under the guise of duty.

Hussam Gujarati made another observation which intrigued me. He said Bahadur showed a strange reluctance to attack the Mughal forces—almost as if he was content to tease them into a confrontation.

Sikandar bin Manjhu

Maybe he was just afraid.

Manjhu

Afraid? Who, Bahadur?

Sikandar bin Manjhu

Then why didn't he attack?

Manjhu

I think he wanted Humayun to parley.

Sikandar bin Manjhu

Did he send an envoy?

Manjhu

No, I think he waited for Humayun to send one.

Sikandar bin Manjhu

Hadn't they had enough of letters?

Manjhu

Perhaps.

Humayun did not share his thoughts with us. I was kept busy with Khwandamir who was a most irritating man, pretentious and pompous, with breath like a four day old corpse.

Now I'll tell you what Bahadur did, and what it cost him.

Bahadur made camp at Mandsaur, on the northern bank of the Teliya Taalab, and we were camped on the southern bank.

Bahadur was 100 kos away from his nearest refuge—his stronghold at Mandu—and we blocked his way.

Under Rumi Khan's advice, Bahadur hunkered down. A moat was dug around his camp, and behind that, araba, a wall of carts and gun carriages. A regular fort!

Humayun sent out forays, but these expeditions were beaten back.

Bahadur was playing the waiting game.

There is a curious element to this.

Humayun considered himself the Padshah of Hindustan, but Gujarat was a much larger empire.

Strange, that Bahadur, with superior gun power, more men and a dazzling military record, should even consider Humayun his equal.

I put it down to Babar's genius.

Was it Khanua? Was it Panipat?

Babar had impressed Bahadur as no soldier had impressed him before.

Bahadur presumed Humayun would be like his father. His father had trusted Humayun as Muzaffar Shah had never trusted Bahadur.

We Mughals were far away from home, in hostile country. Bahadur was practically at his own doorstep. His victorious army would have plunged enthusiastically into any escapade of their Sultân's.

But Bahadur did nothing. He felt his power depended on his guns. And the guns, on their gunner. So he let Rumi Khan decide for him.

And Rumi Khan decided for Humayun.

On the second day our spies brought Humayun a letter from Rumi Khan. The Padshah paid no notice till several of our men returned wounded—to report many others killed.

From the next day onwards we adopted a new tactic. Humayun had his men round up all the locals. He made an example of one unfortunate, flayed him in public and left his body to rot in the sun. He announced that anybody who aided Bahadur Shah with food and provisions would meet a similar fate.

With this fell stroke, Bahadur Shah became the Enemy to the terrified villagers of Mandsaur.

But Bahadur had his loyalists—the poor, the dispossessed, the nameless, the forgotten. All through his triumphs, Bahadur never neglected them. Now it was the banjara who organized provisions, and you know how silently and secretively they work.

Mehtar Banjara told Bahadur he had one million cartloads of grain but dared not lead the convoy towards the Gujarati camp.

Bahadur sent out a detachment of 5,000 horses, but by then the wily Rumi Khan had leaked the news to Humayun.

The Mughals closed in on the horsemen as they were returning with the grain. They massacred them to a man, grabbed as many horses as were still unhurt, and of course we got the grain.

Thus, at every step, Bahadur found Humayun had anticipated his plans, and it still did not occur to him to suspect Rumi Khan.

Yes, the rest of the Gujaratis were not so gullible, and morale fell as they felt their Sultân needed Rumi Khan's approval for every breath he took. Bahadur's madcap courage and daring had won the hearts of his men, and now it appeared his cowardice would destroy them all.

On the eighth day their disaffection grew so intense that Rumi Khan judged it wise to defect.

Rumi Khan arrived at our camp, and was taken right away to the Padshah's pavilion.

Did I tell you we travelled with Humayun's famous movable palace? No. I'm not going to tell you about it. That wretched sycophant has written it all in his *Qanun-e-Humayuni*.

Rumi Khan was housed with the Padshah, an unprecedented honour.

The next day he was put in charge of our guns and artillery, and made no attempt to hide his contempt for our men or their lack of discipline.

I fell into conversation with him.

The Gujaratis were eating rats when he left, he said. Bahadur Shah had antagonized his amirs by sending their rations to the starving troops. 'If my men starve, I starve with them,' he replied tersely, and there was no arguing with that as he had not eaten a meal in days. The weaker horses had been slaughtered and eaten.

Rumi Khan had warned Humayun that Bahadur's men might have a supply source in the temple. Humayun sent for the mahant and had him tortured. When the poor man was at last gasp, he was let go with the warning that the temple wouldn't last an hour if as much as a sack of grain reached the Gujaratis. That is a very ancient temple, that of Pashupatinath. To the Mughals, of course, it was all pagan.

Sikandar bin Manjhu

It should have been to Bahadur too.

Manjhu

No, Bahadur was a two-headed man. I'll explain presently.

Let me tell you what I heard from Hussam Gujarati.

Ten days of starvation had reduced the Gujaratis to abject despair.

All edible animals had been eaten.

Only the more valiant horses, still energetic, despite starvation, were left alive.

Elephants died, their meat too stringy and tough to be roasted, and there being very little fuel left to cook, the huge carcasses were buried untouched.

The horses, Hussam Gujarati told me, went crazy, and began to nibble each others' tails.

Sikandar bin Manjhu

Ha.

Manjhu

I thought so too, at that time. But since then, my son, I have known starvation.

And then Humayun decided to have a little sport.

He sent out a small contingent with an elephant.

The Gujaratis, desperate for rotla, must have imagined the load on the elephant to be grain, for they rushed out in a frenzy.

As instructed, Humayun's troops scattered and abandoned the elephant.

It was captured and brought before the Sultân in triumph.

Bahadur ordered his mahouts to unburden the beast. Its load was opened and found to be nothing more than a flimsy litter with a small box in it.

Hussam Gujarati said by now the Sultân was sweating, his face suffused with rage.

'I'll open it,' he said in a very strange voice. He asked the others to stand back, as if he perceived danger. The others thought there might be a snake in the box, or a poisoned dagger that might spring out when the lid was raised.

Sikandar bin Manjhu

How fanciful.

Manjhu

It would appear so to you, no doubt, never having known the inside of a court.

But it was, as you would expect, an anticlimax.

The Sultân's bellow of outrage could be heard at the farthest limits of the camp.

Sikandar bin Manjhu

Why, what was inside?

Manjhu

A lump of salt to feed a hungry army and a stick of charcoal for the Sultân's face. And, this last was Humayun's touch, some ribbons of blue cloth. Blue being the colour of Saturn, the planet known to delay, prevaricate and disappoint.

Humayun had the kind of malice proverbial with old women, but much more common, really, among kings.

After *maghrib*, Bahadur announced his plan to his ministers. He would make a break for it, steal out and ride alone. In the morning, Sadar Khan would lead the march towards Mandu. Bahadur would take the route north.

Khudawand Khan, the wazir who had served Bahadur's grandfather, and now in his 85th year, said he was against Bahadur's plan. Hussam Gujarati says he advised Bahadur to depend on Humayun's mercy.

Judging by what the old man did later, his advice does not surprise me.

Bahadur rejected it indignantly. Khudawand Khan said in that case, it was time to destroy everything the army could not carry. All the treasure was piled up in the Sultân's tent, and distributed on the persons of the most trusted amirs. You can imagine there was much more than could be stuffed in their saddlebags.

Then Khudawand Khan said the guns would have to be broken. Laila and Majnun, that Bahadur had transported in triumph across his kingdom, and hauled up the crags of Chittorgarh, these were of no use without Rumi Khan, and to leave them behind would be to hand them over to him.

Bahadur wept, but the job was done.

Then came the worst moment of the evening.

Khudawand Khan called for the elephants.

Bahadur's elephants. He was as tender with them, as if they were his own children—Pat Singar and Sharzah.

It was impossible to poison them because there was no food, and it was against all principle to leave them to the enemy. They had to be mutilated, and the mahout refused to carry that out.

Khudawand Khan, infuriated, ordered a flogging.

Bahadur, hearing the commotion, hurried out. He stopped the flogging, and asked the mahout to chain the elephants. Then taking off the necklace of pearls he habitually wore, he gave it to the mahout, and discharged him. When the man was out of earshot, Bahadur stood for a moment with his head sunk between his shoulders. Nobody dared to breathe a word of comfort or consolation, but Pat Singar put her trunk fondly around him. This broke the last vestige of Bahadur's control, and he wept as he had wept for nothing else before.

Hussam Gujarati said all his anguish was in those sobs, all his disappointments, all his loss, all the pain he never expressed at treachery, and all his despair in that smoking *jauhar kund*. It was as if he was reliving every instant of his kingship as he wept—and who knows what else besides?

Then taking a khanjar in each hand, and looking straight at his beloved elephants, Bahadur moved his arms in swift synchrony. Two silver arcs, and two severed trunks had toppled before the outraged scream from the animals deafened them all.

Bahadur, clutching his head, ran from the place. Five minutes later they heard his horse thunder out.

Bahadur did not ride out alone. Five of his loyals went with him.

It was the 20th of Ramadan, 941.[102]

Sikandar bin Manjhu

And so Humayun destroyed the army and let Bahadur escape?

Manjhu

Not at all.

Our spies brought the news late next morning, when the Gujaratis discovered the Sultân had flown.

Sadar Khan organized a force and they had begun the march towards Mandu—but that was only rumour, so we advanced into Bahadur's camp.

For a while it was bloody, but the resistance was weak. The handful of Gujaratis left were so famished they were willing to trade their loyalty for a square meal. Humayun delayed that till he had extracted all information out of them.

I found my old friend Mohammad Hussam [now Hussam Gujarati, historian] crouching in terror in the Sultân's abandoned tent. He was clutching a sackful of precious books. From that moment, till his death two years later, we never spent a day apart.

His books were his ransom.

I made bold to show them to the Padshah, and won sanctuary for him.

---

[102] 25 March 1535

The Padshah held a grand darbar that evening.

The booty we had plundered from Bahadur Shah was magnificent, and Humayun, as usual, was very generous.

And then somebody brought in a bird.

It was a most entertaining bird, a parrot that seemed to have a cultivated wit.

Humayun, delighted, cried out, 'Is this not a clever bird, Rumi Khan?'

And the parrot, taking the cue, cried out, 'Rumi Khan *haram khor!*[103] Rumi Khan *haram khor*!'

Rumi Khan's face fell.

Humayun pacified him by saying, 'If a man had said it, I could have cut off his head, but this is just a foolish bird that doesn't understand its own words.'

And I thought, now Rumi Khan has another king as his slave.

Sikandar bin Manjhu

So what happened next? Bahadur had disappeared into the night; his army, such as it was, set out towards Mandu; but what did Humayun do?

Manjhu

Why, follow the Gujaratis, of course.

He was determined to take Mandugarh.

With Rumi Khan now by his side, the fortress was sure to topple.

Hussam Gujarati would say nothing about Bahadur, and I did not ask.

That old rascal Khudawand Khan, though, wouldn't stop talking.

Humayun treated him with great respect, and flattered him by discussing the Hadith, and feeding him the most delicate fare out of consideration for his great age and position.

The old rogue recovered most marvelously.

Now between Rumi Khan and Khudawand Khan, both of Humayun's ears were filled with outpourings about Bahadur Shah.

It took us nearly a month to get to Mandu.

We received intelligence that Bahadur Shah had already slipped into his stronghold by the time his army got there.

Humayun did not want to confront the Gujaratis. This time he was after Bahadur. His mood had changed. He was ill-tempered and restless. At times, the melancholic malaise of a deprived opium eater overcame him. He lashed out without the least provocation.

I kept Hussam Gujarati hidden in my tent.

Besides him, I also had care of Jam Firoz of Thatta, an ancient too feeble to be part of any campaign. He was, besides, the father-in-law of Bahadur Shah, and for a brief period, this kept him in Humayun's favour.

---

103 Urdu ... حرام خور ... Traitor.

But Jam Firoz was not as forthcoming as either Khudawand Khan or Rumi Khan about his son-in-law, and by the time we got to Mandu, Humayun had begun to get a thoughtful look whenever he happened to notice the old man. So I did my best to keep him secluded. Jam Firoz wasn't ignorant of his likely fate, but he never swerved in his loyalty to Bahadur.

Sikandar bin Manjhu

That counts a great deal with you, doesn't it? Loyalty?

Manjhu

Yes. It sets a good man apart from a bad one.

Sikandar bin Manjhu

You have just categorized yourself.

Manjhu

Because I was disloyal to Humayun?

Sikandar bin Manjhu

Well, weren't you?

Manjhu

Disloyal, yes. Ungrateful, certainly. But no, that does not make me a bad man.

I was loyal to myself.

Perhaps, once my story is told, you might change your opinion of your father.

Sikandar bin Manjhu

You are not my father. Continue.

Manjhu

Mandugarh is even more inaccessible than Chittorgarh.

We camped to the north, at Nalcha.

Humayun's mood improved. He spent most of the time outdoors, walking or riding, delighting in the scenery.

Finally he sent an envoy to Bahadur.

His message was simple: Mandugarh was surrounded. Bahadur had no route for escape. The rains were expected any day now, and his army could not weather that under canvas. Both sides were at a disadvantage. Why not talk it out?

Sikandar bin Manjhu

Whatever you say of Humayun, he was magnanimous.

Manjhu

And drenched. He wrote that after he caught a cold. His famous movable palace wasn't waterproof.

Also, even with reinforcements that had joined him by now, Humayun knew he was no match for that huge fortress with its very alert garrison, commanded by Qadir Khan.

Bahadur was comfortable in his luxurious palace. He agreed to a meeting.

Sikandar bin Manjhu

And so they met, at last?

Manjhu

In person? Not they.

They sent representatives.

Humayun sent a Maulvi, Bahadur sent Sadar Khan.

Now, look at the wiliness of Humayun. He asked for two Gujarati maulvis to accompany Sadar Khan. They met at the Blue Road.

Humayun's proposal was simple—Bahadur could keep Gujarat [as if it was Humayun's to give!] but must surrender Mandu.

Sadar Khan would not agree to Humayun's terms. The two maulvis then set to work on Sadar Khan, and Humayun added Chittorgarh as a sop—

Sikandar bin Manjhu

As a sop? I don't understand. It was already Bahadur's, wasn't it?

Manjhu

Yes, but Humayun was negotiating as a conqueror with a vanquished king.

Technically, all Bahadur's territory was now Humayun's.

So Humayun wrote and sealed the treaty.

It was agreed that Bahadur would leave Mandu peaceably by the Lohani Gate in the west, and Humayun would enter by the Dilli gate in the north.

But things never go according to plan, do they?

Sikandar bin Manjhu

I know that story. That very night Bhupat Rai avenged his parents' death when he opened the fort to the Mughals.

Manjhu

I don't know where that story started!

If it were true, how come Bhupat stuck with Bahadur through thick and thin, dying within a month of the Sultân, and still in his court?

Sikandar bin Manjhu

It is a believable story.

Manjhu

A story, still.

Listen, I was there.

I'll tell you the truth.

Bahadur received the treaty that afternoon at *asar*. He told his men the morning would bring peace.

Now there is a matter of four watches—between *asar* and *fajr*.

Humayun trusted in two things: Bahadur's illiteracy, and his naïveté. Any man who reads would have kept the document with him and read aloud from it, at least to his amirs. Bahadur, with his usual nonchalance, dusted the matter off as done once Sadar Khan had made his report.

Sikandar bin Manjhu

That's not very convincing. Sadar Khan himself could have corrected Bahadur.

Manjhu

He probably did.

And Bahadur must have replied, 'Humayun Padshah is a good fellow. Go to sleep now, and we will send him a couple of bottles of Firangi wine in the morning.'

Sikandar bin Manjhu

Just a drunken sot, wasn't he?

Manjhu

If you say so.

He was fast asleep at an early hour that night.

The Mughals waited till midnight. Then they scaled the fort from the back. They used more than 700 ladders.

When the alarm was given, Qadir Khan rushed to Bahadur's bedchamber.

Valuable time was lost when the valet wouldn't let him in, saying the Sultân was extremely tired and had given instructions not to be disturbed.

The altercation woke Bahadur who was a very light sleeper at the best of times.

It took him perhaps a minute more to mount Kuchak Barq.

Qadir Khan and Bhupat Rai were both already in the thick of it.

Bhupat told Bahadur that earlier that day Rumi Khan had sent a message asking him to avenge his parents—and he had refused. When Bahadur gave them the news of the truce, he had put the matter out of his mind.

Bahadur dismounted from Kuchak Barq and gave him to a groom. He rode out on a piebald horse with Bhupat and gave the order to attack. Perhaps he would have won the sortie, but Qadir Khan panicked. The Mughals were pouring into the fort from every crevice. Humayun himself, it was rumoured, would lead the charge once the fort was forced open. Qadir Khan was under no illusions. This was not a battle for Mandugarh, it was for the head of Bahadur Shah.

Bahadur heeded the counsel, and fled to Sonagarh Qila.

Sikandar bin Manjhu

Where's that?

Manjhu

About a mile to the west. It faces the Lohani Gate through which Bahadur was expected to leave Mandu according to the terms of the treaty. From his vantage Bahadur realized the gate was swarming with Mughals. Leaving Sadar Khan and Alam Khan to hold Sonagarh, Bahadur had Kuchak Barq let down in a rope sling from the top of the citadel. He followed with three trusted officers. Bahadur had ridden but a few paces when he was recognized by an Uzbek soldier called Nuri. The commanding officer Qasim Hussain laughed away Nuri's suspicion. If anybody in Humayun's army could recognize Bahadur, it was Qasim Hussain—he had served under the Sultân not very long ago. Why did he fail to recognize Bahadur now?

Within a few miles Bahadur was surrounded by Humayun's men. He fought his way out leaving behind him a tangle of wounded men.

Humayun occupied the main fort a little after *fajr*.

Lamps were lit everywhere. In the mist, the mahals floated like islands of golden radiance.

Humayun had only one order: 'Kill!'

Not a man or woman was spared.

By the time the sun came up the courtyards were ankle deep in blood.

Down in the city the marketplace was a battlefield. People were dragged out of their houses and butchered.

Sadar Khan and Alam Khan still kept Sonagarh though they were surrounded.

Humayun sent a message offering them sanctuary.

Humayun stood on the battlements in a red robe that showed like a bloodstain against the dark clouds.

Only the skies wept over the dead.

On the second day, hearing of the massacre, Sadar Khan and Alam Khan, in hope of saving their garrison, surrendered.

Under Rumi Khan's advice, they were killed with their garrison. Humayun did sigh, a little, over Sadar Khan.

On the third day, Humayun sent his soldiers further afield. It was his intention to leave Mandugarh an empty shell.

In my tent, Hussam Gujarati wept silently, his face to the wall.

Humayun changed his red robes for one of crimson velvet, sombre and majestic, the exact shade of drying blood.

Such an odour of slaughter hung in the air, we were all choking. None of us could eat, so sickened were we all.

Only the Padshah feasted, his appetite challenging even Rumi Khan's.

A little before midday, an irate Baig brought a complaint. A Hindu had robbed him of his captive, and used his armed guard to threaten and drive him away.

The Hindu was quickly found. He was a small Raja who had command of one of Humayun's more peripheral battalions. He was dragged in, chained along with the man he had protected. He met Humayun's glare with an equally angry one.

'Surrender your captive.'

'He is not my captive, and I will not surrender him.'

'Kill him,' Humayun said wearily. 'Kill them both.'

One of Humayun's guards, Kushal Beg, stepped forward, presumably to carry out the order. Instead, he said, 'Jahan-panah may want to know the prisoner's identity.'

'Raja of Kuchhnakuchh. I'm aware of his identity.'

'Sire, the other one.'

'What, this?' Humayun sneered.

In truth, the Raja's companion was negligible. A weakling with a frightened face.

I thought at first he was a mere boy, but soon realized he was older, one of those men who never seem to age.

'He is the Sultân's musician, Huzoor. I have heard him sing when I visited the court as your envoy. Your humble servant begs that you hear him first. At your command I will cut his throat, but I beg of you to hear him sing.'

Kushal Baig was a brave man to make such a request. In his crimson robes, Humayun looked like Death himself.

'Sing, boy!' he commanded.

'How can I when I'm chained?' the boy shot back.

'Unchain him!'

'You must unchain the Raja too. For as long as I sing, he must be free.'

'You have a lot of nerve to make conditions.'

'And you even more, to think you deserve a song after the way you've treated me.'

Humayun ordered the Raja to be unshackled.

'Fetch him a lute,' Humayun ordered.

'I don't need one. Now be silent.'

The musician sat down cross-legged, and when Humayun started forward angrily, he quelled the Padshah with a gesture.

As he began to draw out his *sur*, a calm descended on my soul. The fear and disgust that crumpled me ironed itself out, and I felt myself again.

Around me too, lined and harsh faces softened and grew thoughtful.

I dared not glance in Humayun's direction.

The boy's voice rose and soared above the assembly, circled it like a bird of prey, tightened in tempo, readied for the kill.

We waited calm and resigned for the song to begin knowing with the first line we would be transfixed by its truth.

Jal jaiyo aiso jeevana bhajana bina, bhajana bina[104]

Truly, we were all cindered, turned to ash by the massacre. What had happened to the song within us?

The mountain is desolate without a tree, desolate the tree without a leaf,
The ocean is desolate without an oyster, the oyster desolate without a pearl.

Many were weeping now.

The sweetness of the singer's voice swept us all in its tide. And I, I only wanted to keep hearing it, my heart heavy with the dread that it might stop any moment now.

The people are desolate without their king, desolate a king without justice!

The line rang out furiously as the boy flung back his head and roared.

It reverberated through the hall, it crashed down the corridors, it ripped the leaves off the trees outside, it struck fire from the stones.

And still he sang.

I don't know when he stopped, for the song continued in my heart, and set me free.

I no longer cared what Humayun did.

The Raja, transfigured with joy, held out his hands calmly for his shackles.

Humayun asked the singer his name.

'Bachchu.'

'Will you stay with me, Bachchu, and sing for me?'

'Only if I may free all my kinsmen. You must order your men not to kill them, and they must live free.'

Humayun beckoned him, and wound his kamarband around the boy's own waist. 'You wear the Padshah's kamarband. Go now, and save all your kinsmen.'

'Here is the first one.' The boy pointed to the Raja.

So the Raja was let go, much to the ire of the Baig, a tone-deaf Uzbek.

Humayun, in high good humour, sat down to eat.

That evening he appeared in robes of bright green to announce a truce.

All killing would stop at sundown. From tomorrow, the people of Mandu could resume their normal lives. No more plundering and looting would be tolerated.

And as for Bachchu, he went about claiming kinship with every inhabitant he met. At the end of the day, he had a family of over a thousand people awaiting the Padshah's mercy.

Humayun only laughed and asked him to go find a thousand more, and for each kinsman he saved he gave him an ashrafi.

All these ashrafis made a pretty big sack, and this sack Bachchu handed over to the astonished Kushal Baig.

---

104 Bhajan [Sanskrit … भजन], a devotional song.
This particular bhajan was composed by the 15th century mystic poet Sant Kabir Das.

'Everything I earn in the Padshah's court is yours,' he said, and set about inventing a new *raag* so full of beauty and despair that nothing mattered to the court but the hearing of it.

Then, one night, Bachchu ran away. He did so quite openly, telling his audience it was time he left.

'The Padshah has been kind to me, but my Sultân needs me, and I must go,' were his words.

Humayun was deeply hurt. His amirs were all for riding after the rascal and bringing back his head on a platter, but Humayun ordered them to leave Bachchu alone.

Sikandar bin Manjhu

As I said before, Humayun was a magnanimous man.

So what did he do about Bahadur? Didn't he pursue him?

Manjhu

He certainly did.

First to Champaner. There he found Bahadur had just departed, taking with him his treasure, that famous belt; his harem and his newborn daughter; leaving the fort in the care of his cousin Raja Narsin Deo and that bookish fool, Ikhtiyar Khan.

When we reached Champaner, the first thing we noticed was a gigantic cannon, identified by Rumi Khan, with a whoop of glee, as Bahadur Shah's cannon, the one he had cast at Diu. Too large to be dragged up into the fortress, it had been abandoned after three holes were punched into it. Rumi Khan was confident he could repair it, and he set about it immediately. Within a few hours he aimed it at the fortress. It discharged such a volley, the shot clean knocked off the gate. A second shot uprooted a gnarly old fig tree at the entrance.

We thought the Gujaratis terrified, but their answer was no less menacing.

A shot from inside the fortress slammed into the cannon straight in the muzzle, and destroyed it beyond Rumi Khan's powers of restoration.

Later, I was told that shot had been fired by Firangi Khan, a Firangi we called Sakta, but his true name was José de Santiago.

Sikandar bin Manjhu

You speak the Frankish tongue?

Manjhu

Fairly well. I can read it better.

I was about to tell you—the next part of Bahadur's history is better heard from the Firangi historians. When I am done here, I'll fetch you the volumes.

Sikandar bin Manjhu

They are of no use to me. I cannot read them.

Manjhu

Then I will read them to you, because they *must* be read. The enemy's point of view is of supreme importance to a historian. Else, your history will be no different from the usual cant— march, besiege, invest, reduce.

March, besiege, invest, reduce.

Sikandar bin Manjhu

You were telling me about Firangi Khan.

Manjhu

Ah. For that feat Ikhtyar Khan gave him a pat on the back and Raja Narsing Deo seven maunds of gold.

The Raja had been left behind because he was dying. His wounds had turned foul, he was running a fever. Sure enough, he died the next day.

Ikhtiyar Khan still held out, so Humayun increased his vigilance at the fort.

Two nights later, a convoy of Kolis were captured when they tried to sneak provision into the fort. Their leader begged for their lives. In return, he promised to show the Mughals a way into the fort. This path was to the west, near Halol, out of the ambit of the sentries.

Humayun had his men hammer a hundred iron spikes into the fort wall at this point. Forty Mughals climbed the wall using the spikes as ladder. Humayun was the forty-first.

There was a satisfactory decoy too: tremendous artillery fire that got the Gujaratis all excited in the wrong direction, while the Mughals took possession of the fort.

The fool Ikhtiyar Khan, who escaped to Pavagadh, was given sanctuary by Humayun. He further endeared himself to the Padshah by first spouting the Hadith and then leading him to the unbelievable treasure trove of Bahadur Shah.

Sikandar bin Manjhu

You said Bahadur Shah took his treasure with him.

Manjhu

Only some of it. Very little of it, actually. Humayun took it all.

Sikandar bin Manjhu

But what of Bahadur?

Manjhu

Indeed, what of him?

Humayun pursued him as far as Khambaiyat. Only to find he had flown to Diu.

Humayun was prepared to sail for Diu. Then he learned that in leaving Bahadur had set fire to the fleet.

Sikandar bin Manjhu

So did he pursue him by land?

Manjhu

No.

As usual, the tribals were all for Bahadur.

They attacked the Mughal camp by night, looting and plundering.

The Padshah nearly had my head—they stole a copy of the *Taimur-nama*, and of course, I was to blame for that!

Now the strange thing is that very evening an old woman had approached the camp and demanded to meet the Padshah. Humayun, who was in a good mood, humoured her. She warned the camp of an ambush.

'Why are you telling me this?' asked Humayun.

'I'm hoping you will free my son as my reward. He is your prisoner.'

The story was dismissed, but Humayun had the woman's son brought out. He placed them both under arrest for spreading a rumour.

But it was no rumour.

The ambush took place a little past midnight.

Humayun's rage knew no bounds.

Of course the woman's son was the first to be punished. Or rather, she was, as she was made to watch. But thereafter, it was *qatl-e-aam*.[105]

Not a citizen in Khambaiyat was spared. The massacre was worse than that at Mandu.

I hid Hussam Gujarati by distracting Humayun.

The Taimur manuscript wasn't really lost, I had found it, dropped and trampled in the mêlée.

I used my panic to attract the wrath of the Padhshah. He had me flogged, but the whip sat light on my back in the knowledge that he had forgotten about Hussam Gujarati.

I was not so lucky with Jam Firoz. He was dragged out and beheaded simply for his lack of judgment in giving his daughter to Sultân Bahadur.

Hussam Gujarati surprised me by saying that now Humayun had made it easy for Bahadur.

'What?' I asked. 'Did he want to be rid of his father-in-law?'

'No, he liked him immensely. I don't mean that. The people are sickened by the Mughals now. They will bring Bahadur back.'

'As if that's in their hands! These poor ignorant people, what can they do?'

Hussam Gujarati merely laughed.

It was only after his death that I understood his wisdom.

But let me get on with my story.

---

105 Urdu … قتل عام … massacre, slaughter.

Humayun returned to Champaner, as I told you, and climbed the fortress.

Sikandar bin Manjhu

That was daring.

Manjhu

Oh yes, he had courage.

And now he had gold as well.

He distributed gold by the shieldful to every man in the army, and of course he was extolled for his generosity.

It takes a Padshah to be generous with the wealth of others.

Hussam Gujarati laughed again when he heard this and said, 'Now Humayun's days in Gujarat are numbered.'

Sikandar bin Manjhu

What, are you trying to tell me Bahadur's treasure wasn't plunder?

Manjhu

Certainly it was. But the treasure wasn't his to give away. It belonged to the people.

Sikandar bin Manjhu

What about the belt?

Manjhu

Patience! I will come to that.

In an attempt to ingratiate the people, Humayun waived the land revenue.

Sikandar bin Manjhu

A masterstroke!

Manjhu

You have the brain of a Mughal.

Sikandar bin Manjhu

And you that of a Gujarati, I suppose. You aren't even from this land.

Manjhu

True. I don't know which land is mine, but this land has accepted me, and I understand its people.

Now that they had a taste of Humayun's cruelty, they remembered that Rana Sanga had *invited* Babar into Hindustan—

Sikandar bin Manjhu

Rubbish.

Manjhu

No, they had a deal, Rana Sanga and Babar.

Rana Sanga, rightly, broke the deal and attacked Babar at Khanua.

But then, everybody invited Babar into Hindustan so that they could be rid of Ibrahim Lodi.

As I was saying, people now saw the burning of Chittorgarh as just punishment to the Rajputs for having invited the Mughals in. So when Humayun refused the land revenue, they knew just what to do with their money. They took it to Diu.

Sikandar bin Manjhu

To Bahadur?

Manjhu

Yes. They went to him and said they had the money, but it was up to him to send a responsible officer to collect it. They had money and they had men, but they needed a king. And so it was done.

Sikandar bin Manjhu

I don't understand. Bahadur got himself an army?

Manjhu

Of course. In his opiate fug, Humayun didn't even consider this a possibility.

The delirium was infectious. His army became an uncontrollable madhouse of drunkenness and debauchery. There was money enough to wash away all guilt, all sins.

Anyway, Bahadur got his army. Imad-ul-Mulk led it against the Mughals at Ahmadabad and was crushed by the sheer numbers of the enemy—

Sikandar bin Manjhu

Oh, the Mughals have become the enemy now, have they?

Manjhu

I was talking about Imad-ul-Mulk. Yes, they were my enemy too, by now.

But I'll come to that later.

Now Humayun asked Khudawand Khan, in my presence, if he thought Bahadur could raise more armies, and that worthy ancient laughed. 'He has no money, and no men. Imad-ul-Mulk was the last of his officers. Rest assured, Gujarat is yours.'

Khudawand Khan, having turned traitor to the kings he had served, now proved himself equally foolish when it came to the people.

Humayun, on the advice of Mirza Askari, did not advance directly into Ahmadabad.

He tarried in Sarkhej.

You must not think Humayun had omitted to make a visit to Batoh, to the tomb of the holy Qutb-al-Qatab, and, naturally, to enrich the khanquah there. As expected, they took his money, gave their blessing, and kept their counsel.

At Sarkhej, Humayun divided up Gujarat among his nobles. His brother, Mirza Askari, he made his Viceroy, and quartered him in Ahmadabad with Hindu Baig as advisor. He put Tardi Baig in charge of Champaner. And off he went to Malwa.

Pleading a fresh crop of boils, I stayed behind.

Within a few weeks, Humayun's officers in Patan and Khambaiyat were beaten by an uprising of Gujarati loyalists.

It was quite funny—they were pursued all the way to Ahmadabad where they rushed for refuge.

Humayun's new empire had begun to fragment.

In Ahmadabad, the Mirza's revels were loud and riotous. His half-brother Ghazanfar defected to Bahadur, and Bahadur turned up with an army. Askari had few sympathizers. He ran to Champaner and begged Tardi Baig to finance his army. There were rumours of Askari trying to set himself up as King of Gujarat and then march on to claim the throne at Agra. Rumours, but Tardi Baig had heard them, so he refused to help.

Bahadur scattered the Mughals with one decisive foray, and chased them all the way back to Malwa.

There is no saying what Humayun might have done—but by then Sher Shah's threat to Agra could no longer be ignored, and Humayun turned his back on Gujarat and went home.

Sikandar bin Manjhu

And you stayed back. You were going to tell me why.

Manjhu

I stayed back because of what Humayun did to my friends.

In your generation, things are different. A great writer like you has no truck with the scribbler of scurrilous verses, or the clerks who take dictation or the accountants who write up reports. In my time it was different. Everybody who read, or wanted to read, was a friend.

No introductions were necessary. Every courtyard was a *mehfil.*[106] All sorts of rubbish was read and discussed, no dream was too trivial and none to grandiose for us to pull to pieces.

---

[106] Urdu … محفل … a formal gathering for poetry, song, music and dance.

Oh, we were terrible fellows!

But we were friends.

Now, after the victory at Champaner, when the army was so engorged with money, we poor scriveners felt injured.

Nobody had rewarded us.

Humayun had dragged us along through mud and mire and blood—plenty of blood.

We had seen things no man should, our skulls had exploded with the screams of the dying, and what had we got out of it all? Not even a pension. We were condemned to this life till we were too old to hold a qalam, or even trace a line with our eyes.

And then—what?

Merciful death would rescue us from the ignominy of want and despair.

Those evenings, all our talk was of this sort.

One evening, the talk was of Taimur and his band of forty. And a bunch of foolish fellows, fired with more wine than ambition, set off to relive that famous tale.

I went home, tired of such follies, my heart aching worse than my head. Those days I dreamt only of escape. I had my own small library, portable in a cart, a little money saved up.

I only needed a safe place to stay—but where would I find that, out of the reach of Humayun?

I went home, despite my disgust, envying these idiots a little.

Imagine my surprise, when I discovered the next morning they had actually set out! Clearly their mad scheme had caught on like wildfire, for not forty but four hundred had ridden out in the small hours.

And the story they had left behind was even more fantastic.

They were off to conquer the Dakshin!

The north was the Padshah's, the Purabiyas were quarrelsome fellows, but the Dakshin was just waiting to be conquered, so why wait?

I laughed heartily.

It was the joke of the day.

Even the employers of these clerks—scriveners, ink horns, paper cutters and bookbinders—chuckled at the thought of their own enjoyment when these rapscallions returned ruined and beaten.

The only one to take the story seriously was Humayun.

He shocked the court by sending out a contingent of ten thousand soldiers—ten *thousand!*

All it would have taken to round up those fools was one soldier on horseback with an order from the Padshah.

They hadn't got very far. Or perhaps the real soldiers themselves joined in a day's carousel with the pretenders, for it was past sundown when they were brought back.

I expected a severe rebuke and then perhaps a fine, but they were thrown into the dungeons and produced in the darbar next morning.

That was a Tuesday, and Humayun entered robed for Mars in blood red satin, with a turban of black. On his sarpech a large ruby shone like a blood drop.

My heart sank, though there was no reason for it, surely.

But once those pathetic adventurers were produced, my fears were justified.

Humayun ordered me to write his judgment.

It kills me, after all these years, to recollect those lines. But I will do so to complete my characterization of Humayun:

Some of you who have stretched your heads beyond the line of duty shall be lightened of the burden of your heads. Others, in their rebellious ignorance appear unable to distinguish hand from foot, and so will forfeit both. Others, who from their conceit had not lent their ears to the Padshah's command, will lose both ears and nose. Others, whose fingertips had strained to touch the forbidden will find their fingers no more in their fists. And as it is unknown to us who began and who followed, the punishments will be distributed randomly amongst you.

And within the hour, before the silent and horrified court, the punishments were carried out, leaving some beheaded, others missing hands and feet, fingertips, ears, eyes, noses.

The amputated parts were all gathered up and given to the only fat fellow in the lot, for him to swallow with a jug of wine.

When he refused both the body parts and the wine, his head was struck off.

The Emperor called for lunch and the rest of us rushed home to vomit.

The day was far from over.

At *maghrib*, the Imam recited the Surah of the Elephant.[107]

It had become second nature with me to read Humayun's thoughts in the shift of his eyes, and during the recitation, I saw the way they moved—from the Imam to his own hands resting on his robe of spotless white.

The Imam droned on and on, though it is quite a short text.

When he was done, the Padshah spoke in a clear low voice.

I couldn't believe my ears. But the shocked faces in the assembly told me they too had heard Humayun's words.

He had ordered the Imam to be trampled to death by an elephant.

'Let it be done within the hour,' he commanded.

Maulana Mahmud Bargholi, he who had bartered peace with Bahadur on the Blue Road in Mandu, spoke up in defense of the Imam. He argued that he was only doing his duty and had no malicious motive in choosing that particular surah. It was no reflection on the Padshah's enlightened judgment earlier in the day.

Humayun heard him out with that cold politeness I had learned to dread. His response was very brief, 'May I remind the respected Maulana that an elephant has four feet. He is free to enlist two more in the criminal's defense.'

The Maulana retreated.

The elephant was brought out.

To all present it was not the unfortunate Imam, but Humayun who was trampled to death that night.

---

107 *Surah Al-Fil* [Arabic الفيل *The Elephant*] is the 105th surah of the Quran.

Sikandar bin Manjhu

And so you left him. But what of the rest? When did you meet Bahadur Shah? What did he say to you?

Manjhu

There are other voices you must hear now.

The rest of my history is personal. It no longer concerns you. You are not my son.

Part Four

33

Oshim and Genda

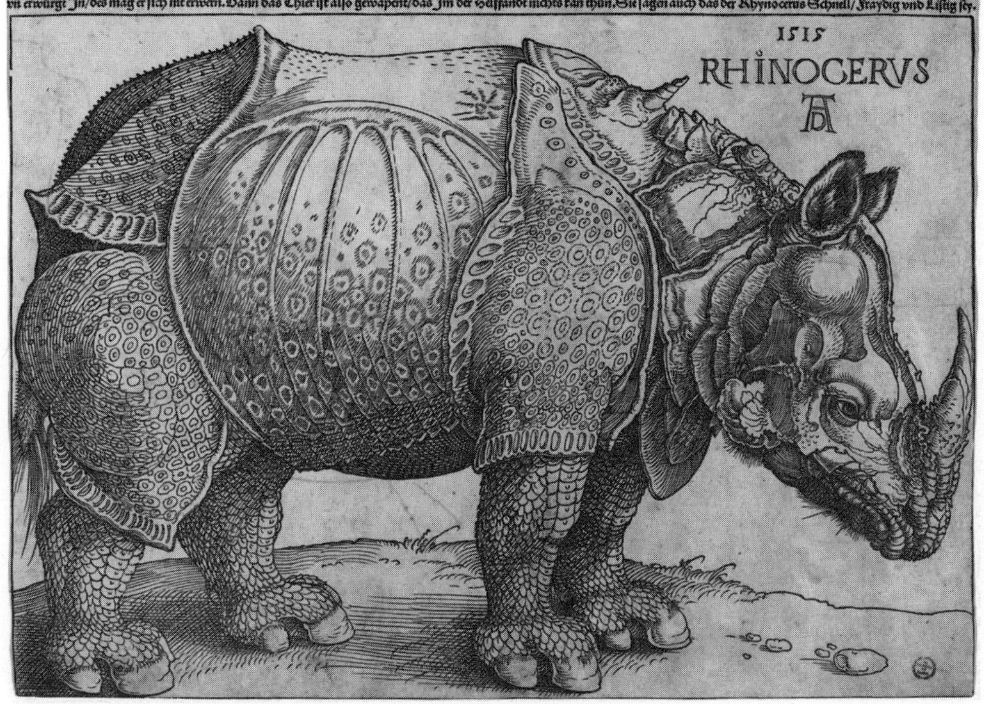

Albrecht Dürer, *The Rhinoceros*, 1515, woodcut[108]

108 On 20 May 1515, the day before Albrecht Dürer's 44th birthday, an Indian rhinoceros arrived in Lisbon from Gujarat. Dürer never saw the animal; he based his woodcut on the description of the animal in a poem by the Italian physician Giovanni Giacomo Penni published in Rome on 13 July 1515.

My name is Ganapati Ramchandra Kudalkar. I am a Kudaldeshkar Brahman from Dabhol, but that is irrelevant to the story you want to hear. I was a witness from beginning to end, and therefore reliable. I told you my name so that you can cross-check in other documents on the matter. There will be many such. The Portuguese are great clerks, they write everything down several times and make their copies in very good paper that survives the damp. I am an interpreter by profession because languages come easily to me. Trade depends on communication, written and spoken, and at all ports, interpreters are in demand. I was one of the first to learn Portuguese well enough to read their books, and that got me noticed. The Firangi do not pay well. They are unclean and cruel in their habits, but I like them. I like their heart for adventure and their curiosity. The world is a bigger place than Goa or Dabhol, and I would like to see it. This is why I stay with the Firangi.

In the year 1514, I was chosen by the Governor D'Albuquerque to accompany his agent Pero de Queimado to the court of the Gujarat Sultân to seek permission for the visit of the Portuguese embassy. This Pero de Queimado was a dull companion. Or perhaps he thought, in common with most Portuguese, that a gentoo was only a savage with no rational parts and no imagination. Well, I could say the same of the Portuguese. And so we made the journey in silence.

We were only a small entourage, on our way to the richest court in Hindustan, but there was no mistaking our swagger. The Portuguese are deeply impressed by themselves, and this, I conclude, is the secret of their success. Think of it. We were on our way to the Sultân's Court to demand, yes, demand, the island of Diu. The official request would be more humble, of course. It would fall to me to draft it. We (I have to side with my employers) would merely request permission to build a fort in Diu.

If you're a mariner, this humble request will make you gasp. If you're a landsman, let me explain. That little jot of land, Diu, brings the Sultân more income than his 86 other ports. That's right, he has 87 ports at his command. Diu is an outpost between the Dakhsin entrepôts and the Red Sea. It commands the ocean. East or west, no other port on our triangular coastline has its vantage. Portuguese forts have nothing to do with trade. You only have to remind yourself of how they wangled their way into Malabar, to understand that. Portuguese forts are like forts anywhere else, bastions equipped for war.

Now consider the nerve of our embassy. Translated it reads:

Kindly permit us to occupy your land with guns which we can point at your people, with cannons which we can fire at your guests. We will, of course, charge a fee for anybody who approaches the port of Diu: be it trade ship, fishing ghurab or even a humble chatur. If they are in our waters, they must pay us, as the ocean is ours, you must agree.

The truth was undeniable. Even the Sultân with his 87 ports and the Mughal with none, must concede that. The Portuguese are masters of the sea. You need to go back six or seven years to understand why.

It is the story of the two Maliks who can make or break our embassy. One has the Sultân's right ear, the other the left. It's also my story. I've been with the Portuguese for so long, I forget that sometimes.

After D'Albuquerque took took Hormuz by shameful murder, he commandeered a ship from Diu. The *Miri* (surely an ill-omened name) had on board goods worth a fortune. D'Albuquerque took it all, and had the Gujaratis thrown in prison. It sent the message. Merchant ships avoided the Diu route. Jiddah, Suez, Cairo, Alexandria—and Calicut, all felt the Portuguese squeeze. And Venice—ah Venice!—traded with Cairo. Naturally, they colluded. Sent from Calicut as envoy by the Samudri four years ago, Mayimamma Marakkar had been cooling his heels at the Mamluk[109] Court for just this development. So the conclave approached Malik Ayyaz of Diu. This is the first Malik of my story.

This Ayyaz, now Malik, you know all about—who doesn't? Diu *was* Malik Ayyaz. His genius had turned a jungle into an international trading centre. In Diu no man was distinguished by language, caste, creed or skin colour. The only currency was money. Everybody was welcomed by Malik Ayyaz whose hospitality was legendary. There were no empty stomachs in Diu. And fortune hunters who arrived indigent, stayed on to prosper. For all his commercial genius, Malik Ayyaz was, primarily, a soldier. And this fact, the Venice-Cairo-Calicut conclave used as a bargaining tool. They would send a navy to Diu, and drive the Firangi away.

The Mamluk Sultân Qansuh al Ghawri and the Portuguese were sworn enemies. The navy was manufactured. Ships were built at Suez by Venetian master shipwrights, but only after the timber had been lugged in overland from Alexandria. Amir Hussain the Kurd, Governor of Jeddah, commanded the fleet.

The Portuguese heard of these stirrings from their reliable network of spies. The Governor, Francisco de Almeida, ordered his 19 year old son Laurenco to cruise about the coast, making warlike noises to scare off Malik Ayyaz and his friends. This Laurenço did, with great plunder and massacre, till he spotted the Calicut fleet near my home in Dabhol—and on the advice of his men, did not engage with it. This enraged his father who denounced him as a coward, or so our chroniclers swear.

No matter. The boy was anything but a coward. When the Mamluk fleet sailed into Chaul, the fighting was fierce and he the most ferocious warrior of them all. Surrounded, shot in the thigh, he ordered himself to be lashed to a chair, and fought on till, wounded in the chest, he died. Malik Ayyaz was gracious in his victory. He maintained his prisoners like guests. To Francisco Almeida, he sent a letter praising his son's heroism. The Mamluks he restrained from further pillaging the Portuguese. His purpose was merely to keep them away from Diu.

The bereaved father, hot for revenge, in November 1508, gathered a huge fleet of nineteen boats, and instead of making straight for Malik Ayyaz, anchored instead at Dabhol. This, I will remind you, is my hometown. I was away, working with a Munshi in Panvel. News travels

109 *Mamluk* [Arabic … مملوک … one who is owned]. The word came to be applied to all non-Arab slave-soldiers in Islamic armies.
In 1206, the Mamluk commander of the Muslim forces in the Indian subcontinent, Qutubuddin Aibak, proclaimed himself Sultân and created the Mamluk Sultânate in Dilli. It ended when Jalaluddin Firuz Khilji overthrew the last Mamluk ruler Muizuddin Qaiqabad in 1290.
The Dilli Sultânate was an Islamic empire based in Dilli that stretched over large parts of the Indian subcontinent for 320 years (1206–1526).
Five dynasties ruled over the Dilli Sultânate sequentially: the Mamluk dynasty (1206–1290), the Khalji dynasty (1290–1320), the Tughlaq dynasty (1320–1414), the Sayyid dynasty (1414–1451), and the Lodi dynasty (1451–1526).

slowly, and it was a week before I learned I no longer had a family. Almeida had landed outside the town with 2000 men. Citizens rushed out and tried to block their way, and their bodies made a wall of corpses. Almeida's men stepped over them, scaled the ramparts and invaded the city. Plunder. Rape. Massacre. It ended in fire. The city was torched. It burned for three days. And all that while Almeida's boats trod water. Finally when the air was too thick with stench and smoke to endure, Almeida weighed anchor.

Then he went on to Diu and there, brought Mallik Ayyaz to surrender. Ayyaz, ruined, offered Almeida the island—which the Portuguese refused. It had been a battle for revenge and Almeida had won it. An unbelievable amount of gold was collected from Ayyaz. Of course it ended with the Portuguese leaving an official in Diu, ostensibly to trade. News of military movements now could move faster to Goa. Almeida, meanwhile, hanged every Mamluk he could find.

What did the battle achieve? Diu recovered, but its official position now was that of a pawn. The Portuguese didn't particularly want Gujarat, but they did want a stranglehold on its trade. They patrolled the coast, demanding a pass or cartaz from every passing vessel, in most cases an excuse to fire upon and plunder the ship.

Which brings me to the other Malik in the story.

Malik Gopi was almost as rich as Malik Ayyaz, but he was a merchant to the soul. He was governor of Surat, and his mercantile interests were centered on the cloth trade in the Malaccas. You must understand that at this time, the Gujaratis ruled in Malacca. To snap the connection would be to ruin both, and that was exactly what D'Albuquerque did. He burnt Gujarati ships in the straits and bombarded his way into Malacca.

Ormuz. Aden. Goa. Malacca. And now Diu. This would give D'Albuquerque complete mastery over the Indian Ocean trade. It was a masterly plan, but one no Indian ruler, Hindu or Muslim, could understand. Conquest to us, is about territory. To the Portuguese, it's about trade.

Malacca was the nerve centre of the Indian Ocean. Through it passed vessels from Coromandel, Ceylon, China. It controlled the markets on the Red Sea. Every Gujarati merchant worth his pagdi had a stake in Malacca.

In 1511, the year following his massacre of Goa, D'Albuquerque occupied Malacca. This made it imperative for Gujarati merchants to ingratiate the Portuguese.

Malik Gopi trembled lest the Portuguese take Surat. He had his friends in Goa, and projected himself as the Gujarat Sultân's right hand man. Our embassy stopped first at Surat, where we were entertained lavishly by Malik Gopi.

Malik Gopi had been in direct correspondence with the Governor D'Albuquerue, assuring him of the return of the Portuguese prisoners held at Champaner, and one of the objects of my visit was to bring them home. Malik Ayyaz was presently at Champaner too, so I would have an opportunity of seeing the two rivals together.

Malik Ayyaz, too, had been active. Being forced to pay the Portuguese was a humiliation. Giving them an inch more of Diu was disaster. He regretted his brief trust in the Mamluks. Most of his time was now spent on making the Sultân realize exactly how dangerous the Portuguese could be. He had sent Sidi Ali to Goa to parley with D'Albuquerque, to gauge the power of the Portuguese on land. I had accompanied D'Albuquerque, as he trotted Sidi Ali through his arsenal. As translator, my job was to interpret the words, but I could leave their menace unstated. What did Sidi Ali make of it all?

Malik Gopi's last letter to Albuquerque had accused Malik Ayyaz of trying to poison the Sultân's mind against the Portuguese.

And this Sultân, Muzaffar Halim, Muzaffar the Clement, what would he be like?

I was eager to see the man between these two contradictory Maliks.

I won't go into the magnificence of the court at Champaner, you know enough about that. Malik Gopi had taken the responsibility of persuading the Sultân to give permission for a Portuguese fort at Diu. What would he get out of it? Wealth? Malik Gopi had enough to buy the Portuguese ten times over. The Portuguese concept of luxury is barbaric. They have no taste and no understanding of beautiful things. Leave that to the Italians.

Have you seen Italian paintings? They are more real than real, lit from within. I knew this Italian in Goa once, a boy called Rainaldo. I offered him good money to do a couple of paintings for my home, Lakshmi, Saraswathi and Ganapathi. And he would have done it too if the clergy hadn't got wind of it. It would have gone severely with me if a fidalgo hadn't intervened. Nevertheless I was produced before the Governor who warned me not to introduce pagan thoughts to Portuguese innocents. But the rebuke was followed by an interrogation which ended in my getting this job.

I was not consulted on the choice of gifts for the Sultân, you may be sure of that, or I would have spoken my mind. The rich collection they had prepared consisted of a gold collar of the sort that a modest householder buys for his daughter, a few yards of black velvet, a few plates of beaten gold and a wash basin of china. I was filled with shame at the thought of being considered part of this embassy when I saw these trifles. It looked as if we had hastily raided a pawnshop on the way and plundered it willy-nilly. And as for that washbasin, the Firangi had captured a Chinese junk long ago, and hoarded the crockery even if most of it was shattered by then.

This Malik Gopi was your usual Marwari potentate, sweating money from every pore, ascetic, even saintly in appearance as long as he was in office, and a cesspit of vice after hours. I would have quit his roof, if it had not been for his lady wife, a most gracious matron. Noting that I avoided the more ebullient entertainments, she led me to the garden, and kindly showed me around. It was a most wonderful place, full of the rarest of flowers, strange trees and pretty shrubbery. 'We have more curiosities,' she smiled when I had expressed my admiration. 'Have you seen our genda?'[110]

The word was a strange one, but the creature so named was stranger still. It looked like a giant boar in a tight achkan of some dull metal—but unlike a boar it had a solitary horn on its snout. It didn't look in the least fierce, just sad and helpless. It had an attendant who looked almost like a twin, except that he was missing a horn. He had the same melancholy eyes.

'Yes, they look like each other, don't they?' My guide said in a low voice. 'The man doesn't speak a word, and the genda can only be managed by him. It pines if separated from him, turns vicious at the approach of any other groom.'

'Is the man dumb?'

'No. He answered me when I enquired his name when he first came. Oshim, he said. Maybe it's Ashwin, or maybe it's Wasim, but it sounds like Oshim. Have you heard such a name?'

'No. Nor beheld such an animal.'

'They come from a different land with different ways and names. But Oshim—is strange.'

In the days that followed, I was kept busy interpreting the many undercurrents at the court so that de Queimado could convey the correct picture to his superiors. I was careful to preface all Malik Gopi's statements with *Malik Gopi says* when I wrote them out. But I fear the agent scarcely glanced at my reports. I did the smart thing. I made copies which I resolved to place directly in the hands of the Governor when I returned to Goa.

The rumours sent by Evangelho, the Governor's agent in Diu, were quite true. Malik Ayyaz would use his considerable military might to keep out the Portuguese. It seemed as if he could summon up large fleets down the Red Sea and up from Malabar at a whistle. Why then did he hold back?

The truth was that Muzaffar Shah didn't want to antagonize the Firangi. Sidi Ali had made a very complete report of the arsenal at Goa. The Sultân reminded Malik Ayyaz of the terrifying massacre D'Albuquerque had inflicted on Goa, and of the Malik's shameful defeat at the hands of Francisco Almeida, following which Diu had tasted the full ferocity of Firangi barbarity.

The reminder hurt. Besides, Malik Ayyaz did not need reminding. He was well aware he nourished a serpent's egg by allowing a Portuguese factor at Diu, but he was damned if he would do more. And even the Sultân acknowledged that Malik Ayyaz *was* Diu.

Malik Gopi kept us simmering in Champaner till the rains set in. I found myself spending all my spare hours in the garden, observing the strange pair. I was not the only audience. Hardly an hour passed without a few gawkers. The animal walked about sluggishly in its enclosure, followed by Oshim. In time a kind of camaraderie sprang up between us. Oshim acknowledged

---

110 Hindi ... गेंडा ... Rhinoceros.

me with a salaam, the animal with a stare. The small gifts of fruit and coin that passed across the fence were, I thought, very welcome, even though Oshim made no thanks. One day he invited me into the enclosure. I went in, eager to get a closer look at the strange beast. Like most strange things, up close it was not strange at all.

Its achkan was not metal but very coarse brownish grey hide. The horn was a small ugly stub. Its melancholy was even more marked as I looked into its orange eyes. Oshim invited me to touch it, which I did, with some trepidation. I was rewarded with a small sound of recognition, but whether it came from Oshim or from the beast, I couldn't tell. Oshim's silence was never breached.

About this time, we received news that the embassy awaiting us was growing restive, and so de Queimado set out for Surat. On his return with the Portuguese ambassadors, I could no longer avoid the formal presentation in court of D'Albuquerque's pitiful gifts. The sultan made his formal acceptance in chaste Persian, which I translated. Then, betraying a faint smile, he asked his court in Gujarati, 'What gift do you think will be suitable recompense for these? I think the usual treasures will not suffice.' In the same breath he ordered the costly khilats readied for the ambassadors and for de Queimado to be given to them. (Naturally, I was excluded.) When the Firangi retired to dress themselves in the finery, Malik Gopi remarked, 'I can suggest a suitable gift for the Firangi, Your Majesty.'

'What is it?'

'Your Majesty's genda.'

It took a moment for Muzaffar to place the word. 'Ah yes, that odd creature. It is housed, I think, in your gardens? Why do you think it will be a suitable gift?'

'I wonder if your Majesty has observed the creature closely. It has a certain resemblance ...'

'To what?'

'To our very honourable Malik Ayyaz.'

It was rudely spoken, delivered with unseemly contempt towards a man who was not there to defend himself. But the Sultân and his court roared in mirth. For the truth was, Malik Ayyaz, short stocky and melancholy of visage, did look a bit like the genda in the tight suit of dull grey he favored in court.

'The resemblance is not perfect,' Malik Gopi continued with a straight face. 'After my last entertainment, my company of paris and apsaras informed me that the honourable Malik is *missing a horn.*'

Next, I was given charge of interpreting the negotiation between the envoys James Texeira and Diogo Beja and the wazir, Khudawand Khan. For some weeks we played cat and mouse—but when it came to the direct question of building the fort at Diu, Khudawand Khan conveyed the Sultân's regrets. Personally, he thought it a good idea, he stated with a flagrant lack of diplomacy, but the Sultân considered Malik Ayyaz's opinion above all else on the question of

Diu. And, in parting, we were given the genda, and though Khudawand Khan and the others persisted in naming it Ayyaz, I made sure that rudeness was lost in translation.

I now come to my role in the tragedy. Oshim was terrified at the thought of leaving the enclosure. The guards hesitated to use force lest the beast retaliate by goring them. It was at this juncture that Khudawand Khan and Malik Gopi sent for me. My friendship with Oshim had not passed unnoticed.

I was reluctant to intervene. I didn't want to be party to displacing the poor fellow from his familiar life. A life incomprehensible to us, as ours might be to him. To my surprise, on seeing me, he came to the fence and expressed his anguish wordlessly. I explained he was required to go on a journey. He asked if I would accompany him, and on my nodding, his face lit up, and he stepped out with great alacrity, the chained beast trotting behind him.

When we reached Goa after a week's misery at Surat, the Governor was in a fury. The envoys had returned empty handed, except for a great hulking beast that might be the very devil in disguise. James Texeira and Diogo Beja being out of countenance, it fell to me to apply the necessary balm. I curse my impertinence now, but then the words were out before I had considered them. 'The beast is a symbol,' I said. 'It is meant to convey a message. It represents the armoured strength of Diu—in fact the animal has long been called Ayyaz. The Sultân is powerless to permit a fort as long as Diu belongs to Ayyaz, but he assures you of his intent and his friendship by giving you Ayyaz himself, which is to say, Diu.'

D'Albuquerque swallowed this outrageous statement whole. Texeira and Beja were let off, and in reward for my services, I was placed in charge of the genda.

Clearly, one place was the same as another for Oshim and his genda. The Firangi crowd was no different from the gawkers at Champaner. The only difference was that, from the ease of long acquaintance, Oshim began to talk with me. At first his words were incomprehensible, but I learnt his language quickly. It is what I do.

Six months passed. The time for ships to set out for Lisbon was fast approaching. As usual, I spent hours on the quay looking at the preparations and wondering what it would be like to leave this land behind and venture into the world beyond the sea. And then all at once, my wonder ceased to be an idle one. The Governor sent for me. I noticed he was sweating. His fingers fumbled at his collar as if it was too tight. He drank thirstily from the glass at his elbow before addressing me. 'I notice you have an extraordinary influence over the Beast,' he said, for so he always referred to the genda.

'Not the animal, no, but I do understand the speech of its keeper.'

'Which nobody else can. Therefore, I require you to accompany the Beast and its keeper to the royal presence in Lisbon. Yes, the Beast is a gift from the people of India to their sovereign King Manuel of Portugal.' He got it all out in one breath. Aha, I thought, this is how the wind sits: he wants me to carry that pretty story, not just the Beast and its keeper. For King Manuel, you see, had been at the Governor's throat all along, clamouring for a fort at Diu.

I was not wrong. He made that clear in the next few minutes. He did not ask if I were willing. He commanded, knowing I had no option but to obey.

Everyone opposed me bitterly when I told them I was leaving for Portugal. I was condemned by the act of crossing the ocean, a stupid belief I had no patience with. I was excited, and couldn't wait to embark.

We had some trouble getting the genda on the ship which was an imposing galleon of 1000 tons, the *Nossa Senhora da Ajuda*.[111] At first it was decided to board it in the hold, but Oshim insisted it was too dark, and the beast might be driven wild. It ended with them being housed above deck, in a special cabin constructed on the forecastle. Its roof had a skylight, and the genda was kept aware of the passage of time, which Oshim said was vital to its health. We left on January 15th, 1515, arriving at Lisbon in the middle of July. Of the three of us, the genda took the journey most manfully.

I will not tell you of the voyage, of my impressions of the wonderful places we sailed through, or of the starlit nights when it seemed as if the purpose of my life was at last revealed. When we disembarked, I made it clear I was not to be separated from the beast and its keeper, at least till they had been introduced to the king.

This important event took place a week after we arrived. It was so cold, I could barely move without my teeth chattering. Oshim and the genda clung to each other for warmth. I was worried about the animal. The cold made it sluggish. I was afraid it would die before I could convey its meaning to the king. But it was done, and I think well done, for the King praised my Portuguese, and asked if I would stay on to instruct some of his scholars in the Indian tongue. He didn't seem to know that there were almost as many tongues as there were Indians.

For a few months, the genda was a sensation. Oshim kept asking me when we would return and I didn't have the heart to tell him we never would. I was busy trying to grasp how this part of the world worked.

First, it appeared that the fidalgoes who cut such capers back home were held in small esteem here. Even the Governor, whose courage (and cruelty) were legendary, was looked upon with a jaundiced eye. The genda was regarded by the King as a promise that Albuquerque still had to fulfill.

I learned also that Portugal and Spain competed for what they called 'conquest.' It surprised me to learn that they regarded not just Goa, but all of Hindustan as Portuguese property, and I couldn't understand the reason for such ignorance for they're an intelligent enough people otherwise. And then the true purpose of their 'conquest' became evident to me. They had 'discovered' new lands, just as I had now, by setting foot in Portugal. By their standards, surely then I was a conqueror! In these 'discovered' lands they planned to either kill or sell the native people, or to establish themselves as kings and keep the rest as slaves. They had very nearly accomplished this last in Goa. They had reduced the temple of my ancestors to ashes, which is why, I jobless Brahmin, took on this life as interpreter.

111 Portuguese for *Our Lady of Mercy*.

And the arbiter in this race for discovery and conquest was a senior sanyasi called the Pope. However, he was not a wandering ascetic as our more revered sanyasis are. He lived in a grand palace in Rome, in Italy, where all the great artists are, and King Manuel kept up a constant flow of gifts in that direction. One such gift was a white elephant, a rare and sacred beast, trapped in Cochin where the Portuguese are in high favor. The Pope cherished the elephant, largely because of its method of introduction—it knelt down before him, and of course that was read as the homage of its pagan land to this great sanyasi.

Which just proves that no man can claim an original thought. My version of this canard was so well received by King Manuel that he now began to voice his impatience for that genda-like fort in every letter he wrote. Because of my penmanship, I was often in demand among scholars, and scholars of the court are the worst gossips in the world.

The King also kept an elephant for his personal amusement, and one day decided to hold a great festival in which the genda would be pitted against the elephant. It would be a fight to the finish—and I had no doubt it would be the genda who would be finished. Oshim was, I think, prepared to defend the genda with his own body. He reacted to the plan with great alarm. I was powerless, unable to reassure him. The night before the fight he gave me the small amulet he wore. He did not expect to outlive the genda.

But Oshim's alarm was set at rest by the peculiar behaviour of the King's elephant. It looked a fine animal, stately and imposing—until the genda was led in. It took one look at our armour-clad Ayyaz—and bolted.

Oshim gave me a dazzling smile as the genda was declared the winner of this strange contest. After that day, King Manuel could not abide the genda. He sent for me, asking me to repeat the intent with which Muzaffar Shah had sent his gift. I repeated the old lie, and the King had it inscribed on a parchment dusted with gold leaf, and illuminated very beautifully. Then he informed me that I would be required to accompany the genda to Rome.

It would be a gift for the Pope, and I would stay there with the beast at the Pope's convenience after I had fully explained the meaning of the gift.

Like Oshim, I too felt one cold place was quite like another. And I would be in Rome, among artists, and I could finally see the wonders Rainaldo had spoken of. As for Oshim, he had only one question: whether I would accompany him.

As it happened, by curious circumstance, I did not. Oshim and the genda were put on one boat, and I in another. Manuel didn't want to risk the genda in Spanish waters. The chance of a sail through the Mediterranean where we might touch Gibraltar and Ceuta was too exciting to refuse. Accordingly Oshim and I were parted.

I have never ceased to curse the moment that I gave in to the temptation and accepted the seat on that boat. I had no reason later to regret my own adventures, but I still hold myself responsible for the tragedy. I embarked on a Saturday, after assuring Oshim I would be there in Rome to welcome him. Their route would be more complicated. By boat till Bordeaux. Then overland to Marseilles. At first Manuel wanted the genda exhibited as the might of Portugal all along the overland route, but when I pointed out that it might not do to trot an exhausted animal into the Pope's presence, he agreed to limiting it to one viewing alone—for which the most august of audience was arranged. The King of France himself would view the beast at the port of Marseilles.

The news reached us at Corsica. The Portuguese Beast had drowned in the Ligurian Sea two days ago, and its carcass was on display.[112]

I begged, bullied and bought my way into a small fishing boat. My only thought was for Oshim. I knew he was a strong swimmer, so he could not have drowned, but I had to get there to make certain he did not die of grief. I wept for the genda, why, I cannot tell. The truth is, its inexpressible sadness had its own shadow in my soul.

When we made port, there was no need to ask for directions. To my horror, there were two bodies laid out in the strand, already bloating with corruption. The genda, and chained to it, shackled and chained leg to leg, the body of my friend Oshim.

They told me later that I needed chains myself in my frenzy of grief, but I have no recollection of it. I do remember being conducted into the presence of King Manuel, so I must have been brought back to Lisbon. I was to conduct the genda once more to Rome.

I stared, uncomprehending. The King smiled. He explained he had expert taxidermists who had stuffed the carcass. It was now my job to introduce this dead animal to the Pope.

My very soul revolted from agreeing to this, but by now I had done too many things that revolted my soul.

I answered Manuel, choosing my words carefully, 'My religion forbids me from traveling with a carcass.'

'You had no such reservation when you arrived at Lisbon clinging to the corpse of your friend. He was an imbecile, I'm told,' the King observed coldly.

'I will explain that, your Majesty. I was then absolved from this restriction by the bonds of affection. I will carry out your wishes now if I may absolve my sin by the compulsions of justice. If you provide justice, I will do your bidding. If not, punish me as you wish, but I will not go to Rome.'

There was an indignant murmur around me, quickly silenced by Manuel's cold command. 'What justice do you seek? Justice for whom?'

'For Oshim the beast's keeper. He was a strong swimmer. The genda could swim too, but I do not blame you for having chained it. It was a beast after all. But what cruelty induced you to chain Oshim to the animal? I saw his wounds. He was chained a long time. He left here in chains. That is the truth, and I want the men who did that punished.'

---

112 On 25 January 1516, in a shipwreck during a storm in the Gulf of La Spezia. Three hundred years later, in perhaps the same spot, another storm would claim the life of the poet Percy Bysshe Shelley on 8 July 1822.

King Manuel laughed. He roared with laughter for so long, I thought he would wet his pants. The court guffawed too. It was Muzaffar's court all over again.

'You fool, the man was an imbecile. This is what we do to the mad in Portugal. We chain them. Don't you do that in your pagan land?'

'No. We let them be.'

'And what if they offend? No, there has been no injustice done, and you, my pagan friend, had best sharpen your Italian, and turn your face to Rome.'

And so I did.

The genda was so far gone in putrefaction that the straw and resin had done nothing beyond stuffing and hardening it in shape. It reeked like a battlefield the day after.

I went to Rome. I was blinded by its beauty and magnificence. I saw the Pope.[113] I said my piece. The Pope had me and the stinking carcass ejected from his presence. But the matter was not let go so easily. I was forced to sit in the public square that day and the next, for the scores of artists who flocked to draw the fabulous beast. I had no intention of returning to Lisbon, so I stayed on in Rome and worked my way on the fleet to Istanbul—but that story doesn't concern you.

Or perhaps it does, for I returned home by way of an Egyptian boat that shook me off at Diu. And there was the genda—a huge fort of stone upreared from the ocean by the Portuguese.

How had Malik Ayyaz allowed this?

But I had been away twenty years. Malik Ayyaz was long dead. Gujarat had a new Sultân. In Goa and Dabhol, nobody knew me. Like Oshim and his genda, Ganpati Ramchandra Kudalkar too, had vanished with the past.

113 Pope Leo X, born Giovanni di Lorenzo de' Medici, was head of the Catholic Church from 9 March 1513 until his death on 1 December 1521.

Part Five

34

The Two-Headed Man

Looking at him asleep in my shade, he seems like the boy he was when we first met, but he's been a king now for ten years, Sultân of Gujarat. Not when he's here, though. Here he's just Bahadur the two-headed man, asleep in the shade of a two headed tree.

The island too is his, although it belongs in perpetuity to Malik Ayaaz, who made it what it is. Diu is the navel of the sea, its point of reference, a place of exits and entrances. Everybody has tried to take the key, but Malik Ayaaz still holds it fast. His son keeps the trust, but he lacks his father's vision. Another has it, though. Khwaja Safar. The fortunes of Div are divided between these two—Bahadur and Khwaja Safar. So far, they've been on the same side.

By 1521, Malik Ayaaz was dead.

The Portuguese sailed into the Gulf, and then south, killing, burning, plundering.

In 1524, when we first met, Bahadur didn't know this island, he didn't know that Malik Ayaaz, our father, would always own Diu. But I got a sense of what he was looking for.

1526

I heard Bahadur was now Sultân. I wondered if I would ever see him again.

1527

There was trouble between the three sons of Malik Ayaaz. Ishaq had been given his father's rights, but Toghan and Iliyas were ambitious. They knew that with Ishaq's madness—for he was mad, insanity ran in the family—they only had to wait. Malik Ishaq went crazy quickly enough: married a Rajputani and plotted against Bahadur and made a deal with the Firangi. But his brothers were loyal to their father's memory. They sent for Bahadur. It was amazing how the very mention of Bahadur's name was enough to make Ishaq panic. He decamped for the desert, his father-in-law's kingdom. Nonetheless, Bahadur did come here. It was some time before he came to see me. He cleared up the mess, gave Toghan the key to Diu. Later, in the quiet of the afternoon, he came to me. I hardly recognized the carefree boy I had known. He had burned his hands, he held them out like claws, coated with some medicine, but it was not as if they pained him. Nothing pained him. He was turned inside out with grief. His friend was dead, killed by Ishaq. I grieved with him. He stayed till his hands healed.

1528

The troublesome Firangi were everywhere. Across the Gulf, in the North Konkan where seven islands mark the southern end of Bahadur's empire, Heitor Silveira and Lopo Vaz de Sampayo attacked Sidi Ali's fleet and captured 73 boats and burnt all the rest. They terrorized the villages, raping, looting, burning Mahim, Bandra, Thana. Rich places, all.

Of course they did all this to extort money. Money is the sap of humans. It has no meaning for us. I heard all this from Bahadur. He had no palace here, but Malik Toghan opened all his houses to him. Most of Bahadur's time here was spent with the sailors, on the wharf. But I had his afternoons. I would throw down some fruit, luscious with honey, and he said they were better than mangoes. Obviously.

1529

The Firangi had a new governor. His name was mentioned often. Nuno da Cunha. He had been sent by the Portuguese King to capture Diu. He filled the Gulf with fast boats bristling with guns, small craft that could beat a quick retreat.

1530

Antonio Silveira. All of Diu spat at the mention of his name. No man was more cursed. This Silveira, under orders from his Governor, entered Surat up the Tapti, and burnt it, killing every man woman and child that crossed his path. Not content with this, he did the same with Rander. The ships from the China trade, he burnt them all. All along the coastal cities, people fled at the mention of Silveira's name. When he harboured at Daman, he found the city empty, but he burnt it anyway.

1531

Nuno organized a huge armada in Bombay harbour—the entire ocean talked about it. The story was that he had opened the prisons, and the asylums. These are places where humans imprison the bad and the mad. Now all these people were free if they would only agree to fight. In addition to the mad and the bad he had 5,000 Portuguese soldiers, 5,000 soldiers on loan from Malabar, and 8,000 slaves. The boats and ships assembled were above number. And all this was meant for Diu.

We trembled.

They came close—but not close enough. They stopped at Shiyal Bet.

I can see Shiyal Bet, a dot in the north, much smaller than even our island. We don't grow there. That year, Toghan was getting the place fortified. It was full of workmen. And maybe a few soldiers, about 800 guards. It was on this place Nuno descended with all his might, around noon.

He called upon the islanders to surrender. Now even I know what surrender means. Men are chained and whipped, and then vanished to be chained and whipped elsewhere.

Who do you think rows all those Portuguese boats? And the women and children I hear are treated much worse. These things are hard for a tree to imagine, but I know something of it from Bahadur's thoughts.

At dusk, the islanders said they would consider surrender only if they were allowed to go free—women and children too.

The Portuguese make most of their money on the slave market, and they were not going to let that go, were they?

So it began.

When darkness lifted, it was not sunrise that coloured the waters. The horizon smouldered red, but it was not fire. When humans are cut, they spill a red liquid and die, even trees know that. And that silence.

Not a bird was left in Diu except the chattering small fry. The kites, the hawks, ravens, crows, they were all circling Shiyal Bet.

When the Portuguese broke in finally, they found dead children, dead women, dead elders, all slain by the fighting men who could not bear to see them enslaved.

Now this I cannot understand with humans, and I think, neither did Bahadur.

Each life—tree or human—must be allowed to meet its destiny.

But who cares what I think?

For reasons beyond my understanding, the Portuguese skulked around Shiyal Bet for more than a week. They had lost men too, despite their guns. *Isla dos Mortos*, they called it. But we still call it Shiyal Bet.

Why did Nuno da Cunha attack Shiyal Bet?

Bahadur said it was an empty show of might.

Now here's something I want you to notice. I hear Bahadur spoken of everywhere as thoughtless, impetuous, impatient, that kind of fly-off-the-handle Sultân. But that's not the man I know. In military matters he was a great strategist—until he gave in to the lure of guns, and he was far more patient with men than many humans I know. Still, a man, like a tree, grows a reputation he's helpless about.

Naturally by now, Malik Toghan was on alert. In addition, Amir Mustafa with Khwaja Zafar[114] took control of the guns. Amir Mustafa? You haven't heard of him? He was from Rum. That's right, the same Rumi Khan who later betrayed Bahadur. But not now. Now he was the very breath of Diu when Nuno attacked. The more the Portuguese cannon blew at us, the more easily they exploded.

I've never seen a gun explode before or after. The Portuguese boats went up in flames, more from their own mishap than from our shots and as for our defense, they found it so close, they gave up trying and fled.

Rumi Khan was the hero of the day.

Bahadur was all for giving him the entire kingdom, I think! But he didn't give him Diu.

Toghan stayed on as Governor. Rumi Khan travelled with the Sultân.

You see now the two-headedness of my friend? Bahadur's generosity knew no bounds, but the Sultân had to be careful.

Rumi Khan cast two enormous guns. Bahadur called them Laila and Majnun and said they would never be separated. He had a Laila of his own by then, so I guess he knew what he was talking about. He told me her name. Nazuk Bahar.

The year ended badly.

In revenge, Nuno let loose a madman (they were all mad men) Antonio de Saldanha. He cruised the coast looting and burning.

He burnt Mahuva.

In the dead of night he surprised Gogha and burnt all the ships in the harbour.

Then it was Bulsar, Tarapur, Mahim-Kelva, Agashi.

Saldanha was given 60 ships to commit these atrocities on the coast, but Nuno, not content with this, kept up a patrol of 12 pirate ships that attacked all ships coming to Diu.

---

114 *Khwaja Zafar* [aka *Khoja Safar*] was a native of Otranto in Italy. Captured in a battle at sea at the age of fifteen he became a confidante of the Ottoman Sultân Selim the First. He converted to Islam. He arrived in Bahadur's court along with Rumi Khan in 1531. After Rumi Khan defected to Humayun, Bahadur gave Khwaja Zafar the military command. He was a canny diplomat who was instrumental in Bahadur's alliance with the Turks.

1532

With every coastal city burnt or pillaged, Bahadur ordered Malik Toghan to fortify Bassein, for the towns south of this were already ruined in paying vast sums to the Portuguese to save themselves. Toghan got about building the fort, but Nuno, hearing of it, attacked with a blaze of gunfire, and brought down the fort. Toghan sued for peace, but Nuno's conditions were impossible and the battle continued. Toghan's troops fled, leaving behind their ammunition, and Nuno used that to completely blow up Bassein. Then he went south along the coast, burning Shashti Island, Bandra and Mahim.

Bahadur, at this time, was occupied in other wars. It was a terrible year—the terrible beginning of a terrible time. When I saw him next, death concealed him in its mask. Only his tortured eyes raked my wood. Somedays he beat his head against my trunk till he bled. He said it was a headache, but I knew better. The things he had done, and the things he had set in motion, they had begun a numbness in him.

1533–34

These things I heard in the two years I did not see Bahadur: the Portuguese had so ravaged the south that the only solution left was to sign over those lands to them.

Bahadur sent Sheikh Iwas to Bassein to sign the treaty. He told me later, all he could think to save were—horses. His horses. From now on, all ships coming and going from Gujarat had to stop at Bassein and pay the Portuguese a tax called the *cartaz.* All the Makkah trade had to be diverted to Bassein for the *cartaz.* If they did not, then the Portuguese would seize the ship with all its goods. Since all the horses came from Arabia, Bahadur made certain his agents would have the first pick of them. He also got such horses as were sent specifically for him, exempted from the tax, at least the first sixty. As an afterthought, he also insisted that the money allotted for oil for the lamps of the mosque at Bassein should continue to be paid as before.

The Portuguese also made him sign a clause that said no warships would be built in Gujarat hereafter. And that all the Portuguese Bahadur had taken prisoner the previous year would be released. Of these, Diogo Misquitta stayed back. A jackal, that one, sometimes here, sometimes there, and false to both, I'd say.

Even a tree could tell this Treaty was an act of desperation. Things were going badly, very badly with Bahadur. You might think it strange that his only thought seems to have been for his horses. It isn't strange at all. Half of him is horse. There are men like that, I've heard tales at the wharf. *Kinnara,*[115] not centaur. A centaur has the head of a man. A kinnara has the head of a horse. Bahadur thinks like a horse, sometimes his horse thinks for him.

1535

Bahadur, fleeing from Humayun, was here during the rains. He sat here, where he sleeps now, day and night, silent, watchful, angry. Food and drink was left for him—no attendant dared approach. I read his thoughts. I don't know if he read mine. Once more he was seventeen, a king without an empire.

The Firangi Nuno da Cunha sent out feelers. The Portuguese would be friends with a friendless Sultân, allies of a king without any land. Bahadur thought that noble. When the rains

[115] In Hindu mythology, *kinnara* is celestial musician—half-man, half-horse or half-bird.

ended, he wrote to a Firangi he had met before, one Martim Affonso Sousa, who made post haste to come here.

This was before the peasants came to Bahadur, you understand. If only he had waited. If only he had trusted his own horse-like brain. If only he had a friend. How could he listen to a tree?

This Martim Affonso Sousa did not come alone, and that, I think, was Bahadur's undoing. He brought his friend, a doctor, a man whose first words won Bahadur's heart, although they were spoken in Portuguese which Bahadur did not understand. I think it was his voice, or his demeanour, or even perhaps the friendship between the two men, brothers almost, that won over Bahadur. Perhaps he was reminded of his lost friend. At any rate, he spoke with them, stating his predicament without hesitation. He had lost his kingdom. He had no army. Above all, he had no guns. He was still the Sultân. The Mughals were marauders, they had to be driven away.

You give us a fort, and we will give an army, Martim Affonso said. I will ride with you. Bahadur laughed at that, and called for a fine brace of horses that he gifted his new friends. And so this new treaty was signed, but even before that, Martim Affonso had picked the spot for the fort and put up a wooden stockade. Indeed it was done the very next day after this meeting. Martim Affonso departed, assuring Bahadur of many guns and many men. Nuno turned up to make the treaty. Bahadur sent Sheikh Iwas as usual. The treaty was one of friendship, or so Bahadur thought. The Portuguese would still give out *cartaz*, but the Makkah trade could pick them up from Div, and there were more horse concessions. In addition, they promised not to war with each other, and the Portuguese were free to kill as many Egyptians as sailed their way. They would be allowed a fort. And Bahadur would have his army.

They sent him 50 men. No guns. By that time, he already had his own army. It happened like this.

An embassy visited Bahadur right here, waiting respectfully for him to emerge from the dargah. They were common folk, dressed in their best, true, but tillers of land, not nobility.

'What do you want?' Bahadur asked. 'As you see, I have nothing to give you. I am a fugitive in my own country.'

'You are our king,' they answered. 'What we have is yours.'

They had taxes to pay. The Mughal had not collected them. Who should they pay to? It would amount to a lot, they reminded Bahadur. And they could pay more. Enough to get him an army. They would send their sons. They would fight themselves, if he could show them how. The sickle and the plough were the only weapons they knew.

So Bahadur had his army, and the Portuguese had their fort.

1536

Bahadur had his kingdom again, and through no help of the Portuguese. The fort of Sao Tome was built, a big bastion of stone, bristling with guns. Not even a tree could suppose that monster was meant for trade.

The matter was plain: the Portuguese meant to be masters of Diu. Their men reeled tipsily through the town.

Worse, our men now reeled tipsily out of the many Firangi taverns. That was their bargaining chip, the wine. Bahadur was a slave to it.

It made me angry. This was the boy who used to gorge on my fruit. What other fruit can possibly hold nectar sweeter than mine?

Bahadur was here when the fort was half done. He tried many times to point out the treaty had agreed to a place for trade, not war. If they were at peace with the Sultânate, whom were they armed against? There were skirmishes. Toghan, worried for the trade, urged

Bahadur to sweeten the deal. Not Bahadur. Not even when his mother visited Diu and commanded him to send rich gifts to the Portuguese. The Portuguese got gifts all the time, and Bahadur's gifts were exceptionally lavish. Bahadur was not going to sweeten anything. He decided to build a wall. It would face the fort and protect the city from the Portuguese.

This brought down the wrath of Nuno da Cunha. Diogo de Misquitta trotted between Goa and Champaner, taking notes. Bahadur stopped his men from completing the wall.

He visits the fort often. I see him return looking betrayed. A month ago, after a day of agitation, he rode into the fort late at night. They let him in, but they did him no harm. Yes, he was a little drunk, but more on sorrow than on wine. His amirs and wazirs were furious with him. You could have been murdered, they said. To walk into the lion's den alone!

They are not lions, he answered. And I'm always alone,

February 14, 1537. Now.

Bahadur sleeps in my shade. He is a light sleeper. His horse is tethered out of sight, but it will whinny the moment he wakes. They are one person.

The Portuguese Governor is in that big caravel you can see heaving on the tide. I have no idea why he doesn't come on land, he's been there for weeks now.

Something is brewing. I'm sure of that. Bahadur knows it too.

He has been remembering all his lost days this afternoon, between sleeping and waking, all his follies, all his pain. I wish he wakes up with the burden lifted.

I haven't heard him laugh in days.

Bacchu, the musician, is the only one who brings a smile. I wish Bacchu would come now and sing for us. He is often here to sing just for us trees. He listens first to our song, and then makes something more of it. To hear him is to hear the tides, the moon's slow drift on the starry skies. He understands one echoes the other.

We are all echoes of one another. I'm an echo of this two-headed man, as he is of me, a two-headed tree. I hope he doesn't wake too soon. It is pleasant here. The air is fragrant with rose and tulsi, and we find ease in each other's thoughts.

I hear the horse whinny.

Bahadur is awake.

35

14 February 1537 [Part iv]

At the dargah, Diu; 3 p.m.

Bahadur woke with a start, his ears ringing with Hari's laugh.

No, it wasn't Hari. Just the wind in the fans of the hokka.

Hari was just a dream. But in that dream, what was Hari laughing about?

Dalbukhidki.

The name brought a sudden chill.

Hari's laugh was not one of amusement. It was the laugh he reserved for anything that made his stomach churn, as if by laughing he could keep from retching his heart out.

Why had he dreamed that now?

These afternoon dreams were the very worst.

But this was no dream, was it? It was memory.

Bahadur lay back again, wide awake, recalling …

36

The Scrivener's Tale

I am here because I can no longer hold a pen. I was told you could enliven my fingers again. Do it, then. I'm in a hurry. I must finish what I started, or someone else will, and that wouldn't suit me at all. The truth is different for different people, and I have engaged to write my own.

What's that?

You cannot help me? Why not? Give me a good reason, or I will have you hanged. A whistle will fetch my men and then let me see how fast your ungodly amirs rush to your rescue.

Yes, that scar is from a sword cut, it nearly severed my wrist.

You're wrong, that can't be the reason. I've had the scar a long while, and it's only been a week since the pen slips from my grip.

What? You must cut into the scar?

At your peril. This hand can still grip a sword.

Very well, you say the scar goes deep, and as it tightens, it strangles the nerve of the hand.

How can I argue with that? But no, I will not let you touch me.

Fetch me a scrivener.

None of our company can write. Among you pagans, I have heard, are scholars who write our tongue. Do you know one such?

Your nephew?

Summon him, then.

Sit down at the desk and show me a fair sample of your hand. Why, you're but a school boy yet. A cabin boy, not yet fifteen.

What is your name?

How do you mean I will *write* it as Ridamuxi? Is that not your name? To save you the impertinence of asking mine, learn it and write it down. Joao Estavao, Master Scrivener of the Flora de Mar. Come here, let me judge your hand.

'Tis fair. It will suffice.

If you are ready, I will begin.

What? You must be paid before you begin?

You would be whipped for that in Goa, but this is Cambaya, and your pagan ways prevail. Here, catch!

What, will you show me the door? You would teach me courtesy, would you? Very well, my young master. Accept this purse. Take from it what you will and return the rest, I am impatient to begin.

The days and events chronicled in the Flora de Mar were made in the presence of the Capito do Mar, later Governor, the great D'Albuquerque.

It only remains for me now to detail how he shaped the fortunes of the world. For in years to come the victories of this pious and benevolent man run the danger of being translated as miracles. Indeed, the sight of him encoffined, his grey beard brushing his armoured knees, made even souls lost to perdition worship him as a saint. Even his last years carried something of this halo. It shone past the crowding clouds of ignominy and scandal that unjustly blotted his fame.

This document, the only page of my chronicle that has escaped his critical eye, will tell the truth of his victorious ways. I have served him loyally. I wrote for him, I fought for him, I supported his failing limbs, I dressed his cadaver for burial. My duties towards him are done.

My loyalty to myself demands this page.

At D'Albuquerque's death, the world was at peace. I was with him in his final illness on board the Flora do Rosa. It is a bitter truth that his greatness was ignored by the King he served, and I have recorded the words that fell unchecked from his lips as he lay dying.

'In bad repute with the men, because of the king. In bad repute with the king because of the men. It were well that I were gone.'

That was untrue.

His bad repute among his men was not because of the King, but because his genius lacked the usual constraints.

He was kindness itself, but never was a man more ruthless. He was merciful, but his mercy was tactical. In his personal tastes he was austere, but he had an iron stomach for blood and corruption. He was quickly moved to pity, yet untainted by guilt. His life was besmirched by murder, but not for an instant did that burden him.

He knew no greed for himself, but for King and country, he was insatiable.

I write this page because, in truth, the great D'Albuquerque lived out the word glory.

Although I have ascribed the reason for mutiny to the greed of the captains, demanding their share of money immediately, and casting a slur on the fair name of D'Albuquerque, that is not the entire truth.

The men—all of us—were sickened by slaughter, and what it had compelled us into becoming. Swinish, drunken, dissolute though we were, we were men still. Something our sober, righteous and pious commander didn't seem to be.

Here, then, is the truth.

We are masters of the sea because we are masters of the ports.

Masters from Ormuz to Serendip, and eastwards to Malacca.

And all these lands are at peace because D'Albuquerque built fortresses strong enough to frighten them into submission, with guns and powder enough to blow up these lands.

At Ormuz. At Socotra. At Cannanore. At Calicut. At Cochim.
At Malacca, he built two.
And Goa, completely fortified.
It was his manner that won him these forts.

His words were simple and direct. This is what he said at Ormuz, but I have heard him say it everywhere.

'Say to the King of Ormuz, that the king Don Manuel, King of Portugal, and Lord of the Indies, desiring greatly his friendship, hath sent me to this his port to serve him with his fleet, and if the king be willing to become his vassal and pay him tribute, I will make peace with him and serve him in everything he shall command me against his enemies; but if he be unwilling, let him know that I will surely destroy all this fleet wherein he placeth his trust, and take his city by force of arms.'

When I handed him this written down (for he inspected every line) he approved saying he had the words memorized, and they came to him like the refrain of an old song, every time he made land.

I then made bold to ask him how, seeing he had never before stepped on that land, it could belong to our king so many miles away who, perhaps, for these were all lands new to us, did not even know its name.

And D'Albuquerque answered me simply saying it was the Law of God, or at least of the Church, which gave to any Christian monarch absolute sway over any land that belonged to a prince who had yet to feel the Light of Christ.

Why then, I pursued, having enlightened these pagan kings and made them Christian do we also take their crown and treasure, even populate their land?

'Keep you eyes open,' he advised, 'and your mouth shut.'

And so I did.

Now I will relate how we acquired those ports.

Having made this demand, D'Albuquerque would wait an appointed time, three days or four, for the tribute. If it didn't come, he wasted no further time.

In Muscat he bombarded the ships in harbour and entered the town, giving orders for a general massacre. We entered houses and rounded up women and children, we pursued the fleeing and returned them to the town square. And then we killed them all.

This being a desert beyond, water was their greatest treasure, and this D'Albuquerque was quick to commandeer, for our men were sent posthaste to pools and water tanks to dispatch their sentries. Having filled our bags for the voyage, he commanded us to fill the pool with rotting carcasses of men, horses, camels, children, so that the water may stay tainted for evermore.

And then we torched the city.

In Muscat, we did not do this immediately as some citizens came down from the mountains to parley, begging us to spare the city now that all the inhabitants were dead. To which D'Albuquerque pointed out it was their own fault these things had come to pass, for disobeying the order of the King and refusing a tribute, but in consideration of their pain he made the further condition of sparing the city if they would but pay ten thousand xerafins of gold by noon next day.

I could have told him these citizens had not ten xerafins between them, leave alone ten thousand, but he paced the deck all morning, glancing at the dial, counting the minutes to noon.

When no gold showed itself at fifteen minutes past the hour, priding himself on his patience, he gave the order to set the city ablaze.

Despite all that slaughter, our men had prisoners too, mainly women and children, and as we could not be burdened with them, D'Albuquerque set them free. He tempered his mercy with a gentle attention, for in departing our ships they left behind a bleeding mountain of ears and noses.

Muscat supplies the port city of Ormuz. In its interior are many rich orchards and fields. This was the Commander's reason for destroying it so completely. Our ship, the Flora de Mar could indeed have blazed all the port towns to ashes and just sailed past, but that was not D'Albuquerque's plan. He had set his sights on Ormuz.

In Ormuz, D'Albuquerque was at his greatest. The story of his second and grand takeover is well known, but his method of parley on his first takeover is what I wish to write about.

When we anchored at Ormuz, there were sixty great ships in the harbour. The biggest was the *Miri,* six hundred tons, belonging to the Sultân of Cambaya, and filled with treasure. The next, likewise laden, belonged to Malik Ayyaz of Diu.

There were besides, two hundred galleons, and the beach was filled with an army of fifteen to twenty thousand men both infantry and cavalry, arraigned for battle and briskly exercising for our benefit, for the news of D'Albuquerque's cruise down the coast had arrived well in advance.

We sent the usual message to the King.

The next morning, when no answer was forthcoming, we fired their ships. The panicked crew finding themselves in the water had barely time to think. The artillery blazed. Smoke filled the air. We rammed the *Miri*. I was the second man to board her. The first, my friend Gaspar Dias, lost his right arm immediately and I sprang in to shield him. There were but sixty men left on that ship, the rest were in the water, and we killed them all.

Then the commander ordered a massacre of those swimming, and in that too we succeeded. Those struggling in the water were quickly encouraged to drown by our cabin boys. Too young to fight, they could still prod the enemy to perdition with oars and grappling hooks, tearing out their bowels and inflicting the greatest torments before death, and this they did with the unthinking cruelty of children. The rest of us were men, our cruelty no less, but more considered.

The sea was swollen with dead shoals. Men, not fish.

Our men were soon sickened by so much slaughter, but not, it seemed our commander.

On the eighth day, the king of Ormuz agreed to parley.

D'Albuquerque named a place. The jetty.

And so it was covered with rich stuffs and draperies of silk and velvet.

Bloated corpses bobbed up lazily all around the two statesmen, one a boy king not fifteen, and the other a seasoned warrior of many battles.

Our men, finding the corpses still accoutered with rich clothing and gold and silver ornaments and daggers, thought nothing of plunging in boat hooks and tearing into their liquefying flesh.

Later, someone recollected, I don't remember who, and then indeed every man agreed he had a seen it too. Every one of those putrid corpses was stuck with arrows.

Need I tell you there were no archers among us?

Our soul had been saved by a miracle, for what could this be but the Lord's sign that our slaughter was just and righteous, our commander very nearly a saint?

We were to encounter many such miracles. You must have heard of the silver crucifix we dug up past the layers of corpses on the streets of Goa, everybody knows that. And so we were saved.

Such things kept us loyal to D'Albuquerque for a while. But in quiet times every man brooded. We returned to that time of waiting on board before the slaughter, cramped and afraid, waiting the time out, one day, two, a week, a month, steeling our souls for murder.

Murder it was.

We killed no enemies, no traitors, no plunderers or thieves.

These words described not those we killed, but ourselves. Each man had become his own enemy, traitor to his soul, plunderer, rapist, thief. We, the soldiers of Christ.

††††

Haridas had recited the Scrivener's tale from memory, word for word, as he had transcribed it in his 16th year while apprenticed to his Vaidya uncle in Surat.

'I think, for all his composure, the man was half crazed with rage,' said Haridas. 'I didn't realize that at sixteen, though.'

'How do you think I'll feel, Hari, about all the men I have killed in battle by the time I'm fifty?'

The question had shot out of him, how many—six?—no, eight years ago. And he still felt that jolt of panic.

'It is not going to stop you from battle, is it?' There was a weary ring to Hari's question.

If Hari were here, he would ask whether he thought of him as the scrivener had thought of Dalbukhidki. But that question was wasted now.

Hari's thoughts about Dalbukhidki mattered not to Bahadur. He was electrified by his own.

That memory explained the moment. Bahadur shut his eyes and envisioned his last glimpse of the horizon. The hulking shape of the *nau*, like a floating fort, meant something else now.

What if the man sulking aboard were not the pusillanimous Nuno da Cunha, but the great Dalbukhidki?

He would have bombarded the harbour by now. The fort would have added to the artillery with its large guns. Not all of Khwaja Zafar's guns would match that combined assault.

Would he have lost Khwaja to the Firangi as he had lost Rumi Khan to Humayun? Malik Vallabh? Perhaps not these two.

But Malik Toghan would have sent cartloads of treasure to the *nau* by now. Anything, anything at all, to save his beloved Diu.

Had Nuno da Cunha been Dalbukhidki, Diu would be burning now.

This Nuno was a bit of slime. Indecisive and weak. But it was such men Bahadur feared more. They vacillated till the last and generally acted in panic. The minds of such men were cesspits, rotting with hate. Nothing was to be gained from confronting him.

Last night Noor Mohammad had been sent as a spy. He should have reported, as arranged, to Malik Vallabh by now.

Since Haridas had left him, Bahadur trusted no one. He had his own *barid*.[116]

Nanu Barq neighed. He had sighted Shaheen.

Bahadur whistled.

An answering whistle, so instant it was almost an echo, travelled on the wind.

The fans of the hokka rustled as Shaheen alighted and then took off almost at once. That meant it was urgent.

Bahadur rose hurriedly and ran towards Barq. Shaheen circled impatiently, and led the way towards Malik Vallabh's palace.

116 Arabic … بريد … courier; messenger.

37

14 February 1537 [Part v]

Malik Toghan's Rest House, Diu. 3.30 p.m.

By afternoon Krishnaji More felt rested enough. Like most villagers, he disliked being indoors in daylight. He wandered out of the rest house and found the garden. It was cheery with flowers but the fence of hokka absorbed all Krishnaji's attention. He was examining the fallen fruit when Malik Toghan's palki was sighted. This threw the staff into a flurry of activity.

Distracted by the voices, Krishnaji turned away from the trees. He caught sight of the palki—it was the grandest he had ever seen. It must be the Sultân—who else could have so luxurious a conveyance?

Krishnaji's eye inventoried the exterior—ivory, gold, silver, gems, and good Vasai teak.

A guard came up to him. 'The Malik would like to speak with you.'

'The Sultân?'

'Sure,' the guard sneered. 'Seeing what a great man you are, the Sultân has come looking for you.'

'Nonetheless, this Malik has,' Krishnaji shot back. Squaring his shoulders, he walked towards the palki.

The man inside acknowledged Krishnaji's greeting, but made no move to emerge.

'So you are from Shashti Pranth, I hear. What village?'

'Mulgaon.'

'Ah.' Toghan couldn't restrain the sigh.

'Huzoor knows my village?'

'I know your mangoes.'

'It is my misfortune to have come empty-handed.'

'Misfortune has made us both empty-handed.'

Krishnaji smiled inwardly at the penury of a man who owned such a palki. Aloud he said, all in one breath, 'Times are hard, we have lost our fields. That is why I'm here.'

'Are you not a *nakhoda*[117] then? I heard you were rescued when your boat capsized.'

'Yes, I was rescued by a most noble Amir, whose name, alas, I do not know. He risked his life to save mine. But I'm not a nakhoda. I owned rice fields and mango orchards. I sold to the Khan at a good price. I was a rich man. Now I'm a pauper and my sons are slaves.'

'Why? The Khan cannot have allowed that.'

'No, he was a good man. Kalu Khan is dead.'

After a moment of silence, 'The news didn't get here—'

'How could it? The first thing the Firangi did was to round up all barids. Now nothing gets out, nothing comes in. I lived with my friends in Vesawe for a year as a fisherman so that I could make this journey.'

'Why did you make this journey?'

'To meet the Sultân. I heard he was here. He comes here at this time every year, that's what I heard.'

'What gives you the idea the Sultân will meet you? He has better things to do than meet every miserable man in his nation.'

'There are many miserable men? Why? Is the Firangi everywhere now?'

'Look to the west. What do you see?'

'The fort? Surely that is the Sultân's?'

'No, it is Firangi.'

'I should have known. They have built such a fort in Vasai too, I've heard. None of us dare to go there now.'

'Why? No matter who rules, it is your country.'

'Is it? When we have to pay for every stream we ford, every field we cross, every hamlet we leave or enter? Gates everywhere with a gun or a whip to squeeze that coin out of you, no matter how ragged you are. And what is it like within Vasai? All Mussalmans are dead. All Hindus have their mouths stuffed with beef, and so, by default, have become Christian. You cannot reason with the Firangi. They have a different dharma. Money is their religion. The Thana Raja sends rich silks and brocades by the bale, gold and silver aplenty, but the Firangi still cannot do without the *damdi*[118] of the poor. It is their way. They don't have stomachs, just bottomless pits. The Firangi are cruel to us, true, but they are cruel to their God as well. They have nailed him up at crossroads everywhere. I asked one fellow, *Is he a God or a criminal?* And he took the skin off my back for that.'

Toghan's bitterness made him a glutton for punishment. 'Sit down. tell me your name first. Then tell me what has happened since the Firangi came. Sit down. I'll ask for sharbat to cool your throat. It is pleasant here in the shade, isn't it?'

'Very pleasant. You have these beautiful trees. Twin *tad*. I have never seen them before.'

'Hokka. Yes, the fruit is delicious too.' Toghan called for sharbat. 'Your name?'

'Krishnaji. Krishnaji More.'

---

117 Urdu ... ناخدا ... sailor; mariner.

118 Hindi ... दमडी ... farthing.

'Very well, Krishnaji. When you have slaked your thirst with the sharbat of this tree, and made yourself comfortable in its shade, tell me everything.'

Krishnaji was silent. Where could he begin? Thirty years ago? When ships like floating forts first appeared on the horizon? In those early days nobody would believe the nakhoda when they swore these ships brought death. Despite their fantastic appearance, those ships were larger boats, that's all, and meant for trade. The nakhoda were simply envious. They feared the trade would be taken away from the Arabs of the Dakshin. That was understandable. What is trade but war without bloodshed?

In Mulgaon, in Kondivti, Majas, Mogra, Veravli, Pratappur, Sahar, Kurla, Bandra, Mahim, they were used to the many colours of trade. Nations paraded through the villages flaunting colours, languages, stories. Always stories. Trade was the very breath of life in Mulgaon, why quarrel with it now?

But the nakhoda turned out to be right.

The ships sent out small swift boats filled with white men with guns.

Nobody in Shashti had seen a gun before.

The Sultân's soldiers fought in the old manner. And it had been a long time since the last battle in these parts. Before his grandfather's time. Cannons, yes, they had heard of cannons, but only in the stories of the marketplace.

The first time they heard gunshots, many Shashtikars died of fright.

Almost every homestead lost an elder or two.

Cattle turned wild.

The Khan's horses, maddened, stampeded to the hills.

Meanwhile the white men leaped ashore and took whatever they could get—beginning with the day's catch, chickens, fruit, flour. They burst into homes and emptied larders. They stopped their plunder only to rape.

Ah, that. There were many raids, many deaths, many rapes, but what of that?

The mountain of misfortune looms unnoticed when a man's life is altered by one incident. Nobody notices that event, or else everybody agrees to forget it. In his case, it was the second. The village forgot it. They didn't have to make a pact to do this. It came naturally to them.

Perhaps because it had been so swift and so brutal and so complete, it was over before they could even take it in. They were past it.

One morning boatloads of men from a ship sailed up-river. This was unexpected, but not unknown. They would grab a fishing boat or two, a ghurab filled with rice and coconut, scramble ashore for a goat or a cow, fuck the nearest woman and leave.

But that morning, it didn't stop there. They sailed into Krishnaji's part of the river, the bend where women bathe and wash clothes.

It was the hour when men tacitly understand they must keep to the fields if they don't want to risk having their ears cuffed by an indignant matron.

The boat sailed right into the creek.

Imagine the moment. Laughter and banter and women singing to the beat of the clothes on the rocks. Women waist deep in water splashing about like children. Some are swimming. With lithe clean strokes their strong brown arms arc through the waves.

Their teasing friends, safe on land, challenge them to a race, call them back, urge them farther.

They are all girls here, six or sixty. They have escaped the men, pacified the children, abandoned their relentless tedium for this hour of pure pleasure. There are no daughters, mothers, daughters-in-law, aunts, grandmothers. Just girls.

A little longer, just a little longer, till someone remembers how late it is getting and there is a mad scramble to retrieve their wet clothes, to abandon names and resume roles, to walk back, consoled, into their lives again.

Just a little while longer ...

Who noticed the boats?

By the time they did, the men were in the water, fording the shallows, scrambling on land, overrunning the rocks, darting into the shadows after the fleeing women.

The boats kept coming. A hundred men. Two hundred.

Some caught their prey in the water, and dragged them through the shallows in repeated frenzy till they drowned.

Others trapped them on the hill, waylaying each terrified cohort till not one could escape.

None did, not a one.

Many drowned, some by the Firangi's violence, some exhausted by his brutalities, others willfully sought the river.

Perhaps they tried to wash themselves free of the filth that had been forced on them, in them. But the water wasn't enough.

Still others wearily went up the hill, they kept walking till they reached a precipice. And then they stepped off it, as if the air alone could sustain their lightness now.

Many died.

They were the lucky ones.

Others like Godavari, Krishnaji's wife, came home in silence.

By then, everybody knew.

Hearing screams, the men had rushed from the fields. Running sickle in hand, lungs bursting, each man knew he was vanquished already.

The Firangi left. When the men were sighted, they backed off, after firing a few cautionary rounds.

The house was dark when Krishnaji arrived, breathless. He slid into the gloom, a shadow among shadows.

Her whispered her name.

Something glinted in the dark.

A knife edge.

She held the knife at arm's length, her face averted.

He took the knife from her and did not approach.

It was understood she would not endure him now.

He was patient.

Months passed. Years.

That knife still glinted in the air between them.

He could no longer endure her. And so they had stayed these long years in the joyless conspiracy of marriage, impossible to endure, and impossible to forsake.

Strange that the death of desire should kill all else in a man's life. All else, but duty.

Krishnaji suspected it was not so with women.

Sometimes, with rising anger, he caught her laughing. At such moments her old beauty shone again, blinding him with anguish.

After *that*—how could she laugh?

There—That was what the Firangi had done to his, Krishnaji More's life, but he was not going to talk about it to a stranger, leave alone to some Malik in a fancy palki.

'You are silent, Krishna.' Malik Toghan sighed. 'No matter. I know you will find words for the Sultân tomorrow. Be sure to tell him what the Firangi have done to Mulgaon—'

'—for they may do that here too. I understand.'

'You are a thinking man, Krishna.'

'The Sultân must break their fort.'

'That's not so easy.'

'Nothing is difficult for Sultân Bahadur. I have heard he is a great warrior.'

'That is true. We have none like him.'

'Then why does he hold back?'

'Perhaps he won't, after hearing you.'

'You shame me, huzoor. I am only a peasant.'

'Well, it was peasants like you who gave Sultân Bahadur his throne. Our farmers put enough heart in him to drive out the Mughal.'

Malik Toghan felt the unexpressed grief of Krishnaji More oppress him. He went home and lumbered towards his rose garden, where he could be certain of being unmolested at this hour.

Bahadur had told him the only way they could stop the Firangi from massacre was by giving them what they had, already, fairly won. Toghan's troops had fled before the Firangi, allowing them to burn Vasai. Every town on the coast had been burnt and pillaged. Who would repair those lives?

'Give in, to fight another day,' Bahadur assured Toghan. 'I will win your islands back for you.'

That also meant a terrible loss of revenue, but Bahadur, fighting the Mughal, barely noticed.

The Portuguese only wanted Diu. All else was pretense.

So they went about burning the coast again.

By now Bahadur was a fugitive himself. Shaikh Iwas, the trusty negotiator, suggested Bahadur write to Martim Affonso, Captain of the Sea. These Firangi loved the grandiose: the man was merely chief of navy. This Affonso was a man after Bahadur's own heart, a skilled warrior. He was good with guns. Now that Rumi Khan had defected to Humayun, Bahadur needed those guns.

Toghan had hosted the meeting. Martim Affonso came with his physician friend Garcia da Orta. Toghan enjoyed trotting him around the garden while Martim Affonso and Bahadur talked through the interpreter Firangi Khan. At that point it was only about a fort to be used as a warehouse. No battlements. And there were concessions.

On his part, Bahadur offered to free the prisoners he had captured. This was the crew of a boat they had boarded.

Bahadur treated prisoners like state guests, and the captain, Diogo Misquitta had become half Gujarati. Now he served as a go between—or spy. Toghan loathed the fellow, laying the entire fort business at his door.

In no time, the Portuguese showed their hand.

Again, Bahadur was distracted, busy reclaiming his empire, while the fort rose impregnable and belligerent, more arsenal than refuge.

What was the use of remonstrance now?

Martim Affonso was out of favour with the Firangi King.

Nuno da Cunha made no attempt to hide his intent.

Bahadur could no longer look away. He had invited Nuno da Cunha to Diu to resolve the matter. The Governor had come alright, but was sulking on his ship. The fort's armoury had been refurbished. There were drills and drumbeats throughout the day. The Portuguese prepared for battle, and Bahadur, the battle-crazed Sultân, prepared for peace.

Malik Toghan would ensure his hold on Diu. Khwaja Zafar had the same motive. Allies now in a common cause, they would be deadly enemies once the cause was won.

Malik Vallabh's Palace, Diu; 3.30 p.m.

Vallabh's father, Malik Gopi, had favoured the Firangi, and most of Sultân Muzaffar's bad decisions were based on his advice.

Malik Toghan and Malik Vallabh—could any two men be more different?

Malik Ayaaz and Malik Gopi had been enemies, but their sons were close friends. Indeed, it was difficult to make an enemy of Malik Toghan. The big man was affable and generous. Only those very close to him knew how astute he was, a huge spider secure in his imperceptible web of spies. In contrast, Vallabh was irritable and reserved. Bahadur read this as defiance of his father's licentious life and inglorious death.

Sultân Muzaffar had ordered a *halan*[119] of Amir Gopi's palace before having him murdered, and his family found themselves paupers. Vallabh had taken matters in hand, proved himself an abler financier than his father. Not only did he recover the family fortune, he had added to it ten-fold.

Lacking Malik Toghan's love for ostentation, Vallabh was often mistaken for a commoner. He dressed, at all times, in homespun cotton. Only his turban of a dazzling white silk betrayed his passion for jewels: the diamond in his sarpech could light up a dungeon.

Bahadur trusted Vallabh's financial genius, and he also had a grudging affection for the man. There was little in his nature that appealed, but his love for music made his home a perpetual darbar for musicians from everywhere. Indeed it was only music that could loosen Vallabh's purse strings.

Today, Vallabh's performer had a powerful voice that rose and fell in a complicated rhythm unfamiliar to his ears. Leaving Nanu with the hostler, Bahadur hurried to the garden where Vallabh's concerts were usually held.

He was early. The audience was just one man, Vallabh. Catching sight of Bahadur, Vallabh rose hurriedly. The singer continued his alaap unperturbed.

'You're here before I could send you news,' Vallabh was surprised.

'Noor Mohammad is back, then? What took him so long?'

'What took you so long?' Vallabh countered. 'I expected you this morning.'

Bahadur related the incident on the beach. 'How dare the Firangi enslave that village? Murder the Khan? Why were we not told of it?'

Vallabh's silence spoke volumes.

Suddenly exhausted, Bahadur looked around for a seat. Wordlessly, Vallabh led him to his chambers.

'I must see Noor Mohammad,' Bahadur protested.

'He can wait.'

Bahadur refreshed himself in the magnificent hamam, soothed by the unusual scent of itr in the water. He submitted to the ministrations of the masseur and donned

---

119 Urdu … حلن … a home raid, usually a punishment ordered by the state.

the suit of white linen Vallabh had thoughtfully provided instead of the usual silk robes kept here for him.

Voices from the hall told him the others had arrived.

Khwaja Zafar, Malik Toghan, Firangi Khan and, hopefully, Noor Muhammad Khalil, the spy.

Malik Toghan's corpulence was legendary in Diu. Carriages snapped at the axle when he but stepped into them. Two trained elephants were kept to convey him around his estate. Six palaces housed his harem of more than a hundred wives. There was a stable of war elephants, and another of camels.

He toured the city on a foul-tempered camel called Farida, caparisoned in blue velvet. Around her neck flashed a Kashmiri sapphire of the purest water strung on a delicate chain of gold. From a distance man and beast appeared fused, lumbering like some fabulous monster, a cyclops with a solitary blue eye.

This morning Malik Toghan was seated on the marble divan, the only piece of furniture that could possibly endure his weight.

Khwaja Zafar, pacing the room, stopped abruptly as Bahadur entered, and made his salaam.

Firangi Khan, till recently John St. Jago, looked exhausted from his journey.

The spy was not among the company.

'So tell us what you have to, Firangi Khan,' ordered Bahadur. 'Were they glad of the venison?'

'Very glad. As you know we Firangi cannot digest Gujarati mutton or beef.'

'Strange!'

'The carcass must be consumed by now, huzoor.'

'Impossible! How many were they?'

'Four at the table.'

'Impossible,' Malik Toghan agreed.

'That is an opinion I cannot disregard.' Bahadur laughed. 'The only competition I can think of is my grandfather, the blessed Sultân Mahmud. He kept two seer of rice on either side of his pillow, one a savoury *pulao*, the other sweetened with *gur*. Sometimes it was *sambusa*—fifty on either side, just in case he got hungry. He got hungry every night. I used to go in to wake him up when I was a little boy, and I can tell you, those plates were always empty!'

'I doubt if by courting the Firangi Governor's stomach you have captured his heart,' Vallabh observed dryly. 'I grew up watching the Firangi in my father's palace, and I know their ways.'

'I fear our careless talk hurts your feelings, Firangi Khan,' Bahadur amended.

'Not at all, huzoor. I was most ill used by the Governor and feel no good will towards his digestion,' Firangi Khan answered with vigour. 'I don't think they intend peace. I fear also the Governor bears some grudge towards your person.'

'Towards me? Whatever for? I've never even met the man. I've done him no injury.'

Khwaja Zafar cleared his throat.

'Yes, Khwaja? You are going to scold me as usual, I take it. Scold away!'

'I would not presume, huzoor. I was going to say that Nuno da Cunha does not see you as either friend or foe.'

'Indeed. What then am I to him?'

'To him, as to your loyal subjects, you are—Gujarat!'

'Khwaja Zafar, I had not counted *you* among my flatterers.'

'Then do not begin now. It is a self-evident truth. Remove Bahadur Shah and the kingdom will splinter into chaos. Nuno has burnt port after port. Our losses are immense, yet the kingdom shrugs off disaster and moves ahead. You are the reason for that. Therefore, the Firangi's next step will be to remove you.'

'I am not so easily removed.'

'Then we must consider why he should think you are.' Khwaja's voice was unusually grave.

'What happened to Noor Mohammad?'

Khwaja smiled and shook his head.

'Dead?'

'He soon will be, or should be. They filled him up with Oporto wine, and you can guess the rest.'

'Why, what does he say?'

'Merely that he exceeded his orders, but I know what that means.'

'Where is he now?'

'In the guard house,' answered Vallabh. 'I had him put there thinking you might want to question him.'

'Indeed I do!' Although he spoke with the righteous indignation they seemed to expect of him, Bahadur felt light-headed with indifference. By the time they had the man brought in, he had already determined to let the fellow go.

What did it matter? He had thought it a stupid idea to begin with.

It had been Toghan's idea—who else would have thought of a feast as an inducement? He had fallen in with it because, really, he didn't know what else to do. So, Noor Mohammad had been sent with a rich gift of jewels and ashrafis to Nuno da Cunha late last evening, with an invitation to *iftar*. The invitation was just an excuse. Noor Mohammad was charged with the impossible duty of discovering the Portuguese Governor's intent.

The Firangi puzzled Bahadur. Bloodshed, plunder, escalating violence to keep up the pressure, these were familiar modes of persuasion. Familiar too was their rule of tyranny—attrition, bloodshed, terror. More puzzling was their greed. It was as though the shiploads of gold and gems, the rich land of Goa, were not enough without the petty fines they squeezed out of every pitiful fisherman or farmer. As rulers they puzzled even more. Dread and tyranny were ways of establishing power. But to maintain power one needed some measure of familiarity with local ways, if only to keep the taxes rolling. They had their scholars, their pundits and munshis, who got them data—which they quickly proceeded to erase. In its place they prepared a narrative that would please their people across the ocean.

Wasn't that what all historians did? Why then did these Firangi seem so different?

To hell with it all! He would—

They brought in Noor Mohammad, handcuffed and dragging chains.

'Set the man free!' Bahadur barked.

The guards removed the restraints and left at a gesture from Vallabh.

'Sit down, Noor Mohammad. You probably have a headache.'

Noor Mohammad did not reply.

'Having lost your head, it can hardly ache, eh? Vallabh, send for that cooling oil your vaid gave me last time, and leave us alone.'

They left.

Noor Mohammad had compacted his tall frame into the smallest chair in the room, his head in his hands, he crouched like a gigantic fetus.

'What happened on the ship? You did go on the ship?'

Noor Mohammad roused himself with effort. 'Yes, God help me, I went on that ship.' He looked Bahadur calmly in the eye and began to speak very rapidly. 'First, it seemed as if they were expecting me. My chatur wasn't even near their ship when they let down the ladder. When I got on board, I was received jovially. I know some of those men. Khwaja Pīr Quli was there. We were wrong to trust that man, huzoor. What am I saying? You were wrong to trust me! They told me the Governor was resting, he was unwell. What is his illness, I enquired. A dog that has bitten every woman in Goa, they laughed. It is true. The Firangi have this loathsome illness they pass on with every fuck. That didn't surprise me. But the familiar manner in which they joked about their master to a stranger, that puzzled me. It should have put me on guard, but it didn't. You see, they had a bottle with them.'

'Ah.'

'There you have the story, huzoor.'

'Indeed. We have shared many bottles, you and I. Continue.'

'Finally, they told me the Governor would see me when we dined. I was impatient, huzoor. Having fasted all day, the wine had gone to my head, and with my stomach on fire, I was impatient. When we dined, and the Governor was among us, I became silent, trying to understand what was going on, but my brain was addled, I understood nothing.'

'What did they ask you?'

'About the dinner, huzoor. When they heard it would be at Malik Toghan's palace, they were eager for details about his food, his paintings, his harem, his dancing girls and their ways in bed.'

'And you enlightened them, I hope.'

'As much as I could, yes. Then the conversation turned to you. They asked me the same questions, but this time I did not answer them.'

'I do not doubt you.'

'I wouldn't have answered them sober, huzoor, but by that time I was senseless.'

'So you do not know how or what you answered.'

'That is the truth, huzoor.'

'What happened next?'

'I passed out. I woke up soaking wet—a Firangi had emptied an ewer on my head. By the smell it wasn't water. I was still at the table which was messy and stank like a filthy outhouse. Rats frolicked among the debris. The rascal who had woken me up so shamefully dragged me on to the deck. It wasn't dawn yet. I saw my chatur bobbing in the water, and my first thought was to thank Allah they hadn't cut the painter. My second was to reproach Him for what I knew the Firangi would do next. My third was a prayer that I might have the strength to get into my boat—for by then I was in the water, pushed overboard. That too was a blessing, huzoor, for I came ashore washed and cleansed of their stinking foulness. Thereafter I went home and bathed. After *fajr* I bid goodbye to my family and blessed my children. Then I sought out Amir Vallabh, knowing I was a dead man already.'

'You are in my service to carry out orders, not to draw conclusions.'

'True. And I failed to carry out your order.'

'Try this one. Go home, pack your belongings, tell your wife you are going to Ahmadabad. Take the road to Sihor, change horses, then take the road to Porbandar and find a boat to Mandvi. Stay there at my house until you hear from me. You will tell anybody who asks that you have been sent to Ahmadabad. I'll look after the rest.'

Noor Mohammad hesitated.

'Now what?'

'I have not deserved this kindness, huzoor.'

'We will both deserve kindness, Noor Mohammad, when we swear off the Firangi *pari* trapped in their casks and bottles. Send the others in now, and get on your way.'

Bahadur disposed of Noor Mohammad with a terse comment to the others. 'The man is an idiot. He is safer at court in Ahmadabad, far from these pirates. See that he's given a good horse, will you?'

Khwaja Zafar shrugged. 'An idiot can be the most dangerous of adversaries.'

'I agree,' Vallabh joined in.

'You want him hanged, eh?'

'It would be politic.'

'Done publicly after denouncing him as a spy.'

'I'll keep that in mind for next time. So, my friends, what shall we do with this Firangi, this Nuno da Cunha, who lies groaning in his ship with a sore on his stinking prick?'

'Keep a magnificent dinner ready for tonight,' observed Khwaja Zafar sourly, 'and wait for him to arrive, I suppose.'

'But is that Firangi etiquette?' asked Vallabh. 'To insult the envoy and accept the invitation? I read that as a refusal.'

'Noor Mohammad was entertained,' Khwaja pointed out. 'Wined and dined with every courtesy last night.'

'And doused with a full chamberpot this morning,' Vallabh reminded him quietly.

'A prank. A common one among sailors.'

'Noor Mohammad is not a sailor. He cannot be expected to understand such courtesies.'

Bahadur held up a hand. 'Leave it, Vallabh, let it go.'

Vallabh, his face suffused with rage, moved a pace away. 'For now, yes.'

'Very well, Khwaja, what if he does not turn up?' asked Bahadur. 'I don't think he will.'

'With respect, huzoor, it is not what you think, but what he thinks that must advise us. Noor Mohammad Khan has not been forthcoming. With your permission, I will have him put to the question.'

'Tortured, you mean? I don't like your euphemisms. Permission denied. I have questioned him already, and he was most forthcoming.'

Khwaja Zafar bowed and retreated a pace.

Bahadur, looking away, smiled to himself. It needed just that peeve to unite these two enemies. They would have had Noor Mohammad's beard in a mangle if he hadn't sent him away. He hoped Noor Mohammad would keep his wits about him and ride hard.

'Come, Toghan will give us a feast that historians will write about, and I shall fill this Nuno's glass myself. Khwaja will provide the bottle, a slender bottle of green glass such as you gave me last week—and Vallabh will fill it up with a rare vintage.'

'I, huzoor?' Vallabh the teetotaller was puzzled.

'We must avenge poor Noor Mohammad's humiliation. Let yourself go, man! I promise to make certain he drinks the whole bottle.'

Bahadur joined in the laughter easily enough, but it was a mirthless laugh. The night would end with the kind of wildness he had grown tired of. A wave of exhaustion washed over him, and he sank abruptly into a chair.

Vallabh remarked that his guests must be tired. On that hint, the others took their leave. It was understood Bahadur had matters to discuss with his financier.

Vallabh saw his guests out and returned a few minutes later looking disturbed.

'What is it?'

'My mother would speak with you, huzoor.'

'With pleasure, I shall visit her at *maghrib*.'

'Huzoor, she waits outside. I explained, but she would not be refused.'

'For shame, Vallabh. Goda Maasi, this son of yours has forgotten all his manners—'

Smiling, Bahadur welcomed the stern woman who entered. Emaciated almost to a skeleton, she looked much older than her sixty years. Her luminous eyes made an ornament out of every wrinkle and crease in her visage. In all the years he had known her, Bahadur had never seen her smile. She was the most loving woman he knew. Her kindness extended to everyone who came her way, but for Bahadur she had a special tenderness. She was one of the two people who could bring his turmoil to a halt. The only one now, since Sheikh Jiu was dead.

'Go do something, child,' she dismissed Vallabh, and waved Bahadur's assistance away as she walked painfully to a comfortable chair.

'I am well, Bahadur, don't concern yourself about me. It is you I'm here to talk about.'

Bahadur threw up his hands. 'What now, Maasi? I haven't done anything!'

'That's how our conversations always begin. This time it is not you, but me. I've done something, and I'm here to ask for pardon.'

'A child cannot judge his parent. But we were always conspirators. Go on, tell me, what have you done now?'

'Yesterday I had a visit from your mother.'

'Ah.'

'Then you guess what it was about? No, don't look away, child, it must be said. Your mother asked me to talk about it.'

'Then you've done it already. The matter is over! Tell me why have I not had any of your *gorkeri* at *iftar*? I looked for it yesterday.'

'Ramzan is but three days old. The pickle can wait till your stomach is used to fasting. Your mother said—'

'That my wives complain? I know. That isn't true. My wives are quite content. It is my mother who complains that they are still in Jiddah and I haven't sent for them yet.'

'True, your wives are content, weighed down with your generosity and kindness. Wait—I haven't yet told you what I've done.'

'What?' Bahadur could not keep anger out of his voice.

'Bahadur.' Godavari took his hand. Her fingers, light as leaves, traced the lines on his palm. 'I told your mother you have your reasons and she should not interfere. How do you know, she asked me, has he told you what those reasons are? Yes, I said, he has told me, but I am not at liberty to speak of them to you. There! I have presumed. I have lied. Nonetheless I spoke nothing but the truth.'

Bahadur, profoundly touched, pressed her hand to his heart. If only life could be as simple as this moment.

'If I knew the reason, you would be the first person I would tell,' he said in a whisper, letting go of her hand. 'It seems as though you know the reason. Tell me.'

'You are the reason. Bahadur is the reason the Sultân neglects his wives.'

'Bahadur will have his way.'

'Bahadur must always have his way, but the Sultân doesn't always let him.'

'You don't blame me, then?'

'Blame you? Oh no, no.'

Goda stood tiptoe and kissed his forehead. 'There, child! Your headache will vanish.'

Aboard Nuno da Cunha's galleon, Diu; 3.30 p.m.

Khwaja Pīr Quli blinked as he emerged into sunlight.

He had been imprisoned in the hold since the dinner with the spy. The night had passed in a frenzy of hate and self-loathing that robbed him of fatigue. He had touched nadir, in abject degradation emptied his bowels right there, without shame, without disgust, left a mound of shit between two enormous crates. That horror peeled off the moment the door was unlocked. He aimed a kick at the guard who gagged at the stink, his wily eyes leaping underneath their grey overhang of hair. He spat on the deck within an inch of the Governor's foot.

'Explain why you kept me prisoner in that foul place. I could not breathe for the stench!' he barked without salutation, and to further expunge his shame, retched over the ship's railing.

'The ship is a foul place,' Nuno da Cunha replied wearily. 'I should have gone on land long ago. You kept me here. Why?'

'I? Your fear kept you here.' Pīr Quli straightened up, energized. 'Let us not say fear. You are the great Nuno da Cunha. Your historians will so preface your name. Fear is alien to you. Let us say your intelligence kept you here.'

'You are my intelligence.'

'In this matter, yes. You evade my question. Did I or did I not get the spy talking last night? Was it just to imprison me?'

'Just? No. Politic? Yes. Tell me again what the spy said. What is planned for me tonight by this blackguard Sultân?'

'You will be attacked at the feast. Surrounded and attacked.'

'Impossible. I have guards.'

'Good with guns. Useless in hand to hand combat. In Bahadur's camp even cowherds fight.'

'You are certain the spy didn't lie?'

'Are you certain that I'm not lying?'

'No.'

'Then I must answer no, too.'

'You have no doubt at all, that his intentions are evil.'

Khwaja Pīr Quli stared insolently.

Disconcerted, Nuno stammered, 'What of this Egyptian business? What have you heard?'

'What of the treasure, I think you mean to ask? You are determined to burn Diu if you have to, but possess that treasure you will.'

'It is the rightful property of his Most Christian Monarch Manuel of Portugal.'

'As it was once the rightful property of the many infidel kings of Rajputana and Gujarat who looted it from some Dakshin Raja. Then it travelled from one Mussalman king to another till it came to Bahadur Shah. And he moved it before the Mughal could grab it. I have news for you, Nuno da Cunha. Prepare yourself. I have letters. Copies of letters that have passed from the Sultân—'

'To the King? I have seen those already.'

'Ah. You know then that Bahadur holds you to no account.'

'If I'm replaceable, why kill me?'

'True. That is a matter I had not considered. However, the treasure is lost to you. It has been, for the past year, in the possession of Sultân Suleiman in Istanbul.'

'What? You told me he had sent it to Makkah with his queens. And it will return when they do.'

'That is correct. But there were letters. I have copies. Letters from Bahadur to Suleiman, letters from Asaf Khan to Suleiman—'

'Who is this Caferçao?'

'Asaf Khan is the man who conducted the queens and the treasure to Makkah.'

'So you think it is lost to us? The belt? I promised my king that belt! I promised!' Nuno's voice cracked as he struck impotently at the railing. Khwaja regarded him with pity.

'Depends on how we play the cards,' he said slowly. 'All is not lost to us. There is still Zaman Mirza.'

'I thought that sly fox escaped—'

'To Lahore, yes. He is a jackal, not a fox. When he has eaten the leavings there, he will come running for pickings here. We should be ready for him.'

'What do you mean?'

'We want the same things, don't we? We want him. He wants Gujarat.'

'Does he? But he has no stomach for a fight.'

'True. But he will have no problem occupying an empty throne.'

'Are you suggesting—'

'You do what the great D'Albuquerque did at Ormuz? Great deeds can only be done by great men. Who can aspire to the greatness of D'Albuquerque?'

And turning on his heel, Khwaja Pīr Quli called to a sailor to lower a boat for him.

Nuno da Cunha made no attempt to detain him. The Khwaja's last jibe had gone very deep. In Hormuz, twenty years ago, D'Albuquerque had engineered an assassination in open court. That story had been told many times since. It was shocking, thrilling, game changing.

Rais Husein, the powerful noble, controlled the boy king. D'Albuquerque arranged a banquet. He invited Rais Husein, and the king. Rais Husein strode in, followed by the snivelling king. The interpreter Alexandre de Athayde, grabbed Rais Husein by the sleeve and pushed him to the floor at D'Albuquerque's feet. D'Albuquerque reproached him for coming armed to a friendly dinner. Rais Husein had begun to deny this when he realized he was surrounded. He clutched at D'Albuquerque's cloak, begging for mercy, but the great D'Albuquerque said to the man next to him, his own nephew, 'Kill him!'

At the order, all the Portuguese jumped on the fallen man with their daggers, literally tearing him to shreds. (They carried home bits of bloodied clothing as souvenirs). The terrified young king was permanently enslaved to D'Albuquerque, and the Portuguese had claimed Ormuz as their own.

If D'Albuquerque had done that, why couldn't he?

Nuno da Cunha sent for Manuel de Sousa, Captain of the fort. He had his suspicions about de Sousa. Twice he had let Bahadur walk unarmed into his fort, and twice he had let him go. He had defended himself by saying it was against the tenets of a fidalgo to harm a guest. Nuno wondered if he could trust Manuel de Sousa with his plan, but the messenger had left already.

Nuno da Cunha stared at the Goghla shore. The Sultân was lodged somewhere behind those trees, in one of Malik Toghan's luxurious palaces. What was he up to?

Malik Vallabh's Palace, Diu; 4 p.m.

Malik Vallabh's clock strikes four as Bahadur enters, laughing. 'That's two hours to *iftar*! What has happened, my braves? Why so grave? Who has seen Bachchu? I've been looking for him.'

'He is with the swans,' Vallabh says. 'I'll send for him.'

'No, no, I will go to him—'

And turning back he says over his shoulder, 'I have a plan, wait for me.'

Does he have a plan?

Bahadur has said the words before he has considered them. No, there is no plan. Since he woke up from that dizzying nap, he has made no plans, no decisions, but he feels compelled to hurry. As if Bachchu is part of this haste, he runs towards the pond.

Bachchu is in the water, the swans circle him. Bahadur stops, an unbearable pressure in his chest, wanting to cry out to Bachchu, not knowing what he must say.

Bachchu begins to sing. His voice follows the swans in slow, majestic, ever-widening circles.

This is how I should live, Bahadur thinks, like this *raag*, advancing not with war but with grace. He is done with war. That is certain now. No more battles. He shouts out a greeting to Bachchu and hurries back to the council.

Vallabh meets him half way. A moment of silence opens like a flower.

Bahadur says, 'Tomorrow I'll send for the Begums. I had thought of making the Hajj this year, and bringing them back myself. But that must wait. Asaf Khan can bring them back. They can leave Jiddah after Eid.'

Vallabh knows Bahadur is thinking of his wives and his daughter with guilt, not longing, and wonders if his mother had something to do with this decision. They have been away more than a year, the child must be nearly two. Vallabh cannot bear to be parted from his children even for a day. He says quickly, lest Bahadur sense a rebuke, 'Yes, the ship leaves tomorrow at *asar*, but the birds are quicker. I'll send the munshi early to you.'

Bahadur, lightened, walks into the room whistling. He senses their anxiety, Toghan has given them news about the ailing Firangi.

Firangi Khan says, 'In the fort they think Noor Mohammad Khalil is dead.'

'A predictable conclusion. Their friends threw him overboard,' Bahadur reminds them.

'Nuno da Cunha has sent for Manuel de Sousa.'

'Why, is he taken worse? We should send our vaid and hakim. These Firangi doctors are useless. Vallabh, will you—'

'No, I don't think he's worse,' Khwaja Zafar says.

'You're worried, Khwaja. He refused Toghan's invitation to dinner because he is ill. Even a jogi will overeat at Toghan's banquets. And Nuno da Cunha, by all accounts, feeds uncommonly well. Naturally, if he banquets with us, his physician will rebel and his liver will go to pieces.'

'I think otherwise,' Khwaja Zafar's voice is grave.

'Well, what do you think?'

'I think he's afraid we will murder him.'

'Murder him?' Bahadur is startled. 'One doesn't murder a guest. It simply isn't done.'

'Ormuz?'

'Ah, that. Those were barbarians.'

'It was the great—'

'Dalbukhidki. I know! He was a barbarian, but an intelligent one. This one's an idiot. My friend Martim Affonso Sousa told me so. Which is why I wrote directly to the king of Portugal. Naturally, the letter was leaked, and now we'll see a difference in this Nuno's behaviour.'

'Will we? He came in response to your invitation, Huzoor,' maintains Khwaja Zafar doggedly, 'yet he refuses to meet you,'

'Oh, stop scolding, Khwaja Sahab! You make too much of it. Why won't he come to us? Let's find out! I'm going to him.'

The Khwaja's jaw drops. 'Now?'

'Why not?'

'Don't go, Bahadur,' Vallabh says quietly.

'You too?'

'I don't advise it either,' Firangi Khan says. 'I don't believe a word they say.'

'And you a Firangi!'

'Alas. I know what they want, so I know how they think.'

'What do they want, Firangi Khan?'

'You.'

Bahadur laughs. Toghan joins in, a little too easily, it seems to Khwaja Zafar.

'Ask them to ready a boat.'

'I'll arrange it,' Toghan says. 'We'll have a grand expedition tomorrow on a special barge. I'm having one made just like the Mughal's. It is almost ready. The menu—'

'Malik! No. No arrangements, no fanfare, no food. I'm going there to talk with him man to man. It is time to end this game now. You know Martim Affonso agreed with me when I told him Portugal can profit more without bloodshed. Tell them I'll be at the wharf in ten minutes.'

'If you must go, let me come with you,' Khwaja Zafar says. 'You must not go alone.'

'Ten guards, armed to the hilt. At least,' Firangi Khan adds.

'No guards. Five friends and a page to hold my weapon, for I want to be unarmed.'

'We are all coming then,' Vallabh says.

'Vallabh, not you. You don't fight.'

'I thought you said this was a diplomatic mission. I'm a diplomat.'

'Oh, very well.'

They avoid looking at Malik Toghan. Any boat smaller than a galleon will sink with him in it.

'Malik, you will await us with your choicest delicacies,' Bahadur smiles. 'Where is that boy of yours?'

'Sabrang?'

'The very same. I'll take him. He can be my page this evening. Have him meet me at the boat.'

The chatur is ready. Bahadur asks for its canopy of brilliant white to be removed. They will travel in an open boat. The galleon is about three miles away.

The boy Sabrang hangs back. Bahadur notices him and throws him his sword. The boy catches it with a gasp of wonder. Bahadur unbuckles his quiver, hands him the bow.

'Stay by my side,' Bahadur says, but the boy doesn't need to be told. There is nowhere else in the world he would rather be. His eyes are wide with adoration.

Khwaja Zafar has brought his son-in-law Babbar Jehan, a man who has, on more than one occasion, lived up to his name.

The galleon is anchored in their view. By now the Firangi must have noticed them. As Firangi Khan unfurls his red silk kerchief to wave, Khwaja Zafar stops him. He says, 'I still think this is a bad idea, huzoor. We should turn back.'

Bahadur surprises them by considering this. He says, 'If anything should happen to me, send for Meeran Mohammad before the Mirza gets here.'

Vallabh frowns and is about to speak, but Bahadur silences him with a gesture.

It is just a reminder. He had done well by naming Meeran Mohammad his heir in open darbar, seating him on the throne, and making all the amirs swear fealty. A Sultân not yet thirty does not appoint his nephew as successor without good reason.

The retreating beach brings the morning's adventure to mind. 'Vallabh, has that man I sent you recovered? Krishnaji More?'

'I looked in on him. He was asleep after a good meal.'

'Good. I'll see him in the morning.'

'I'll send him to you. At what hour?'

'No, don't bother. I'll ride out to him.'

Bahadur falls silent. The rise and fall of oars makes sweet music. The island, tasseled with hokka is like a beautiful girl marred by some fatal disease. The ugly Portuguese fort bulges out like a tumour.

Khwaja Zafar hands Bahadur a monstrous pair of glasses. 'Try them, huzoor, They arrived yesterday from Venice.'

'But I don't need them, Khwaja, everything looks clear to me.'

'Clear, but not near.'

Through Khwaja's spectacles the galleon leaps into focus, bigger, closer, almost within spitting range. There is a scurry of men on the deck, but no, the gunwales are not manned. As Bahadur watches, men line up, a ladder is lowered. One of them, the captain perhaps, waves a welcome.

Yes, it is the captain, but not the captain of the ship. It is the captain of the fort, Manuel De Sousa.

Bahadur is relieved. This Manuel is a good fellow. With him is Diogo de Misquitta. Not such a good fellow.

They are close before they know it.

The next few minutes are spent in securing the chatur and the Khwaja goes first, with Firangi Khan. Bahadur smiles at the boy Sabrang, rigid in attention, struggling to keep his balance in the swaying boat. And if he mistakes not, struggling to overcome a growing nausea as well.

'First time on a boat?'

'Huzoor.'

'There is no shame in feeling queasy. I still do after many voyages. I am still scared of the ocean.'

'You?'

'Why not? I'll be sailing again one of these nights. I'll be needing a page.'

Leaving the boy effulgent with delight, Bahadur runs up the ladder with a monkey's agility. Oh, to be fifteen again—what scamps they had been, he and Haridas!

But now it is all a clumsy flurry of welcome, and here is Manuel de Sousa greeting him. Here is Diogo de Misquitta, nicknamed Qazi, making his obeisance in Gujarati.

Time now to put Bahadur away.

The Sultân of Gujarat says, 'We are most concerned to learn your honoured Governor is ill. When we received his regrets, we decided to come right away to enquire how we can ease his suffering. What do your doctors say?'

Firangi Khan is a while translating all this.

Bahadur does not fail to note the uneasy looks Manuel de Sousa keeps darting in the direction of the cabin where, presumably, the Governor is resting.

'Why not nurse the Governor on land?' asks Bahadur. 'My palace is his home till he recovers. There is no need for him to suffer the rigors of the fort.'

Manuel de Sousa thanks the Sultân with forced grace and says he will see if the Governor can receive so honoured a visitor. Qazi says he has waited all afternoon, but the Governor has been too ill to see him. This is a lie, as Bahadur discovers from the sudden tightening of Vallabh's face.

Bahadur does not doubt for a moment that Nuno da Cunha dived into bed when the chatur was sighted.

The captain's cabin is a small octagonal chamber lit with a single lamp. Bahadur would have been ashamed to nurse a dog in it. The air stinks with stale liquor and the usual odour of unbathed Firangi. Nuno da Cunha clutches his bedclothes and murmurs a tepid welcome.

'I'm sorry to see you so ill,' Bahadur says. 'You must have a high fever, your face is so very red.'

'It is an old malady.'

'Indeed? I remember you from our last meeting as rather pale. You will be better on land. I will make you comfortable in my palace, and your own doctor shall consult with our hakims and vaids.'

'That's very kind, but I should be up and about very soon. You said you had business to discuss?'

'I said so in my letter, yes. But that was more than a month ago. We can discuss everything once you are better.'

'Oh, I have nothing to discuss, only plenty of complaints.'

'Indeed. Perhaps I have my share of them too, so let's wait for a more felicitous hour.'

With Firangi Khan translating to and fro, and the hovering shadows of the company crowding the door, this exchange is growing tiresome.

Nuno da Cunha has gone pale again, and is sweating profusely. Perhaps the man really is ill.

A young Firangi approaches the sick man and whispers in his ear. Nuno nods, glances at the door.

Bahadur rises abruptly. 'It appears we have taken too much of your time, and I am in a hurry too.' He bows stiffly, every nerve alert.

Nuno da Cunha, whiter than his soiled sheets, mouths something, but Bahadur strides out. Brushing past Manuel de Sousa, he slides down the ladder, impatient for the others to join him. Vallabh and Babbar Jehan get in. Khwaja Zafar joins them after a brief delay.

They are silent, trapped in a web of anger and uncertainty, each man unsure of what the other makes of the encounter. As if in keeping with their discomfort, the sea churns in deep turmoil that augers a swift and treacherous undertow. The Khwaja trains his spectacles on the galleon and utters an exclamation. He hands the glasses to Bahadur. Qazi is back again on deck with Manuel de Sousa.

A boat is lowered for them. They row towards Bahadur's chatur. Bahadur stalls to allow them to approach. Meanwhile, six more boats fill up with fidalgoes. They row straining against the tide, making little headway. Manuel de Sousa and Qazi have a third man with them. Firangi Khan says it is Antonio Correa. The name means nothing to Bahadur. He is trying to explain the sudden flurry of fidalgoes, without concluding the obvious. Something in him, something so alien to himself, refuses to countenance the possibility of treachery.

'We should never have come,' Khwaja Zafar says.

'Let them come, I am waiting,' Babbar Jehan assures his father-in-law.

'You're waiting, and what about my daughter?' the Khwaja exclaims. His eyes spill over without warning.

'Be tranquil now, Khwaja. Let us hear what they have to say.' Bahadur's voice is gentle.

Bahadur leans forward into the wind to hear what Manuel de Sousa is shouting, but he cannot make out the words. He beckons the boat closer, invites Manuel into the chatur.

Manuel de Sousa has one leg in the chatur when he overbalances and falls. His legs stick out in a comic V that wins a guffaw of laughter from Bahadur.

De Sousa is rescued within seconds by the oarsmen. They seat him on the cushions, a cloak is thrown over him with much merriment. It is the laughter of relief, a bare hairsbreadth away from terror.

'What is so urgent that it has you pursuing us?' Bahadur smiles. He sees only Manuel's dripping face, but he feels that prickling urgency he knows better than his own heartbeat.

The other boats draw closer, the fidalgoes shout out to Manuel de Sousa.

'Your friends are anxious about you, it seems,' Bahadur drawls, and turns away, disinterested. In a whisper he primes the page. 'When I say your name, shoot an arrow in the air. Do you know how to do that?'

'Yes.'

'Good. Wait for my signal.'

The others are at the ready. Menace flashes between the boats like electricity. Bahadur notes the fidalgoes have no guns. Manuel de Sousa stands up and raises a hand.

'Sabrang.'

Bahadur is on the second syllable when the arrow flashes into the air. It catches fire from the sun, a streak of light in its graceful plummet into the water. Till it strikes the roiling tide, nobody moves. Every man's eye follows it, mesmerized.

It comes, Bahadur thinks, preparing for the roar in his blood, the joy of combat, that brilliance of death at the shining edge of life, the tremor that has thrilled him all his life.

It does not come. Instead, an acuity of observation brands his brain.

He sees the filthy skin with pustules and warts, the matted beard, the broken teeth in a Firangi face and only later recognizes it as Qazi, and thinks *I must tell him to bathe.*

He sees Babbar Jehan clench his jaw, throw back his shoulders, become a column of steel.

He sees Vallabh empty his face of all emotion as his eyes turn towards home.

He sees Khwaja Zafar narrow his eyes as his fingers grip his dagger.

He sees all this and yet makes no move towards his sword. Something nudges him. He recognizes it from habit. His fingers curl around it, feeling its reassuring curve, but his arm is still slack, unwilling to heft its weight.

The boy has placed the unsheathed sword in his grip, and has fit another arrow to his bow. All this Bahadur sees in the time it takes for the arrow to hit the water.

His eye sweeps the chatur, engaging every man in silence.

The fidalgoes shout out to Manuel de Sousa.

'Why don't you go to them?' Bahadur asks.

If Manuel de Sousa leaves the chatur, there can be no quarrel anymore.

Bahadur understands that Manuel will never leave the chatur. Manuel is the bait, and the Sultân has bitten.

Bahadur grasps Manuel by the arm and pushes him towards the nearest boat. Qazi shouts something at him, the words are lost in the wind.

Bahadur leans forward to hear better.

In that instant, Qazi plunges a dagger into him.

Bahadur is caught in the ribs, no, darn, between the ribs. That means a lung tear and ten minutes to keep his breath going for the fight—the thought is a lightning flash in Bahadur's brain, but as always, his arm is quicker, and Qazi topples into the ocean in a red haze, a look of surprise on his face.

The Firangi have boarded the chatur now. Sabrang works his bow almost as fast as Bahadur's sword. Babbar Jehan whirls like a steel windmill, spinning out scarlet skeins.

Manuel de Sousa dies, transfixed by Khwaja Zafar's kris.

Bahadur catches a glimpse of Vallabh, still standing empty-faced in the mêlée. Why isn't he dead yet, Bahadur wonders—and realizes how very dead he is, hammered to the mast by an iron pike.

They are seven against seventy or more.

Bahadur flings himself in front of Sabrang, and catches the arrow in his thigh. His breath is coming in painful rasps now. He needs to get away. He is slowing down, too slow, almost surrounded now.

He hears Sabrang cry out urgently, '*Huzoor!*'

But it is not a warning, it is Subrang's death cry. The child's eyelids close like petals as he falls.

And I'm still alive, Bahadur marvels, what more will it take to make me die?

His boats have set out from the shore. They will be here soon. He feints, escapes a stranglehold, dives overboard, sights his rescue half a mile away, forgets everything but the salty beat of water he must move with, stay with and persuade to keep him afloat.

But he can no longer ignore the undertow. The Firangi pursue him. There are others in the water with him. He discerns Khwaja Zafar, Firangi Khan—but where is Babbar Jehan?

The boats crowd them, he is almost there, almost—when the current pulls him in possessively and he disappears, holding what little breath is left him, holding it till his brain is ready to burst with unbearable pressure, and up he comes, crying out in relief.

Too late he remembers the battlefield is no place for relief, not even to a drowning man. He hears them exclaim his name *Soltao, Badur, El Rey.*

A man leans out towards him, holding out an oar.

All he has to do is grasp it, all he has to do, but even that is too slow, too difficult, there he has it, almost ...

... almost, and at that moment his head explodes into blood and bone and brain, battered by a halberd.

As a hand reaches down into the water and tugs at his waist, for one moment, through unbearable anguish, he feels the tug of hope, but as something gives, he understands. It was not hope, but greed, that tugged him briefly towards life.

There, they have the gold dagger from his waist. They will let go now. There is nothing more left to steal.

They let go, he is free, his arms flail out as he sinks. A spume of red bubbles is erased by the next swell of grey waves.

38

Coda

And so I lost him, my two-headed man.

I lost him to the sea, as I lose my seed every year.

The sea carries my seed to some other island. Somewhere there is another me.

That happens not with men.

As long as there is memory, men may hope for immortality.

So I remember him. I murmur his story when the wind lets me. The tides spring up like his laugh. At night the stars wheel about like the roads he loved to wander, with only the moon for lamp.

Someday at dawn he'll return to his refuge just as the roses open. And we will look at each other and think each other's thoughts until he thunders away again on a new Barq, one I have yet to see, a hokka for hire on another new dare.

Sultân al-Barr, Shaheed al-Bahr.[120]

Bahadur, Shah of Gujarat.

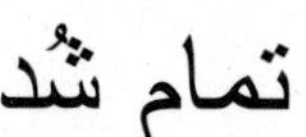

120 Urdu … سلطان البر … King of the Land … شہید البحر … Martyr of the Sea.

Maps

INDIA in 1525

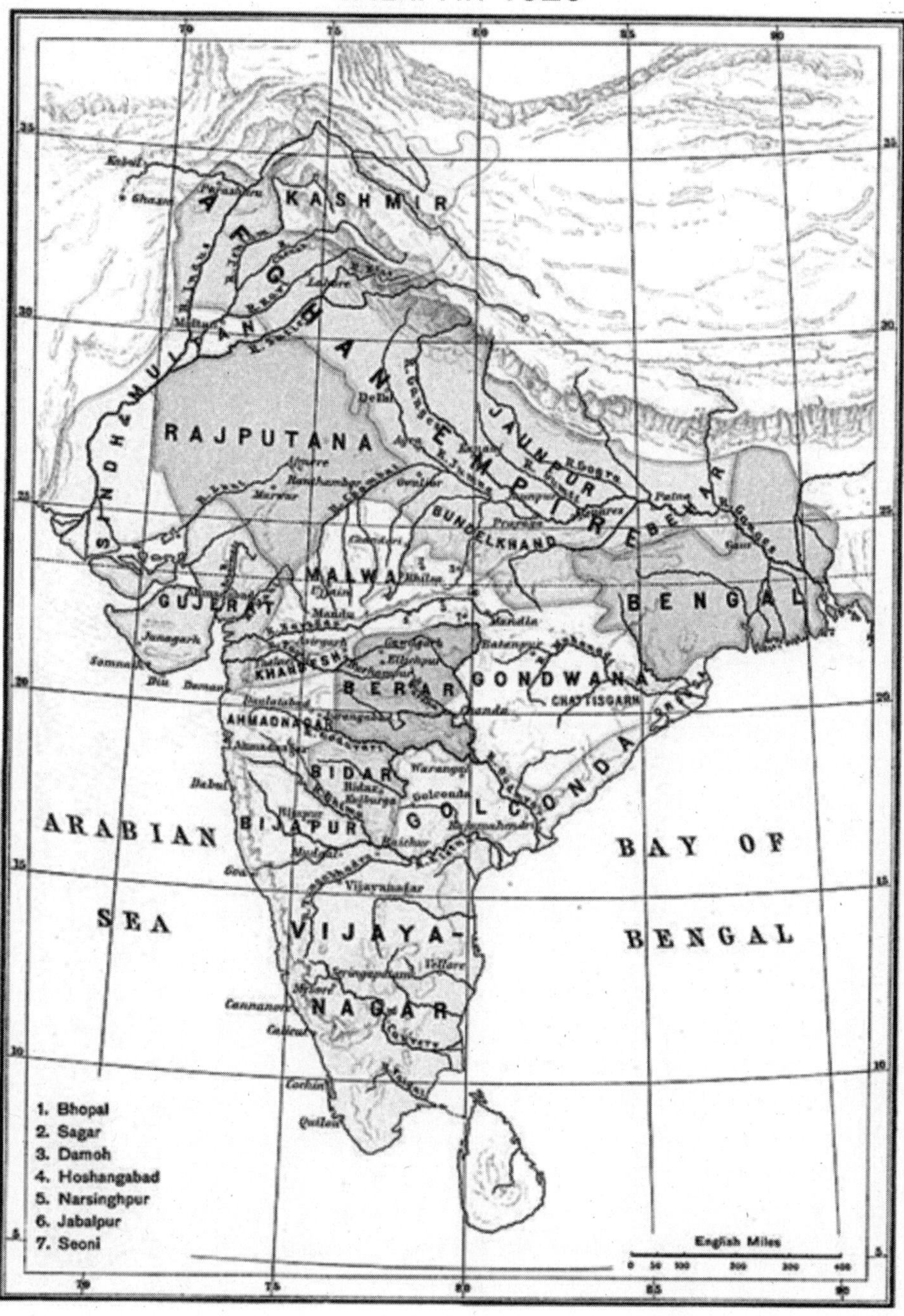

N
Multan
Ajudhan
Uchch
Delhi
Nagaur
Bayana
Sehwan
Mandor
Ajmer
Ranthambor
Umarkot
MEWAR
Jhalawar
Thatta
Chittor
SINDH
Sabarmati River
Mandasor
Patan
Idar
RANN OF KACHCHH
GUJARAT
Mahi River
MALWA
Ahmadabad
Sarkhej
Bhadreswar
Gulf of Kachchh
Khambayat
(Cambay)
Champanir
Dvaraka
Baroda
KATHIAWAR
Narmada River
Gulf of
Khambayat
Porbandar
Bharuch
Junagadh
Rander
Tapti River
Burhanpur
Mangrol
Veraval
Surat
Somnath Patan
Diu
Daman
GUJARAT
ARABIAN
SEA
Bassein
INDIAN
OCEAN
Ahmadnagar
Chaul
0 50 100 mi
0 50 100 150 km

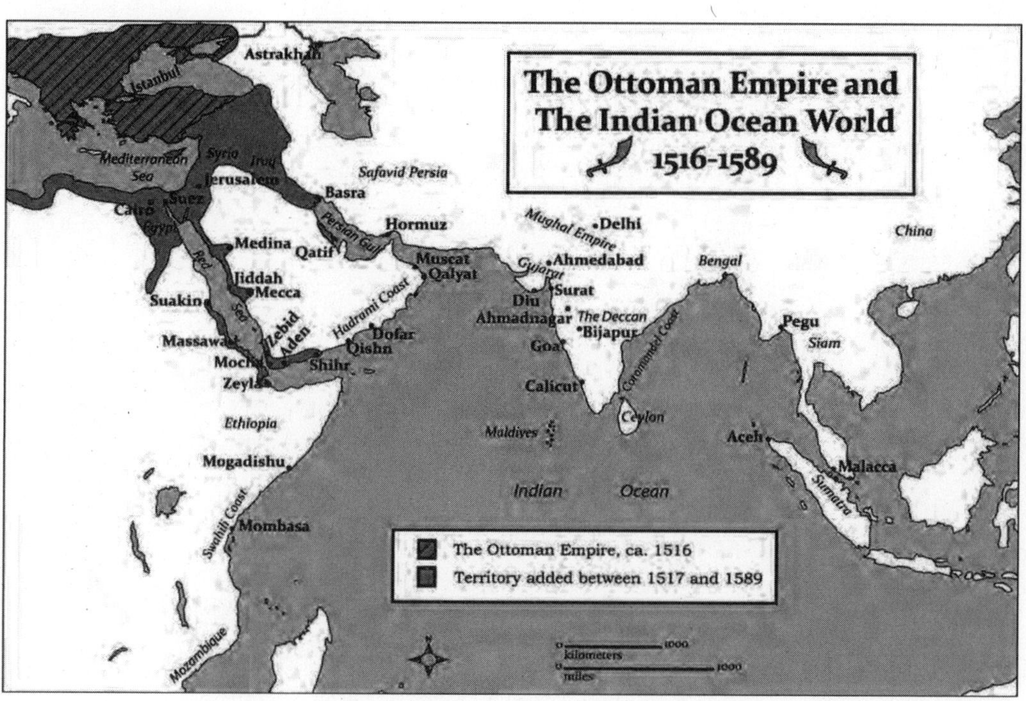
The Ottoman Empire and
The Indian Ocean World
1516-1589
Astrakhan
Istanbul
Mediterranean Sea
Syria
Iraq
Jerusalem
Safavid Persia
Basra
Cairo
Suez
Egypt
Hormuz
Persian Gulf
Medina
Qatif
Red Sea
Jiddah
Mecca
Muscat
Qalyat
Suakin
Hadrami Coast
Zebid
Aden
Dofar
Qishn
Massawa
Mocha
Shihr
Zeyla
Ethiopia
Mogadishu
Swahili Coast
Mombasa
Mozambique
Mughal Empire
Delhi
Gujarat
Ahmedabad
Surat
Diu
Ahmadnagar
The Deccan
Bijapur
Goa
Calicut
Coromandel Coast
Ceylon
Maldives
Bengal
Pegu
Siam
China
Aceh
Malacca
Sumatra
Indian Ocean
The Ottoman Empire, ca. 1516
Territory added between 1517 and 1589
kilometers
miles
1000

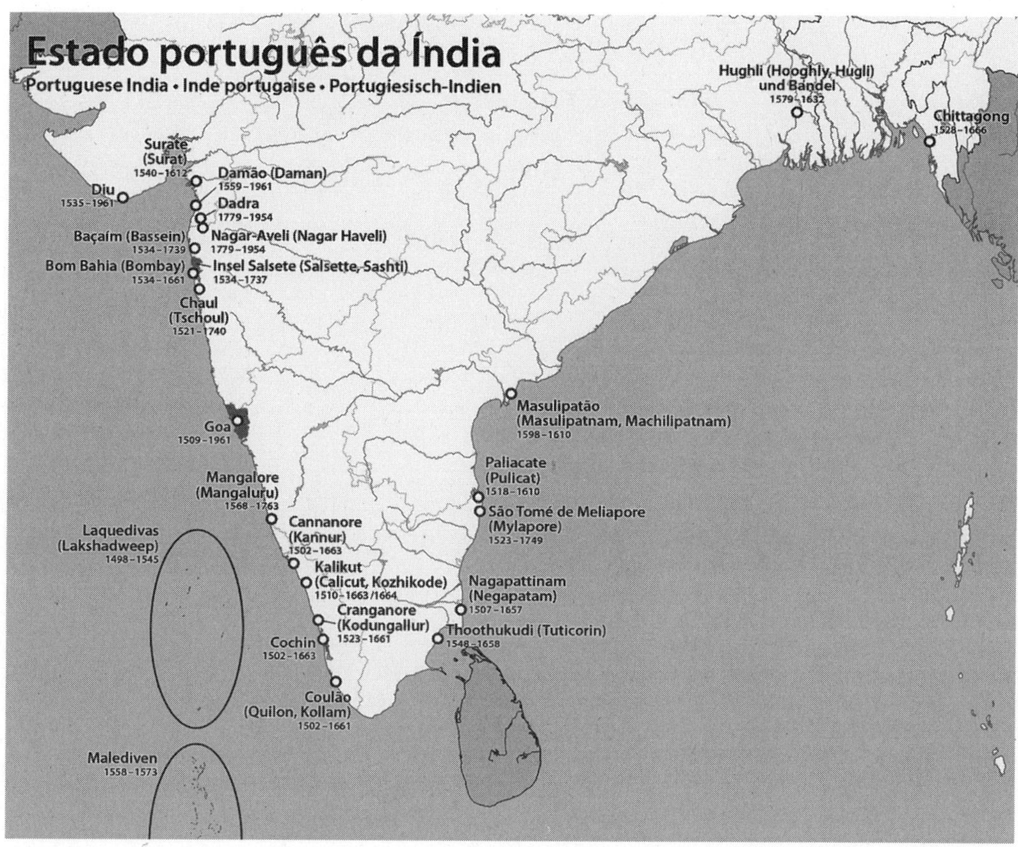
Estado português da Índia
Portuguese India • Inde portugaise • Portugiesisch-Indien
Hughli (Hooghly, Hugli) und Bandel
1579–1632
Chittagong
1528–1666
Surate (Surat)
1540–1612
Diu
1535–1961
Damão (Daman)
1559–1961
Dadra
1779–1954
Baçaím (Bassein)
1534–1739
Nagar-Aveli (Nagar Haveli)
1779–1954
Bom Bahia (Bombay)
1534–1661
Insel Salsete (Salsette, Sashti)
1534–1737
Chaul (Tschoul)
1521–1740
Masulipatão
(Masulipatnam, Machilipatnam)
1598–1610
Goa
1509–1961
Paliacate
(Pulicat)
1518–1610
Mangalore
(Mangaluru)
1568–1763
São Tomé de Meliapore
(Mylapore)
1523–1749
Cannanore
(Kannur)
1502–1663
Laquedivas
(Lakshadweep)
1498–1545
Kalikut
(Calicut, Kozhikode)
1510–1663/1664
Nagapattinam
(Negapatam)
1507–1657
Cranganore
(Kodungallur)
1523–1661
Thoothukudi (Tuticorin)
1548–1658
Cochin
1502–1663
Coulão
(Quilon, Kollam)
1502–1661
Malediven
1558–1573

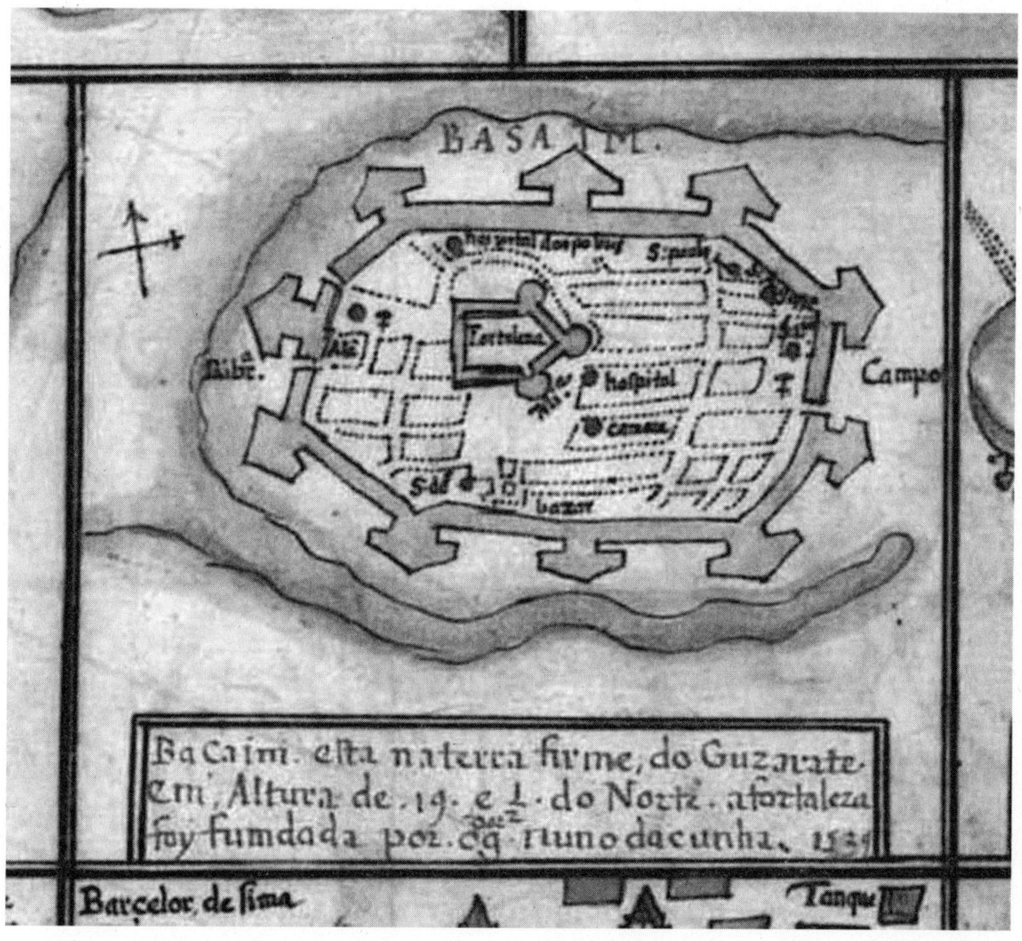
BASAIM.
Fortaleza
hospital
camara
bazar
Campo
BaCaim. esta naterra firme, do Guzarate.
em, Altura de .19. e 1/2 . do Norte . afortaleza
foy fumdada por. cg nunodacunha,
Barçelor, de sima
Tanque

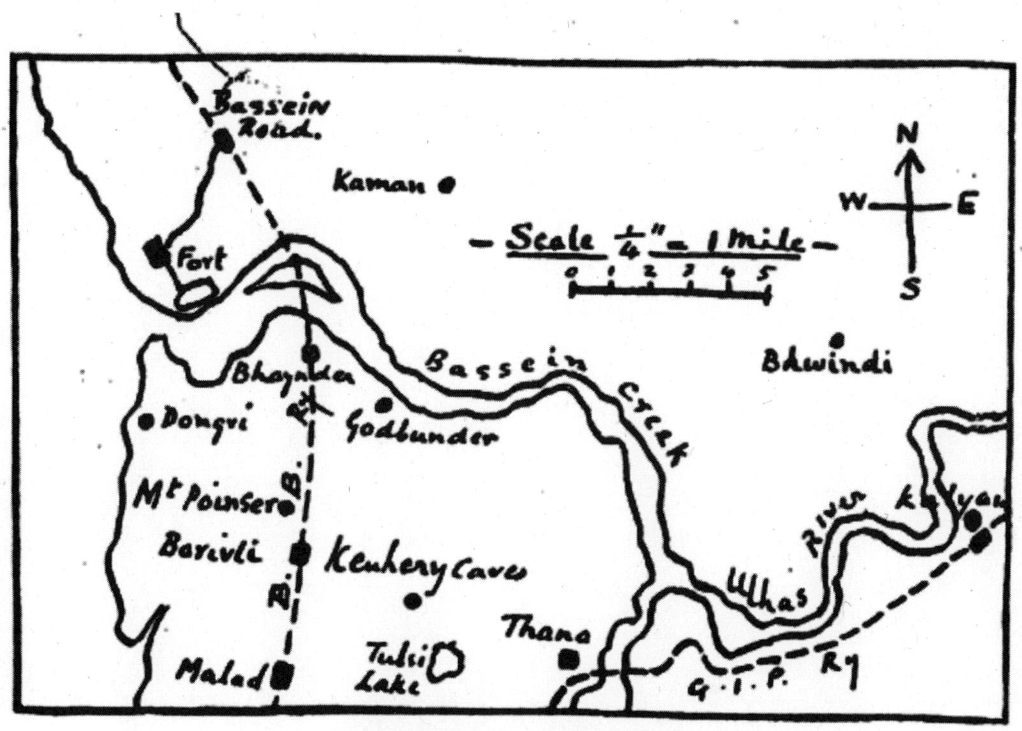

ENVIRONS OF BASSEIN

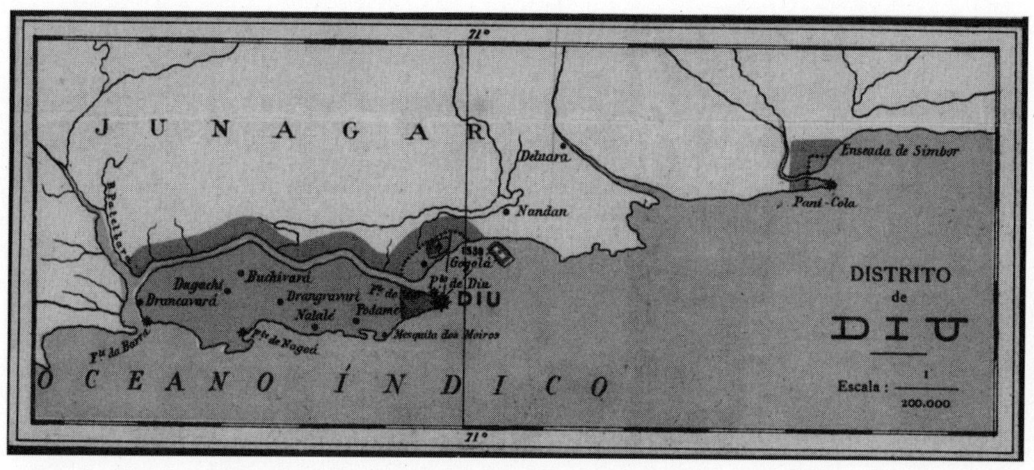
71°
J U N A G A R
Deluara
Nandan
Enseada de Simbor
Pant-Cola
R. Patelbar
Buchivará
Dugachi
Brancavará
Drangravari
Natalé
Podame
1538
Gogolá
Pta de Diu
DIU
Mesquita dos Moiros
Pta de Nagoá
Pta da Barra
O C E A N O Í N D I C O
DISTRITO
de
DIU
Escala : 1/200.000
71°

Sources

1. *The Babar-nāma in English* [Memoirs of Bãbur] translated from the original Turki text of Zahiru'd-din Muhammad Babur Padshah Ghazi by Annette Susannah Beveridge; Luzac & Co., London, 1922.

2. *The Baburnama: Memoirs of Babur, Prince and Emperor*; a new translation by Wheeler Thackston Modern Library Classics; September 2002.

3. *The History of India as Told by Its Own Historians. The Muhammadan Period.* Edited from the posthumous papers of the late Sir Henry Miers Elliot, K.C.B., East India Company's Bengal Civil Service, by John Dowson, M.R.A.S. Volumes I-VIII, London: Trübner & Co., 1867–1877.

4. *A History of Gujarat—From A.D. 1297-8 to A.D. 1573* by Manekshah Sorabshah Commissariat; Longmans & Green; 1938.

5. *Portuguese and the Sultanate of Gujarat, 1500-1573* by Kuzhippalli Skaria Mathew; Mittal Publications, 1986.

6. *Notes on the History and Antiquities of Chaul and Bassein* by Joseph Gerson Da Cunha; Thacker, Vining & Co.; Bombay, 1876.

7. *Writing the Mughal World—Studies on Culture and Politics* by Muzaffar Alam and Sanjay Subrahmanyam; Columbia University Press, 2011.

8. *Humayun Badshah* by S. K. Banerji [Introduction by Sir E. Denison Ross]; Oxford University Press, 1938.

9. *Gujarat—The Local Muhammadan Dynasties* by Sir Edward Clive Bayley; W. H. Allen & Co.; 1886.

10. *Ras Mala Vol. I: Hindoo Annals of the Province of Goozerat in Western India* by Alexander Kinloch Forbes; Oxford University Press, 1924.

11. *The Mīrat-i-Sikandari: A History of Gujarat from the Inception of the Dynasty of the Sultans of Gujarat to the Conquest of Gujarat By Akbar of Shaikh Sikandar Ibn Muhammad Urf Manjhu Ibn Akbar* edited by S.C. Mishra and M. L. Rehman; The Maharaja Sayairao University of Baroda; 1961.

12. *Mirat-I-Ahmadi : a Persian history of Gujarat* by Ali Muhammad Khan; Oriental Institute of Baroda, 1927.

13. *Maharana Sanga—The Hindupat* by Sarda Har Bilas; Scottish Mission Industries Co., Ajmer, 1918.

14. *Tareekh e Gujarat by* Shah Abu Turab Wali; English Translation by Shahin Ghias; M.Phil. Dissertation; Aligarh Muslim University, 1980.

15. *Annals and Antiquities of Rajasthan* by James Tod & William Crooke; Motilal Banarsidass, 1998.

16. "*Tarikh-i-Firishta*," of Mohammad Qasim Hindu Shah Astarabadi 'Firishta'; translated by General John Briggs as The History of the Rise of Mahomedan Power in India in 1829; Kuzhippalli Skaria Mathew; Mittal Publications, 1986.

17. *Medieval Malwa; A Political and Cultural History 1462-1501* by Upendranath Day; Munshilal Manohar Lal Publishers, Delhi, 1965.

18. *Medieval India: from Sultanat to the Mughals, Volume 2* by Satish Chandra; Har-Anand Publications 2005.

19. *The History of Gujarat* (The Gazetteer of Bombay Presidency, Volume 1, Part 1 by James Campbell; The Government Central Press, 1896.

20. *The Humayun Nama by Gul Badan Begam*; translated by Annette S. Beveridge; Royal Asiatic Society, 1902.

21. *The Tezkereh al Vakiat*; or, Private Memoirs of the Moghul Emperor Humayun: Written in the Persian Language, by Jouher, a Confidential Domestic of His Majesty; translated by Major Charles Stewart; [originally published by John Murray, 1832]; Cambridge University Press; Illustrated edition, March 28, 2013.

22. *Storia do Mogor—Moghul India 1653-1708* by Niccolo Manucci; Royal Asiatic Society, 1900.

23. *Notes on the History and Antiquities of Chaul and Bassein* by Joseph Gerson Da Cunha; Thacker, Vining & Co.; 1876.

24. *Tārikh-i-Salātin-i-Afghāniyah* by Ahmad Yadgar; in *The History of India as Told by Its Own Historians. The Muhammadan Period.* Edited from the posthumous papers of the late Sir Henry Miers Elliot, K.C.B., East India Company's Bengal Civil Service, by John Dowson, M.R.A.S. Volumes I-VIII, London: Trübner & Co., *1867–1877.*

25. *Camoens: His Life And His Lusiads* by Sir Richard Francis Burton;[first published in 1883]; Nabu Press, 27 March 2012.

26. *A History of India Under the first two Sovereigns of the House of Taimur—Babar and Humayun* by William Erskine; Longman, Brown, Green and Longmans, London, 1854.

27. Indian Sufism since the Seventeenth Century—Saints, Books and Empires in the Muslim Deccan by Nile Green; Routledge, 2006.

28. *The Portuguese in India* by Michael Pearson; Cambridge University Press, 2006

29. *The Portuguese in India: Being a History of The Rise and Decline of Their Eastern Empire* Volumes I and II by Frederick Charles Danvers; first published by W. H. Allen & Co., 1894; Asian Educational Services, 1992.

30. *The Rise of Portuguese Power in India, 1497-1550* by R. S. Whiteway; first published by Archibald Constable & Co., Westmister in 1899; Asian Educational Services 1989.

31. *Vasco da Gama and his Successors, 1460 —1580* by K. G. Jayne; Methuen, London, 1910.

32. *The Career and Legend of Vasco da Gama* by Sanjay Subrahmanyam; Cambridge University Press 1997.

33. *The Three Voyages of Vasco da Gama, and His Viceroyalty.* From the Lendas da India of Gaspar Correa, accompanied by original documents (translated from the Portuguese, with notes and an introduction by the Hon. Henry E. J. Stanley). The Hakluyt Society, London, 1869.

34. *Lendas da Asia 1497—1550* Vol III Chapter XCV by Gaspar Correa; Goa State Central Library, Panjim.

35. *Decadas da Asia 1497—1539* by João de Barros; Goa State Central Library, Panjim.

36. *Decada Quinta (Dos feitos...em quanto governaram na India Nuno da Cunha, Garcia de Noronha, Estevão da Gama e Martim Afonso de Sousa), Lisboa 1612* by Diogo do Couto; Goa State Central Library, Panjim.

37. *The Commerce of Cambay—From the earliest period to the Nneteenth Century* by V.A.Janaki; The Department of Geography, MSU, Baroda Geography series; Number 10, 1980.

38. *An Arabic History of Gujarat : Zafar Ul-Walih Bi Muzaffar Wa Alih* Vol. I by Abdallah Muhammad Bin 'Omar Al-Makki; edited by E. Denison Ross; John Murray, London, 1910.

39. *A Description of the Coasts of East Africa and Malabar in the Beginning of the Sixteenth Century* by Duarte Barbosa; Edited by Henry E.J. Stanley; Hakluyt Society, 2010.

40. *Qanun-e-Humayuni* (Also known as *Humayun-Nama*) *of Khwandamir*; translated with notes by Baini Prashad; The Royal Asiatic Society of Bengal, 1940.

41. *Narrative Pasts: The Making of a Muslim Community in Gujarat, c. 1400—1650* by Jyoti Gulati Balachandran; Oxford University Press, April 2020.

42. *The Ottoman Age of Exploration* by Giancarlo Casale; Oxford University Press, 2010.

43. *Writing the Mughal World; Studies on Culture and Politics*; Muzaffar Alam & Sanjay Subrahmanyam; Columbia University Press, 2012.

44. *Gazetteer of the Bombay Presidency: Vol 1V*; Ahmadabad; Government Central Press, 1879.

45. *Music Patronage and the Sultans of Gujarat* by Francoise Delvoye in *New Developments in Asian Studies* edited by Paul van der Velde and Alex McKay; Routledge, 1998.

46. *Forging a Region: Sultans, Traders, and Pilgrims in Gujarat, 1200-1500. by* Samira Shaikh; Oxford University Press, 2010.

47. *The Botanical Treasures of Tutankhamun by* Charlene Herselman; Lecture at the University of Pretoria on 1 October 2010.

48. *Unraveling the Strands of Diplomacy in the Contest for Coastal Gujarat in the Sixteenth Century* by Shounak Ghosh; Ex Historia, vol. 9 (2017).

49. *Luso-Muzaffarid Encounters: A Study of the Diplomatic Strategies of Malik Gopi;* Proceedings of 76th Session of the Indian History Congress, Aligarh, 2016.

50. *SocioPolitical Condition of Gujarat in the 15th century;* PhD Dissertation of Ajaz Bano; Aligarh Muslim University, 1988.

51. *New evidence on Maritime Archaeology around Mul Dwarka (Kodinar), Gujarat. Coast, India* by A.S. Gaur, Sundaresh and Sila Tripati; *Man Environ., vol.34(2); 2009; 72-76.*

52. *Archaeological Evidence for Modern Coastal Uplift at Diu, Saurashtra Peninsula, India* by Miklos Kazmer, Nilesh Bhatt, Vishal Ukey, Siddharth Prizomwala, Danko Taborosi and Balazs Szekely; *Geoarchaeology: An International Journal* 31 (2016) 376–387

53. *Maritime Archaeology of Gujarat: Northwest coast of India* by A.S. Gaur and Sundaresh; Asia-Pacific Conference on Regional Underwater Cultural Heritage Proceedings; 2011.

54. *A Short Guide to Bassein* by Father Hull; 1941.

55. *Note Towards a Marxist Perception of Indian History* by Irfan Habib; *The Marxist*, XXVI 4, October—December 2010.

56. *A Possible Medieval Lighthouse at Mul Dwarka (Kodinar) Saurashtra, India* by A. S. Gaur, Sundaresh, B. R. Rao, Sila Tripati, V. D. Khedekar; International Journal of Nautical Archaeology, 3 August 2010; https://doi.org/10.1111/j.1095-9270.2010.00281.x

57. *Essays in Indian History: Towards a Marxist Perception* by Irfan Habib; Anthem Press, 2002.

Notes

Damu

After two years of plunder and destruction by the Portuguese, on 23 December 1533, aboard the Portuguese galleon *Sao Matteus* off the coast of Vasai [Bassein] a Treaty of Peace was signed. The signatories were the representatives of Bahadur Shah, Sultân of Gujarat and the King of Portugal. Sheikh Iwas signed on behalf of the Sultân, and Nuno da Cunha, Governor of Estado da Inde for the King of Portugal.

By the terms of the Treaty, Vasai, with its mainland and islands, and their revenues, were given over in perpetuity to the King of Portugal. The territory so made over included the prosperous district of Shatshashti, comprising 66 villages, which formed the principality of Shashti Pranth, soon to be garbled as Salcette. Today it comprises the western suburbs of Mumbai city, bounded in the north by Bassein Creek, and separated from the mainland to the east by Thane Creek.

[*Titolo do Livro do Tonbo da fortaleza e cidade De Baçaim O Tombo do Estado da India' por Simao Botelho* in Roderigo Josa de Lima Felner (ed) op.cit. pp 132-33; quoted in *Portuguese and the Sultânate of Gujarat (1500-1573) by* K. S. Mathew; Mittal Publications, 1986.]

The Shining Sword of Samarqand

Zahiruddin Bābar was born on 14 February 1483 [6 Moharram, 888 Anno Hegirae] in Andijan in the Farghana Valley [present day Uzbekistan].

Umar Sheikh Mirza II, his father, ruled Andijan and Farghana.

In 1494, Umar Sheikh died in freak accident when the dovecote for his pigeons collapsed on him and Babur, aged 11, assumed the throne.

[*It has been mentioned that the fort of Akhsi is situated above a deep ravine; along this ravine stand the palace buildings, and from it, on Monday, Ramzan 4, (June 8) Umar Shaikh Mirza flew, with his pigeons and their house, and became a falcon.*] *Bāburnama*, page 13.

[*One of those things was this: Qaba has a stagnant, morass-like Water, passable only by the bridge. As they were many, there was crowding on the bridge and numbers of horses and camels were pushed off to perish in the water. This disaster recalling the one they had had three or four years earlier when they were badly beaten at the passage of the Chir, gave way to fear. Another thing was that such a murrain broke out amongst their horses that, massed together, they began to die off in bands.*] *Baburnama*, page 31.

[*Another thing was that the young sons of the townsmen and shopkeepers, nay! even of Turks and soldiers could not go out from their houses from fear of being taken for catamites.*] *Baburnama*, page 41.

[*Few amongst women will have been my grandmother's equals for judgment and counsel; she was very wise and far-sighted and most affairs of mine were carried through under her advice.*] *Baburnama*, page 43.

Hijrah

The Islamic calendar [Arabic ... التَّقْوِيم الْهِجْرِي ... *Al-Taqwīm al-Hijrī*] begins its count from the day Muhammad and his followers fled from Makkah to Yathrib [today's city of Madinah] and established the first Ummah [Arabic .. أمة], Muslim community. This event is called the Hijrah, 'flight' [Arabic ... هِجْرِيَّة] and is denoted in the West as A.H., [Latin ... *Anno Hegirae*, 'In the year of the Hijrah'].

The Islamic calendar is a lunar calendar and consists of 12 months— Muharram, Safar, Rabi-ul-Awwal, Rabi-ul-Thāni, Jamadi-ul-Awwal, Jamadi-ul-Thāni, Rajab, Shabān, Ramadan, Shawwal, Dhul Qādah, Dhul Hijjah—in a year of 354 or 355 days.

~~~~

Namāz [Farsi نماز] from Proto-Indo-Iranian *námas* [to bow, prostrate] is the word for Islamic prayer. In Arabic it is called ***Salāt*** or ***Salāh*** [صَلاة].

According to the time of day there are five prayers:
Fajr [فجر] the prayer before dawn
Dhur or ***Zohr*** [ظهر] the prayer when the sun passes its zenith
Asar [عصر] the prayer in the late afternoon
Maghrib [مغرب] the prayer just after dusk
Isha [عشاء] the night prayer, between sunset and midnight.

~~~~

Hokka

Hyphaene thebaica, the *Doum* palm [Arabic دوم], is native to the Arabian Peninsula and Northern Africa. It has become naturalized in Gujarat, India, where it is called *Hokka* [Urdu هوکا]. In Nigeria, among the Hausa people, it is known as *Goruba.* It is called *Arkobkobai* in the Tigrayit language of Eritrea; *Mkoma* in Swahili; and *Zembaba* in Amharic.

The genus name *Hyphaene* is from the Greek *hyphaenein*, to weave, which refers to the fibers of the leaves and fruit which are used for weaving. The species name *thebaica* harks back to the city of Thebes along the banks of the Nile in Upper Egypt. In heiroglyphs, the Egyptian name for Thebes was:

It depicts the sceptre of the pharaohs, a long staff with an animal's head and a forked base.

H. thebaica is one of the 11 species of the genus found in Africa.

This palm flourishes in hot dry regions where groundwater is present and where little else grows and the tree is valued for the shade it provides. Every part of the tree is useful, and perhaps the most important are the leaves. The fibre and leaflets are used by people along the Niger and the Nile to weave baskets, mats, coarse textiles, brooms, ropes, roofings, string and thatch. Its timber is used for posts and poles, furniture and beehives, and is resistant to termites and borers. It provides wood for fuel. The dried bark is used to produce a black dye for leatherwear. Its spiny leaf stalks are used in fencing. It is very resistant to bush fires. Its roots are used in the treatment of bilharzia, its fruit pulp is chewed to control hypertension. Sore eyes in livestock are treated by using charcoal from the seed kernel. The hard seed inside the fruit, known as 'vegetable ivory,' is used to make buttons and tiny carvings and as artificial pearls. Ashes from the stipes of the tree can be used as a substitute for salt.

It yields edible fruit [pulp and kernel], palm wine from its stem, and juice from its young fruit. In Kenya, a powder made from the outer covering of the fruit is added to water and milk and left to ferment to produce the mild alcoholic drink, *mnazi.*

It was considered sacred by the ancient Egyptians in the belief that it protected and supplied people with shade, water and food after death. Its seeds have been found in many pharaonic tombs. Egyptian archaeologists, led by Zahi Hawass, announced the discovery of eight baskets of 3,000-year-old doum fruit in King Tutankhamun's tomb on September 24, 2007.

~~~~
~~~~

Diu

The early history of Diu is obscure. But marine archeological findings tell us the nearby port at Kodinar, Mul Dwarka was an active trading post since 2,000 BCE. Mul Dwarka has a limestone tower which probably functioned as a lighthouse. The local term for it is Div-Dandi—which may be the origin of Diva. What better site for a lighthouse than Diu?

~~~~

Muzaffar Khan, a lieutenant of Mohammad Tughlaq II of Dilli, was appointed Viceroy of Gujarat in 1391. Five years later, he proclaimed himself **Muzaffar Shah**, King of Gujarat. In 1402 he defeated his old enemy Runmal, Rai of Idur, at Somnath and pursued him to Diu. The Rai and his family were trampled to death by elephants and the city was burnt to the ground.

Diu was still in ruins when Jalal Khan, recognizing its geographic vantage, resurrected the city.

~~~~

The *Miri* and Vasco da Gama

Vasco da Gama in his 2nd visit to Calicut, he set fire to the *Miri*, a ship full of Hajjis, off the coast of Anjediva. Deaf to the cries of the trapped women and children, he gleefully watched it burn. As he neared the coast of Calicut, the particularly Portuguese brand of cruelty made the Samudri Rajah send a Brahman envoy with a conciliatory proposal. It was rejected outright, and the answer reached Calicut in a manner which was, by now, the recognized brand of Portuguese diplomacy.

Da Gama captured two large ships laden with rice, took the goods, systematically amputated the hands and ears and noses of the 800 member crew, then tied their feet together after knocking out their teeth. The dying men were thrown on deck and the ships were set afire. Their amputated body parts were packed in a sack.

The Samudri's envoy had his hands, ears and nose amputated, and the sack was draped around his neck with a terse message to the Samudri that he should make a curry out of the contents and eat it.

~~~~

The Ottomans at Diu in 1531. The Arrival of Rumi Khan

Mustafa Beyram was part of the expeditionary force of Salman Reis. After Salman's murder, his loyalists fled to Gujarat, and arrived there towards the end of 1531, just as Nuno da Cunha's forces were gathering for an attack on the harbour. Malik Toghan put Mustafa incharge of the defense with the superb cannon Majnun that Beyram had brought along. The Portuguese were routed and Mustafa rose in royal favour. Now titled Rumi Khan, he was responsible for commanding the artillery in the siege of Chittorgarh.
~~~~

A Brief Chronology of Gujarat's Sea Trade

Gujarat's maritime trade with the Red Sea and Persian Gulf ports dates back to 2,500 BCE when the Indus Valley Civilization traded with Mesopotamia, Oman and Bahrain. These sea routes continued to be active after the decline of this civilization.

321—250 BCE: In Mauryan times, trade extended as far as the Mediterranean in the west and China in the east.

70 BCE: The Kushans in the Indo-Gangetic Valley, along with their parent branch the Parthians, controlled the land routes between the Persian Gulf and India, and Egypt controlled the traffic on the Red Sea to Indian ports.

78—110 CE: Nahapana, the most famous of Gujarat's Kshatrapas, owed his riches to the sea trade. Nahapana's kingdom was at Mandsaur, where 1,500 years later, Bahadur's luxurious pearl-embroidered tent would draw this envious comment from Humayun: 'Truly is this the abode of the King of the Sea?'

110—158 CE: The Chashtanas, who followed the Kshatrapas, were opposed by the Andhra kings at sea as well as on land. After their defeat by Gomatiputra Satkarni in 119 CE, they lost control of the Red Sea trade. But Rudradaman (145–158 CE) recovered the trade by a canny treaty with the Andhras, which lasted till his death.

100—200 CE: Writing soon after, the Unknown Sailor of *The Periplus of the Erythrean Sea* mentions the Andhras as the most adventurous sailors.

320 CE: Gujarat was soon challenged by the Gupta Empire (320–330CE), and its ports Bharuch and Suparika were controlled by Samudragupta (330-0380 CE).

319—638 CE: The Vallabhis prosperous ports attracted Arab attacks. Despite such attacks, trade flourished, challenged only by central Indian dynasties, principally the Chalukyas. The competition soon led to a power struggle between the Chalukyas, the Vallabhis and Harshavardhana. In 636 CE, the Arabs attacked the capital of Vallabhi.

900 CE: The Gujarat branch of the Chalukyas, the Solankis, had control of the ports of south Gujarat as well.

Al Masudi, who visited Khambat in 913-914 CE wrote that the Indian fleet was so powerful that the entire strength of the Abbasids was needed to counter it.

1,000 CE: The Solankis were the most powerful kingdom in Western India. Following Mahmud of Ghazni's raids on Somnath Patan, the Solankis moved their principal port to the Gulf of Khambat which soon became an entrepôt of renown.

Through the next three centuries, harassed and marauded, first by the Ghaznavids, then by the Mongols and the Dilli Sultâns, the Solankis still managed to retain their grip on the sea trade.

~~~~
~~~~

14 February 1537 [i]

The Portuguese navigator Bartolomeo Dias sailed around the Cape of Good Hope in 1488, opening the sea route to India. Just east and southeast of the Cape, is the deadly convergence of the warm Agulhas current and the cool Benguela current, a deterrent to mariners. Dias originally named his discovery Cabo Das Tormentas [Cape of Storms]. The discovery opened a new route to India, bypassing the Red Sea, and freeing European trade from Arab control.

~~~~

The Red Sea and Persian Gulf Trade in the 15th and 16th centuries

With Vasco da Gama's discovery of the sea route to India, the Portuguese set about consolidating their maritime presence along the Indian coastline with raids on ports and attacks on Indian ships. Their purpose was to monopolize the spice trade by capturing strategic ports along the Persian Gulf and Red Sea routes.

Aden was captured in 1505, effectively blocking the Red Sea trade.

Ormuz was captured by Alfonso de Albuquerque in 1507.

Goa was captured from the Bijapur Sultânate in 1510 and soon became the centre of Portuguese power in India.

Raids on the west coast of India continued. Indian ships were captured or fired, their merchandize looted, the local population terrorized till Bahadur Shah ceded the port of Bassein and its hinterland of Shasti Pranth in 1535.

The Portuguese capture of Malacca in 1511 cut off Gujarati monopoly of the eastern trade—there were more than 5,000 Gujarati merchants thriving at Malacca at the time of Portuguese take over. Since the capture of Istanbul by the Ottomans in 1453, the spice routes to India had been largely under their control.

The principal outlets for the distribution of spices through Europe and Asia were Hormuz, Aden and Malacca. After the Portuguese takeover no ship could call at these ports without paying a duty (the cartaz), and spices could only be shipped to Europe by the Cape route.

However, Diu still eluded the Portuguese.

The Gujarat Sultânate was ambivalent in its response to the Portuguese during the reign of Mahmud Begada. One of the Sultân's advisors, Malik Gopi, whose wealth depended on the Malacca trade, did his best to persuade the Sultân to permit the Portuguese to build a fortress at Diu. Malik Ayaaz, who practically ran Diu, was adamant in his refusal to let the Portuguese in.

The Ottoman Empire, under Sultân Selim, allied with Muzaffar Shah of Gujarat under the aegis of the canny merchant and diplomat Malik Ayaaz, who had cultivated a strong Turkish presence among the capitalists of Diu. In the early 1500s, Malik Ayaaz had also formed ties with the Mamluk admiral Hussain al Kurdi, who sent a fleet to help oust the Portuguese in March 1508 in the decisive Battle of Chaul. But Hussain's motives seemed suspicious, and Malik Ayaaz transferred his interest to the Ottomans. Indeed, his alliance may have led Sultân Selim to invade Cairo in 1517. His victory over the Mamluks established the Ottomans as the official Protector of the Holy Cities of Mecca and Madina in the Hejaz.
~~~~

The Portuguese blockade controlled the pilgrim traffic to Mecca and Madina, another reason for the Ottomans to ally with Gujarat against the Portuguese.

In the 1520s, under the Grand Vazir Ibrahim Pasha, and with master navigator Selman Reis, the Ottomans established a customs house at Bab-al Mandab where ships coming from India would have to pay duty. This meant they effectively controlled both ends of the Red Sea. Their supremacy was short-lived. Internal conflicts soon exposed these ports once more to Portuguese assaults.

~~~

Chaghtai [Urdu … چغتائی]

Chaghtai was Genghiz Khan's second son. He formed the Chaghtai Khanate, a territory that extended from the Amu Darya to the Altai in the 1300s. In 1363, Transoxiana was lost to the Timurids. This reduced territory was henceforth called **Moghulistan**.

Moghulistan extended over modern Kazakhstan, Kyrgystan and the Xinjiang Uighur Autonomous Region of China. In the fourteenth century, inhabitants of Moghulistan were called **Mughal**, (the Persian version of Mongol). They used the titles Mirza and Baig.

The Mongol tribe, Barlas, who traced their roots to Genghis Khan, settled in Moghulistan and absorbed the local culture. They spoke Chaghtai, a Turkic language, and adopted Islam.

Two Barlas chieftains have left their mark on world history: Taimur-Lang [Tamerlane] and Zahiruddin Bābar.

By the 1400s, the Timurid Empire had fragmented, and the centre of Persian culture had shifted to Herat and Samarqand. The Timurids referred to themselves as **Gurkani**, (from *Gurkan*, for son-in-law). Taimur adopted this title to stress his kinship with Genghis Khan through his marriage with Saray Mulk Khanum, a direct descendent of Genghis Khan.

Bābar's father, Umar Sheikh Mirza, was Taimur's great-great-grandson, and his mother Qutlugh Khanum, was a direct descendent of Chaghtai Khan.

The Mughals never titled themselves thus. Their preferred title was Gurkani, but history chose otherwise.

~~~

Khwaja Zafar

One of Salman Reis' most trusted loyals, he hunted down the assassins of his master. Later, he accompanied Rumi Khan to Gujarat.

After Rumi Khan's defection to Humayun, he became a trusted aide to Bahadur Shah, both as a soldier and as a diplomat.

Portuguese histories (which call him a renegade) list him as a native of Otranto, Italy and condemn him for converting to Islam and siding with 'pagans and infidels.'

The Ottomans and Bahadur in 1536-37

Ibrahim Pasha, the brilliant vazir who won so many victories for the Sultâns, was executed by Suleiman the Magnificent for insubordination in 1536—before he could accomplish his goal of driving the Portuguese out of the Indian Ocean. His successor, Hadim Sultân, was in the confidence of Khoja Zafar. Through them, Bahadur maintained a growing relationship with the Ottomans in Egypt.

In his last effort to be rid of the Portuguese, soon after signing the treaty at Diu in 1535, Bahadur had his family sent to Mecca, presumably on Hajj, but carrying with them an incredible amount of treasure including the famous belt. They travelled with Asaf Khan who was charged with sending an envoy to the Ottoman Sultân in Istanbul, offering the treasure in payment for naval aid.

The envoy, Umdet al Mulk, arrived in Istanbul in mid-1536.

The treasure consisted of two hundred and fifty chests containing one million two hundred and seventy thousand and six hundred measures of gold. It was eagerly accepted. But it was the belt, impossible to describe and always undervalued, that gave the Ottoman Sultân his title of Suleiman the Magnificent.

Batoh

Batoh/Batwa is the present day Vatva, an eastern suburb of Ahmadabad. It is where the founder of the Bukhariya sect of Gujarat, Burhanuddin Qutub-e-Alam is buried. His son, Syed Sirajuddin Muhammad, was the renowned early 15th century Muslim teacher and scholar a.k.a. Shah-e-Alam.

The saint Jalaluddin Bukhari, who had predicted the Sultânate of Gujarat as Zafar Khan's destiny, continued his spiritual teachings in the person of his grandson Abdallah Qutab-i-Alam and his great grandson Mohammad Shah-i-Alam.

Sheikh Qutub-i-Alam established the Khanquah at Batoh.

~~~~

Qizilbash [Farsi … قزيل باش] dates to late 15th century Turkey when the head of the Safaviyya Sufi order Shaikh Haydar organized his followers into a militant mercenary group. They wore a distinctive twelve-gored crimson headwear called titled تاج حيدر [*Tāj-e-Ḥaydar*], Haydar's Crown. Qizilbash literally means 'red head.'

The appellation was a pejorative label given to them by their Sunni Ottoman foes, but they adopted it as a provocative mark of pride.

~~~~

Khanquah [Urdu … خانقاه]— a Sufi school and seminary.

Dargãh {Farsi درگاه / *Hindi* दरगाह] is a tomb built over the grave of a revered religious figure, a saint or a dervish.

Its etymology is significant. The Farsi word درگاه is a composite of *dar* (در) —'door or gate' and *gãh* (گاه) 'place.' It may have its origin in the Arabic *darjah* (درجه) which means 'stature, prestige, order, or place.'

Sufis believe that these places are portals where they can invoke the deceased saint's intercession and blessings in their quotidian affairs. Consequently, these places have become sites of pilgrimage and spiritual uplift.

~~~~

Mleccha Indo-Aryan term for 'foreigner'—possibly from native of Meluha or Melakka which was the Sumerian word for the Indus Valley people.

Initially the term identified those who spoke a different language, but it soon became pejorative, distancing Aryans from 'foreigners'—many of whom were indigenous non-Aryan Indians.

~~~~

Gujarat

Kheda, the name is derived from the Sanskrit क्षेत्र ... literally, 'a field or tract of land.' Kheda lies on the belt of a dinosaur nursery. Fossilized eggs are a common find.

[*Upper Cretaceous dinosaur egg clutches from Kheda district (Gujarat, India). Their distribution, shell ultrastructure and palaeoecology* by Srivastava, S.; Mohabey, DM.; Sahni, A.; Pant, SC.; Palaeontographica, A Palaozoologie, Stratigraphie 193(5-6): 219-233; 1986; https://eurekamag.com/research/022/063/022063837.php]

~~~

The Myth of Sati:

Finds its first mention at the end of 2nd Millennium BCE in *Taittiriya Samhita*, part of the *Yajurveda*.

Sati, the daughter of Daksha, was Shiva's first wife. Her father disapproved of Shiva, the wild wanderer, and so excluded him from an invitation at a grand *yagnya* (sacrifice). Anguished, Sati killed herself. Shiva, in his grief, would not be separated from her and clutching her corpse he danced the *tandava* of destruction. The sun was obscured. Life stopped. The desperate gods appealed to Vishnu who sent his Sudarshana Chakra spinning to sever the corpse of Sati into many pieces that fell to earth. These places, where pieces of her dismembered body fell, are scattered over the subcontinent, and are revered as Shakti Peethas, places of the divine feminine and Shakti worship.

~~~

Piram Island

A small Island near Ghogha, off the Gulf of Khambat.

In the 14th century it was the headquarters of Mokhdaji Gohil who captured Gogha and Piram Island in 1325 and exacted toll from ships approaching Khambat. His successful piracy induced an attack from Muhammad bin Tughlaq. Mokhdaji put up a fierce fight, but was eventually killed and Piram Fort was destroyed.

Piram Island is of great paleontological interest. Miocene fossils of *Sivatherium* ['Shiva's beast'], an ancestor of today's giraffe, have been found on the island.

~~~
~~~

1525

Music & The Gujarat Sultâns

Music flourished under the patronage of the Gujarat Sultâns, many of whom were musicians themselves.

Ghunyat al-Munya, an Indo-Persian treatise on Indian music, was compiled in 1344-45 by the Governor of Gujarat to introduce his nobles to the Indian system of music.

Important musical texts in Sanskrit extant at that time were; *Sangitopanisat* (1324) and the *Sangitopanisatsaroddhara* (1350).

Gujarat's contribution survives in ragas with toponyms: *Saurashtram* (Sorathi in Hindustani music), *Bilawal* (for Veraval), *Khambayati* (Khambat). 700 years later, these ragas are still popularly performed in both Hindustani and Carnatic music.

Many dhrupad compositions bearing the *takhallus,* [signature] of Sahi Bahadur or Sultân Bahadur have been discovered. But they may equally be dedications to the king by the composer. Several such have also been found naming Sultân Mahmud.

Sultân Mahmud was an expert player of the rubab (today's sarod & sitar). His court historian Udayaraja composed the chronicle *Mahmudasuratrana charitra.* Predictably hagiographic, the poem expresses not only the Sultân's musical leanings, but his patronage to musicians at the court.

Muzaffar the Clement was acknowledged as a musician of great repute. Music festivals were held annually during his reign, and the Sultân himself participated.

Bahadur Shah had several dhrupads written for him by the great poet-musician Nayak Bhakshu. In these beautiful compositions, Bahadur appears in the role of *nayak* or hero.

O my beloved how can I impress you who excel in every art? asks the lovelorn *nayika,* heroine.

These are among the 1,000 dhrupads collated in the reign of Shah Jahan, himself a great patron of music. At Shah Jahan's behest, the original dedication and *takhallus* on each song was erased and the emperor's own was substituted. Nonetheless, these originals are still apparent in the manuscript.

[*Music Patronage in the Sultânate of Gujarat: A Survey of Sources* by Françoise Delvoye in the book *New Developments in Asian Studies* edited by Paul van Der Velde & Alex McKay; Routledge, 1998]

~~~

Flight

Bhadar

Ahmad Shah 1 built his new capital at the site of the historic city of Asaval, in 1411, and named it after four Ahmads, as Ahmadabad. The citadel he built was named after the old citadel of Patan, Bhadra, later familiarized as Bhadar. Its magnificent architecture shows Indo-Saracenic design at its most delicate and aesthetic best. For the next two centuries it was the showpiece of the Gujarat Sultânate. Sultân Mahmud Begada made it the centre of Gujarat's traditional crafts as well.
~~~

The Tale of the Kamarband

Dewal Rani

The daughter of Raja Karna of Anhilwara.

In 1296, Alauddin Khilji sent Aluf (Alp) Khan to invade Anhilwara. Rani Kamaldevi was captured and became the third wife of Alauddin Khilji, and very soon his favourite. Dewal Rani, her daughter, was brought to Dilli at her request a few years later, and married to Alauddin's son Khizr Khan. Following Alauddin Khilji's death, Mubarak Shah who succeeded him, had Khizr Khan blinded and murdered, and made Dewal Rani his queen. He was soon murdered by his lover Khusro Khan, and Dewal Rani became, once again, the wife of a Sultân.

Her story has endlessly fascinated writers, from Amir Khusrow in the 14th century, who wrote the romance of Dewal Rani and Khizr Khan as *Ishquia*, to Nandashankar Mehta's 1866 Gujarati classic *Karan Ghelo*.

~~~~

The Khiljis

The Khilji [Urdu … خلجی] dynasty ruled the Indian subcontinent from Dilli between January 1290 and September 1320.

They were the Khalaj, the earliest tribe to cross the Amur Darya from Central Asia into present day Afghanistan.

Jalal-ud-din Khalji became the first Khilji ruler when he displaced the last Mamluk Sultân Muiz ud din Qaiqabad.

His nephew and son-in-law, Alauddin Khalji, murdered and succeeded him and ruled tyrannically for 20 years. After his death in 1316 chaos reigned. There were successive coups and assassinations until Ghayasuddin Tughlaq displaced them to found the Tughlaq Dynasty.

[Alauddin Khalji's taxation system was probably the one institution from his reign that lasted the longest, surviving into the nineteenth or even the twentieth century. From now on, the land tax (*kharaj* or *mal*) became the principal form in which the peasant's surplus was expropriated by the ruling class.]

— from *The Cambridge Economic History of India*

[Irfan Habib (1982). "Northern India under the Sultânate: Agrarian Economy". In Tapan Raychaudhuri; Irfan Habib (eds.). *The Cambridge Economic History of India*. Vol. 1, c.1200–c.1750. CUP Archive. ISBN 978-0-521-22692-9.]

~~~~

How the belt came to Rana Sanga

It happened thus.

When Mahmud Khilji was Rana Sanga's prisoner, the Rana treated him with great affection, even seating him on the same cushion he sat on, an honour given to very few.

On one such occasion, the Rana, coming in from his famous rose garden, held out a bunch of roses to Mahmud.

That prisoner Sultân said, 'There are two ways of giving a gift; raise your hand and bestow it as a blessing on your inferior. Or else lower your hand and place it at the feet of your superior. I am your prisoner, true, but how can I extend my palm merely for a bunch of flowers?'

The Rana laughed and said that with the roses he offered Mahmud half the kingdom of Malwa too.

The delighted Sultân accepted the roses, and on the third day after this incident, the Rana despatched Mahmud back to Mandu with an escort to seat him on the throne of his ancestors. Mahmud later sent Rana Sanga the kamrband and a jeweled crown as *nazrana*— [Urdu نذرانہ … bestowal]—a mark of his regard.

~~~~

Mahmud Khilji II

Mahmud Khilji II was the last of the Khilji Kings of Malwa. He gained the throne through the support of the Rajputs, led by Medini Rai, against the promoters of his brother Sahib Khan. This Rajput influence was resented by his amirs, many of whom were supporters of Sahib Khan. The nobles sought help from Dilli and Gujarat to rid the court of Rajputs and depose Mahmud.

Farishta describes Mahmud as 'a fool in the cabinet, but had not his equal in courage in the hour of danger.' He sought to rid himself of the Rajputs and arranged for the murder of Medini Rai. The plot failed, Medini Rai was wounded, but escaped. His loyal Rajputs attacked Mahmud, but fighting single-handedly, he beat them back.

Captured by Rana Sanga, he was treated with great courtesy, nursed by the Rana himself at Chittor, and sent back to Mandu with his kingdom restored to him.

His reign was full of impetuosities, madcap ventures, and shameless betrayals. He had given sanctuary to Chand Khan and evaded Bahadur as he was plotting a coup with Chand Khan for the throne of Gujarat. Bahadur, sensing this, marched to Mandu. Chand Khan fled to the Deccan and Mahmud was forced to surrender.

Bahadur was prepared to restore his kingdom to Mahmud, but Mahmud insulted him, and Bahadur took him hostage, along with his seven sons. On the way to Ahmadabad, the carriage conveying the Khiljis was ambushed by Bhils. In the mêlée the guards, fearing their prisoner might escape, killed Mahmud.

And, with the death of Mahmud, the Khilji dynasty came to an end.

~~~~

Chittorgarh

Chittorgarh

The capital of Mewar.

The fort has existed since Mauryan times and has witnessed several changes of power. It was supposedly built by Chitrangada Mori (Maurya), and later conquered by the legendary Gohil hero Bappa Rawal in the 8th century CE.

Allauddin Khilji conquered it in 1303, and gave the fort to his son Khizr Khan who was soon deposed, and the fort reverted to the Rajputs. It would remain with them till Bahadur's campaign in 1535.

Among Chittorgarh's famous personages are Rana Kumbha and Rana Sanga and the mystic saint Meera Bai. Its infamous history of Jauhar, surely the most unthinkable ritual of misogyny, is still regarded as heroic. It is particularly poignant that the Jauhar prompted by Bahadur's assault was on 8 March, 1535, a day that is celebrated today as International Women's Day.

Every historian has recorded Bahadur's efforts to prevent so heinous a deed, by offering safe conduct to the women.

~~~

Meera bai, Mihira Devi

The Rathor Princess who married Rana Sanga's son Bhoj Raj in 1519, is India's most popular and revered mystic Bhakti poet. Her devotion to Krishna found expression in passionate love poems that are sung today as bhajans.

Widowed in 1521, she was part of Rana Sanga's household. After his death following the battle of Khanwa, Meera was constantly persecuted, and spent the rest of her life wandering in search of her beloved Krishna. Her last years were spent in Brindavan where she attained samadhi in 1547.

~~~

Jauhar

The mass self-immolation of Rajput women in the face of certain military defeat. The earliest accounts of *jauhar* are from Alexander of Macedon's assault on India's northwest in 327 BCE.

The word has its roots in the Sanskrit *jatugrha* [जतुगृह]— *a house plastered with combustibles for burning people alive.*

The Farsi word *jauhar* [جوہر] has multiple meanings. Principally, it refers to something precious, a *jewel,* an *adornment.* But it can also connote skill, worth, and virtue.

Dilli/Lodi Bãgh, 1526

The Dilli Sultânate

The Dilli Sultânate was an Islamic empire based in Dilli that stretched over large parts of the Indian subcontinent for 320 years (1206–1526).

Five dynasties ruled over the Dilli Sultânate sequentially:

the Mamluk dynasty (1206–1290),
the Khalji dynasty (1290–1320),
the Tughlaq dynasty (1320–1414),
the Sayyid dynasty (1414–1451), and
the Lodi dynasty (1451–1526).

~~~

Mamluk [Arabic مملوك … one who is owned]. The word came to be applied to all non-Arab slave-soldiers in Islamic armies.

In 1206, the Mamluk commander of the Muslim forces in the Indian subcontinent, Qutubuddin Aibak, proclaimed himself Sultân and created the Mamluk Sultânate in Dilli. It ended when Jalaluddin Firuz Khilji overthrew the last Mamluk ruler Muizuddin Qaiqabad in 1290.

~~~

The **Lodi** dynasty ruled the Dilli Sultânate from 19 April 1451 when Bahlul Khan Lodi ascended the throne after the last Sayyid ruler Alauddin Alam Shah abdicated in his favour.
It ended on 20 April 1526 when Ibrahim Lodi lost to Babar in the First Battle of Panipat. It marked the end of the Dilli Sultânate and the beginning of the Mughal dynasty.

~~~

Lodi Bãgh, spread across 90 acres in Dilli is a garden complex that contains the Tomb of Muhammad Shah [the third Sayyid dynasty ruler], the Tomb of Sikandar Lodi [the second Lodi ruler and father of Ibrahim Lodi], Shisha Gumbad which contains multiple unidentified graves [originally it was decorated by enameled tiles that glittered like glass, hence the appellation] and Bara Gumbad—the large dome—that served as a passageway to the Jama Masjid and Sikandar Lodi's *mehmãn khãna* … Urdu … مہمان کھانا

~~~

The Lodi Sultâns

The Afghan Lodis were independent chiefs in Multan since 970 AD.

Bahlol Lodi assumed the throne of Dilli on April 19, 1491.

There was constant conflict with the Jaunpur Sharqui Sultâns.

The real generals in these wars were the queens of both Sultâns.

Bahlol was succeeded by Sikandar, a puzzling character who combined great wisdom and valour with compulsive violence and insensate bigotry. Ibrahim and Jalal were his sons.

On the death of Sikandar, his sons Ibrahim and Jalal Khan divided the Sultânate, with Ibrahim getting the throne of Dilli and Jalal that of Jaunpur.

Ibrahim was reproached by his nobles for so dividing the kingdom, and recalled Jalal under the pretense of urgent affairs of state to discuss.

But Jalal, scenting danger, hurried to Jaunpur where he declared himself Sultân Jalaluddin.

Ibrahim now set about bribing Jalal's faithfuls with huge sums and jagirs, and most of them, predictably, abandoned Jalal.

It ended with Jalal being driven from Kalpi to Agra, and there he was offered a truce which he cravenly accepted.

Ibrahim, meanwhile, imprisoned his four other brothers in Hansi, and hearing Jalal had sought refuge at Gwalior with Raja Bikramjit (possesor of the Kohinoor), stormed and conquered Gwalior by blowing up the outer fort of Badalgarh with gunpowder.

Jalal Khan escaped to Malwa where Mahmud Khilji refused sanctuary.

In his flight, Jalal was captured by Bhils who handed him over to Ibrahim in return for a handsome reward.

Jalal was condemned to be jailed at Hansi along with his brothers—but was quickly strangled en route.

This ferment, adding to Ibrahim's paranoid cruelties towards the nobles of his father's time, made him deeply unpopular.

His deputy, Azam Humayun Khan Sherwani led the assault on Gwalior. Raja Bikramjit capitulated with the offer of seven maunds of gold, his elephant Shyamsundari, and his daughter in marriage. (The famous diamond was probably still with Bikramjit).

Azam Humayun was summoned to Dilli and jailed along with his son Islam Khan. The younger man escaped and revolted.

Ibrahim, finding the rebels were gaining support, vented his rage on his most trusted and senior nobles by inviting them to a newly constructed house to discuss the situation. He did not, of course, tell them the basement was packed with gunpowder which caused a most convenient combustion.

Events of this sort compelled Daulat Khan Lodi of Multan to send Babar in Kabul a present of mangoes preserved in honey and the ritual *paan* as invitation to invade Dilli.

~~~

Mahmud Shah Sayyid

December 1398 was the most terrible month in Dilli's history. Taimur left the city full of rotting corpses (100,000 prisoners were slaughtered in one evening because they were inconvenient baggage). The city did not recover for years from famine, disease and poverty.
~~~

The Sultân Mohammad Shah fled and on his death, Khizr Khan, a tributary of Taimur, established himself as King, and, in tracing his origins back to the Prophet himself, he styled himself Sayyid. He had the *khutbah* [Arabic … خطبة]—sermon—read in Taimur's name, and gained the respect of the people by restoring peace and normalcy.

Mahmud Shah, his grandson, was a weak king who recognized the ambition and talent of a young horse trader called Bahlol Lodi, and gradually allowed him to usurp power. His son, the last of the Sayyids, Alam Shah, only asked for a quiet life, and abdicated.

~~~

Untgar (Hunwantgar)

In 1505, Sikandar Lodi besieged the fort of Untgar which would provide him access to Gwalior. The Rajput stronghold was strongly defended, but eventually Sikandar prevailed. On his return to Agra through rugged terrain, famine and drought overtook the army. A cup of water sold for 15 tankas. Of the massive army, only 800 survived the march.

~~~

The Khanquah of Nizamuddin Auliya

Hazrat Nizamuddin Auliya [1238 – 1325]—The most revered Sufi saint of India. He founded the Chishti *silsila* [order]. Among his more ardent disciples was the poet Amir Khusro. Today, Hazrat Nizamuddin's khanquah in Dilli lends its name to the District.

~~~~

The Basti

A *Qawwāl* [Urdu … قوال] is a performer of *qawwāli* [Urdu … قوالی]—a religious musical form introduced in the subcontinent by the Sufis in the 13th century.

Qawl [Arabic … قوْل] is 'an utterance of the Prophet Mohamed.'

Qawwāli can embody all human emotions and is a very popular genre of Indian music. Nusrat Fateh Ali Khan was perhaps the best known qawwāli singer of our age.

~~~~

Ghilmān [Arabic … غلمان] is the plural of **Ghulām** [Arabic … غـلام]— They were slave-soldiers taken as prisoners of war from conquered regions in Central Asia.

Can refer to young boys recruited as slaves or servants. In this context: catamite.

~~~~
~~~~

The Lodi Camp/Bãghpat/The Road Home

The Jaunpur Sultânate [Urdu … سلطنت جونپور], ruled by the Sunni Sharqi [Eastern] dynasty, was an independent Islamic state in North India between 1394 and 1479. It was founded by Khwajah-i-Jahan Malik Sarwar, a vizier of Mohammad Shah Tughlaq when the Tughlaq dynasty fractured.

Jaunpur was founded in 1359 by Feroz Shah Tughlaq. He named it in memory of his cousin and predecessor 'Jauna Khan' who ruled Dilli as Muhammad bin Tughlaq from 1325 until his death in 1351.

In 1479, the Sharqi Sultân Hussain Khan was defeated by Bahlol Lodi and thereafter Jaunpur was part of the Dilli Sultânate.

The Sharqis were patrons of music, art and architecture. The last Sharqi King, Hussain Khan was a great musician. To him we owe the musical form of Khayal [Urdu … خیال].

[*Imaging Sound* by Bonnie S.Wade, University of Chicago Press, 1998]

~~~

The Myth of Shiva and Kamadeva
[*Matysa Purana*, 1st Millennium BCE]

Mahadev (Shiva), deep in meditation, takes no heed of the lovelorn Parvati. Spring is in the air, and Kamadeva, the God of Love, is busy shooting his flowery arrows in every direction. One of them strikes Shiva and he wakes from his meditation. Spotting the culprit, he opens his third eye in rage, and Kamadeva is reduced to ashes.

The world stops turning.

All living creatures wither.

The gods panic and cast about for some way to restore Kamadeva to life.

Rati, the Goddess of Desire, pleads for her husband's life through the pall of smoke, but Shiva is unmoved. Then the smoke clears and he sees Parvati. She joins Rati in pleading for Kamadeva's life. Shiva, enchanted by Parvati's allure, relents.

Love is restored and the world turns again.

And Parvati's long penance to gain Shiva's love is fulfilled.

~~~

Tandava

The energetic dance form attributed to Shiva as Nataraja, or Lord of the Dance, Tandava has an important place in Bharata's *Natyashastra* from which all Indian dance forms have evolved. It is depicted iconically in Chola bronze sculptures as the Tandava Murti. The representation is interpreted in the poem *Chidambara Mummani Kovai*:

Thy hand holding the sacred drum has made the universe.
Thy lifted hand protects the conscious and unconscious.
All these worlds are transformed by Thy hand bearing fire.
Thy sacred foot is refuge for the tired soul.
Thy lifted foot points the path to eternal bliss.
These Five Actions are indeed Thy Handiwork.

The Tandava represents five aspects of divinity:

Shrishti (creation);
Sthiti (preservation);
Samhara (destruction);
Tirobhava (illusion); and
Anugraha (grace).

As colloquialism, tandava is passed off as tantrum.

~~~~

The Battle of Panipat

From 12th to 19th April, 1526 the two armies faced each other, motionless. On the night of the 20th, Bābar sent out a small force which was repulsed.

The battle began at daybreak, on the 21st.

Ibrahim Lodi had an army of 100,000 men and 1,000 elephants.

Bābar had 24, 000 men.

Bābar stationed himself in the centre, Humayun on the right and his Chief Minister, Mir Ali Khalifa on the left.

There were two flying columns, right and left. All along the front line were *araba*—carts lashed together with hide and supported by crickwork. Behind them was the artillery: matchlock men and musketeers.

The Afghans made a central assault.

In no time at all the two flying units closed around them; this was *tulghuma*, the prized tactic of a small army.

The Afghans were surrounded. The elephants panicked under gunfire, and trampled their own men.

The battle was over by noon.

Ibrahim Lodi died on the battlefield.

Survivors fled.

Bābar marched to Dilli.

A week later, on 27th April the *khutbah* was read in his name.
~~~~

Rana Sanga

Maharana Sangram Singh, surely the greatest of Rajput warriors, was the third of Rai Mal's sons by his Jhali queen, Ratan Kanwar. The eldest, Prithviraj, was a great hero. The second Jai Mal was forgettable, and Sanga was brave, but not as impetuous as his brothers. Their constant companion was Suraj Mal, an uncle, of their own age. The four chafed under their enforced passivity, and each longed to claim the throne of Mewar.

This made them natural enemies.

To end this conflict they approached a sybil and demanded an augury.

Prithviraj planted himself on the pallet in front of the sybil with Jai Mal by his side. Sanga chose to sit on a panther hide, and Suraj Mal jostled one knee onto the same hide.

Before they could complete their question to the sybil, she pointed to the panther hide—delivering her prophecy that Sanga would be king, with Suraj Mal sharing the honour.

This provoked Prithviraj into a rage and he attacked Sanga. Jai Mal threw himself between them and prevented the murder. But Prithviraj had already blinded Sanga in one eye.

Sanga left, followed by Jai Mal, to seek refuge elsewhere.

Rathod Bida, seeing the bleeding boy, offered him aid.

Prithviraj sent his men, demanding Sanga, but Bida refused to give up his guest.

The soldiers murdered Bida and his son, but by then Sanga had fled. He was engaged by a cowherd for some days, but was considered too stupid even for that menial task. Sanga then rode to Ajmer, serving the Paramar chieftain Karam Chand, without divulging his identity. When Karam Chand learned who his new recruit was, he maintained the secrecy to protect him from Prithviraj's ire.

Prithviraj, whose deeds of chivalry eclipse his asinine cruelties, died when he was poisoned by his brother-in-law. His grief-stricken father soon followed, and Sanga became Rana of Mewar on 4 May, 1508, at the age of 27.

Dilli, Malwa and Gujarat were all Muslim kingdoms, and Rana Sanga waged war against them relentlessly, gaining their respect and friendship even through his avowed enmity.

And how did he get the famous belt out of Mahmud Khilji? [See notes on *Tale of the Kamarband.*]

At the time of the Battle of Panipat, Rana Sanga's kingdom extended through most of Malwa, Ranthambore, Bhilsa, Kalpi, Chanderi, Ajmer, Abu, Mewat, Gwalior, Ambar, and Marwar to stop at Agra on its eastern border. The three sultanates that surrounded him—Dilli Gujarat and Malwa—had been kept quiescent in a kind of grim friendship.

This was what Babar had to contend with at Khanua.

Rana Sanga's defeat at Khanua was caused by an accident—an arrow pierced his forehead and he slumped unconscious on his elephant. The Rana was quickly taken off the field and a substitute rode his elephant to keep up morale. But the news got about and without its leader, the composite force fragmented, and the battle was lost.

When the Rana regained consciousness, he was reproachful at having been taken off the battlefield and remained isolated and depressed for months. Soon, so goes the tale, the song of a *chaaran** revived his spirits—he began planning a second confrontation with Babar.

This did not suit his nobles. Almost inevitably, they poisoned him.

Rana Sanga, magnanimous victor over many enemies, died at the hands of his own people whom he had cherished as family.

~~~~

Chaaran [Urdu … چارَن] [Hindi … चारण]—literally, 'he who chants'—a bard.

~~~~

Meru Prastara [Hindi … मेरु प्रस्तार]:

Known today as Pascal's Triangle, the mathematical formula for binomial expansion was independently discovered by a number of mathematicians long before the French savant, Blaise Pascal described it in 1654.

The earliest description is from the Indian mathematician Pingala, 2 BCE. It was revised and completed in 505 CE by the Ujjaini polymath Varâhamihira. It was named Meru Prastara, the staircase to Mount Meru, by Halayudha four centuries later, who presented the formula as a triangle. Five hundred years later, it was described in Persia by the poet Omar Khayyam, and in Iran, it is known as Khayyam's Triangle.

~~~~
~~~~

Khanua, 1527

The Battle of Khanua was fought between Zahiruddin Bābar, recent Padshah of Dilli and a large confederation made up of almost every ruler in North India. The Western Afghan confederacy, with their leader Hasan Khan Mewati, and the Eastern Afghans joined Rana Sanga with the promise to be his feudatories.

Bābar tried to win over Hasan Khan Mewati to no effect, but he did succeed with the chiefs of Dholpur and Gwalior.

Bābar then tried his luck with Raja Shilajit (Silhadi) Tomar of Raisin by sending him as an envoy to Rana Sanga suggesting a settlement.

Rana Sanga refused.

Rana Sanga's troops captured Bayana and on 21 February 1527 completely routed Bābar's advance guard.

Bābar, as a diversion and a last ditch attempt to get Hasan Khan Mewati on his side, sent a raiding party into Mewat, ordering total destruction.

It did not work.

The morale in Bābar's camp burned low. To inspire them, he forswore drink.

They were impressed, but continued disheartened.

Bābar then made his appeal to them in stirring words:

Noblemen and soldiers! Every man that cometh into this world is subject to dissolution. When we are passed away and gone God survives. One and Unchangeable. Whoever sits down to the feast of life must, before it is over, drink of the cup of death. He who arrives at the inn of mortality, the world, must one day, without fail, take his departure from that mansion of sorrow. How much better then is it to die with honour than to live with infamy.

Give me but fame, and if I die 1 am contented. If fame be mine, let death claim my body.

'The most High God has been propitious to us. He has now placed us in such a crisis that if we fall in the field we die the death of martyrs; if we survive, we rise victorious, the avengers of His sacred cause. Let us, therefore, with one accord swear on God's holy word, that none of us will for a moment think of turning his face from this warfare; or shrink from the battle and slaughter that ensue, till his soul is separated from his body.

Twenty thousand soldiers swore on the Qur'an to fight to the death.

[Queen Elizabeth I, taking a leaf from Bābar's book, would make a similar appeal at Tilbury on 9 August 1588, to rally her troops against the Spanish Armada.]

Once again, Bābar sent Silhadi to negotiate for peace by offering an annual tribute to Rana Sanga if only he would leave Dilli and its dependencies, and suggested the boundary line should be Peela Khal at Bayana.

The Rajputs treated the messenger with scorn.

Silhadi, understanding that the Rana might have taken up the offer had it not come through him, was an embittered man. He had brought 35,000 horse to the field, did that count for nothing?

Bābar had his army arrayed as it had been at Panipat, with a steady centre of artillery behind *araba* and moveable flanks.

The battle opened at 9.30 in the morning with the Rajputs charging the right and centre.

The artillery opened fire, and undaunted, the Rajputs kept up their pressure.

Silhadi chose this moment to betray the Rajput cause.

He wheeled around and joined Bābar, with all his 35,000 horse.

In the confusion, Rana Sanga was struck in the forehead by an arrow and slumped unconscious on his elephant. He was hurriedly dismounted and a substitute was installed to keep up the morale.

But word had spread that the Rana had left the field.

It was the signal for general chaos.

The battle folded by late afternoon, and the field was Bābar's.

Bābar knew that Rana Sanga's threat still loomed large, and passed the next few months planning against a reprisal. But the wounded Rana was destined never to fight again.

~~~~

The Rann

Kos Minar [کوس مینار]—Milestones. [literally, mile pillar]

1 kos = 1.8 miles = 1/4 yojana.
Minar = tower/pillar.

Although *Kos minars* as milestones are linked to Sher Shah Suri's magnificent road planning, they have been part of the Indian landscape since Mauryan times [4 BCE].

The Grand Trunk Road, Sadak-e-Azam [Urdu … سڑک اعظم], runs 1,491 miles from Teknaf in Bangladesh in the east to Kabul in Afghanistan in the west.

~~~~

The Mirror of Sikandar bin Manjhu

Mīrāt [Urdu … میرات] — mirror.
When used as a Muslim name for boys, it means 'wish'.

~~~~

Tarīkh [Arabic … تاریخ] — literally, 'date,' but in usage it means history, annals, chronicle.

Tarikh-i-Ahmad Shahi, Tarikh-i-Mahmud Shahi, Tarikh-i-Bahadur Shahi

Tarikh-i-Ahmadshahi, written soon after the foundation of Ahmadabad, is now lost. But its contents have been quoted extensively, particularly in the *Mirat-i-Ahmadi.*

Mirat-i-Ahmadi, written between 1748-1762 by Mohammad Ali Khan, the revenue minister of Gujarat and his assistant Mittha Lalli Kait, is a collation of extracts from the *Mirat-i-Sikandari, Akbar-nama, Jehangir-nama* and *Padshah-nama.*

Tarikh-i-Bahadurshahi, written by Hussam Gujarati is now lost. It has been extensively quoted in *Mirat-i-Sikandari.*

~~~~

Manjhu

Humayun's librarian. His origins are obscure, and his fame rests on his son's achievement, the *Mīrat-i-Sikandari.* From this document we learn of his 'previous friendship' with Hussam Gujarati whom he saves from the Mughals. The observations in *Mīrat-i-Sikandari* are Manjhu's, but much of what he recounts he had gleaned from Hussam Gujarati.

~~~~

Sikandar bin Manjhu

Born in Mahmudabad in 1558, he completed his history of the Gujarat Kings at the age of sixty.

~~~~

Shah Tamasp

Farsi … طمعیپٹ … 'he of the valiant horses.'

He was the second Shah of Safavid Iran (1524-1576). He gave Humayun sanctuary when he fled Sher Shah Suri. In return for this favour, Humayun converted to the Shia faith.

When he left Shah Tamasp for India, Humayun was accompanied by poets banished by the royal bigot.

The Diamond

Later known as the Koh-i-Noor [Farsi کوه نور]— 'mountain of light.'

Perhaps the largest cut diamond in the world, weighing 105.6 carats, it was mined in the Kollur mines of Golconda.

Its recent history is well known. It resides now in the Jewel House of the Tower of London.

~~~

Mohammad Hussam Gujarati

A scholar of Bahadur Shah's court, probably a noble, he was a close associate of the Sultân and penned the *Tarikh-i-Bahdur Shahi* during that time. The rest of his history is told in the *Mirat-i-Sikandari.*

Nothing further is known of him.

~~~

Mahmud Shah III of Gujarat

The son of Bahadur's brother Latif, he was the worst of the Gujarat sultans. He gained the throne on 10 May 1538, at the age of eleven, and for the next 18 years proved himself a tyrant and bigot.

~~~

Itimad Khan

Abdul Karim, a confidante of Mahmud Shah III, he was given free access to the harem, despite the Sultân's pathological jealousy.

~~~

Tānk [Taank]

Hindi … टांक … people of the Tonk river.

A tribe of Gujarat.

The story behind the Gujarat Sultânate is a Tānk tale.

A cousin of Mohammad bin Tughlak, Firoz Khan, when hunting in the environs of Thanesar, accepted the hospitality of two prosperous Tank brothers Sadhu and Sadharan. He kept quiet about his identity.

Sadaharan's wife noticed signs of nobility in their guest, though he was clothed like a commoner. She sent in a *surahi* of wine with Sadharan's beautiful sister. After Firoz's third cup of wine 'the rosebud of his disposition began to unfold' and he noticed the beautiful *sāqi* [Urdu ساقی]—wine-server.

Sadharan's wife made bold to question the visitor, and when his identity was revealed, the family happily consented to an immediate marriage between Firoz and the young lady.

In time, Sadharan converted to Islam and, assumed the name Wajih-ul-Mulk and became a confidante of Firoz Khan. Wajih-ul-Mulk and his family became disciples of a Sheikh of Bukhara.

In return for an act of charity, Zafar Khan, son of Wajih-ul-Mulk received as blessing from the Sheikh, 'the whole country of Gujarat.' His wife pointed out the oversight: Zafar, already fifty, could hardly hope to rule for a decade or two. And, such blessings were best kept in the family.

Zafar returned to the Sheikh the next day, and begged that the blessing be transferred to his children. The Shaikh placed 13 dates in a dish before him and pronounced that as the number of his progeny that would wear the crown. [The Gujarat Sultâns were 13 in all.]

When Mohammad bin Tughlaq died at Thatta in 1351, Firoz Khan assumed the crown of Dilli as Firoz Shah Tughlaq.

In 1407, Zafar Khan proclaimed himself Sultan of Gujarat and assumed the title of Muzaffar Shah I of Gujarat.

~~~

Auzbegs [Uzbeks]

Mohammad Shaybani, an Uzbek who united several warring tribes into a nation which was later to become the Khanate of Bukhara. He was Babar's nemesis. He captured Samarqand and later wrested Herat and Bukhara from Babar.

As the price for Babar's liberty, Babar's sister Khanzada Begum was married to Shaybani.

Shaybani was killed on 2 December 1510 in the Battle of Marv, with the result that Shah of Persia, Ismail I ruled Khorasan. At Babar's request, Ismail I sent his sister and her son back to Babar's court.

Shaybani's corpse was beheaded, and his skull used as a drinking cup, a prevalent rite of victory. Later, Ismail passed on the cup to Babar in a gesture of royal brotherhood.
~~~

Mahmud Khilji

Mahmud Khilji (1436–69), a.k.a. Alauddin Mahmud Shah I was a 15th century Sultân of the Malwa Sultânate, a small kingdom in what is now Madhya Pradesh.

~~~~

Mandu

Capital of Malwa Sultânate.

In historic India, first under the Mauryas, and then under the Guptas, Malwa was the centre of culture and learning, with Ujjain as its epicentre.

From the mid 10th to the 14th century, Malwa was ruled by the Paramaras.

Raja Bhoja 1010-1055 CE, soldier and polymath who wrote treatises on a variety of subjects, was both critic and patron to poets and intellectuals.

In 1305, Malwa was conquered by the Dilli Sultânate. After Taimur's invasion in 1401, the Dilli Sultânate fragmented, and Dilawar Khan established an independent kingdom, the Malwa Sultânate with its capital at Mandu.

The Sultâns of Mandu were renowned for their architecture. In the 16th century, Mandu was synonymous with beauty and luxury.

~~~~

Mandsaur

Archeological finds from Mandsaur in Madhya Pradesh, establish it as the site of the Battle of Sondhani in which the Huna general Mihirakula was routed by King Yashodharaman in 4 CE.

The Pashupatinath temple dates to 6 CE, or earlier.

~~~~

Kalinjar

Originally *Kalanjara,* [Hindi … कालिंजर] for Shiva.

Celebrated as a Shaivite shrine from ancient times.

The fortress of the Chandela kings of Bundelkhand stood at 1500 ft above a deep ravine, making it one of the most impregnable bastions of medieval India. It had been unsuccessfully besieged by Bābar.
~~~~

In 1531, Humayun made a bid for it as a strategic move for acceptance from a very divided nobility. The Raja of Chandela offered 6,720 tolas of gold in return for peace, and Humayun accepted, assuming the title of Ghazi for having 'subdued an infidel.'

Ghazi—[Arabic ... غازی]—'warrior'—the title given to a Muslim soldier who undertakes an expedition for religion and domain.

~~~

Tanka

Coinage first introduced by Muhammad bin Tughlaq in the 14th century, it soon became the international currency of trade. It was minted in copper and brass against a reserve of gold. That was soon replaced by silver. After the collapse of the Tughlaq dynasty, tankas were minted by regional rulers.

The Gujarat Sultâns minted tankas to inaugurate a new Sultân's reign.

~~~

Mohammad Zaman Mirza

Bābar formally nominated Humayun his successor on 23 December, 1530 CE.

Bābur died on 26 December, 1530 CE.

The three days in between were fraught with drama.

Bābar's principal adviser, the Khalifa, was dead set against Humayun's coronation. Humayun's plunder of the Dilli treasury without the king's permission had made him untrustworthy.

The Khalifa also resented the power the Queen, Maham Begum, had wielded over Bābar and he dreaded her control over Humayun. Maham Begam was the only queen to have shared Bābar's throne. Bābar also gave her the charge of two children by another wife, Dildar Begam: Hindal Mirza and Gulbadan Begam, who would grow up to write that beautiful memoir, the *Humayun-nama.*

Khalifa promoted instead, Bābar's brother-in-law, Sayid Mahdi Khwaja. This worthy could hardly wait for the King's demise. When visited by a minister, thinking the man was beyond earshot, he said, 'My first act as king will be to flay men like you.' When he noticed the minister hadn't left, Khwaja menaced him with the warning:

زبانِ سُرخ سرے سبزی دھد برباد

An infelicitous tongue destroys the callow head.

The story spread, and the Khalifa, embarrassed, withdrew his candidate.

Soon after Humayun was crowned, his brother-in-law, Mohammad Zaman Mirza, rebelled. This was quickly suppressed, but the Mirza's discontent showed itself sporadically. In

1534, in another, better planned rebellion, Zaman Mirza allied with his brother and nephews to defy Humayun.

This time the Mughal army broke their resistance. The rebels were imprisoned and Humayun ordered them to be blinded with a 'fire pencil.' Zaman Mirza charmed his jailer into letting him escape, eyes intact, and fled to Gujarat, seeking sanctuary at Bahadur's court.

~~~~

Ghyasuddin bin Hummamuddin [Khwandamir]: 1475/6 – 1535/6.

Persian Historian.

He wrote a universal history of monarchs while in Herat in Shaybani Khan's court—*Ḥabīb al-Siyar fī Akhbār afrād al-Bashar* [حبیب السیر فی اخبار افراد البشر] *The Beloved Report on the Multitudes of People.*

After Ismail I took over Herat, Khwandamir was invited by Bābar to join his court. He did so in 1528. He then wrote *Qanun-e-Humayuni* [قانون ہمایونی], *The Edicts of Humayun,* a biography of Bābar's son and successor.

He died soon after the events described by Sikandar bin Manjhu.

He is buried in Dilli in the environs of the dargah of the Sufi saint Hazrat Nizamuddin.

~~~~

Surah of the Elephant:

The 105th Surah [Arabic سورة] or chapter of the Qur'an is *Al-Fīl* [Arabic الفيل]—The Elephant. Revealed in Mecca, the Surah has five verses or ãyah. [Arabic: آية *āyah*, plural آيات *āyāt*)].

أَلَمْ تَرَ كَيْفَ فَعَلَ رَبُّكَ بِأَصْحَٰبِ ٱلْفِيلِ
أَلَمْ يَجْعَلْ كَيْدَهُمْ فِى تَضْلِيلٍ
وَأَرْسَلَ عَلَيْهِمْ طَيْرًا أَبَابِيلَ
تَرْمِيهِم بِحِجَارَةٍ مِّن سِجِّيلٍ
فَجَعَلَهُمْ كَعَصْفٍ مَّأْكُولٍ

Transliteration:

Alam tara kayfa fa'ala rabbuka bi'aṣḥābil-fīl
Alam yaj'al kaydahum fī taḍlīlin
Wa'arsala 'alayhim ṭayran ababīl
Tarmīhim biḥijārati min sij-jīlin
Faja'alahum ka'aṣfim mākūl

Translation [mine]:

Did you not see how the Lord dealt with the Army of Elephants?
Did He not foil their treacherous intent?
He sent against them a flight of martins
To pelt them with a hail of stones;
And mowed them down like a field freshly grazed by cattle.

This Surah refers to specific events in the year of Mohamed's birth, also known as the Year of the Elephant.

Islamic tradition holds that Abrahah, the Aksum general and Christian zealot who ruled Arabia and Yemen, had built a cathedral in Sana'a and wanted it to be the world's principal site of pilgrimage. When Abrahah realized that the Ka'aba in Mecca drew pilgrims from all over, he led a military invasion of the Hejaz in 570 CE to destroy the Ka'aba forever, divert all pilgrims to his cathedral, and reap the profits thereof.

Abrahah's army of elephants was besieged by a mighty flock of martins [Arabic ابابيل ... *ababīl*] that came from the Red Sea and showered a rain of stones on them. The maddened elephants trampled and killed the entire Aksumite battalion.

~~~
~~~

Oshim and Genda

The Requerimiento:

It reads like a dystopic myth today, but in 15th century Europe, the Requerimiento was a fiat from the Pope. The Doctrine of Discovery was recited by European explorers as they touched foreign soil. Irrespective of whether the natives understood them or not, the recital was all that was needed to claim the land as their own. This is how the Americas were 'claimed'. This is his how Vasco da Gama 'claimed' Calicut for his sovereign. And just so the Spaniards and the Portuguese didn't quarrel over territories, the Treaty of Torsedillas of 4 June 1494 stated that all territories east of a line drawn 100 leagues west of Cape Verde would belong to the Portuguese. Anything west of this was Spanish. This neat division of a thickly populated world was permissible as all lands which lacked a 'Christian Monarch' were, in the eyes of the Church, empty land —*Terra Nullius.*

Paranoia on so grand a scale has seldom been witnessed at any time in history.

'Terra Nullius' was finally erased as a concept by the Mabo case, a legal fight for indigenous rights of the Meriam people of the Murray islands. Eddie Mabo was the plaintiff. The judgment annulled the concept that the islands were Terra Nullius or 'lands belonging to nobody' when the British occupied them in the 18th century.

Here is a translation of the Requerimiento:

* On behalf of the king and the queen, subjugators of barbarous peoples, we, their servants, notify and make known to you as best we are able, that God, Our Lord, living and eternal, created the heavens and the earth, and a man and a woman, of whom you and we and all other people of the world were, and are, the descendants. Because of the great numbers of people who have come from the union of these two in the five thousand year, which have run their course since the world was created, it became necessary that some should go in one direction and that others should go in another. Thus they became divided into many kingdoms and many provinces, since they could not all remain or sustain themselves in one place.

* Of all these people God, Our Lord, chose one, who was called Saint Peter, to be the lord and the one who was to be superior to all the other people of the world, whom all should obey. He was to be the head of the entire human race, wherever men might exist. God gave him the world for his kingdom and jurisdiction. God also permitted him to be and establish himself in any other part of the world to judge and govern all peoples, whether Christian, Moors, Jew, Gentiles, or those of any other sects and beliefs that there might be. He was called the Pope. One of the past Popes who succeeded Saint Peter, as Lord of the Earth gave these islands and Mainlands of the Ocean Sea [the Atlantic Ocean] to the said King and Queen and to their successors, with everything that there is in them, as is set forth in certain documents which were drawn up regarding this donation in the manner described, which you may see if you so desire.

* In consequence, Their Highnesses are Kings and Lords of these islands and mainland by virtue of said donation. Certain other isles and almost all [the native peoples] to whom this summons has been read have accepted Their Highnesses as such Kings and Lords, and have served, and serve, them as their subjects as they should, and must, do, with good will and without offering any resistance. You are constrained and obliged to do the same as they.

* Consequently, as we best may, we beseech and demand that you understand fully this that we have said to you and ponder it, so that you may understand and deliberate upon it for a just and fair

period, and that you accept the Church and Superior Organization of the whole world and recognize the Supreme Pontiff, called the Pope, and that in his name, you acknowledge the King and Queen, as the lords and superior authorities of these islands and Mainlands by virtue of the said donation.

• If you do not do this, however, or resort maliciously to delay, we warn you that, with the aid of God, we will enter your land against you with force and will make war in every place and by every means we can and are able, and we will then subject you to the yoke and authority of the Church and Their Highnesses. We will take you and your wives and children and make them slaves, and as such we will sell them, and will dispose of you and them as Their Highnesses order. And we will take your property and will do to you all the harm and evil we can, as is done to vassals who will not obey their lord or who do not wish to accept him, or who resist and defy him. We avow that the deaths and harm which you will receive thereby will be your own blame, and not that of Their Highnesses, nor ours, nor of the gentlemen who come with us.

~~~~

The Treaty of Tordesillas

On 7 June, 1494, the Treaty of Tordesillas, a town in Central Spain on the banks of the river Douro, divided the newly discovered lands outside Europe between the Portuguese and Spanish Empires along a meridian 1,184 nautical miles west of the Cape Verde islands, off the west coast of Africa with the approval of Pope Alexander VI. This imaginary line came to be known as the Tordesillas Meridian.

A new conflict began when expeditions of both kingdoms reached the Pacific Ocean and no agreed meridian of longitude establishing spheres of influence had been established in the Orient. The source of dispute were the 'Spice Islands' of Maluku, then the singular source of the world's nutmeg and cloves. To resolve this 'Moluccas Issue' a treaty was signed on 22 April 1529 by King John III of Portugal and the Castilian emperor Charles V at Zaragoza in Aragon. **Pope** Clement VII was the Vicar of Rome. The Treaty of Zaragoza established the eastern border between the two domain zones at longitude 17° east of the Maluku Islands, the Zaragoza Antimeridian.

~~~~

Mayimama Marakkar

The Calicut Samudri's ambassador to the Mamluk court, he was instrumental in organizing naval aid against the Portuguese. He brought a Mamluk fleet of 12 ships to the Battle of Chaul in 1508. He was killed in that battle.

~~~~

The Battle of Chaul, 1508

The battle was fought by the combined forces of the Samudri Rajah of Calicut, Malik Ayaaz of Gujarat and the Mamluk fleet under the captaincy of Amir Husain Al-Kurdi, brought in by Mayimama Marakkar, against the Portuguese.

The engagement between the Mamluk fleet and the Portuguese was indecisive, until Malik Ayaaz's navy routed the Portuguese. The Portuguese Governor's young son Lourençao Almeida, fought courageously, but was killed.
~~~~

The outcome crippled the Portuguese temporarily, and stopped their incessant assaults on the west coast. It also resulted in serious disaffection between the Mamluk captain and Malik Ayaaz.

The Portuguese Governor Francisco Almeida challenged Malik Ayaaz: 'He who has swallowed the chick must now digest the cockerel or pay for it.'

Malik Ayaaz had the prisoners treated with honour and returned them to the Portuguese who responded by torturing and hanging the prisoners they had in their power.

~~~~

The Battle of Diu:

On 3 February 1509 the Mamluk-Diu-Calicut combine faced a Portuguese armada commanded by Francisco Almeida.

For Almeida it was a battle of revenge. For the Portuguese King, victory would mean practical control over the Indian Ocean.

Malik Ayyaz was fighting to keep the Portuguese off Diu; the Mamluks and the Calicut Samudri, to stop their spice trade from being commandeered by the Portuguese.

Also in the fray, though remotely, was Venice, which had provided the ships and naval expertise to the Mamluks in the hope of cornering the European spice market.

The Portuguese won--bloodily.

They arrived at Diu after having unleashed terror at Dabul to leave the city smouldering, and all life extinct.

Much to Malik Ayyaz's relief, the victorious Almeida refused Diu, contenting himself with extracting more gold out of the merchants than they even knew they had. For his own personal satisfaction, Almeida enjoyed the spectacle of gruesome forms of torture and execution of the prisoners.

The Battle was decisive. It opened the Indian Ocean and the Indian coastline to Portuguese domination for the next century.

~~~~

Malacca

Named for Amlaki, *Phyllanthus emblica,* [Sanskrit … आमलकी] Amalaka was founded in the early 1400s by Parameswara, also remembered as Iskandar Shah. The population then was a mixture of Buddhist, Hindu and Muslim, and the canny ruler organized them all into a network focussed on trade.

Within a few years, Malacca was established as the leading trade post of the east with Chinese, Arab, Persians and Indians calling at the port and soon establishing themselves on the islands as traders.

Raja Tengah who followed Parameswara, converted to Islam, and became known as Sultân Muhammad Shah.

In mid-15th century, Gujarati merchants made up a large part of the population. Malik Gopi's wealth was heavily invested in Malacca, which had, by now, become the centre of the spice trade.

The Portuguese were intent on breaking the Arab-Venetian-Indian monopoly. Alfonso D'Albuquerque correctly deduced that acquiring Malacca would break the back of the spice trade. In August 1511, he fought his way in, bloodily as usual.

Portuguese fortunes at Malacca, though, were severely fraught. But that's another story.

The Two-Headed Man

Treaty of Diu

Signed at Diu on October 25, 1535 by Nuno da Cunha for the Portuguese King and Sheikh Iwas for Sultân Bahadur Shah. It granted the Portuguese permission to build a fortress at Diu for the purpose of trade. The King of Portugal would not receive any customs duties, but ships may not call at Diu without receiving a Portuguese *cartaz*. The Portuguese would not attempt to convert Muslims to Christianity, nor would Christians be permitted to convert to Islam.

~~~~

Diogo de Misquitta

This questionable character, sometimes mentioned as James Misquitta, and nicknamed 'Qazi,' was a Portuguese prisoner who stayed on in Bahadur's court voluntarily, and with the blessing of the Portuguese. He adapted quickly to Gujarati ways and served Bahadur as a soldier and the Portuguese as a spy. His *Chronico do Reyno de Gusarate* is a record of his time with Bahadur Shah, whom he accompanied on his last visit to Diu. The Chronico signs off on 17 November 1535.

Subsequently, historical events identify him on Nuno da Cunha's galleon on 14 February 1537. They all agree that Diogo de Misquitta was the first to attack Bahadur with a knife and Bahadur's instinctive riposte with a sword thrust killed Diogo de Misquitta.

~~~~

14 February 1537 [iv]

The Siege of Bassein

In 1532, the Portuguese renewed their raids on the Gujarat coast. Nuno da Cunha appointed Diogo da Silveira to strike terror on the coast. Gogha, Taloja, Agashi and Bandra were plundered and burned. Assaults continued on Agashi, Bandra, Thana, Surat. Malik Toghan's luxurious *jagir* [estate] in Bassein had an imposing fortress and Bahadur ordered him to mobilize troops to defend it against the Portuguese. Malik Toghan's forces were routed and the Portuguese massacred the populace and set fire to the city. The ensuing alarm spread through Shashti Island and Bahadur had to sue for peace. The Treaty of Bassein was accordingly signed, with Sheikh Iwas standing in for Bahadur, and Bassein and its adjoining islands passed into Portuguese control.

~~~~
~~~~

14 February 1537 [v]

A Chronology of the Gujarat Sultânate

1391

Muzaffar Khan, Viceroy of Gujarat under Mohamad Tughlaq II, declared himself King of Gujarat and took the name of Sultân Muzaffar Shah I.

1411

Ahmad Khan, grandson of Muzaffar I, assumed the throne as Sultân Ahmad Shah. He founded the city of Ahmadabad at Asaval. He died in 1443, after an outbreak of plague.

1443

Sultân Qutub Shah assumed the throne.

On Feb 11, 1453, Sultân Qutub Shah won a battle with Mahmud Khilji I of Malwa—but was robbed of his crown jewels, including the Kamarband. The Kamarband was now the property of the Khiljis.

1458

Sultân Mahmud Shah I assumed the throne at the age of 14 and within weeks he quelled a rebellion and inaugurated a long and adventurous reign which made him one of the greatest kings in Indian history, for certain the most prominent of the Gujarat Sultânate. His capture of the forts of Pavagadh and Junagadh gave him the moniker 'Begada' [Urdu گڑھ meaning 'fort']. He made Champaner his capital. He died on 23 November 1511 after forty-four years on the throne. In death his legacy was honoured by the title Khudāigān-i-Halīm [Urdu خدا ئے گان حلیم], the Benevolent Lord. He is buried at the Sarkhej Roza near Ahmadabad. Sarkhej Roza is a corruption of Zarkhez Rauza [زرخیزروضة] meaning 'evergreen shrine.'

1511

Sultân Muzaffar Shah the Clement, the eldest son of Sultân Begada, assumed the throne and ruled until his death on 5 April 1526.

1526

Sultân Sikandar Shah, crowns himself in February, and is killed on May 30, of the same year. After only six weeks as king, he was murdered in Champaner while he was sleeping after a game of chaugan.

August 3, 1526

Bahadur is crowned Shah of Gujarat.

Syphilis

Syphilis was introduced into India by the Portuguese.

Its first subcontinental mention is in 16th century Ayurvedic texts, where predictably, it is called Firangi Rog—the Foreigner's Disease.

~~~~

Meeran Mohammad

Bahadur's nephew, he was the ruler of Khandesh in the Deccan, under Bahadur's patronage.

He accompanied Bahadur on his campaigns to Chittorgarh and Mandu.

After Humayun's victory over Gujarat, he sent a force to subdue Khandesh, but recalled his army when his attention was diverted by Sher Shah Suri.

Meeran Mohammad, at Bahadur's behest, attacked the Mughal forces at Malwa and recovered Mandu.

He was in Mandu when he was proclaimed Sultân of Gujarat after Bahadur's murder.

Consumed by grief at Bahadur's death, he fell dangerously ill, and died on May 4, 1537 while on his way to claim his throne.

~~~~

About the Authors

Kalpana Swaminathan and **Ishrat Syed** are surgeons who write together as **Kalpish Ratna**, an almost anagram of their first names. Melding Farsi and Sanskrit, it means 'the pleasures of imagination.'

Kalpish Ratna have written novels, short stories, nonfiction and essays over the last three decades. Their acclaimed writings include *The Quarantine Papers*, shortlisted for the Crossword Fiction Award in 2010; *The Nalanda Chronicles*; the short story collection *Synapse.*

Uncertain Life & Sure Death, *Once Upon A Hill* and *Room 000* look at Bombay with new eyes.

Fat, *The Secret Life of Zika Virus, A Crown of Thorns*, and *Gastronama* examine the entanglements between our bodies, disease and the environment.

Kalpish Ratna have also written stories for children: *Doctor Wrasse of Crystal Rock*, *Nyagrodha*, and *A Pandemonium in Pakshila.*

For more on their work, visit www.kalpishratna.com